YOU CAN GET MUCH FURTHER WITH A SMILE, A
KIND WORD AND A GUN THAN WITH JUST A SMILE
AND A KIND WORD.
AL CAPONE

👋 BOOKS BY TROY TAYLOR 👋

DEAD MEN SO TELL TALES SERIES
Dead Men Do Tell Tales (2008)
Bloody Chicago (2006)
Bloody Illinois (2008)
Bloody Hollywood (2008)
Without a Trace (2009)
Blood, Guns & Valentines (2010)

HAUNTED ILLINOIS BOOKS
Haunted Illinois (1999 / 2001 / 2004)
Haunted Decatur (1995 / 2009)
More Haunted Decatur (1996)
Ghosts of Millikin (1996 / 2001)
Where the Dead Walk (1997 / 2002)
Dark Harvest (1997)
Haunted Decatur Revisited (2000)
Flickering Images (2001)
Haunted Decatur: 13th Anniversary (2006)
Haunted Alton (2000 / 2003 / 2008)
Haunted Chicago (2003)
The Haunted President (2005 / 2009)
Mysterious Illinois (2005)
Resurrection Mary (2007)
The Possessed (2007)
Weird Chicago (2008)

HAUNTED FIELD GUIDE BOOKS
The Ghost Hunters Guidebook
(1997/ 1999 / 2001/ 2004 / 2007 / 2010)
Confessions of a Ghost Hunter (2002)
Field Guide to Haunted Graveyards (2003)
Ghosts on Film (2005)
So, There I Was (with Len Adams) (2006)
Talking with the Dead (with Rob & Anne Wlodarski) (2009)

HISTORY & HAUNTINGS SERIES
The Haunting of America (2001 / 2010)
Into the Shadows (2002)
Down in the Darkness (2003)
Out Past the Campfire Light (2004)
Ghosts by Gaslight (2007)

OTHER GHOSTLY TITLES
Spirits of the Civil War (1999)
Season of the Witch (1999/ 2002)
Haunted New Orleans (2000)
Beyond the Grave (2001)
No Rest for the Wicked (2001)
Haunted St. Louis (2002)
The Devil Came to St. Louis (2006)
Houdini: Among the Spirits (2009)
And Hell Followed With It (with Rene Kruse) (2010)

WHITECHAPEL OCCULT LIBRARY
Sex & the Supernatural (2009)

STERLING PUBLICATIONS
Weird U.S. (Co-Author) (2004)
Weird Illinois (2005)
Weird Virginia (Co-Author) (2007)
Weird Indiana (Co-Author) (2008)

BARNES & NOBLE PRESS TITLES
Haunting of America (2006)
Spirits of the Civil War (2007)
Into the Shadows (2007)

HISTORY PRESS TITLES
Wicked Washington (2007)
Murder & Mayhem on Chicago's North Side (2009)
Murder & Mayhem on Chicago's South Side (2009)
Murder & Mayhem on Chicago's West Side (2009)
Murder & Mayhem in Downtown Chicago (2009)
Murder & Mayhem in the Chicago Vice Districts (2009)
Wicked New Orleans (2010)
Haunted New Orleans (2010)
Wicked Northern Illinois (2010)

STACKPOLE BOOKS TITLES
Haunted Illinois (2008)
True Crime Illinois (2009)
Big Book of Illinois Ghost Stories (2009)

THE DEAD MEN DO TELL TALES SERIES

BLOOD, GUNS & VALENTINES

BY TROY TAYLOR

- A WHITECHAPEL PRESS PUBLICATION FROM DARK HAVEN ENTERTAINMENT -

TO ALL OF THE HISTORIANS, WRITERS AND RESEARCHERS WHO LIVE AND
BREATHE AL CAPONE IN THE SAME WAY I DO GHOSTS, HAUNTINGS AND THE
UNEXPLAINED. THANKS FOR LETTING ME INTRUDE INTO YOUR WORLD FOR A
LITTLE WHILE!

ORIGINAL COVER ARTWORK DESIGNED BY

©Copyright 2010 by Michael Schwab & Troy Taylor

Visit M & S Graphics at http://www.manyhorses.com/msgraphics.htm

THIS BOOK IS PUBLISHED BY:

Whitechapel Press
A Division of Dark Haven Entertainment, Inc.
Chicago, Illinois / 1-888-GHOSTLY
Visit us on the internet at http://www. American Hauntings .org

First Printing -- September 2010
ISBN: 1-892523-71-X

Printed in the United States of America

DEAD MEN DO TELL TALES:
BLOOD, GUNS, & VALENTINES

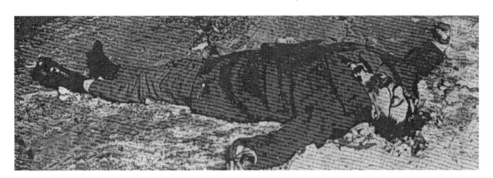

WHEN I SELL LIQUOR, THEY CALL IT BOOTLEGGING. WHEN MY PATRONS SERVE IT ON SILVER TRAYS ON LAKE SHORE DRIVE, THEY CALL IT HOSPITALITY.
AL CAPONE

I HOPE WHEN MY TIME COMES THAT I DIE DECENTLY IN BED. I DON'T WANT TO BE MURDERED AND LEFT FOR DEAD BESIDE THE GARBAGE CANS IN SOME CHICAGO ALLEY.
GEORGE "BUGS" MORAN

NOBODY WAS EVER KILLED EXCEPT OUTLAWS, AND THE COMMUNITY IS BETTER OFF WITHOUT THEM.
AL CAPONE

NO USE BRINGING ANYONE ELSE IN HERE. I WON'T RAP ANY OF THEM. I WOULDN'T LAY THE FINGER EVEN ON THE GUILTY MAN. I KNOW THE MEN WHO SHOT ME.
JOHN TORRIO

O'BANION WAS A THIEF AND A MURDERER, BUT LOOK AT HIM NOW, BURIED EIGHTY FEET AWAY FROM A BISHOP
CAPTAIN JOHN STEGE

THREE HUNDRED DOLLARS TO THEM BUMS? I CAN GET THEM BUMPED OFF FOR HALF THAT MUCH!
DION O'BANION

PROHIBITION? PROHIBITION WILL NEVER MAKE THIS COUNTRY DRY. YOU THINK LAW CAN QUENCH A MAN'S THIRST? A MAN CAN'T DRINK LAW. PEOPLE ARE BORN THIRSTY, AND THEY ARE GOING TO STAY THAT WAY.
"POLACK" JOE SALTIS

SUMMER 1930

The Lexington Hotel opened in 1892 on the near South Side of Chicago. The ten story brick and terra cotta building that stood at the corner of Michigan Avenue and Twenty-Second Street first served the crowds who came to the city for the World's Columbian Exposition of 1893. These were boom years on the city's South Side and the luxurious hotel attracted scores of wealthy and famous visitors, including President Benjamin Harrison. But by the late 1920s, the hotel boasted another famous resident, a stocky, moon-faced man with thick eyebrows and a receding hairline who was registered under the innocuous name of George Phillips. After abandoning the Metropole Hotel, located one block to the south, in 1928, "Mr. Phillips" began using the Lexington as his Chicago headquarters.

George Phillips may have been the name he signed on the guest register, but the people of Chicago knew him as Public Enemy No. 1 – Al Capone.

Capone's wealth allowed him to act as if he owned the Lexington. Anyone who walked through the front doors and into the lobby would find it occupied by the gangster's bodyguards, all of whom were making a concerted attempt to appear inconspicuous. Some, like Tony "Joe Batters" Accardo, were seated in deep leather armchairs, appearing to read newspapers while loaded Thompson submachine guns lay concealed in their laps. When a stranger approached, a telephone call was placed upstairs and gunmen were put instantly on alert. Other sentries stood watch by the elevators. To approach Capone's fourth-floor suite, a visitor would have to pass between rows of casually posed bodyguards, each of whom carried a sidearm under his jacket in a holster that hung, according to the prescribed style, four inches below the armpit.

The hub of Capone's empire was Room 430, the command center of his six-room suite. From there, he directed – with help from his friend and financial manager Jake "Greasy Thumb" Guzik – a vast syndicate that owned or controlled breweries, distilleries, speakeasies, gambling houses, horse and dog tracks, nightclubs, brothels, labor unions, business and industrial associations, and much more. Together, these various legal and illegal enterprises produced annual revenue in the hundreds of millions of dollars. Cash was often stacked in Room 430 in padlocked canvas bags, waiting to be transferred to banks where accounts were set up under scores of aliases.

As protection and enforcement for his organization, Capone controlled as army of sluggers, bombers and torpedoes, numbering between 700 and 1,000 men. Some of them were under his direct command while others were available through allied gang leaders. In order to keep himself from being arrested or prosecuted, Capone relied on an intricate connection with City Hall, involving a range of officials from aldermen to police officers, detectives, precinct captains and even the mayor himself.

At the Lexington, once a visitor passed inspection on reaching the fourth floor, he was admitted to an oval vestibule where a crest containing the initials "A.C." had been inlaid in the oak parquet floor. To the left was a bathroom containing an immense lavender sunken tub with gold-plated faucets. The walls were tiled in Nile green with purple and tan trim and the floor tiles were a contrasting shade of green. Another, smaller bathroom was located off Capone's office, which occupied a corner of the building where a rounded bay window commanded a sweeping view of Michigan Avenue. The office was papered in a pattern of large flowers of uncertain botanical origin on a beige background. Other walls throughout the suite were painted rose or gold. Clearly, the ruthless crime lord had an eye for over-the-top interior design as it was interpreted by the popular "Florida" style of the day. An exquisite Oriental rug covered the floor of Room 430, the high ceiling of which was painted with an elaborate design of leaves, branches and foliage. A chandelier dripping with amber and smoked glass prisms shed a soft light over the surroundings. The fireplace contained a heap of artificial coal interspersed with light bulbs that blazed orange and red in imitation of flickering flames. An expensive radio set had been built into the wall above the mantel.

In addition to the fourth-floor command center, Capone and his entourage spread out through much of the hotel, with his henchmen using the second floor ballroom as a gym. Other rooms on the third, fourth, and fifth floors were set aside as Capone's private movie theater, kitchen and dining room. A private chef tasted all the food and drink before it was served to Capone. There were bedrooms for bodyguards and a block of rooms set aside for use by visiting family members. Secret stairways and escape routes led out of the building or to other parts of the hotel, including a two-room suite occupied by one of Capone's mistresses, which could be reached through a staircase hidden behind a bathroom medicine cabinet.

The crime boss was a late riser. He probably slept better knowing that his trusted gunsel, Louie "Little New York" Campagna, slept on a cot outside the door with two automatics within reach. Capone usually stayed up past dawn, eating, drinking and visiting his clubs and brothels. Visitors who called on him before noon would find him in a robe and silk pajamas, which were monogrammed like the silk sheets he slept on. He ordered the French pajamas in lots of a dozen at $25 each, preferring royal blue with gold piping. He favored colored underwear made from Italian silk that cost $12 a pair, an exorbitant amount in the 1920s. But money wasn't an issue for the man whose henchmen affectionately called "Snorky," slang for a sharp dresser. His suits, custom-tailored at Marshall Field for $135, with the right-hand pockets reinforced to support the weight of a gun without destroying the line of the garment, ran to light colors – pea green, light blue, lemon yellow – and he delighted in matching ties and socks, snappy fedoras and pearl-gray spats. A diamond sparkled in his tiepin and affixed to his vest was a platinum watch chain that was encrusted with diamonds. On his middle finger, he wore a flawless, eleven-carat, blue-white diamond ring that cost $50,000. There was little that Capone could not afford.

By the summer of 1930, Capone was 31, but he appeared much older. Countless plates of pasta and numerous bottles of wine had deposited layers of fat on his body, but under that fat was rock-hard muscle. When he was angry, he could inflict brutal punishment. He stood five feet, ten-and-one-half inches tall and weighed 255 pounds. He walked with an assertive thrust to his upper body, his shoulders sloping like a bull's. His large head sat on a short, thick neck that could barely be distinguished from his torso. His face appeared congested, as if too much flesh had been pressed onto his skull. His hair was dark brown, his eyes startlingly pale gray under thick eyebrows. His nose was flat, his mouth wide and fleshy. Three scars -- one running along his left cheek from ear to jaw, another across the jaw and a third below his left ear – were souvenirs, it was said, from a long-ago knife fight. He was embarrassed by his disfigurement and frequently considered plastic surgery but instead applied a layer of white talcum powder to his entire dark-complexioned face, hoping to hide the paleness of the scars. To photographers, he always presented his right, unmarked profile. He hated the nickname that had been given to him by the press – "Scarface" – and no one used it in his presence if they valued their life. He allowed his pals to call him "Snorky" but that was the only moniker that anyone dared.

Although Capone was not a physically attractive man, he radiated power. He started out as a street thug and worked his way into the one of the most powerful positions in the American underworld by sheer force of will. Despite his looks, women desired him and men wanted to befriend him, all because of his power, his wit and his charm. Even those who wanted nothing more than to destroy him understood his appeal. Capone ran the city of Chicago – and his rise to greatness was not achieved by bloodshed alone.

A visitor was likely to find Capone in his office, seated behind a long, mahogany desk with his back to the bay window, a cigar clenched between his teeth. On the desk in front of him sat an ornate telephone, a gold-plated inkstand and a herd of miniature ivory elephants with upraised trunks – good luck pieces. There was a bronze paperweight in the shape of the Lincoln Memorial and a pair of field glasses that he liked to use to scan the headlines of newspapers stacked on the newsstand on the street outside the hotel. On a nearby wall were three portraits depicting Abraham Lincoln, George Washington and Chicago's Mayor William "Big Bill" Thompson. On the wall next to the picture of Lincoln was a framed facsimile of the Gettysburg Address. On the opposite wall was an an eclectic assortment of objects -- painting of Cleopatra, three stuffed deer heads, and photographs of Capone's favorite movie stars – comedian Roscoe "Fatty" Arbuckle and the sultry Theda Bara. A hand-carved cuckoo clock chimed four times each hour.

A half-dozen of Capone's henchmen usually lingered in the suite, attentive to their boss' every whim. When his cigar went dead, he never needed to speak or gesture to get it re-lit; someone automatically sprang to his side, lighter flaring. When he swallowed the last drops in the bottom of a glass, someone was there to re-fill it. When Capone wanted someone beaten, stabbed, threatened or killed, there was always someone willing to do his bidding. When an election needed to be bought, voters needed to be intimidated, or a union boss needed to cough up Capone's share of cash, there was always someone around to take care of it.

Al Capone ran the city of Chicago. He controlled the mayor, the police, the state's attorney's office and just about every alderman and official in the city. There was no doubt about it: things in Chicago didn't get done without permission from Al Capone. At the height of his power, no one could touch him.

Or so it seemed. By the summer of 1930, wheels were already in motion to bring him down. Agents from the Treasury Department were working around the clock to gather enough evidence to charge him with tax evasion, a crime that paled in comparison to the scores of murders and violent acts that he had committed and ordered carried out over the years. Capone's swift rise to supremacy was coming to an end.

He was the most powerful man in Chicago – but he was a man who lived in fear. It was not the threat of arrest and prosecution that terrified the gangland boss. It was not prison that caused him to awaken in the night, screaming for help. He cowered in the darkness because he knew that the gunmen under his command could not protect him from the man who stalked his dreams and lurked in the shadows during his waking hours. There was no way that bullets could kill this man who stalked Capone – because bullets had already killed him in February 1929.

Al Capone was being pursued by a ghost.

1. CAPONE

Alphonse Capone was born in Brooklyn, New York, on January 17, 1899. His father, Gabriele, a barber, and his mother, the former Teresina Raiola, had come to America from Castellammare di Stabia, a town about fifteen miles south of Naples, Italy, in 1893. The family's surname was an Americanization of the original "Caponi," from an augmentative of *capo,* or head, meaning someone who was stubborn or arrogant, rather than the literal sense of someone with a large head. The Capones settled in an apartment in Brooklyn at 95 Navy Street in the chaos of the borough's largest Italian neighborhood. Rent in the brick and wood-frame tenements ran around $4 a month and none of the flats had heat, running hot water or bathrooms. Water had to be heated on potbellied coal stoves, which also provided scant protection against cold weather.

After working as a grocer for a short time, Gabriele opened a barbershop at 69 Park Avenue, a short distance from his home. He and Teresina, who was usually called Teresa, eventually had nine children, eight of whom survived to adulthood. In order of birth they were Vincenzo (renamed James), Ralph, Salvatore (Frank), Alphonse, Amadeo Ermino (later John, nicknamed Mimi), Umberto (Albert), Matthew, Rose (who was born and died in 1910) and Mafalda, who was named for Italy's royal princess.

Gabriele was a literate man who wrote poems and stories in his spare time. Teresa had been a seamstress in Italy and she continued to do sewing piecework after she came to Brooklyn.

The Capones were just like the other thousands of poor, uneducated Italians who had been pouring into American during the first mass migration from their country that began in the 1880s. The Italians had a harder time assimilating than the other immigrants of the era. They were, especially the Southern Italian peasants and craftsmen who made up the majority of the new arrivals, clannish and wary of outsiders. Centuries of problems caused by foreign invaders and domineering domestic masters had taught them to mistrust authority. They considered the police and the politicians their natural enemies. The laws, they believed, had been made to protect the rich and to take advantage of the poor. Italian immigrants tended to place loyalty to family and community above allegiance to their adopted country. For this reason, they did not necessarily look down on those who broke the laws of the new society, even the gangsters and racketeers, and sometimes invested them with heroic stature, as long as they were loyal to their people and, above all, good family men.

The hardships and prejudice endured by the Italian immigrants in the "land of opportunity" confirmed their suspicions about the new country. With their lack of formal education, their inability to speak, read or write the language, and their past employment limited to farming and shop-keeping, they found, as city dwellers, only the lowest-paying jobs were available to them. They became ditch-diggers, brick-layers and stone-cutters; they laid pipes and railroad ties; sold rags from street carts and stands; ran

ITALIAN IMMIGRANTS FACED MANY HARDSHIPS WHEN THEY ARRIVED IN AMERICAN, FROM LANGUAGE BARRIERS TO HARSH STEREOTYPES.

small fruit and vegetable stores; and, like Gabriel Capone, they plied scissors and razors to put food on the table. But what these jobs made was not enough and consequently, a man's wife and children worked, too. The Capone children were working odd jobs before they entered their teens.

Years of labor in the old country gave the typical Italian immigrant the physical stamina to withstand the hardships of the city slums, but the health of the children suffered. Undernourished, overcrowded in dingy cold-water tenements, lacking adequate sanitation, clean water, fresh air and sunlight, the first-generation Italians had the poorest health of any foreign group in New York. Infant mortality was almost double that of the rest of the city's population with the greatest killers being respiratory diseases, diarrhea and diphtheria.

LIKE THE CAPONE FAMILY, MANY ITALIAN AND SICILIAN IMMIGRANTS LIVED IN POVERTY IN THE ROUGH TENEMENT SLUMS OF BROOKLYN.

Illiteracy among the Italian-Americans ran to almost sixty percent, highest among all of the immigrant groups, and because their children had to go to work, very few of them ever made it to high school. By the second generation, though, compulsory education largely eliminated the illiteracy problem. During the boyhood of the Capone brothers, however, it was, together with truancy, commonplace. Except for Matt, the youngest brother, none of the Capones ever finished high school.

The Italians also had to deal with a myth that continued to plague their descendants for generations to come. According to this myth, they had criminal instincts. Mayor Joseph Shakespeare of New Orleans, another city that was flooded with thousands of Italian immigrants, wrote that the Southern Italians and Sicilians were ".... the most idle, vicious and worthless people among us." Many New Yorkers shared this view, although largely for reasons that were more fiction than truth. In fact, based on the menial jobs they took and the prejudices against them, it's surprising that more Italians didn't enter into a life of crime. Those that did, however, garnered a lot of attention. These younger immigrants, tired of hard work for little pay, found that crime opened the door to the "opportunities" that had been promised when their parents arrived on American shores. They joined the ranks of professional gunmen and bombers, extortionists, vice peddlers, labor racketeers, gambling house operators and bootleggers. It was this lawless generation that began to combine the methods of predatory Italian secret societies like the Mafia with American big business tactics to create one of the most efficient enterprises in the history of organized crime.

Gangsters and lawbreakers made up a small percentage of the Italian-American population and yet the criminal few reinforced the prejudices already in place. Many saw the "dago" as not only criminal by nature, but physically unclean and mentally inferior. The effect of these prejudices caused the Italian-American community to draw even more tightly together in a way that no outsider could penetrate. The enclaves were further divided among the traditional lines of class and regional origin – Sicilians stuck together and refused to trust Neapolitans and Romans viewed Calabrians with suspicion. The sense of community ran so deep among some Italian-Americans that they were likely to keep in touch all of their lives, no matter how widely their careers diverged. This often explains why the pallbearers at a gangster's funeral have been known to include judges, district attorneys and priests and why, at testimonial dinners for a retiring city official, police inspectors may sit next to hardened gunmen.

This was the world that shaped the life of Alphonse Capone.

However, Capone was unusual when it came to Italian-Americans of his day. He took little pride in his foreign roots. "I'm no Italian," he often said, "I'm from Brooklyn." The press often labeled him as being from Sicily or Naples but Capone was born in New York and was baptized at St. Michael's Church at the corner of Tillary and Lawrence streets, just a block from his parents' home.

Life in the neighborhood where Capone spent his first 10 years was rough, but it was never dull. Hordes of ragged children played stickball, dodged traffic and ran wild as their mothers, dark women with thick black hair, walked the streets with baskets on their heads that were filled with groceries for the day's meals. Fruit and vegetable carts lined the curbs and the completion of the Williamsburg Bridge in 1903, the greatest suspension bridge in the world at that time, brought hordes of people to the area, looking for cheap housing.

During the warm weather months, the corner of Sands and Navy streets was often the scene of music shows, attended by hundreds of people. It was during these shows that Capone acquired his passion for Italian opera. At night, Sands Street catered to darker tastes as sailors came ashore, looking for liquor and women. It was an area that was one of the roughest in the city, where murder and mayhem constantly occurred. The bars were filled with drunken sailors, stacked three and four deep and if their money ran low, there were pawnshops that stayed open all night. There were tattoo parlors, gambling dens, dancehalls, fleabag hotels that rented rooms by the hour and a legion of gaudy whores who were always available.

Capone's schooling began not far from Sands Street at P.S. #7 on Adams Street. His teacher, a 16-year-old girl named Sadie Mulvaney, had received her training from Catholic nuns and despite her youth and general unworldliness, she managed to keep order among some of the toughest boys in the neighborhood. One of them was Salvatore Luciana, who would become better known later in life as Charles "Lucky" Luciano. He and Capone took to each other and they remained lifelong friends. Sadie Mulvaney would later remember Capone as a "swarthy, sullen, troublesome boy," but he was no more trouble than any of her other students. He was big and strong for his age, quick to anger and when provoked, would fly into a murderous rage.

After school, Capone liked to hang around the docks. He never tired of watching the change of the U.S. Marine Guards behind the main Navy gate. The recruits, many of them new, had to mark time in drill formation before they could be relieved. If a raw recruit was out of step, their corporal would keep the entire detail marking time until the blunderer caught on. One afternoon, Capone, who was 10 years old but looked about 14, came to the gate with several friends. Having watched the whole routine for several weeks, he understood the corporal's strategy. On this occasion, there was one particularly inept guard who, even after three of four minutes, still didn't understand what was going on. After several minutes, Capone called out to the man and told him to get in step because he was holding up his comrades. The recruit finally changed step and the detail was dismissed. Burning with anger, the red-faced recruit charged up to the fence, making as if he planned to spit at Capone. Al flew into a rage and even though the guardsman was twice his size, challenged him to a fight. The corporal intervened and ordered the recruit back to the guardhouse. He told Capone that if the young man had actually spit on him, he

THE BROOKLYN NAVY YARD, A FAVORITE HANGOUT FOR BOYS IN CAPONE'S NEIGHBORHOOD.

would have put him on report. But Capone told him not to. He said that if the Marine stepped outside the gate, he would take care of him. He walked away with his fists clenched and his face reddened with anger.

Not long after, the corporal discussed the cocky Italian boy with the sergeant of the guards, "If this kid had a good Marine officer to get hold of him and steer him right, he'd make a good man for the Marines. But if nothing like this happens, the kid may drift for a few years until some wiseguy picks him up and steers him around and then he'll be heard from one day."

The corporal's prophecy, which he recalled in 1947 to a reporter for the *Brooklyn Eagle*, came true much sooner that he likely imagined. Capone fell under the influence of an older, Navy Street gangster named John Torrio, who had been born in Naples in 1882. By the time that he met Capone, Torrio had already established himself as an underworld figure of some note. Torrio, who stood no higher than Capone's upper chest, was a pallid little man with delicate hands and feet. He seemed to be mild-mannered and quiet, but appearances were deceiving. He had belonged to Manhattan's famous Five Points Gang for seven years until the bloodthirsty hoodlums began to dwindle in ranks, headed

JOHN TORRIO IN 1903

for either prison or the grave. He then joined another gang with headquarters in a saloon that he ran on James Street. Although calm and reflective, he made a name for himself as having no compunctions about murder and would order the execution of an enemy without hesitation – even though he himself never carried out the violence. He claimed that he had never fired a gun in his life and had practical objections to most acts of violence. He considered it a poor solution to business problems and preferred alliances, meetings and diplomacy. There was, Torrio believed, enough money in the rackets for all to share in peace without risking injury or death. Torrio, in his heyday was the closest thing in the underworld to a criminal mastermind from the pages of detective fiction. His methods greatly influence his young protégé and Capone would often remark that by imitating John Torrio, he solved many problems without bloodshed.

In 1907, the Capones moved to another Italian neighborhood about a mile south of Navy Street. The family moved into a flat on the second floor of a cold-water tenement at 38 Garfield Place in Brooklyn's Park Slope, which is now an upscale neighborhood but at the time was a rough area. All eight of them (the oldest son, James, vanished at the age of 16 and it would be many years before the family learned what had happened to him) shared the crowded space.

Al maintained his contact with his friend John Torrio. At the corner of Fourth Avenue and Union Street, above a restaurant that was within sight of Garfield Place, Torrio started a "social club" with his name in gilt letters on the window. Capone passed by the place every day on his way to school.

Capone began second grade at P.S. #113 on Butler Street, six blocks from his home. He maintained a B average all of the way up to sixth grade, when he fell behind in math and grammar, mostly due to truancy, and had to repeat the grade. During the year that he turned 14, he missed 33 days out of a possible 90 and when his teacher admonished him for skipping class, his got angry and struck her. After being thrashed by the principal, he quit school, never to return. He worked sporadically as a clerk in a candy store, then as a pinsetter in a bowling alley and finally as a paper and cloth cutter in a book bindery. There was a poolroom at 20 Garfield Place where Capone and his father both played and Al became the neighborhood champion.

Capone found that he could not roam very far from home without crossing into territory that was run by various street gangs. Any stranger was liable to arouse their suspicion and trouble often developed between Sicilians and Neapolitans. An area near Flushing Avenue was dangerous for anyone not from Sicily. The Sicilian gangs were vicious knife fighters and had brought to the Brooklyn streets an Old World tradition of disfiguring their enemies, especially informants. They would cut his face from eye to ear and this "rat" work became so well known that other gangs began imitating it to divert suspicion from themselves. Knives were a used by just about all of the Italian gangs.

The Irish gangs dominated the area near the Navy Yard. To them, especially those who worked on the docks where their leaders monopolized the labor market, the Italians were cheap competition who threatened their livelihoods. The preferred weapons of the Irish were fists and canvas sacks filled with stones and pieces of brick. Garbage can lids were used as shields. They made formidable opponents on the battlefield.

The Jews occupied the territory in the northeast section of Brooklyn known as Williamsburg. They despised the Italians for their excessive loyalty to Italians alone, which made them indifferent to group efforts toward the general betterment of all of the gangs. The Jewish gangs were less violent than most, with the exception of the Havemeyer Streeters, who waged war on all non-Jewish gangs. They repeatedly smashed the windows of the Williamsburg Mission for Jews because it advocated conversion to Christianity.

The gangs offered an escape to the young men and boys of the tenements. They offered freedom and an outlet for stifled energies, plus a camaraderie that was missing in a home where both fathers and mothers worked long hours to feed and clothe their large broods. The agencies that might have kept the boys off the streets, the schools and churches, lacked the money and support to do so. Few schools in the slums had a gym or a playground or any kind of after-school recreation programs. The average teacher was poorly trained, unimaginative, and deadly dull, mostly thanks to the uninspired curriculum. The religion taught in the churches failed to reach the young and few religious organizations had the money to offer any sort of activity that would compete with the lure of the streets. In the gangs, the boys formed their own street society, independent of the adult world around them. Led by some older, forceful boy, they pursued the thrills of shared adventure, engaging in horseplay, gambling, pilfering, vandalizing, drinking, smoking and fighting with rival gangs. Not all of the gangs were criminal. Some developed into social or athletic clubs, approved and assisted by adults in the community. For many boys, though, it was a small step from random mischief-maker to professional criminal. Practically every racketeer, Capone included, spent his formative years in a street gang.

Nearly every street gang enjoyed the protection of the local ward boss. It wasn't necessary for its members to have reached voting age at election time. They could still render valuable service by intimidating voters, slugging or kidnapping them and stealing ballot boxes. The ward bosses spared no expense securing young allies. They leased clubhouses for them, bought sports equipment and uniforms, and gave them steak dinners, picnics and tickets to ball games and prizefights. If a gang member was arrested he could count on his ward boss to furnish bail and a lawyer. If convicted, the ward boss could often get his sentence reduced or dismissed altogether.

The gang that Capone and Lucky Luciano joined as teenagers was the Five Points Gang, into which Torrio introduced them both. The gang was based on the Lower East Side of Manhattan and named for the convergence of five streets, which were Mulberry; Anthony (now Worth); Cross (now Park); Orange (now Baxter); and Little Water (which no longer exists). This was an area known as the "Five Points" and it lay between Broadway and the Bowery in present-day Chinatown. By the 1820s, this district was already starting to fall into disrepair and disrepute, filled with gambling houses and brothels and all manner of criminals. In 1842, Charles Dickens visited Five Points and in his book *American Notes* wrote how appalled he was at the horrendous living conditions he found there. Reform of the district was attempted by various religious groups, but to no avail. The district was at the heart of the "Bloody Old Sixth Ward," which had a notorious reputation for political corruption. One glaring example was an election in which the number of

THE INFAMOUS FIVE POINTS NEIGHBORHOOD IN NEW YORK GAVE BIRTH TO SCORES OF STREET GANGS, DATING BACK ALL OF THE WAY TO THE FOUNDING OF THE CITY. CAPONE AND TORRIO JOINED UP WITH THE REMNANTS OF ONE OF THE SURVIVING GANGS.

ballots that were received was higher than the number of actual registered voters in the area at the time.

For nearly a century, Five Points spawned the most brutal gangs to ever terrorize New York City. The Forty Thieves were the first, formed in 1825, and they were followed by the Shirt Tails, so named because they wore their shirts outside of their trousers; the Plug Uglies, Irishmen who protected their heads in combat with leather plug hats, felled their victims with clubs and stomped them to death with hob-nailed boots; and the Dead Rabbits ("rabbit" being a slang term of the era for ruffian), whose standard bearer led them into the fray with a dead hare impaled on a stick. After the Civil War, the Whyos emerged. Legend gave the origin of the name to a owl-like cry of "Why-oh!" they uttered while fighting. Membership in the gang required a recruit to commit at least one homicide for murder was their main source of business. A price list found on a gang member when he was arrested in 1884 details the going rate for acts of murder and mayhem the Whyos were willing to commit, ranging from $1 for a "punching," $7 for "nose and jaw broke," $15 for "ear chewed off" and $100 and up for "doing the big job" (i.e. murder.)

A gang member named "Dandy" John Dolan is credited with several macabre inventions for inflicting mayhem including a pair of shoes with pieces of ax blade embedded in them for use when kicking an opponent, and a copper eye gouger to be worn on the thumb.

The Five Points Gang, a successor to the Whyos, was in its heyday around the turn of the twentieth century under the leadership of a former prizefighter named Paul Kelly, whose given name was Paolo Vaccarelli. From the New Brighton Dance Hall, a club that he owned on Great Jones Street, he directed operations for more than 1,500 gang members and laid claim to all of the territory bounded by the Bowery and Broadway, Fourteenth Street and City Hall. A quiet, cultured man, Kelly was better educated than most gangsters of his day. He spoke English, Italian, French and Spanish and always dressed with great style. No gang leader could keep his power if he did not prove himself politically useful and Tammany Hall was in debt to Kelly for the many times when his men gave support to its candidates on election

PAUL KELLY, ALSO KNOWN AS PAOLO VACCARELLI

day.

By the time that Capone joined the Five Points Gang, Kelly no longer had the prestige that he once did. Years of warfare with Monk Eastman's Bowery gang had strained his resources and then his own lieutenant, Biff Ellison, had started to resent Kelly's leadership. One night in the winter of 1905, Ellison and a member of the rival Gopher gang burst into the New Brighton Dance Hall with guns blazing. A Five Points man named Harrington went down with a bullet in his head and Kelly himself stopped three slugs. He somehow survived the attack, and three months later opened another dance hall, Little Naples. A reform group managed to get it padlocked and Kelly retreated to Harlem, where he set up a new racket organizing labor unions. He eventually became president of the International Longshoremen's Association.

Despite his move to Harlem, Kelly did not sever his connections with what was left of the Five Points organization. Though the membership had drastically dwindled, the remnants included a core group of tough guys that a man with Kelly's business and political aspirations found worth preserving. On Seventh Avenue, close to the Broadway Theater, he set up a new headquarters for them, which he named the New Englander Social and Dramatic Club. While the name seemed innocuous, what went on there was anything but tame. Police repeatedly raided the club during investigations of knifings, beatings and shootings and while arrests were sometimes made, the charges never stuck. Capone was arrested three times during his days with the Five Pointers, once for disorderly conduct and twice for suspicion of murder. No evidence was ever produced to support the charges.

One of the main uses that Kelly found for the remaining Five Point men were their affiliations with other gangs and gang leaders. John Torrio and his friends often worked with Frank Yale, a Sicilian from Brooklyn. At the time, Yale was only 25 years old and was already making his mark in the Brooklyn rackets. Before long, he would dominate them. His specialty was murder contracts and he was quick to admit it – "I'm an undertaker," he often quipped. But he believed in diversification, owning a dancehall, the Harvard Inn, on the Coney Island waterfront that turned out to be a strategic location when Prohibition came into effect. He quickly became the first New York gangster to distribute liquor from coastal rum-running ships. Yale also rented out gunmen for labor-management disputes, working as either strikebreakers or union goons. He forced Brooklyn tobacco shops to stock cigars of his own cheap manufacture. His portrait adorned each box and soon a "Frankie Yale" became a slang term for a bad smoke. Race horses, prizefighters, nightclubs and a gangland funeral parlor were all part of Yale's operations but his single greatest source of profit and power was the Unione Siciliane.

Over the decades, the Unione Siciliane has been described as everything from a secret criminal society with close ties to the Mafia to a much-maligned fraternal organization. It eventually became a sort of twisted combination of both. In the late 1800s, the Unione Siciliane originated in New York as a lawful fraternal organization, the first to advance the interests of Sicilian immigrants. For modest dues, its members received life insurance and various social benefits. Branches began to spring up everywhere there was a sizable Sicilian community. Gradually, the organization developed enough strength to swing local elections, which is probably how it first gained the attention of gangsters. Soon, a group of New York racketeers began to infiltrate the Unione Siciliane. Their leader was Ignazio Saietta, known as Lupo the Wolf, a

FRANKIE YALE

bloodthirsty killer and leader in the Black Hand extortion rings of the early 1900s. Through Saietta's maneuvers, which started in New York and extended out to branches in other cities like Chicago, the Unione Siciliane acquired a Jekyll and Hyde nature, with one side the open and respectable organization that did good works for needy Sicilians, and the other, hidden and malevolent, dealing in prostitution, extortion, kidnapping, racketeering and murder. It became commonplace for the president of the association to be a gangster. During a six-year period, the U.S. Secret Service traced sixty murders to members of the Unione Siciliane. Saietta himself maintained a "murder stable" in Harlem with meat hooks on which he hung his victims and a furnace that he used to burn them alive. According to one of the only Unione members that police were able to persuade to talk, recruits had to submit to a blood ritual to become part of the inner circle. Led to an altar, the recruit had to prick his finger with a stiletto and swear fidelity and secrecy to the organization.

The reputable officers of the Unione Siciliane, the businessmen, judges, city and state officials, claimed to know nothing about how the gangsters were exploiting it. They owed the association too great of a debt to even endanger it. The frequent fund-raising functions provided opportunities for the politicians and business owners to meet and make deals with people in whose company they couldn't ordinarily be seen – which allowed them to make even more money.

In the 1920s, hoping the shed the unfortunate image that it had gained, the Unione changed its name to the Italo-American National Union, but the name change did nothing to alter its character. Law enforcement officials were skeptical about the statements and disclaimers issued by union officials that professed to be disheartened by those who felt the organization bred crime and disorder. Executive officer Constantino Vitello wrote: "Our officers are strong business and professional men. Our members are honest Americans. The constitution of the Unione, strictly enforced, declares that no man who has a blot on his character may enter and those who are proved to have committed a felonious act while members may be expelled."

At the time this statement was issued, Frankie Yale had been the national head of the Unione Siciliane for nearly a decade.

Yale hired Capone as a bouncer and bartender for the Harvard Inn, positions which suited the young man. When required to break up a fight in the club, he was quick to use a club or his large fists. He was also fast and accurate with a pistol, having perfected his skills shooting beer bottles in the basement of the Adonis Social Club, a favorite Brooklyn hangout.

It would be during his time at the Harvard Inn that Capone gained his trademark facial scars. The incident took place one night when Frank Galluccio, a petty felon from Brooklyn, dropped into the club with his sister. Capone made a remark to the girl that Galluccio found offensive and he whipped out a knife and went for Capone's face. When the wounds healed, they left brutal scars. Capone, normally vindictive, chose to forgive Galluccio, perhaps knowing that what he said to the girl had been out of line. Some years later, in one of those magnanimous gestures that he had learned could win him admiration, Capone hired Galluccio as a bodyguard for $100 a week.

Many young and rising mobsters of the day started what were called "cellar clubs," which were usually rented storefronts where, behind closed blinds, the members gambled, drank and entertained girls. In 1918, during a party at a cellar club on Carroll Street, Capone met a tall, slim, blonde named Mae Coughlin. She was 21, two years older than Capone, and worked as sales girl in a department store in the neighborhood. Her parents, Michael Coughlin, a construction worker, and her mother, Bridget, were respected in

A YOUNG AL CAPONE, ALREADY SHOWING THE SCARS THAT WOULD EARN HIM THE DESPISED NICKNAME THAT WOULD FOLLOW HIM THE REST OF HIS LIFE.

the Irish community for their hard work and religious devotion.

Despite the antagonisms between the Irish and the Italians, young Irish girls often showed a preference toward Italian men, mostly because they were willing to marry young, while Irish boys tended to wait until they were settled and secure in their occupation. John Torrio, for example, had married a young Irish girl from Kentucky, Ann McCarthy. Capone was apparently so eager to marry Mae that he obtained a special dispensation from the Church, eliminating the necessity to publish *banns*, a public announcement of an impending marriage that enabled anyone to raise a legal impediment to it. This prevented marriages that were legally invalid, either under Church or civil law. Presumably, the difference in their ages embarrassed the bride because on the marriage certificate she lowered her age by one year and Capone raised his by one. The ceremony took place on December 18, 1918, and was performed by Reverend James J. Delaney, pastor of the St. Mary Star of the Sea Church, where Mae's family worshipped. The bride's sister, Anna, and a friend of Capone's, James De Vico, were witnesses. The following year, Mae bore her first and only child, Albert Francis, nicknamed Sonny. Torrio was his godfather and on each of Sonny's birthdays, he bought him a $5,000 savings bond.

Torrio had been spending more and more time in Chicago, starting in 1909, when his uncle, James "Big Jim" Colosimo, first brought him there. Although he continued to pursue ventures in New York, Chicago was now his home. Capone's fortunes, meanwhile, had not changed and the money that he craved to take care of his wife and son still eluded him. Already suspected of two murders, he faced indictment for a third if a man that he sent to the hospital during a bar brawl should die. The man lived, but Capone was no longer around to hear about his recovery. A message had come from Torrio, summoning him to Chicago.

With his wife and son, he fled New York and headed west to the Windy City.

2. COLOSIMO

The most important criminal in Chicago during the early 1900s was Big Jim Colosimo, who ruled the underworld for a longer period of time than any man in the history of the city. The money that he raked in from the many immoral and illegal enterprises that he controlled was conservatively estimated at $50,000 a month for about eight years, an enormous take at that time, although small compared with the haul made by the bootleggers and racketeers of the 1920s. Colosimo was a great spender. He built a fine home for his father, and an even grander one for himself, filled with an assortment of expensive and gaudy furniture. He supported a horde of relatives, some of whom worked in his various brothels and saloons. He maintained a large staff of servants, including two uniformed chauffeurs to drive his lavish automobiles. He kept his massive girth clad in white linen suits and he had a fixation on diamonds. He wore a diamond ring on every finger, diamond studs on his shirt front, a huge diamond horseshoe pinned to his vest, diamond cufflinks, and belts and suspenders that were fitted with diamonds. He bought the stones from thieves and needy gamblers and hoarded them like other men collect books and paintings. He often carried loose stones in a small bag in his pocket and when bored would pour them from hand to hand or would lay them out on a black cloth to watch them sparkle in the light. Colosimo was a strange character and a man who helped to usher in the era of organized crime in Chicago.

Colosimo was 10 years old when his father brought him to the United States from Italy. He spent all but two or three of his remaining thirty-nine years in the red-light district of Chicago's South Side. He began his working life as a newsboy and bootblack but quickly changed careers when he saw the money that could be made in crime. At 18, he was an accomplished pickpocket and pimp with a half-dozen girls working for him. By the late 1890s, after several brushes with the law, Colosimo abandoned his life of crime and became a street-sweeper, the only honest job he ever held. By 1900, he was promoted to foreman of his crew and had organized his fellow workers into a social and athletic club that eventually became a labor union. At this point, Colosimo was befriended by the two most powerful political bosses in Chicago: First Ward Committeeman Michael Kenna and Alderman John Coughlin. Within the First Ward lay the notorious Levee District, a vice-laden area filled with whorehouses, saloons and gambling parlors. Kenna and Coughlin employed Colosimo as their collector in return for the votes of all of the members of his unions.

In 1902, Colosimo married Vittoria Moresco,

COLOSIMO WITH HIS ATTORNEY, CHARLES E. ERBSTEIN

(LEFT) COLOSIMO'S OLDER, AND QUITE UNATTRACTIVE, WIFE, VITTORIA MORESCO. (RIGHT) THE SOUTH SIDE LEVEE DISTRICT

who ran a brothel on Armour Avenue. By 1912, he and his wife owned 35 brothels, catering to all income levels. He also organized a white slavery ring with another brothel owner named Maurice Van Bever, a fellow dandy who was transported around the Levee in a red carriage driven by a liveried coachman. Perhaps the crowning achievement of Big Jim's career was the opening of Colosimo's Café in 1910 at 2126 South Wabash Avenue. The café became the premiere nightspot in the city and no other club could compete with its star entertainers, the beauty of its chorus girls or the skill of its acclaimed orchestra. With musical attractions, good food and a wide array of vintage wines, it attracted the rich and powerful from all over the city – all of whom had to brave the wickedness of the Levee district to get there.

COLOSIMO'S RESTAURANT ON SOUTH WABASH, IN THE HEART OF THE LEVEE.

Bounded north and south by Twenty-Second and Eighteenth streets and east and west by Clark and Wabash, the Levee took shape during the World's Columbian Exposition in 1893, also known as the Chicago World's Fair, when thousands of people from all over the world descended on the city. It became one of the best-known concentrations of crime and vice. Visitors to the district could partake of just about every form of sin imaginable and in addition to Colosimo's, there were two other vice rings that formed the criminal organization that ruled the Levee and which provided the area's various forms of "entertainment."

Maurice Van Bever and his wife, Julia, who operated an interstate white slavery ring that extended from St. Louis to

Chicago, controlled one of the Levee's vice rings. Their operation inspired the passage of the Mann Act in 1910. Representative James Robert Mann of Illinois introduced the legislation that made it illegal to transport women across state lines for immoral purposes. It was believed that operators in the Levee had imported more than 22,000 young women into the United States to work in their brothels.

Charley Maibum, who ran a pay-by-the-hour hotel where the local streetwalkers could take their clients for a quick rendezvous, operated the city's third vice ring. He often served as "muscle" and protection for other brothels that ran into trouble with competitors or law enforcement officials.

In addition to these, there were scores of independent operators in the district. The Levee featured a number of "dollar a girl" joints, where the women provided services on a volume basis. Many of these unfortunate young ladies ended up on the Levee thanks to the smooth charm of oily con men, who lured them away from small-town life with promises of romance and marriage in the big city. Instead of a love and excitement, they ended up robbed, beaten and "broken in" at the hellish dives of the Levee. In those days, most could see the need for organized prostitution but the methods used to induce women to become prostitutes were looked upon as unwholesome. In Chicago (and in every other major city of the day), vice operators had no problem paying off police officers and politicians for permission to run houses of prostitution. However, the officials were less tolerant of what was called the "procuring" of the girls, although the right amount of money could always get them to look the other way. Chicago's vice trade required so many women that procurers operated with or without approval, and the city became a supply point for other cities in the Midwest.

But not all of the bordellos in this part of town were cheap dives that were filled with "white slavery" victims and broken-down old whores. It was also home to the famed Everleigh Club and a number of other brothels that, while certainly not in the Everleigh Club's league, were not exactly flophouses either.

The Everleigh Club, run by two sisters, Ada and Minna Everleigh, was perhaps the finest brothel in the United States at the time. Lavishly decorated and filled with only the most beautiful and most cultured working girls, the Everleighs charged exorbitant rates and offered customers not only sex, but a complete experience with meals, music and more. The bordello became nationally known and attracted visitors from all over the country. There was nothing quite like it, before or since.

Other high-end brothels were operated by Vic Shaw, Zoe Millard, and Georgie Spencer, a trio of madams who were in constant competition with the Everleighs. Shaw was a prominent red light district fixture for almost forty years and even after the Levee was shut down, she continued to operate brothels and out-call operations until she was well into her seventies. Millard was inclined to blame anything bad that happened in the Levee on the Everleighs, and once inflicted a terrible beating on one of her girls for defending the sisters. Spencer, whose brothel was on South Dearborn Street in the same block as the Everleigh Club, flaunted her operation and was eventually driven out of business by the police, who usually turned a blind eye to vice operations. Spencer was so abrasive, however, that they refused to look the

THE EVERLEIGH CLUB, THE SWANKIEST BROTHEL IN THE CITY.

(LEFT) INFAMOUS MADAM, VIC SHAW. (RIGHT) HER BORDELLO ON THE LEVEE, WHICH WAS IN CONSTANT COMPETITION WITH THE EVERLEIGH SISTERS. A LONG-STANDING FEUD BETWEEN THE TWO BORDELLOS WENT ON FOR YEARS.

other way.

Despite the almost frantic efforts of these three madams, the Everleighs always maintained that their biggest problems came from Ed Weiss, who, with his wife, ran a brothel next door to the Everleigh Club. Weiss had married a former harlot who had worked for the Everleighs, Aimee Leslie, and the pair bought out the brothel next door, which had belonged to Julia Hartrauft. They remodeled the place, creating sort of a scaled-down Everleigh Club, which irritated the sisters. The success of the place was due to in part to its luxury and the beauty of the girls Weiss hired, but most of it came from Weiss' shrewdness in putting most of the Levee cab drivers on his payroll. When a drunken spender got into a cab and asked to be driven to the famed Everleigh Club, he would be taken to Weiss' place instead. Most of them never knew the difference.

The brothel on the other side of the Everleigh Club was called the Sappho, and was owned and operated by Weiss' brother, Louis. It was also a better class of resort but it was never as popular as Ed's. There were a number of other, cheaper brothels, like the Casino, which was run by Vic Shaw's husband, Roy Jones; the Old Ninety-Two; French Charlie's, and the California, which was run by Blubber Bob Gray and his wife, Theresa McCafey. The California was one of the toughest parlor houses in the district. There were about thirty or forty girls who worked there at one time, wearing shoes, flimsy chemises and nothing else. They stood naked in the windows and doorways whenever a policeman was not in sight and two men worked the sidewalk outside, inviting in any man who passed by. When customers appeared, the girls were brought into a large room that was empty except for a couple of benches along one wall. The girls were paraded past and the customers were allowed to choose. The going rate for a tumble was $1, but fifty cents would do if the man turned out his pockets and proved that he didn't have a dollar to his name. The California remained one of the seediest dives in the district until 1909, when it was raided by federal immigration agents who were searching for foreign women who had been brought to the United States for "immoral purposes." They found six "white slaves" at the California. Blubber Bob, who weighed over three hundred pounds, tried to escape when the authorities burst in, but he got stuck in a window and it took three men to pull him out.

There were several other celebrated houses in the Levee during its heyday, including that of Frankie Wright, who called her brothel the Library. It got its name for the single case of well-worn books that graced its parlor. Big Jim Colosimo owned two large brothels in the district: the Victoria and the Saratoga. The Victoria was named in honor of Colosimo's wife, Victoria (Vittoria) Moresco. Colosimo himself spent most of his time at his restaurant on Wabash Avenue, near Twenty-Second Street.

At one end of the district was a notorious saloon called the Bucket of Blood, which stood across the street from Bed Bug Row. Nearby was a brothel called Black May's, which offered light-skinned African-American girls for white customers and allegedly presented "animal acts" for those with a taste for such things. There was also the acclaimed House of All Nations, which featured prostitutes from foreign countries. The place boasted a $2 entrance and a $5 entrance, although the same girls worked both sides of the house.

The Levee ran wide open for years, under the protection of its vice lords, well-paid Chicago cops and, of course, corrupt politicians, who made sure that the necessary money made it into the right hands. Reformers, especially religious ones, constantly hampered operations in the Levee and eventually, the crusade (and propaganda) against "white slavery" would get the better of the district.

During the heyday of the Levee,

ADVERTISING FOR COLOSIMO'S RESTAURANT

Colosimo's Café was the heart and soul of the district. It was a place of gaudy opulence, from its gilded doorknobs to the massive mahogany and glass bar. Green velvet covered the walls and gold and crystal chandeliers hung from a sky-blue ceiling where cherubs cavorted on cotton-white clouds. The restaurant was a dazzling dreamscape of gold mirrors, tapestries and murals of tropical vistas. With the flick of a switch, a hydraulic lift raised or lowered the dance floor. Festivities seldom got underway before midnight and often continued until well past dawn. In a suite of rooms on the second floor, gamblers could find any game they fancied from faro to roulette to high-stakes poker.

Colosimo's Café enjoyed national renown and it was a place where local dignitaries and businessmen might rub elbows with killers and thieves. It catered to visiting celebrities like Al Jolson, George M. Cohan, John Barrymore and Sophie Tucker, whose "coon-shouter" songs with gestures (like the "Angle Worm

Wriggle") had caused the normally permissive Chicago police to place her under arrest for indecency. Colosimo loved the opera and no matter how packed the place was, he could always find a seat for a member or guest of the Chicago Civic Opera Company. He considered acclaimed tenor Enrico Caruso a close friend.

But as profitable as Colosimo's was, it produced only a fraction of the fortune that allowed Big Jim to maintain two limousines, each with its own chauffeur, homes for his father and himself, a wife and a mistress. The chief sources of his annual income were white slavery and his chain of brothels.

Colosimo had actually met his wife because of the Levee's sex trade. In 1902, while working as a bagman for ward bosses Kenna and Coughlin, he made the acquaintance of Victoria Moresco, a fat, unattractive, middle-aged madam who operated a second-rate brothel on Armour Avenue. She offered Jim the position of manager and he accepted. Two weeks later, they were married. Under Colosimo's management, the brothel prospered and he soon acquired a brothel of his own, then another, until before long, he owned and controlled scores of them. Out of every $2 that his girls made, Colosimo kept $1.20. Like many of his competitors, he also ran a number of saloons near, or connected by passageways, to his bordellos.

The supply of available prostitutes never really met the demand for the turnover was far too rapid. The average parlor house whore seldom lasted more than five years. As she aged quickly, she would sink to cheaper and cheaper houses until she hit bottom on Bed Bug Row or became a streetwalker. Drink, drugs and disease usually completed her destruction. So, to replenish their stock, the vice controllers of the Levee turned to white slavery.

The origin of the term "white slave" is usually associated with Mary Hastings, a Chicago madam of the

ONE OF THE THOUSANDS OF "WHITE SLAVES" AND PROSTITUTES THAT WORKED THE BROTHELS OF THE LEVEE. COLOSIMO NOT ONLY OPERATED A NUMBER OF SPORTING HOUSES, HE WAS ALSO INVOLVED IN BRINGING FRESH GIRLS AND MAKING SURE THEY WERE "BROKEN" TO WORK IN THE BROTHELS.

1890s who lured many young Midwestern girls to her brothels in Chicago's notorious Custom House Place vice district. Seeking out girls between the ages of 13 and 17, she promised them jobs in the big city. To their alarm, the girls were instead taken to one of the brothels, where they were locked up, stripped and "broken in" by professional rapists. The broken girls that Mary did not employ, she sold to other brothel-keepers at prices that varied depending on the girls' ages and looks, very young girls being the most sought-after. In the midst of all of this, one of her victims managed to scrawl on a piece of paper, "I'm being held as a slave," and tossed the note out of a window. Found by a passerby and taken to the police, who raided the brothel and rescued the girl, the note supposedly inspired a newspaper reporter to coin the term "white slave." Incidentally, the raid didn't do Mary Hastings any serious damage. She continued to operate at the same address for several more years until four of her captives escaped and finally brought about her downfall.

Colosimo was deeply involved in Chicago's white slave traffic. In 1903, he had joined forces with Maurice and Julia Van Bever. They organized a new gang to handle fresh stock, established connections with white slavers in New York, St. Louis and Milwaukee, and over the course of the next six years imported hundreds of girls, either putting them to work in their own establishments or selling them off

to other brothels.

Vice made Colosimo a vast fortune, which, in turn, made him one of Chicago's wealthiest Italians. Thanks to this, he became a natural target for Black Hand extortionists.

The Black Hand first emerged as an organized crime entity around 1900. Because of the isolation caused by their lack of language skills, Italian immigrants were easy prey from criminals within their own ranks. Suspicious of authority, they were at the mercy of groups like "La Mano Nera," the Black Hand, a shadowy society that terrorized poor and working-class Italians. In fact, the "society" was simply a collection of criminals, and the name was created by journalists, but the notion of it inspired real terror.

The way the Black Hand operated was both simple and direct. First, a victim who showed signs of prosperity would be chosen from among the Italian immigrant population. For instance, if a man purchased any property and that fact became public knowledge, he could almost count on the attention of the Black Hand. A letter, bearing a signature of the Black Hand was sent to the victim demanding money. If the letter was ignored, or the victim refused to pay, his home, office or business would be bombed. If he still refused to pay, he would be murdered. Most of the letters were blunt instructions about sums of money and where they were to be delivered. Others were more clever and worded with deference and Italian courtesy. No matter how they were phrased, each brought the promise of death if the instructions were not carried out to the letter.

Hundreds of threat letters were received and countless murders were carried out between 1900 and 1920. Despite the magnitude of these operations, none of the extensive investigations conducted by the police ever revealed a Black Hand organization that reached national or even citywide proportions. The "Black Hand" was not an actual group, but a method of crime. It was used by individuals, by small groups,

TENTH VICTIM OF BLACK HAND MURDERS

ASSAILANTS SHOOT MAN IN BACK AND ESCAPE.

Slayers Leave Victim Bleeding in Street to Be Picked Up by Police.

BLACK HAND EXTORTION LETTERS BEGAN TO BE SENT TO COLOSIMO, THREATENING DEATH AND BOMBINGS IF THEIR DEMANDS WERE NOT MET.

and by large, organized gangs. In Italy and Sicily, the tactic was employed by the Mafia and called the Black Hand because as a general rule, extortion letters, which formed the initial phase of the terrorism, bore the imprint of a hand in black ink. The letters were also sometimes marked with crude drawings of a skull and crossbones or, for variety, crosses and daggers.

Between 1900 and 1920, there were an alleged 400 murders in Chicago ascribed to the Black Hand. The gangs that made up the Black Hand preyed on the Italian and Sicilian immigrants and many murders occurred. One vicious and mysterious killer was called the "Shotgun Man." He was believed to be responsible for at least one-third of the thirty-eight unsolved murders that occurred between January 1910 and March 1911.

As the police attempted to combat the Black Hand gangs, they were faced with impossible obstacles. Hundreds of arrests were made but suspects were usually released within hours because there was no evidence connecting them with specific crimes. Many cases of murder and extortion were brought into the courts but convictions were nearly impossible to obtain and those few who were sent to prison were usually quickly paroled thanks to payoffs to corrupt politicians. The reason it was so hard to prosecute the Black Hand gang leaders was the same reason they were so terrifying in the first place: as soon as a Black Hand suspect was arrested, witnesses and members of the victim's family were threatened with death if they gave information to the police. Judges, jurors, members of the prosecutor's staff, and even their families received threats. In one case, a witness was about to give the details of a Black Hand extortion plot when a man entered the courtroom and waved a red handkerchief at him. The witness froze and refused to speak. The state had to abandon the case.

By the late 1910s, police officials were forced to try and downplay the Black Hand. They simply had no way of controlling the situation and no way to combat the threats or apprehend the killers when the extortion went one step too far. Most Chicago cops paid them a grudging respect as an elusive and resourceful prey, while others denied their existence altogether, as the FBI would do a few years later when forced to confront the reality of the Mafia. The prejudices of those in the city government who sought to dismiss the Black Hand failed to take into account the helplessness and despair of the Italian immigrants as they tried to cope with the hardships of life in a new and unpredictable country, only to be faced with being terrorized on top of it.

Because of this, some of the Italian business and professional men decided to try and take matters into their own hands. They formed what was called the White Hand Society, an organization that was sponsored by wealthy businessmen, the Italian Chamber of Commerce, Italian newspapers, and several fraternal orders of Italians and Sicilians. It was formed to work with the police and to try and exterminate the Black Hand. Although virtually every member of the society was threatened with death at one time or another, it was active for several years. Private detectives were employed to help the police investigate Black Hand cases and agents were even sent to Italy and Sicily to look into past histories of the most notorious gangsters. They also arranged

"DEATH CORNER" AT OAK AND MILTON STREETS, WHERE A NUMBER OF UNSOLVED MURDERS TOOK PLACE, INCLUDING THOSE CARRIED OUT BY THE MYSTERIOUS "SHOTGUN MAN"

for the protection of witnesses and their family members. Several murderers and extortionists were sent to prison through the efforts of the White Hand, but they were soon paroled and resumed their activities. For this reason, this society of neighborhood vigilantes was more of a symbolic gesture than anything else. Their intentions were good but they were up against a much too powerful adversary. The White Hand faded out of existence around 1912.

The Black Hand gangs endured for about another eight years until finally a federal law that forced them out of existence. Once the federal government began prosecuting extortion as the misuse of the United States mail, dozens of Black Hand gangsters began to be convicted, fined and sent to federal prisons. The corrupt politicians were unable to help them and most of the convicted men served their full sentences. Thanks to government intervention, the bombings, murders and extortion that still took place were carried out by other methods than through the use of the mail and soon the Black Hand began to disappear.

By 1920, and the coming of Prohibition, most of the extortionist gangs found that bootlegging and rum-running was a more profitable field for their talents and the Black Hand became a thing of the past. There is no doubt that the Black Hand, believed by the general public to be a sinister Italian criminal conspiracy, set the stage for the heyday of organized crime that was to come.

In 1909, Colosimo received his first Black Hand extortion letter. He knew what to expect and at first, he went along with it. He met demands for as much as $5,000 but as the extortionists continued to plague him, demanding more and more money each time, he decided to fight back. He commanded plenty of tough gunmen and at the next attempt, Colosimo wrapped up a bundle of plain paper, armed himself with a revolver and, accompanied by an assortment of muscle concealing sawed-off shotguns, set out for a rendezvous under a South Side bridge in advance of the appointed time. After dropping off the bundle as directed, Colosimo and his men hid in the shadows across the street. At midnight, three men approached the bundle. Before they could examine it, they were blasted to death amidst the roar of the shotguns.

After that, Colosimo enjoyed a moment of peace, but it did not last long. He soon received a demand for money from yet another Black Hand gang. He decided that he needed someone to work with him in Chicago who was smarter and more ruthless than he was. Vittoria convinced her husband to call John Torrio, her nephew in New York.

3. TORRIO

John Torrio was 31 years old when he came to Chicago in 1909. Soon after he arrived, three more Black Hand extortionists were slaughtered under the Rock Island Railroad overpass on Archer Avenue. Torrio, with his personal aversion to bloodshed, had arranged the massacre. Other killings followed until finally, Colosimo was free of his tormentors.

But Torrio's service to Colosimo went far beyond planning the murders of Black Handers. He was an organizational genius. Years later, Elmer L. Irey, chief of the Enforcement Branch of the U.S. Treasury Department, called him "the father of modern American gangsterdom." This was no exaggeration for within months, the cool, soft-spoken New Yorker had consolidated Colosimo's holdings in such a way that he became the foremost Chicago racketeer of his era. Starting with the Saratoga brothel, of which his grateful uncle made him the manager, Torrio was soon supervising all of Colosimo's brothels and getting them on a sound financial footing. He next organized the saloons and the gambling dens. He guided the Colosimo-Van Bever white slave ring into the dominant force in the Levee and personally saw to the bribing of police and public officials. When Colosimo branched out into the protection racket, Torrio collected the payments, using no other persuasion than a quiet word of warning, a thin smile and an ice cold stare. He suffered a slight setback when he was arrested, along with other members of the white slave ring, after the transporting of a dozen girls from St. Louis to Chicago. Maurice and Julia Van Bever paid a $1,000 fine and went to jail for a year. Five others received lesser sentences, among them the prosecution's main witness, a pimp named Joe Bovo, who had delivered the St. Louis merchandise. Torrio, however, was freed because Bovo would not testify against him. Colosimo, shielded by his political connections, was not even questioned in the case.

JOHN TORRIO AROUND THE TIME HE ARRIVED IN CHICAGO TO HELP COLOSIMO WITH HIS BLACK HAND EXTORTION THREATS.

In the same year that Torrio came to Chicago, reform movements began gathering strength. The Levee's vice rings began to fall apart, but Torrio managed to steer his uncle safely through all of the problems. On the night of October 18, 1909, evangelist Gipsy Smith led 2,000 of his followers into the red-light district. By the time they made it to Twenty-Second Street, more than 20,000 curious Chicagoans were marching with them. As the whores and their madams looked on in stunned disbelief from behind closed doors, three Salvation Army bands struck up and the congregation joined Smith in the hymn "Where He Lead Me I Will Follow." Marching back and forth through the red-light district, they knelt in prayer before the most notorious brothels. Smith ended the protest with a prayer for all of the Levee's fallen women.

RELIGIOUS GROUPS MARCHED ON THE LEVEE AND INSPIRED REFORMERS TO SHUT DOWN MANY OF THE CLUBS AND BROTHELS IN THE DISTRICT. SOON, THE REFORMS BEGAN TO HAMPER COLOSIMO AND TORRIO'S VICE OPERATIONS.

The immediate result of the protest was not what Smith had in mind. Many of the young men in the parade crowd, who might have never set foot in the Levee, stayed behind to sample the wares of the various houses of ill repute. Once the religious folks were gone, the party in the district really began. Minna Everleigh wickedly told a newspaper reporter, "We are glad of the business, of course, but I am sorry to see so many nice young men coming down here for the first time."

But it was not meant to last. In 1910, white slavery itself was crippled (although not ended) by the passage of the Mann Act. The famous Everleigh Club was closed down in 1911 and the reform movement dealt a final blow to the Colosimo-Van Bever white slave ring. In New York, a girl who had been part of the ring defied threats of death and publicly exposed the system. Pending indictments against the white slavers, she was whisked away for safekeeping in Bridgeport, Connecticut. There, according to witnesses, two men came for her in a car. They showed her Department of Justice credentials and told her that she was needed for the signing of an affidavit. The next morning, her bullet-riddled body was found in a cemetery outside of Bridgeport. The case against Colosimo collapsed and soon after, he handed Torrio a percentage of all of his brothel and gambling interests.

After closing down the Everleigh Club, the Chicago police investigations stalled out. But Torrio was not optimistic about the future of the Levee. He convinced Colosimo that the days of wide-open vice were numbered and that they should plan for the future. What prompted their next step was the new mobility of the average American. In six years, from 1908 to 1913, the number of automobiles in the country increased tenfold and became more affordable than ever before. One of the by-products of this new mobility was the roadhouse, an isolated establishment for drinking, gambling and prostitution that was usually outside the jurisdiction of most police forces. It occurred to Torrio that the countryside offered massive room for the expansion of the vice industry. Colosimo agreed and they established their first roadhouse in Burnham, a tiny city on the Illinois-Indiana border. The president of the unincorporated village was 20-year-old John Patton, who had been working in a local saloon since age 14. He proved a willing pawn and by the time the next reform wave swept over the Levee, Colosimo and Torrio were ready.

The next attack on the Levee began with a massive civil welfare parade that was organized on September 29, 1912. This protest spurred grand jury indictments and complaints to be filed against property owners in the district, followed by the padlocking of many of the district's resorts. But the vice lords fought back. A meeting was held at Colosimo's Café and soon after, the Levee girls donned their gaudiest clothes and scattered through Chicago's most respectable residential districts. Hips swaying and voices loud and raucous, they sashayed into fancy restaurants, tried to book rooms in elegant hotels, rang doorbells and generally made a nuisance of themselves. The authorities were forced to concede that a mass eviction from the Levee would be a mistake and so they suspended the raids – but only temporarily.

The reformers continued their fight until, in November 1912, Chicago put an end to segregated vice in the city. However, the Levee did not completely disappear. Many of the famous houses of ill repute were bulldozed, as they stood in the way of an important east-west railroad corridor, but others remained and became the jazz clubs of the 1920s. In addition, new bordellos opened in the suburbs and in other parts of the city and some of the original spots also opened their doors again, now disguised as hotels, saloons and cabarets.

In Burnham, Colosimo's first roadhouse was doing brisk business. It was open 24 hours a day with ninety girls working in three shifts. It took in more than $9,000 per month, of which Torrio took half. They next acquired the Speedway Inn and the Burnham Inn, both of which Torrio supervised. None of the sporting houses stood more than a few feet from the Indiana line and in the event of a raid, the girls and their customers could easily avoid arrest by scurrying across the border. Warnings of police activity came through a network of gas station attendants, short order cooks and operators of roadside produce stands along the route to Burnham. The customers, mostly laborers in the area's steel mills and oil refineries, were a rough lot, but they were free with their money.

Other vice operators set up under the protective wing of Burnham's young mayor until finally, the small community, which measured barely a mile wide, was nothing but a cluster of buildings that offered booze, gambling and whores. Nobody did business there for long without Torrio's consent. One night a hoodlum named "Dandy Joe" Fogarty drunkenly threatened Torrio in the Burnham Inn. He was found later with his body riddled with bullets. Two of Torrio's men, Sonny Dunn and Tommy Enright, were briefly detained by the local constabulary but were soon let go.

W. C. DANNENBURG, HEAD OF
THE NEW MORALS SQUAD.

Things were not going as well for Colosimo and Torrio in the remnants of the Levee. One police inspector had been sentenced to Joliet Correctional Center, two others suspended and a superintendent of police was dismissed for accepting graft. Mayor Carter Harrison, Jr. had appointed a retired Army officer, Major Mettellus L.C. Funkhouser, to the newly created post of Second Deputy Police Commissioner, with the power to investigate and prosecute vice offenders independently of the regular police department. Funkhouser established the Morals Squad and chose as its director Inspector W.C. Dannenburg, the man who had been successful in locking up the Van Bevers.

Disturbed by these new appointments, the Levee vice bosses convened again at Colosimo's place. They agreed that the Morals Squad must be stopped, if not with bribe money, then with murder. One of the operators was given the task of offering Dannenburg $2,000 a month to protect the brothels, but the inspector arrested him for attempted bribery. During the weeks that followed, the Morals Squad arrested more than 2,000 vice operators and brought charges of graft against the regular police officers assigned to the Levee. Colosimo and his colleagues voted to kill Funkhouser, Dannenburg and various other members of the Morals Squad. At the same time, Torrio sent for Roxie Vanilli, his cousin and a veteran of the New York gangs.

Among those present for the vote was Roy Jones, who ran a saloon at 2037 South Wabash Avenue. In April 1914, a man named Isaac Henagow, suspected of being a Morals Squad informant, dropped in for a drink. He was shot to death in the bar. Mayor Harrison revoked Jones' license and when the Levee politicians failed to get it restored, Jones came to believe that he had been double-crossed. He soon began making threats that he would reveal the plot to kill off the members of the Morals Squad. Colosimo offered him $15,000 to leave the country but Jones refused. Colosimo then tried to frame him on a white slavery charge and Jones finally fled to Detroit. By this time, though, his stories of planned assassinations had reached the ears of Inspector Dannenburg.

A short time later, a police sergeant from the Morals Squad was knifed to death while investigating Henagow's murder. Then, on July 16, Dannenburg led a raid on the Turf, a brothel at 28 West Twenty-Second Street. After the raid was over, and the girls

ROY FRANCHE BEING LED TO THE POLICE WAGON AFTER BEING ARRESTED FOR THE MURDER OF ISAAC HENAGOW, A MORALS SQUAD INFORMATION, AT THE SALOON OF ROY JONES. THE SALOON WAS CLOSED DOWN, CAUSING JONES TO BELIEVE HE HAD BEEN DOUBLE CROSSED BY TORRIO. HE THREATENED TO TELL ALL THAT HE KNEW ABOUT THE SOUTH SIDE VICE OPERATIONS AND HE WAS SOON "CONVINCED" TO LEAVE TOWN.

were loaded into a paddy wagon, Dannenburg and his men were standing outside when they were confronted by an angry, shouting mob. Hoping to get away gracefully, they started walking toward Michigan Avenue, but the mob followed, still shouting but now also throwing stones at the officers. Dannenburg, obviously not liking where things were going, hurried to catch up with the paddy wagon. He climbed aboard and took off toward the station house. As the Morals Squad officers continued to walk, they drew their revolvers in hopes that a threat of possible force might get the mob to back off – it didn't work. Moments later, a red automobile appeared and parked near the back of the unruly crowd. John Torrio, Roxie Vanilli and a tough named Mac Fitzpatrick got out. At that moment, two regular police sergeants, Stanley J. Birns and John C. Sloop, came around the corner of Michigan and Twenty-Second. Seeing guns and mistaking Dannenburg's men for thugs, they also drew their revolvers. By this time, Vanilli and Fitzpatrick had mixed in with the mob and seconds later, shots rang out. Who fired the first shots – and who they were aimed at – has never been determined. But when the gunfire ceased, Sergeant Birns lay dead and three of Dannenburg's men had been hit several times. The red auto was gone. A third officer from the Twenty-Second Street Station, Sergeant Edward P. O'Grady, arrived after the shooting and he ran into Torrio and Fitzpatrick as they were helping a wounded Vanilli back into the car. They claimed to have no knowledge of the skirmish and he let them drive away. Witnesses later reported that shots had been fired from the direction of the automobile. An autopsy that was performed on Birns seemed to confirm this. The bullets extracted from his corpse were dumdums (soft bullets meant to expand on impact), a type commonly used by gangsters, whereas regulation police issue ammunition was always .38-caliber at that time. Most likely, Birns had been accidentally killed by dumdums that were intended for Dannenburg.

The authorities rounded up all of the usual suspects after the shooting and for the first - and last - time in his life, Colosimo was jailed on conspiracy charges. He spent a half day in the police station lockup before being released on bail. The police also arrested Van Bever, Joe Moresco, Vanilli and several others, but the court released them on the same day. No one was ever indicted and the state's attorney closed the investigation for lack of evidence. The only one ever prosecuted from the whole mess was Jim Franche, the man who shot Isaac Henagow in Jones' bar. He stood trial for the murder, was found guilty, and the judge sentenced him to hang. However, he obtained a new trial because of technical irregularities and the jury acquitted him on his plea of self-defense – even though every eyewitness testified that Henagow had never raised a hand toward him.

Among Mayor Harrison's last acts in office was the transfer of some of the gangster's police cronies to precincts far from the Levee and the withdrawal of Colosimo's liquor license. But the splendid café did not stay closed for long. The mayoral election of 1915 brought a new Republican mayor into office, William "Big Bill" Thompson, who was destined to become the hero of every pimp, whore, gambler, gangster and bootlegger in Chicago.

WILLIAM "BIG BILL" THOMPSON

William Hale "Big Bill" Thompson served as the mayor of Chicago during what was likely the city's most corrupt and violent period. When he finally left office after three terms, the *Chicago Tribune* wrote that Thompson's rule had meant "filth, corruption, obscenity, idiocy and bankruptcy" for the city that he had sworn to serve. They added that he had "given the city an international reputation for moronic buffoonery, barbaric crime, triumphant hoodlumism, unchecked graft, and dejected citizenship. He nearly ruined the property and completely destroyed the pride of the city."

In Thompson's defense, he served as mayor through the most difficult era in Chicago history. In those days, Chicago seemed to be filled with gangsters - gangsters who slaughtered one another (214 dead in four years); gangsters killed by the police (160 during the same period); gangsters shooting up buildings, throwing bombs, and speeding away in big automobiles; gangsters bribing city officials, ward bosses and aldermen; gangsters dining in expensive restaurants and attending plays, operas and baseball games; gangsters armed with shotguns, rifles and machine guns, convoying beer trucks – in short, pretty much gangsters everywhere -- except in jail. "That's all newspaper talk," scoffed Mayor "Big Bill" Thompson. Although, just for the record, according to the Illinois Crime Survey, Al Capone was one of the largest contributors to Thompson's mayoral campaign, which leads most to believe that his ties to gangland were not just rumors.

But how corrupt was Thompson? Did he purposely allow the criminal element of Chicago to run unchecked during his terms of office? Or was he just so inept that he had no idea of the lawlessness around him? Who can say? But we should note that when he first started his political career, one of his supporters stated, "The worst thing that you can say about him is that he's stupid."

Thompson's early life was spent avoiding education. He went out West as a young man to become a cowboy, but returned to Chicago after the death of his father. He later achieved a small amount of fame as captain of the Chicago Athletic Club's water-polo team, which was his only qualification for office when he ran for the first time. He first ran for alderman in 1900 after making a $50 poker bet with friends who said that he was too afraid to run. His speeches were dull, his delivery was listless, and he had little idea what he was talking about. In fact, he was so clueless that when it was time during a speech for him to smile or laugh, a friend would let a brick fall to the floor as a signal.

Thompson ran for mayor with the naiveté of a champion athlete on the side of truth, justice and the

American way. He actually vowed in this first campaign that "I am going to clean up Chicago" but by this third campaign, his picture was hanging in Capone's inner sanctum and the gangster was donating as much as $260,000 for Thompson's re-election. After winning that first election, Chicago became a wide-open town once again as far as vice and crime were concerned.

But Thompson's ability to win elections did not always come from Chicago's criminals. People actually voted for him, although for whom they thought they were voting is anyone's guess. During his initial run for office, every position in Thompson's platform invalidated some other position. Chameleon-like, what he actually said depended on where he was campaigning. In German neighborhoods, newspapers said that he sounded like "Kaiser Bill," and he later generated a lot of controversy when he refused to invite Marshall Joffre, hero of the Marne, and Rene Vivani, the French Minister of Justice, to Chicago as part of their national tour to drum up American support for their side in the Great War. Thompson noted that Chicago was the "sixth largest German city in the world" and added that he didn't think many of the residents would be interested in having the Frenchmen there. In the German-hating Polish neighborhoods, his campaign workers passed out flyers that called his opponent "the German candidate." In the Protestant neighborhoods, a vote for the opponent was "a vote for the Pope." In the Irish wards, he lashed out at the English and when addressing American audiences, he wrapped himself in the flag and invoked the spirit of George Washington.

He promised the reform groups strict enforcement of the anti-gambling laws, and he promised the gamblers a wide-open town. To black audiences, he told them to shoot craps – "When I'm mayor, the police will have something better to do than break up a friendly little craps game" – and promised them jobs. To the wives and mothers of the upper-class neighborhoods, he swore to clean up the city and drive out the crooks, making Chicago the cleanest city in the world. He told the anti-saloon groups that he would enforce the state's blue law and continue to prohibit the sale of liquor on Sunday. He promised the "wets" that he would oppose all of the Sunday blue laws, and he won over the saloon owners by signing a pledge to that effect. "I see no harm in a friendly little drink in a friendly little saloon," he said.

Needless to say, Big Bill Thompson won the 1915 mayoral election with the largest vote ever recorded for a Republican in Chicago.

Within six months, he had violated every campaign promise that he made, except for one – he did keep Chicago a wide-open town. After a few token arrests on the Levee and elsewhere, a new "live and let live" policy began to prevail. Slot machines that were manufactured by Chicago's Mills Novelty Co. began clattering away all over the city, with politicians at City Hall getting a cut of the profits. The Sportsmen's Club, a Republican organization, was used as a collection agency for graft. Membership in the club swelled after gamblers, gangsters, brothel-keepers and saloon-owners received a letter on club letterhead bearing Thompson's name that offered $100 lifetime memberships. Some of the top members in the club included the Mayor; Chief of Police Charles C. Healey; Herbert S. Mills, president of the slot machine company; gambling magnate Mont Tennes, and Jim Colosimo, whose liquor license had been restored by Thompson.

Instead of the large, easily raided whorehouses that they formerly operated, vice operators had started maintaining numerous discreet "call flats." The prostitutes would seek out their customers in the dance halls, also owned by the vice operators, and then take them to the flats, or apartments. In an attempt to expose this scheme, Major Funkhouser published a piece that estimated the number of these places in Chicago at 30,000. Soon after, Mayor Thompson stripped him and his Morals Squad of all authority.

The first eight months of Thompson's time in office produced twice as many complaints about the police as the entire preceding year. Police Chief Healey, who had begun his tenure with a declaration of war against the underworld, ended it by being exposed as the boss of the city's largest graft ring and on intimate terms with some of the most notorious gangsters in the city. In January 1917, he was indicted on bribery charges along with three other members of his department, an alderman and four underworld vice operators. As its main exhibit during the trial, the prosecution produced a notebook that had been

THOMPSON'S POLICE CHIEF CHARLES C. HEALEY, WHO WOULD LATER STAND TRIAL ON CORRUPTION CHARGES.

confiscated from a North Side police lieutenant. The first pages listed shady hotels and their weekly tributes, ranging from $40 to $150. Next came sporting houses and gambling dens, some marked, damningly, as "chief's places," which meant that the money went directly to Healey. Others were marked "three ways," which meant that Healey shared the take with Police Captain Tom Costello, underworld character Mike "de Pike" Heitler, and Billy Skidmore, a bondsman, gambler and saloon owner. Another list named the saloons that the police allowed to operate illegally after 1:00 a.m. and on Sunday. There were also lists of gambling and disorderly houses that were headed "Can't be raided" and "Can be raided," with appropriate warning, of course.

Healey retained two of Chicago's most successful criminal attorneys for his defense, Charles Erbstein and Clarence Darrow. They managed to get him acquitted. The jury, in fact, acquitted all nine defendants.

Alderman Charles E. Merriman, a political science professor at the University of Chicago and a leader in the reform faction, wrote: "Chicago is unique. It is the only completely corrupt city in America."

Johnny Torrio watched the emergence of Big Bill Thompson's regime with great interest. He knew that the time was coming for even bigger money to be made in the Chicago underworld. Interestingly, he catered to the vices of others while he himself seemed to have none. He never smoked, drank or gambled and took no interest in any woman but his wife, Ann. He kept a daily routine like any banker or professional

JOHN TORRIO, WHO TURNED VICE INTO BIG BUSINESS.

man, leaving home in the morning and either walking to his office on South Wabash or driving to Burnham. He spent nine or ten hours attending to the details of the brothel business, which mean moving whores from house to house to make sure that customers saw fresh faces. His workday also involved purchasing food, drink and linens for the whorehouses, and calculating the profits from the night before. If he didn't encountered any problems that needed to be dealt with, he returned home each night by 6:00 p.m. and had dinner with his wife. Unless they attended an occasional play or concert together, he stayed home until morning. He had no interest in nightlife. He and Ann played cards or listened to the phonograph. Torrio loved music and knew a lot about it. He could follow a score and hold a conversation with a professional musician. Ann once said, "He is the best and dearest of husbands. My married life has been like one long, unclouded honeymoon. He has done everything to make me happy. He has given me his wholehearted devotion. I have had love, home and contentment."

Johnny Torrio was a family man, a devoted husband, a quiet and contented businessman – and one of the most cold and calculating gangsters in Chicago history. He routinely ordered the deaths of rivals, thought nothing of directing beatings, bombings and shootings, and ascribed no humanity to the prostitutes he handled. He regarded them simply as a commodity, to be bought, sold and replaced when they ran out. Crime was just business to Torrio and in his case, crime definitely paid.

Torrio was an exemplary business manager. Because of his hard work and the leniency of the Thompson administration, Colosimo had become the top Chicago vice lord. His political value extended far beyond the Levee and with his City Hall connections. He no longer depended on the ward politicians for protection; in fact, they came to him for favors. The café was Colosimo's pride and joy, perhaps even his obsession. He dealt with all of the minutiae of running the restaurant and was happiest there, fussing over customers and celebrities and being flattered and admired by them in return. He gave virtual autonomy to Torrio when it came to all of his other business dealings – his first serious mistake.

His second mistake was a romantic one.

One evening in 1913, Jack Lait, a reporter from the *Chicago Daily News*, came into Colosimo's and began telling him about a girl that he had heard singing in the choir at the South Park Avenue Methodist Church. Lait told him that the girl was talented and a knockout and he thought she deserved a better place to showcase her talents. Why not Colosimo's? Big Jim agreed to give her an audition and the next evening, Lait introduced him to Dale Winter, described as a "slender, demure brunette with blue eyes and skin like rose petals."

Dale was only 19 years old. She had been born in Ohio and dreamed of a career in opera. Her father had died when she was only five and after high school, her mother took her to New York. She auditioned for producer George Lederer, who was casting a road company version of the operetta *Madame Sherry*, which had been a smash hit. Dale won the ingénue role, which was essentially the part of an innocent young girl. Chaperoned by her mother, she traveled across the country to San Francisco, where the tour ended. Hoping to stay on the road, she put together a vaudeville sketch with another actress, sold it to a company that was about to depart for Australia, and went along to play the main part. In Australia, the venture collapsed, stranding Dale and her mother 6,000 miles from home. Luckily, they were able to borrow money from a sympathetic actor and managed to get back to San Francisco. A booking agent sent them on to Chicago, where, he assured them, Dale could find work with a newly organized light opera company. Unfortunately, they arrived to find that the company had disbanded without ever staging a single performance. The two women were penniless, but the South Park Avenue Methodist Church kept them from starving when they hired Dale as a soloist.

Colosimo found that Dale Winter was everything that Lait had promised. He needed no convincing to hire her for his stage show and she soon became his star attraction, enchanting the customers every night

COLOSIMO AND HIS NEW LOVE, SINGER DALE WINTER.
IRONICALLY, THE ONLY DECENT GIRL HE EVER KNEW WOULD
LEAD HIM TO HIS DEATH.

with a repertoire of operatic arias. She did not want to leave the church choir, though, and she continued to sing hymns by day until the congregation discovered that she moonlighted at Colosimo's. They were scandalized and demanded her immediate dismissal. The church pastor was more tolerant and chose as a theme for his next sermon the Bible passage of John 8:7 – "He that is without sin among you, let him cast the first stone at her." But the congregation was not moved by his defense and he had no choice but to let Dale go.

Dale was upset by this turn of events. She was not happy with the atmosphere of the Levee, but felt she had no choice but to work there. She promised herself that she would quit as soon as she had enough money saved up to get herself and her mother back to New York. Grand opera was still her dream, not singing in a café. As the star of Colosimo's floor show, many better job opportunities came her way. The Broadway impresario Morris Gest offered her a contract, as did Florenz Ziegfeld, whose dazzling shows featured stunning girls. Dale had been looking for a way back to New York and any of these opportunities would have gotten her there. However, by the time they came along, it was too late. She no longer planned to leave Chicago because she had fallen in love with Big Jim Colosimo and he had fallen in love with her. Big Jim left his wife, confiding in Torrio that his love for Dale was "the real thing."

"It's your funeral," Torrio replied, which would turn out to be prophetic words.

THE FOUR DEUCES AT 2222 SOUTH WABASH AVENUE

With Dale's gentle guidance, Colosimo began to acquire a little polish. He learned to moderate his loud, overbearing voice and to clean up his language. He hired a tutor to help him perfect his English. He began to dress more conservatively, leaving his diamonds at home. He began spending more time with artists and his wealthy customers, neglecting the politicians and underworld characters with whom he normally fraternized. Dale liked to ride horses in the city parks and Colosimo, attired in equestrian gear, would trot along beside her. He badgered his friend Caruso for an opinion about Dale's voice and when the great tenor found it pleasing, he asked for an audition with the opera company. The conductor also liked her voice but found it needed training, so Colosimo enrolled her at the Chicago Musical College.

It was ironic that Dale Winter, the only decent girl that Colosimo ever knew, would be the reason for his death. Emotional vulnerability was seen as a weakness in the underworld and word began to spread that Colosimo was getting soft. The Black Hand extortionists resumed their demands and now Colosimo paid them off out of fear that something might happen to Dale. They plagued him constantly until the day he died.

Meanwhile, John Torrio, while continuing to take care of Colosimo's affairs, slowly and quietly began to build his own organization. He began making plans for other vice spots besides Burnham and found that officials in Stickney, a small village about eight miles outside of the city, were open to his ideas. At the edge of the Levee itself, a block from Colosimo's Café, he took over a four-story red brick building located at 2222 South Wabash Avenue. It would

GHOSTS OF THE FOUR DEUCES ✋

Made famous by Al Capone and Johnny Torrio, the building that was home to the infamous Four Deuces had a history in Chicago before – and after—the Outfit's tenancy in the place. It had rumors of a haunting that can be traced back both to the time of Four Deuces and possibly, to a horrific incident that occurred long after the mob was gone.

The building that would gain a reputation as the Four Deuces, in the heart of the South Side Levee District, was built around 1880. It was part of a block of buildings and the four-story structure held four apartments, one on each floor. In 1901, the building was purchased during a foreclosure auction by the Northwestern Mutual Life Insurance Co. They in turn sold it to Solomon Friedman, who opened a saloon on the main floor. It joined the dozens of other saloons already operating on the Levee. In 1903, Mayor Harrison sent out a notice to the owners of saloons on South Wabash warning them to respect the midnight closing law. If they did not, they could be shut down for good and their liquor licenses revoked. Friedman was one of those who received a notice.

A number of unsavory establishments opened nearby, offering gambling and prostitution. Sol Van Praag, a First Ward politician who also dabbled in gambling, opened a cigar store at 2226 South Wabash, which he used as a front for various operations. The place was often raided, including one raid in 1917 when seventeen people were arrested for being involved in an open craps game. Van Praag eventually rented the place to Martin Guilfoyle, who shot and killed a hoodlum named Peter Gentleman in the store in 1919.

Soon after, John Torrio took over the entire building at 2222 South Wabash and opened the Four Deuces. The establishment offered drinking, gambling and prostitution, and it was where Al Capone had his first job in Chicago, working as a capper for the brothel.

According to gangland rumor, a torture chamber was located in the basement of the building where rival gangsters were forced to give up information – and sometimes their lives.

After repeated raids during the tenure of Mayor Dever, the Torrio-Capone outfit moved their operations to Cicero and the Four Deuces was closed down. It later became an apartment building but was still the scene of horror. On April 9, 1932, a woman who lived in a third floor apartment ended her life by setting herself on fire in a bathtub filled with kerosene.

The building was torn down in the spring of 1964, but that didn't put an end to the rumors that circulated around the neighborhood. According to tenants during the last decades of the building's existence, the place was haunted. Stories claimed that screams, moans and wails could often be heard coming the basement – where gangsters once met violent ends during extended torture sessions.

Another story claimed that the sound of a woman screaming was sometimes heard in the third floor apartment. According to a witness who lived there, he once heard a blood-curdling scream echoing from his bathroom. When he dared to look, he found the room empty – but he swore that the faint smell of burning flesh was still in the air. "I served in France during the war," he told a reporter. "I know what death smells like and that was in the air of that room."

The bathroom was the same one in which the woman set herself on fire in 1932.

be known thereafter as the Four Deuces. On the first floor, he opened a bar and office. The second and third floors were used as gambling rooms and the fourth floor was a brothel. The cellar of the Four Deuces was a torture chamber. According to Judge John H. Lyle in his book *The Dry and Lawless Years*, hapless individuals from whom the mobsters wanted information were taken down to the cellar and tortured until they talked. Afterward, they were killed and their bodies hauled out through a trap door at the back of the building, to be dumped along a country road or sunk into the deep waters of a rock quarry.

Around the time that Torrio opened the Four Deuces, in late 1919, he sent for his friend from Brooklyn, Al Capone. The young man's initial duties were humble ones, working as a bodyguard, chauffeur, bartender and as a capper for the brothel, working out on the street to lure men inside.

Shortly after Capone came to Chicago, a momentous event occurred. It was an event that Torrio had long been planning for and he had been trying, without much success, to get Colosimo to exploit. The profits, Torrio was convinced, would be many times more than anything they had ever made with their vice operations. But Colosimo was not convinced – gambling and whores had made him a fortune, why risk the unknown? Torrio finally had to accept the fact that Colosimo's days were over. It was a new era for American crime.

Prohibition had come to pass and American had just gone dry.

4. AMERICA RUNS DRY

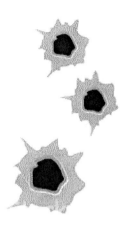

When the 18th Amendment to the Constitution, which abolished the sale and distribution of alcohol, took effect on January 17, 1920, many believed that it would cure the social ills of America. Little did they know at the time, but it would actually do just the opposite. America's great thirst for the forbidden liquor bred corruption in every corner. Law enforcement officials became open to bribes because the majority of them did not agree with the law. Worse yet, Prohibition gave birth to the great days of organized crime. The gangsters of America had previously concerned themselves with acts of violence, racketeering and prostitution but the huge profits that came to be made with the sale of illegal liquor built criminal empires.

Prohibition was not something that came quickly to America. It took a long, hard fight before the "dries" had their way and imposed their well-intentioned but misguided legislation upon the country. Alcohol was a powerful and well-entrenched part of American culture and one could find beer, imported rum or locally made liquor and cider in almost every frontier household. Almost everyone, young and old, drank. A pitcher of beer was often found on the family supper table simply because the local water was unfit to drink. Alcohol was a basic ingredient in most old medicinal remedies and many mothers put cranky babies to sleep by adding a few drops of whiskey to their milk. When neighbors got together to raise barns, harvest crops or merely to socialize, there were always jugs of whiskey on the table next to the platters of food.

Even America's greatest heroes were proponents of alcohol. Daniel Boone operated a store that sold liquor. Davy Crockett found that taking a jug of whiskey along when he went "electioneering" helped him win votes. George Washington, Thomas Jefferson and Benjamin Franklin all brewed or distilled their own alcoholic beverages, and the young Abraham Lincoln operated a tavern. A daily ration of rum was given to American soldiers and sailors. Frontiersmen felt so strongly about their liquor that in 1794, the farmers of western Pennsylvania almost went to war with the federal government over a tax on whiskey.

This is not to say that the founders of our country were drunks. Even a man who could hold his liquor with the best of them was not likely to prosper if he were drunk half the time. Public drunkenness was, in most cases, socially frowned upon and could lead to a reprimand from the church pulpit, a fine, a flogging, or banishment from the community. Religious leaders called for moderation, not total abstinence.

In spite of this, there were those who felt that alcohol was simply evil. There were early, localized attempts at Prohibition. The colony of Georgia tried it from 1733 to 1742, only to see an increase in the number of illegal mountain stills. Small towns, cities and counties all over the country tried, and often failed, to prohibit alcohol. In those cases, it was easy for residents to travel over the county line, or to the next town, for a drink, so it was hard to see any long-term success.

Alcohol began to gain its questionable reputation with the coming of the nineteenth century. As the country expanded and immigration increased, there was a rise in the consumption of hard liquor as opposed to beer and wine. While many white settlers saw nothing wrong with using alcohol to cheat and

CARRIE NATION

THE TEMPERANCE MOVEMENT - URGING THE CLOSURE OF SALOONS AND THE BANNING OF ALCOHOL - BEGAN GATHERING STEAM IN THE LATE 1800S AND THE EARLY 1900S WITH THE FOUNDING OF THE WOMEN'S CHRISTIAN TEMPERANCE UNION, THE ANTI-SALOON LEAGUE AND OTHERS. CRUSADERS LIKE CARRIE NATION GARNERED ATTENTION BY SMASHING UP SALOONS AND MAKING SPECTACLES OF THEMSELVES.

demoralize the Native Americans, the more conscientious took issue with it. Evidence also started to emerge that showed alcohol, once thought to have numerous medicinal qualities, could be hazardous to one's health. Few stopped to consider that it was overindulgence that was the problem, not general consumption.

An influx of lager-drinking German immigrants in the mid-1800s brought about a revival in beer consumption. American brewers began taking advantage of the new railroads to open up chains of taverns across the country in which they could sell their own brands. Saloons sprang up on every city street corner, while small towns with one church and one schoolhouse might have a dozen or more saloons in their midst. With competition high, bar owners wanted to keep the booze flowing as much as possible and resorted to sidewalk hawkers and free lunches (well-salted to induce thirst) to entice men into their establishments. While some of the saloons were clean, respectable spots, many were dirty eyesores, operating on a shoestring budget, the hangouts of bums, thieves and prostitutes. The opponents of alcohol needed no further evidence that liquor was causing the country's moral decay.

Alarm over the increase in drunkenness, along with the growing political power of brewing and distilling companies, led to an increase in activity for the Prohibition movement. The American Temperance Society was founded in 1826, the Women's Christian Temperance Union in 1874, and the Anti-Saloon League in 1892. These were three of the many organizations dedicated to a total ban on alcohol. To gain more attention, and greater political leverage, these groups often joined with other, more worthy causes, like the abolition of slavery or women's suffrage.

The prohibitionists did not believe in moderation. You either did not drink or if you did, you were doomed to damnation along with the gamblers, heathens, fornicators and godless foreigners. Women temperance fighters marched with banners emblazoned with slogans that proclaimed sentiments like, "Lips that touch liquor will never touch ours." Preachers claimed that the "wine" that Jesus and his apostles drank was only grape juice and ranted about the dangers of drinking, which included blindness, insanity, poverty and babies that were born sickly, already addicted to the devil's brew. They plastered walls with posters of bartenders who were actually demons in disguise; hopeless drunks staring in despair at empty liquor bottles; and ragged children standing outside the doors to taverns, watching in despair while their fathers were inside drinking away the grocery money. They dragged derelicts out of gutters and put them on display as examples of what alcohol could do to a man. A "literary work" called *Ten Nights in a Barroom*, which damned alcohol and saloons, was read in churches and in schools across the country and was even made into a musical drama designed to win support for the cause.

One of the most colorful and fanatical soldiers for the Women's Christian Temperance Union was Carrie Nation. Standing nearly six feet tall and weighing 180 pounds, armed with a Bible and a hatchet, this grim, dour-faced woman was determined to destroy the "wicked, riotous, rum-soaked, beer-swilled, bedeviled publicans of Kansas." She would stride into a saloon and wreak havoc, smashing mirrors, windows and bottles with her hatchet. The more times that she was arrested for the destruction of property, the more she seemed (to her supporters, anyway) like a martyr to the cause.

The "wets," those opposed to Prohibition, made the mistake of ridiculing the Prohibitionists, instead of taking them seriously. Their jokes were no defense against the self-righteous solemnity of the movement. It was not long before state after state, and finally, the entire country adopted Prohibition.

The Volstead Act, which brought about national Prohibition in America, went into effect in 1920 and lasted until 1933. It stopped the manufacture, transportation, importation and sale of alcoholic beverages. The making of small amounts of home-brewed beer and wine for personal consumption in one's own home was permitted and so stores selling home-brewing equipment and supplies opened up everywhere. Many of them did most of their

THE AUTHORITIES OFTEN MADE BIG PUBLIC DISPLAYS OF THE SEIZURE OF NOW ILLEGAL BOOZE -- WHILE THOSE WHO WATCHED KNEW QUITE EASILY WHERE MORE LIQUOR COULD BE PURCHASED.

business with bootleggers. Medicinal alcohol could be purchased at a pharmacy with a doctor's prescription, a loophole that many doctors and pharmacists exploited, until the government took steps to close it. The only alcoholic beverage that could be legally sold was "near beer," which had an alcoholic content that was so small that most drinkers didn't consider it worth the trouble, especially when the real thing was available from the friendly neighborhood bootlegger.

Today, we can look back at the advocates of Prohibition and call them naïve and misguided. We can also say that many of the politicians who supported them were hypocrites who were primarily interested in garnering votes. However, the majority of the Prohibitionists sincerely believed their cause was just and that the movement would solve America's problems. They believed that people would have more spending

STILLS AND LIQUOR-MAKING DEVICES THAT WERE IMPOUNDED DURING THE EARLY DAYS OF PROHIBITION.

money; crime rates would fall so drastically that police forces could be trimmed down to the bare minimum and jails and prisons could be closed down; poverty would be abolished; corn and grain that had been "wasted" on making alcohol could be used to feed the hungry at home and overseas; and men who once staggered home from the saloon on a Saturday night would now be up bright and early on Sunday morning to take their wives and children to church. It seems like wishful thinking to us now but to the Prohibitionists of the day, it was a bright vision for the future.

But, of course, Prohibition didn't stop anyone from drinking. In fact, it made drinking the "in thing" to do, simply because it was not allowed. Across the country, more than 200,000 "speakeasys" opened. These drinking establishments were so named because many of them were located behind, above or below legitimate businesses and patrons often drank in silence to avoid discovery. Huge bootlegging operations sprang into existence to supply the speakeasys and those who chose to ignore Prohibition and buy booze for home consumption. Disrespect for the law became the fashion as people who would never before have dreamed of doing anything illegal were now serving illicit liquor in their homes or drinking in the neighborhood speakeasy. As one man put it at the time, "Anybody who says they can't find a drink ain't trying."

By outlawing alcohol, the authorities made criminals out of millions of otherwise law-abiding citizens. They seriously undermined the respect those people had for law and order and worst of all, they offered the criminal underworld the chance to make more money than they ever dreamed possible. All of the money that had been made by robbery, prostitution, loansharking, bookmaking, extortion and other criminal pursuits was nothing compared to the windfall of bootlegging. Organized crime that was syndicated on a national, corporate scale was born and became so powerful that it has never been shut down.

Prohibition was widely considered to be doomed by 1928, but it hung on for another five years before being repealed in 1933. By then, it had taken its toll. The court systems had become clogged; the jails and prisons were filled, often with people who had never been in trouble with the law before; trusted politicians, officials and police officers had been corrupted; and millions of dollars had been spent hiring new Prohibition agents, coast guard officers and cops. The drunken violence associated with seedy bars was nothing compared to the bloodshed that erupted in city streets as bootleggers battled for control of the liquor trade.

OUTLAWING ALCOHOL MADE CRIMINALS OUT OF MILLIONS OF LAW-ABIDING CITIZENS -- AND MADE BREAKING THE LAW THE "IN" THING TO DO.

Prohibition went into effect at 12:01 a.m. on January 17, 1920 and in less than an hour, the new law had been violated no less than three times in – of course – Chicago. The first violation occurred before 1:00 a.m. when a truck rolled into a railroad switching yard and six masked men, brandishing revolvers, jumped out. They bound and gagged a watchman, locked six engineers in a shed and, after breaking into two freight cars, removed $100,000 worth of whiskey in cases that had been stamped "for medicinal use." At almost the same time, another Chicago gang stole four barrels of alcohol from a warehouse, while a third gang hijacked a truck that was loaded with whiskey. This was the first known instance of what would soon become a common gangster practice.

Needless to say, no one was ever arrested for these violations.

John Torrio studied the new law and surveyed Chicago and the rest of the country with impatience. He had seen this coming. He had predicted it to his friends and business associates and knew that this was going to be the way that organized crime could amass untold amounts of wealth. To take something that had always been legal, and make it illegal - especially something as pervasive as alcohol - and then expect Americans to adhere to the letter of the law was incredibly naïve. Torrio knew that by taking advantage of Prohibition, and providing the people with what they wanted, the mob could reach new levels of power. This was a way for men like himself to become millionaires – and yet, his hands were tied. He was unable to rouse Colosimo into action. Big Jim was too entranced with Dale Winter and had lost all interest in business.

Torrio was fuming. He was desperate to get organized and start filling the need that had been created. Most of the saloons and roadhouses in and around the city had stayed open with expectations of obtaining liquor somehow. Torrio (and many others) believed that the risk of supplying alcohol was very small compared to the rewards. To cover the entire state of Illinois, as well as Iowa and part of Wisconsin, the Prohibition Unit had assigned a pathetic force of only 134 agents. As for the Chicago police, Torrio anticipated no more difficulty in getting protection for bootlegging that he had for running prostitutes and gambling joints. And he turned out to be right – Charles Fitzmorris, Chicago's police chief in the early Prohibition years, once publicly admitted that, "sixty percent of my police are in the bootleg business." Best of all for the bootleggers was Big Bill Thompson and his "wide-open town" policy. Despite the public embarrassments, the various buffooneries, the raping of the city treasury and the rampant lawlessness that occurred during his first term, Thompson managed to win a second term by a slim margin. He still had the support of the most powerful political machine in Chicago history (backed by gangland) and a fat campaign chest to which his thousands of civil service appointees were compelled to contribute.

The way had been paved for the underworld to reap huge benefits from Prohibition and Torrio wanted to take advantage of the situation. He was not the only one – most of the gang leaders in the city planned to go into bootlegging. Some of them had laid away stocks of liquor months before the Volstead Act went into effect and then sold it for at least twice the price after Prohibition began. Others had arranged for deliveries from moonshiners, smugglers and secret distillers. Torrio planned, with his usual attention to detail, a method to avoid hostilities between the various gangs by creating territories and trade agreements among them. Colosimo, as long as he received his share of the earnings, left Torrio free to act in the way that he thought best. He had no interest in the details, which was unfortunate, because what was needed to keep everyone in line was a reassertion of Colosimo's old forceful leadership, which, in turn, would have brought back his former prestige. Instead, he continued his passive disinterest in everything but his pretty, young girlfriend.

Torrio knew that Colosimo's time was coming to an end.

Colosimo, meanwhile, was dealing with his domestic drama. He had been living apart from Victoria Moresco for three months by this time and had offered her $50,000 if she would not contest his divorce action. She agreed and the decree became final on March 20, 1920. Within three weeks, Victoria had married a Sicilian hoodlum twenty years her junior named Antonio Villani. Big Jim married Dale. They honeymooned at a fashionable spa in French Lick, Indiana, and then returned to Chicago, where they settled into Colosimo's ornate mansion at 3156 Vernon Avenue. He had no idea that his domestic bliss was to be short-lived.

A week after Colosimo's return, on Tuesday, May 11, Torrio telephoned to announce the delivery of two truckloads of whiskey at the café. The trucks would be there, he stressed, at 4:00 p.m. and Colosimo needed to be on hand for the delivery. Colosimo left his house a few minutes before the hour and climbed into a car, driven by his chauffer, a man named Woolfson, which was waiting at the curb. Dale asked him to send the car back so that she and her mother could go shopping. He promised to do so, kissed her goodbye and drove away. Woolfson later reported that Big Jim muttered to himself in Italian, a language that the chauffeur didn't understand, for the entire drive.

There were two entrances to the café on South Wabash Avenue, about fifty feet apart. Woolfson dropped Colosimo off at the arched north entrance and then drove back to Vernon Avenue to pick up Dale

THE END OF JIM COLOSIMO, RIGHT IN THE ENTRYWAY TO HIS OWN RESTAURANT -- "BEAUTY KILLED THE "BEAST", SO TO SPEAK.

and her mother. Colosimo pushed open the glass-paneled door and walked across a small, tiled vestibule, passing a coatroom, a telephone booth and a cashier's cage. He then walked through the main dining room, went through an archway into the second dining room, which was often used for overflow crowds, and entered his office in the back. A few moments later, a porter, who was coming up from the basement, noticed a stranger enter the vestibule near the doors, as if he had followed the boss in off the street. The man seemed to know where he was going so the porter returned to his duties downstairs, where four other staff members were also working.

In Colosimo's office, his secretary, Frank Camilla, and Chef Caesarino were discussing the night's menu. Colosimo asked them if anyone had called. No one had, which seemed to trouble him. He tried unsuccessfully to reach his attorney, Rocco De Stefano, on the telephone and then sat at his desk and listened to the dinner plans. The three men chatted for a few minutes and then Colosimo walked back toward the vestibule through the two dining rooms. Camilla and Caesarino both later stated that they had the impression Colosimo intended to wait for the man with the whiskey delivery either in the vestibule or on the sidewalk outside. Camilla recalled glancing at the clock – it was 4:25 p.m. – and then he continued his discussion with the chef. A moment later, the men heard two sharp cracks. Caesarino dismissed them as a backfiring automobile, but Camilla decided to investigate. When he did, he found Big Jim lying face down on the cold tiles of the little vestibule. Blood was streaming from a bullet hole behind his right ear. The second bullet had cracked the glass of the cashier's window and had buried itself in the plaster wall. Colosimo was dead.

Camilla immediately called the police. Thanks to Colosimo's political clout, Chief of Police John J. Garrity personally rushed to the scene. The chief of detectives was also called in, as were several detectives from the state's attorney's office. Camilla called Dale to tell her the news and she fainted.

The police questioned more than thirty suspects, including Torrio and Capone, both of whom were occupied elsewhere at the time of the shooting – in view of a large number of witnesses. Torrio's eyes filled with tears when he was notified of his uncle's death. "Big Jim and me were like brothers," he said in an uncharacteristic display of emotion.

The investigation into Colosimo's murder was hastily conducted and uncovered no real leads, except for one. During the dragnet that followed the murder, the police stumbled onto veteran Five Points gang member Frankie Yale at Union Station. Yale had been in town for a week and was just about to board an eastbound train when the police stopped him. There was nothing to connect him to the murder, so he was allowed to leave for New York. Soon after, the porter came forward with his description of the stranger that he saw in the vestibule of the café, a description that eerily resembled Frankie Yale. Rumors were already swirling in the underworld that Torrio had paid Yale to bump off his uncle, so detectives from Chicago contacted New York and asked them to pick up Yale and hold onto him until they could get there with the porter to see if he would identify Yale as the mystery man. The porter was brought to New York but when he was face-to-face with the Yale, he froze and swore that he could not identify him as the man he had seen. Later, this condition of not being able to remember the faces of killers would be dubbed "Chicago amnesia." The investigation foundered after that but the police never doubted the guilt of Torrio and Yale. Officially, Colosimo's murder still remains unsolved.

Colosimo's funeral was held on May 14 and became the first of the gaudy gangland affairs that would be held throughout the 1920s. The lavishness of the floral tributes (with wreaths from Johnny and Al among the largest), the costly bronze casket, the size of the cortege and the sordid mix of politicians and mobsters set the standard for gangster funerals to come. No rites were held in a Catholic church or cemetery because Archbishop George Mundelein forbade them, not because Colosimo was a murderer, a whoremonger or white slave trafficker, but because he divorced his wife to marry Dale Winter.

In the end, a Presbyterian minister, Reverend Pasquale De Carol, performed the funeral rites in Colosimo's Vernon Street mansion. Dale was in attendance, barely able to stand. Hymns were sung, Hail

Marys were recited and the Catholic Prayer for the Dead was intoned. Ike Bloom, who managed one of the Levee's most disreputable dancehalls, offered a heartfelt eulogy. "There wasn't a piker's hair on Big Jim's head," he said. "Whatever game he played, he shot straight. He wasn't greedy. There could be dozens of others getting theirs. The more the merrier as far as he was concerned. He had what a lot of us haven't got – class. He brought the society swells and the millionaires into the red light district. It helped everybody, and a lot of places were kept alive on Colosimo's overflow. Big Jim never bilked a pal or turned down a good guy and he always kept his mouth shut."

More than 1,000 people preceded the cortege as it wound its way through the Levee to Oakwood Cemetery. They paused for a moment before the crepe-draped entrance to Colosimo's Café while two brass bands played a dirge. Dale rode behind the hearse in a car with drawn curtains. More than 5,000 mourners followed behind her. The 53 pallbearers and honorary pallbearers included, in addition to criminals, nine aldermen, three judges, two congressmen, a state senator, an assistant state's attorney and the state Republican leader.

Colosimo was laid to rest in the family mausoleum at Oakwood Cemetery and Dale lay grief-stricken for the next 10 days. She learned that her marriage to Colosimo had not been legal under Illinois law, which at that time required a one-year interval between divorce and re-marriage. Colosimo had no will and Dale had no claim to his estate. His family nevertheless gave her $6,000 in bonds and diamonds. Victoria Moresco was given $12,000 and the remainder of his money went to his father, Luigi.

Dale tried briefly to manage Colosimo's Café but she had no experience in running a business and it was eventually taken over by Mike "The Greek" Potson, a professional gambler who had long been a minority partner with Big Jim. Dale and her mother returned to New York. She took back her maiden name and stepped into the leading role in a popular musical called *Irene* at the Vanderbilt Theater. She continued in the role for several years in New York and then took it on the road. She was in San Francisco in 1924 when she married actor Henry Duffy. They ran a large and successful string of theaters on the West Coast and appeared in numerous shows together until the 1930s, when Dale finally left the theater and turned her energies to raising their two children. The Depression and the popularity of movies closed many of the couple's theaters in the late 1930s. They were forced to file for bankruptcy in 1941. In 1945, they divorced. Dale appeared in a few forgettable film roles and went on to marry and survive two wealthy men, Herschel McGraw and Edward S. Perot, before her own death in 1985.

Mike Potson purchased the remaining shares of Colosimo's Café in late 1920 when Luigi Colosimo returned to Italy. He kept the restaurant going but the wet bar and the gambling at the café attracted the attention of federal enforcement agents during Prohibition. In 1926 and again in 1928, a federal judge padlocked the place for violations of the Volstead Act. It was raided several more times before Prohibition finally came to an end. After that, Potson kept the club popular with musical reviews and performances and it continued into the middle 1940s, although by then, Potson's reputation as a gambler had started to get in the way of good business. Hollywood comedians Abbott and Costello sued Potson over gambling losses they sustained on the second floor, adding to the place's bad publicity. In 1948, Potson was indicted on a broad range of gambling charges and ended up going to prison. He died in 1955.

After several failed attempts by outside interests to purchase Colosimo's and get it going again, a fire swept through the property in January 1953. The Church of Divine Science then purchased the building, tried to clean it up a little and started holding services there. However, the rundown condition of the building forced the city to take action and a suit was filed to raze the property. The wrecking ball came for Colosimo's on February 7, 1958, marking an end of an era in South Side Chicago history.

 5. GANGS OF CHICAGO

Colosimo was barely cold in his grave when Torrio, assisted by Capone, began his grand plan for expansion. The first thing that Torrio did was to try and win recognition as Colosimo's successor. Aldermen Kenna and Coughlin approved of him as did most of the other key figures in city politics and the local underworld. Having secured a home base on the South Side, he and Capone proceeded to expand their suburban gambling and whorehouse interests. This was easily accomplished through bribery. Town and

 village officials eagerly accepted whatever was offered and while property owners near some of the prospective sites initially protested, their resistance melted when Torrio offered them money to pay off their mortgages, repair their homes, buy new furniture or simply put food on their tables. Within two years, careful planning and corruption transformed a chain of once law-abiding small towns – stretching from Chicago Heights in the south to Cicero in the west – into bastions of vice.

In Chicago Heights, Torrio opened the Moonlight Café and to the two thriving roadhouses in Burnham, he added the Coney Island Café and the Barn. In Posen, he established the Roamer Inn, under the management of Harry Guzik, one of three brothers who had been long entrenched in the rackets, and his wife, Alma. In Blue Island, he opened the Burr Oak Hotel; in Stickney, the Shadow Inn; in Cicero, a number of gambling houses and cabarets.

The Roamer Inn became a strong test of Torrio's political connections in 1921. The Guziks placed an advertisement for a housemaid and when a pretty, young farm girl applied, they stripped her naked, made her a prisoner and had her broken in as a prostitute. After five months in captivity, she managed to get word to her family. By the time that her brothers rescued her, she was a mental and physical wreck. In court, her father told how the Guziks had tried to bribe him not to testify. They were convicted and sentenced to hard time. While free on bail, pending an appeal to the Illinois Supreme Court, they came to Torrio for help. Torrio, in turn, approached Walter Stevens, one of the most respected gunmen in Chicago.

Stevens had been a lieutenant for Maurice "Mossy" Enright for many years and was considered a pioneer in labor union racketeering, slugging, bombing and killing during the industrial strife problems of the early 1900s. He was the last survivor of the Enright gang after Mossy himself was killed as a favor to rival labor racketeer Big Tim Murphy in 1920. Stevens, like Torrio, lived a much different personal life from his professional one. He was a devoted husband and dearly loved his wife. When she became incurably ill, he nursed her for twenty years until she died. He adopted three children and sent them all to good schools. He was an educated man and a student of military history. As a voracious reader, his favorite authors included Robert Louis Stevenson and Jack London. He never touched alcohol and rarely smoked. His daughters were forbidden to wear short skirts or use makeup.

When Mossy Enright was killed in 1930, Stevens joined up with the Torrio-Capone gang. He had many contacts but perhaps his greatest was Illinois Governor Len Small. A few months after Small, a Kankakee farmer and crony of Big Bill Thompson, took office, he was indicted by a grand jury for embezzling $600,000 while state treasurer. Working behind the scenes for the defense were Walter Stevens, "Jew Ben"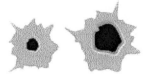

Newmark, a former investigator for the state's attorney as well as a thief and extortionist, and Michael "Umbrella Mike" Boyle, a business agent for Electrical Workers' Union No. 134. Boyle's nickname came from his practice of standing at a bar on certain days of the month with his umbrella partially open so that contractors who wanted to avoid union problems could drop off cash. As the governor's trial progressed, the three men kept busy bribing and intimidating jurors. Small was acquitted and he did not forget the men who helped him. When they later went to jail – Newmark and Boyle for jury tampering and Stevens for an old murder – Small pardoned them. Stevens now drew Small's attention to the Guziks' unfortunate situation and before the Supreme Court could hand down its decision in their case, the governor pardoned them. Within three months, the Guziks were running a new brothel, the Marshfield Inn, just outside the city's southern limits.

In the third, and most important phase of the expansion, Torrio and Capone assembled a formidable array of gangs without whose alliance and cooperation they could not hope to succeed.

DION O'BANION'S NORTH SIDE GANG

On the Northeast Side of Chicago, between the Chicago River and Lake Michigan, there was the gang run by Dion O'Banion, who was potentially Torrio and Capone's most dangerous opposition. O'Banion was an often reckless Irishman who always carried three guns with him. He could shoot accurately with either hand. Chief of Police Morgan Collins once called him "Chicago's arch criminal" and stated that O'Banion "has killed or seen to the killing of at least twenty-five men."

O'Banion never spent a day in jail for shooting any of those men. His political usefulness was too great. O'Banion controlled the Irish vote in the city and while bribery and intimidation usually did the trick, he and his men never hesitated to beat, kidnap and murder. He always

DION O'BANION

delivered his district and the Democratic bosses of the Forty-Second and Forty-Third wards prized O'Banion's vote-getting abilities so much that they once gave him a testimonial dinner at the Webster Hotel and presented him with a gem-encrusted platinum watch. Among those present at the dinner were Colonel Albert Sprague, the Cook County commissioner of Public Works and a Democratic candidate for U.S. Senate; Robert M. Sweitzer, then Cook County Clerk; and Chief of Police Michael Hughes. Ironically, O'Banion personally always voted Republican.

To offset his violent involvement in the rackets, O'Banion loved flowers. He acquired a half interest in William Schofield's flower shop at 738 North State Street, directly across the street from Holy Name Cathedral, where he once served as an altar boy. On most days, he could be found in the shop, cutting flowers, potting plants and putting together arrangements for weddings and burials. He became gangland's favorite florist, which was a lucrative business because underworld etiquette required both friends and foes of a fallen gangster – including the man who killed him – to honor him with elaborate floral creations. Everyone ordered from O'Banion and the moment that word reached him of a gangster's demise, he was on the telephone to his wholesale supplier. At the same time the undertaker was starting to prepare the corpse, and before the orders even started coming in for flowers, O'Banion and his staff were already at work making wreaths and elaborate bouquets and choosing banners that could be gilded with suitable sentiments like "Sympathy from the Boys" and "Gone, but not Forgotten". All a caller had to do was telephone the shop, identify himself and name the amount he wanted to spend. O'Banion would take care of the rest.

O'Banion was happily married and his wife, Viola, who called him by his given name of "Dean," insisted that he was a devoted family man: "Dean loved his home and spent most of his evenings in it. He loved to sit in his slippers, fooling with the radio, singing a song, listening to the player piano. He never drank. He was not a man to run around nights with women. I was his only sweetheart. We went out often to dinner or the theater, usually with friends. He never left home without telling me where he was going and kissing me goodbye," she told an interviewer.

Dean and Viola never had children. They occupied a twelve-room apartment on North Pine Grove Avenue. He drove a late-model Locomobile and his proudest possessions were a player piano, for which he had paid $15,000, and a Victrola. He was constantly setting them up to play the same tune and trying to synchronize them. Sadly, he died before the invention of stereophonic sound systems, for a set of speakers would have produced the effect that he sought. He dressed stylishly, always wearing a tuxedo when he attended the theater or went out to dinner. He spoke well, minding his grammar, and

DEAN AND VIOLA O'BANION

insisted that his associates follow proper etiquette. O'Banion walked with a limp, his left leg being shorter than his right, the result of a boyhood fall from a streetcar, but he was otherwise unremarkable. He was strong and fit with a round face, cleft chin and a genial personality.

Dean (he later adopted the name Dion) Charles O'Banion had been born in 1892 in the small Central Illinois town of Maroa. His father, Charles, was a barber by trade who hailed from Lincoln, Illinois, and his mother, the former Emma Brophy, was the Chicago-born daughter of an Irish immigrant father and American mother. She had been just eight months old when the Great Chicago Fire leveled the city in 1871. Charles and Emma married in 1886 and moved to Maroa the following year, where Charles' parents lived.

Dean spent the early years of his life in Maroa but soon after the birth of his sister, Ruth, his mother contracted tuberculosis and died in 1901. Dean was only nine years old at the time and the loss was a devastating one. The remaining family members packed up and moved to Chicago, where Emma's parents had a place for them. With the move came the end of Dean's innocent years. The hard times, and the legend, were about to begin.

Upon moving to Chicago, O'Banion found himself turning to the streets for a playground. The family settled in a tenement flat on the edge of the North Side's Little Sicily, a maze of narrow, dirty streets that reeked of smoke from the nearby factories. The flames from a gasworks chimney that reddened the sky at

THE SLUMS OF LITTLE HELL IN CHICAGO, WHERE O'BANION AND MANY OTHER MEMBERS OF THE NORTH SIDE GANG GREW UP.

night gave the neighborhood its nickname – Little Hell. It had formerly been an Irish neighborhood dubbed Kilgubbin and about a 1,000 Irish remained. The Sicilians started arriving around 1900 and were soon the majority. Although only a square mile in size, Little Hell was one of the most dangerous spots in the city and averaged between 12 and 20 murders each year. One spot, the intersection of Oak and Milton streets, became known as "Death Corner" after 38 people were gunned down there in just over a year. Thirteen of the murders were attributed to a Black Hand assassin who was never identified. The press simply called him the "Shotgun Man." O'Banion became involved with a junior street gang known as the Little Hellions and began picking pockets and rolling drunks. At the same time, he sang in the choir at the Holy Name Cathedral and, on Sundays, he served as an altar boy. Some of the priests at the church believed that perhaps his devotion might lead to a calling to the priesthood but O'Banion soon learned to ration his religion to Sundays and to devote his remaining time to robbery and, as he reached young adulthood, to burglary, what he called "a man's profession." He soon hooked up with a number of other hardcase young men, including George "Bugs" Moran, Earl "Hymie" Weiss, Vincent "The Schemer" Drucci and Samuel "Nails" Morton. With these toughs at his side, O'Banion put together one of the most devastating gangs in Chicago history. They devoted themselves to burglary, safecracking, and after 1920, to bootlegging.

In 1909, O'Banion served three months in the House of Correction for robbery and two years later, another six months for beating a victim. Those short sentences turned out to constitute his entire prison record. He soon demonstrated his ability to bring in votes and he was able to count on his political patrons to keep him out of jail.

A handful of missteps were all that ever gained the attention of the police. He was not always the most subtle of safecrackers. Once, when attempting to open a safe with a stick of dynamite, he blew out the entire side of an office building but barely put a scratch on the safe. In 1921, Detective Sergeant John J. Ryan caught O'Banion, Hymie Weiss and a couple of other men in the act of blasting open a Postal Telegraph safe. O'Banion cheerfully told the police officer things weren't as they appeared – they were actually in the office late that night applying for jobs as apprentice telegraph operators. An alderman furnished a $10,000 bond for O'Banion and another $30,000 in bribes to make the case go away. Not long after, the fingerprints of O'Banion, Weiss, and Vincent "The Schemer" Drucci, were found on the dial of an empty safe in the Parkway Tea Room. A jury acquitted them. O'Banion spoke to a reporter when he left the courtroom: "It was an oversight. Hymie was supposed to wipe off the prints but he forgot."

O'Banion might have had a questionable reputation with the authorities, but was well liked in the neighborhood. As his fortunes soared, his acts of charity went beyond those of a man just trying to make himself look good. He had genuine feelings for poor and miserable people such as his parents had been. Often, the police would get excited when they saw O'Banion's car cruising about in the shabby districts and suspected that a crime was in the wind. In truth, he was merely out on an expedition of charity, his car filled with food and clothing. He visited the slums, dropping off money for widows, the elderly and the orphans. He gave groceries to those who couldn't afford them, bought shoes for ragged children and kept many men and women from the poorhouse. A newsboy would sometimes be stunned to find that O'Banion gave him $100 for a two-cent paper. He sent many sick children to the hospital and paid their medical bills. He once sent a crippled boy to the Mayo Clinic and, when told that neither surgery nor medication could cure him, set up a trust to take care of him for as long as he lived.

O'Banion also had an odd sense of justice. After an altercation at the LaSalle Theater that put a man named Dave Miller in the hospital for several weeks -- O'Banion later apologized, saying, "it was just a piece of hot-headed foolishness," -- Miller's brother, Hirschie, was approached by someone who offered to kill O'Banion for money. The would-be assassin's name was John Duffy and he came to Chicago after killing a policeman in Philadelphia. He was a blustering, swaggering fellow who was proud of the fact that he had committed four murders. He had earlier met O'Banion and the Millers (who were usually friends – the Millers declined to prosecute Dean for the shooting) and all of them sized Duffy up as a drunken braggart and wanted nothing to do with him. Duffy approached Hirschie about killing O'Banion and Hirschie turned him down cold. He later told O'Banion about it and while angry, he vowed to watch his back around the man. He and the Millers were convinced that Duffy was crazy and Hirschie warned him, "Lay off that guy. He'll kill somebody yet."

Duffy continued to throw his weight around in Chicago with no thought of danger. He was oblivious to the fact that his situation was growing precarious. He brought it to an abrupt climax with an impulsive but brutal crime that offered O'Banion the perfect excuse to revenge himself on Duffy.

At the time Duffy was living with a likable young woman named Maybelle Exley in a little apartment on Carmen Avenue on the North Side. They had a volatile relationship, mostly caused by Duffy, who sometimes flew into terrible rages when he was drinking. One night, a pal named Billy Engelke was drinking with them in their apartment and Duffy went into another of his alcohol-fueled outbursts. Suddenly, he pulled out a revolver and shot Maybelle in the head. She was dead before she hit the floor.

Duffy snapped. He began to weep as though his heart was broken and began rushing up and down the room, waving his arms and crying. He couldn't believe what he had done. Billy Engelke later said that he was sure the man had gone insane. Duffy picked up Maybelle and gently laid her down on the davenport. He bent down and kissed her on the forehead before covering her with a sheet. "Goodbye Maybelle," he said.

Panic-stricken, Duffy knew that he had to get out of Chicago. Not knowing what else to do, he went to see O'Banion. He told O'Banion that he had "accidentally" killed his sweetheart and needed money to leave town. O'Banion listened in silence and then told him that he would meet him later that night. O'Banion drove up alone to where Duffy and Engelke waited for him, arriving around midnight. He had a few words with Duffy, told him that he had a plan for him to escape, would stake him some money and drive him to an outlying railway station where he could board a train without worrying about the police finding out. Duffy, feeling better with the prospect of a safe getaway, climbed into the car with O'Banion and they drove off into the night.

Duffy was found dead the next morning with three bullet holes in his head. O'Banion had his revenge – and he managed to get a little justice for the poor farm girl who had died at Duffy's hand.

O'Banion surrounded himself with men who were just as eccentric as he was. Perhaps one of the most colorful was Earl Wojciechowski, the son of a Polish immigrant and better known as Earl "Hymie" Weiss. Hymie coined a term that would become one of gangland Chicago's best-known traditions when he murdered a fellow gangster named Stephen Wisniewski in 1921 – the "one-way ride." After Wisniewski hijacked some of O'Banion booze, Weiss was tasked with teaching him a lesson. He took the gangster for a ride along Lake Michigan and somewhere along the way, Wisniewski was murdered and his body dumped on the roadside. Afterwards, Weiss was said to have bragged, "We took Stevie for a ride, a one-way ride!"

EARL "HYMIE" WEISS

Weiss was born on January 25, 1898, the son of Walenty and Mary Wojciechowski, who Americanized their names to William and Mary Weiss. He had two brothers, Bruno and Frederick and a sister named Violet. Two other siblings died as children and Weiss' parents separated while he was still young. Weiss began his criminal career as an "auto pirate," stealing cars and cutting them up for their parts. In May 1919, after two stolen cars were found at 128 North Cicero, police captured Weiss, along with James Fleming and Alfred Marlowe, as they drove up in a third stolen car. They had been chopping up the cars at 317 North Avers, where they kept tools to dismantle car chassis, strip them for parts and then sell the stolen license plates. Weiss later became friends with O'Banion and the two of them went into the burglary and safecracking business.

Like O'Banion, Weiss attended Holy Name Cathedral and always wore a crucifix around his neck and kept a rosary in his pocket. Thin and wiry with coarse, dark hair, hot black eyes and a notoriously short temper, he was easily the smartest member of the gang and the most arrogant. Many people told stories of his kindness but those who disliked him shuddered in fear at his very presence (Rumor had it that he was one of the only men whom Al Capone feared). Weiss' frequent mood swings may have been caused by the fact that he   suffered from severe migraines. A sofa was installed for him in an upstairs office at Schofield's flower shop and he would sometimes lay there for hours, wracked with pain and completely immobilized in the darkness.

When feeling well, Weiss was described as "generous to a fault." Like O'Banion, he often helped out poor people in the neighborhood, contributing food and money to those who fell short on their grocery bills. He not only paid all of his parents' food bills and expenses, but he took care of their friends and neighbors, as well. Once while staying overnight with the family of a fellow gangster, he heard a noise in the kitchen and went in to find his friend's son trying to get into a cookie jar on the kitchen counter. Weiss laughed and lifted the boy up so that he could snag a snack, a welcome favor that the child would remember many years later as an adult. Weiss made many friends growing up and a number of his classmates from St. Malachy's School, which he attended as a child, were honorary pallbearers at his funeral. He shared an apartment with a Ziegfeld Follies showgirl named Josephine Libby, who called him "one of the finest men in the world."

But Weiss, like so many other gangsters of his era, had a dark side. On election days, he worked hard for whatever political party he had been hired to support, clubbing his way from polling place to polling place with a revolver. He seemed to relish beating up election officials while his thugs stole the ballot boxes. One example of his fiery temper occurred in June 1921 when he shot his brother. Fred had just returned from France after completing his military service and made an unwise comment to his brother about the fact that he had failed to serve his country. Earl whipped out a gun and shot him. The Weiss family tried to cover up the incident and Fred pleaded with his doctor at Washington Boulevard Hospital not to tell the police. Everyone claimed it was an accident. The truth of what really happened did not come out until after Earl's death, when Fred finally admitted that his brother shot him.

During their safecracking expeditions, O'Banion and Weiss usually brought along two friends and fellow gang members, Vincent "The Schemer" Drucci and George "Bugs" Moran.

Born Vincenzo D'Ambrosio in Caltagirone, Sicily, very little is known about Drucci's early life other than he grew up in Chicago and was a boyhood friend of Dean O'Banion. After serving in the U.S Navy, Drucci returned to Chicago and started robbing pay telephone coin boxes. He earned his nickname "The Schemer" because he loved to concoct outrageous and ridiculous plans for robbing banks, kidnapping millionaires, overthrowing the government and becoming president of the United States. Chicago mythology has it that O'Banion hated Italians, but he certainly liked Drucci, which seems to disprove this notion. It also argues against the fact (like Weiss, who was Polish) that the North Siders were an "Irish gang." It certainly had Irish members, but the gang also welcomed members of other ethnicities, as long as they were loyal to the other members.

VINCENT "THE SCHEMER" DRUCCI

To rival gangs, Drucci was a tough, brutally dangerous gunman against whom few dared to tangle. As far as the other North Side gang members were concerned, he was a fun-loving practical joker who was definitely on the eccentric side. One of his favorite pranks was to dress as a priest and as a couple passed him on the sidewalk, he would blurt out, "You have a nice ass!" When the couple turned around to face him, Drucci would say, "Not you lady, your fellow." On one occasion, O'Banion joined in the fun by pretending to beat up Drucci while he was wearing the priest outfit.

Drucci would sometimes play jokes on the drivers who made booze deliveries for the gang. The driver would arrive at Schofield's and park his car in back while he drove a delivery truck out to pick up bootleg liquor and deliver it to warehouses on the North Side. One winter day, Drucci filled one of the driver's cars with snow. When the unsuspecting driver went to leave in his car, he discovered the interior was packed full of snow. The driver was steamed and Drucci was nowhere to be found. O'Banion thought the joke was hilarious, but in sympathy, he paid to have the car cleaned.

Another joke that was frequently played by Drucci involved fellow gang members' new shoes. Whenever he discovered that someone was sporting new footwear, Drucci would yell out "shoes!", tackle the wearer and hurl the shoes as far as he could. Hymie Weiss fell victim to this one day on the second floor of Schofield's flower shop. Drucci saw that Weiss had on a shiny new pair, so he immediately tackled Weiss to the ground, removing his shoes and throwing them out the open window. One of the gang's drivers was outside at the time and knew to duck when he heard the shouted, "shoes!" Hymie stuck his head out the window and asked the driver to kindly retrieve the shoes and bring them up.

One evening, Drucci got so drunk and out of hand that the gang had to throw him in the trunk of a car to keep him from killing someone. They drove home, and when they opened the trunk, they discovered to their shock that he had fallen out along the way. He was later found, bruised and battered, but otherwise in one piece. He remembered nothing of the trip.

Drucci was arrested numerous times on gun charges and the police always knew that he was armed if they saw him on the street. Every time that he was frisked for weapons, he always asked the cop, "Is this Russia?" After a while, he went to great lengths to avoid being arrested. One night, two police officers spotted   Drucci in his car. They knew that he has forfeited his bond on a charge of blowing up a safe. Drucci, realizing that he was about to be nabbed, stepped on the gas – only to be stopped by the Michigan Avenue Bridge as it slowly started to open to let a steamship pass. In desperation, he floored the gas pedal and made a spectacular jump over the open drawbridge. But he didn't count on the cops to be just as daring. They also made it across and managed to corner Drucci just a block away. He was arrested for attempting to evade the police.

Vincent Drucci was probably Chicago's most entertaining gangster, but he could also boast something that no other local gangster had done – in 1923, he appeared in a "blue movie" (early porn) that was shot in Chicago called "Bob's Hot Story."

GEORGE "BUGS" MORAN

George "Bugs" Moran was born Alelard Cunin in Minnesota in 1891, the son of a French stone mason named Jules Cunin, and his wife, Marie. His father was later recalled as a mean-tempered man and the two never got along, although he and his mother stayed on good terms throughout this life. He ran away in 1910 and adopted the name of George Moran. He became involved with a gang of young toughs who began specializing in stealing horses. In 1912, Moran was arrested for the first time. He spent several stints in jail after that for other crimes, including larceny and burglary.

Moran made friends in Joliet Correctional Center and began hanging around the North Side after his release. One day, Moran was listening to a speech given by an outdoor orator and became annoyed when a man in the crowd started heckling him. Moran confronted the heckler and a fight broke out. As a result, Moran's chest and neck were badly slashed with a knife and he spent the rest of his life wearing high-neck collars to hide the scars. His nickname of "Bugs" was probably created by newspaper writers (as most gangsters' more colorful handles were) but it was noted that Moran had a fiery temper, which led to the moniker.

Following the knife attack, and after recuperating for several weeks in the hospital, Moran began hanging around McGovern's, a cabaret at 666 North Clark Street, where Dean O'Banion was currently working as a singing waiter. Many criminals who were just starting out hung around the place and Moran became friends with many of them. One of them was O'Banion and the two began working together, robbing warehouses, with other members of what would become the North Side gang. After one fouled-up job, Moran was captured. He kept his silence and served two years in Joliet without implicating O'Banion in the crime. After he was released, he went back to work with his friend. He was soon captured again and, once more, he kept silent about who he worked with. He stayed in jail this time until 1923.

When Moran got out the last time, he joined back up with O'Banion's now formidable North Side gang. They had become a powerful organization, supplying liquor to Chicago's wealthy Gold Coast. Moran became a valuable asset, hijacking liquor trucks at will. He became known as O'Banion's right hand man, always impeccably dressed, right down to the two guns that he always wore.

Moran fell in love with a showgirl who had recently arrived in America from Turkey. Her name was Lucille Bilezikdijan and she had a child from a previous relationship, which she feared would turn Moran away from her. Instead, he raised the boy as his own and not long after, he fathered his own child with Lucille. Like so many other gangster wives, Lucille averred that her husband was, "one of the best men she had ever known."

Years later, Moran would be the last surviving member of the Moran gang.

O'Banion's most devoted follower was Leland Varain, better known as Louis Alterie. He was born in Northern California, the son of French ranchers, and moved to Chicago as a young man, where he joined up with the North Side gang. Befitting his California background, Alterie was a Western enthusiast who wore a ten-gallon hat and two holstered Colt .45 revolvers. He owned a ranch near Sedalia, Colorado. As well as being a top gunman for O'Banion, he also formed the Theatrical Janitors' Union and used his position as union president to extort money from theater owners. With Hymie Weiss, he perfected yet another widely imitated murder technique – the rented ambush. They would rent an apartment within gun range of a place that the target frequently visited and keep vigil near an open window until they had the marked man in their sights.

The killer received his famous nickname of "Two Gun" Louis during the gaudy funeral of Dean O'Banion in 1924. While other members of the North Side gang wept openly next to O'Banion's casket, Alterie paraded back and forth in front of the Sbarbaro funeral home on Wells Street, wielding a pair of six-shooters and vowing to shoot it out with his O'Banion's killers in broad daylight at State and Madison. No one took him up on the offer.

Alterie had a predilection for blondes -- but only natural blondes. On one occasion, he discovered that a girl who was traveling west with him got her blond hair color from a bottle and he threw her off the train. The parting occurred while he was on his way to his Colorado ranch. Alterie often hid out fugitive criminals at the ranch and during the fall, he always invited O'Banion, Weiss and other members of the gang out to the ranch for deer hunting. Among his favorite hunters was Samuel "Nails" Morton, one of the gang's few Jewish members.

LOUIS "TWO GUN" ALTERIE

Samuel Morton earned his famous nickname for being "tough as nails" fighting bullies in the old Maxwell Street neighborhood of Chicago. He was a bit of an oddity among local gangsters in that he was a bonafide war hero. The son of Jewish immigrants who scraped out a miserable living in the cold water tenements of the West Side, he joined the army at the start of World War I and was assigned to the 131st Infantry, the Rainbow Division. Morton sustained a bullet wound in his arm and shrapnel in his leg and while laid up in a field hospital, begged his commanding officer to let him rejoin his unit. When he did, he was given the Croix de Guerre for heroism in combat after leading a raiding party against a German position. He was the only member of the group to return from the raid with his life. For his gallantry, he was promoted to lieutenant and went home to Chicago a hero.

Morton hooked up with O'Banion, Weiss, Alterie and other names familiar to the Chicago police and began helping the North Side outfit to set up a profitable gambling and bootlegging syndicate. Within two years, "Nails" had moved into a suite at the Congress Hotel and was enjoying the fast life. In October 1921, he and Hirschie Miller were acquitted on charges of murdering Police Officers William Hennessey and James Mulcahy at the Pekin Inn, a notorious South Side jazz and gin cabaret. Charges were made that key witnesses in the case had been paid off by state's attorney (and Thompson crony) Robert Crowe, but a "thorough investigation," run by Crowe's own office, failed to uncover anything illegal.

One morning in early 1923, Morton made a date for a horseback ride with O'Banion, his wife and a mutual friend, Peter Mundane. Morton had been taken with horses after visiting Louis Alterie's Colorado ranch. After returning to Chicago after one trip, he outfitted himself with jodhpurs, a

SAMUEL "NAILS" MORTON

riding jacket and black derby. The men liked to rent horses from the Brown Riding Stables at 3008 North Clark (later the site of the old Ivanhoe Theater) and then go riding in Lincoln Park.

On this morning, Morton mounted a frisky colt named "Morvich" after a famous jockey of the day. The plan was for "Nails" to ride east down Wellington toward the Lincoln Park bridle path, where he would rendezvous with his companions. Unfortunately, the nervous horse began behaving erratically and as Morton rode away from the stable, Morvich bolted south down Clark Street. Near the intersection of Clark and Diversey, Police Officer John Keyes saw how fast the animal was approaching and tried to curb him when he realized the rider has lost control. Then suddenly, the left stirrup gave away and fell to the ground. Morton clung to the horse's neck, and then decided to take a chance and jump to the ground. He landed headfirst on the street and on the way down, one of the horse's hooves hit him in the head, causing a skull fracture that would turn out to be fatal.

The police officer rushed to the fallen man, who was lying unconscious on the street. He recognized him immediately. "Why, it's 'Nails' Morton!" he gasped. "He was my lieutenant in France!"

Morton was rushed to the hospital and died on the operating table. Within hours, hundreds of friends and admirers crowded the undertaking parlor at 4936 North Broadway to pay their respects. Gangster or not, the war hero was remembered as a friendly and likable man.

As far as his pals were concerned, "Nails" had been murdered – a crime that could not go unpunished.

Led by Morton's best friend, Louis Alterie, several members of the North Side gang broke into the Brown Riding Stables and executed the guilty horse. Alterie later telephoned the stable manager and told him "we taught that horse of yours a lesson."

Dean O'Banion threw a party in celebration of this unusual act of vengeance.

WILLIAM "KLONDIKE" O'DONNELL

THE WEST SIDE IRISH

The West Side of Chicago, in the area around Madison Street and Chicago Avenue (regarded today as the West Loop), was the domain of the O'Donnell brothers – William "Klondike," Myles and Bernard – and their strictly Irish gang. Their territory covered this section of the city and extended as far out as Cicero, a township bordering Chicago's southwestern limits. The gang was usually referred to as the Klondike O'Donnell mob, although all three brothers led it.

"Klondike" O'Donnell was a husky, red-faced Irishman who acted as the unofficial mayor of Cicero. Joseph Z. Klenha, who actually held the office, always deferred to him. He operated alongside two other Cicero racketeers: Eddie Vogel, who ran a slot machine operation, and Eddie Tancl, a powerful saloon operator. In those days, Cicero was still a relatively crime-free town. Aside from a little political corruption, most of the inhabitants enjoyed a glass or two of O'Donnell beer after work and played Vogel's slot machines whenever they wanted a thrill.

They had no idea that the quiet town would be turned into a battleground for the mob.

THE GENNAS OF LITTLE ITALY

Little Italy, on Chicago's near Southwest Side, was the territory of the six Genna brothers – Sam, Jim, Pete, Angelo, Tony and Mike, who were known as the "Terrible Gennas." The Gennas made their headquarters along Taylor Street, an area where they had lived their entire lives. Their father, a railroad section hand from the Sicilian port of Marsala, had brought his family to America in 1894, when Sam, the eldest, was 10 and Mike was an infant. Both parents died young, leaving their sons to fend for themselves

THE "TERRIBLE GENNAS" WITH THEIR FAMILY: (LEFT TO RIGHT) SAM, ANGELO, PETER, TONY AND JIM

in the squalor of the tenements. They soon made a life for themselves in the underworld and they, along with their gunmen, became some of the most feared criminals in Chicago. Through Black Hand extortion they amassed a small fortune and through service to ward bosses they gained the political connections needed to operate a gambling den, a pool room, a cheese and olive import company and the largest bootleg operation in the city.

Five of the six Gennas were typical Sicilian killers – overbearing, savage, treacherous and dangerous and at the same time, devoutly religious. They went regularly to church and carried rosaries and crucifixes in their pockets, right next to their guns. The exception was Tony, known as "Tony the Gentleman," who studied architecture and built model tenements for the poor. He was a patron of the opera and lived elegantly in a suite at the Congress Hotel. He never killed, but attended all family councils at which murder was planned, and had a voice in all decisions. The Gennas' main gunmen were as dangerous as Tony was civilized. They included Sam "Samoots" Amatuna, an accomplished musician and murderer; Giuseppe Nerone; and the ferocious killers John Scalisi and Albert Anselmi, who were known for teaching Chicago gangsters to rub their bullets with garlic, to increase the chances of gangrene. Garlic has no such toxicity, but the legend spread and soon the practice gained popularity throughout gangland.

Early in 1920, the Gennas' political connections made it possible for them to get a government license for handling industrial alcohol. They purchased a three-story warehouse at 1022 West Taylor Street (about 600 feet from the Maxwell Street police station) and started out with about $7,000 worth of alcohol that had been purchased legally from federal sources. Only a small amount was ever distributed to legitimate purchasers. The rest was re-distilled, colored and flavored to imitate whiskey, brandy and other liquors and sold through bootleg connections.

Their manufacturing methods were very dangerous to their customers. Rendering out the wood alcohol content, which would make it drinkable, required not only more chemical knowledge than the Gennas had, but also more than they cared to invest in. As a result of their ignorance, the end product contained a poison that could, depending on the amount ingested, produce horrific pain that lasted for three or four days, cause permanent blindness or even kill the drinker. The coloring and flavoring process only increased the dangers. The alcohol manufactured by the Gennas gave rise to the expression "blind drunk" and was

JOHN SCALISE AND ALBERT ANSELMI WERE SICILIAN KILLERS IMPORTED BY THE GENNAS, WHO LATER WENT TO WORK FOR CAPONE. THEY INTRODUCED THE IDEA OF RUBBING THEIR BULLETS WITH GARLIC TO CAUSE GANGRENE, A PRACTICE SOON ADOPTED BY OTHER ITALIAN GANGSTERS.

believed to cause an insanity that was characterized by sexual depravity, hallucinations, paranoia and homicidal impulses.

But no matter how noxious the Gennas' liquor was, their Taylor Street warehouse couldn't keep up with the demand for it. They quickly came up with a solution and put hundreds of poverty-stricken Sicilians and Italians to work cooking corn sugar alcohol in the nearby tenements, homes and shops. The cookeries and stills produced thousands of gallons of raw alcohol, which was cut, flavored, colored and sold as brandy and whiskey. The entire neighborhood was drenched with the smell of fermenting mash – which should have been obvious to those who were supposed to be upholding the Prohibition laws. However, the lucrative operation was protected by Torrio, who received a monthly sum and passed on payments to the authorities. It was reported that five police captains were on the Genna-Torrio payroll, along with four hundred uniformed patrolmen, mostly from the Maxwell Street station. In addition, plainclothes officers from headquarters and the State's Attorney's office called at the Genna warehouse each month to collect their own bribes. The police also received their alcohol at discounted prices.

The "alky cooking" could also be dangerous, both to the cookers and the customers. The cookers received $15 a day to keep the fires burning under their stills and to skim off the distillate. It was then collected in five-gallon cans by Genna drivers. But the cooker faced serious risks. If he used gas for fuel, he might have to tap a main to get it, not because the Gennas wouldn't pay for it, but because an abnormal increase in gas consumption might arouse the suspicion of the meter reader, who might then demand

A LIQUOR STILL LIKE THE ONES USED TO COOK ALCOHOL IN LITTLE ITALY.

payment to keep quiet. A clumsily executed theft from the gas main might release a rush of gas, which could kill the cooker. Worse yet, a badly constructed still was liable to explode, scalding its operator to death. For the customer, the physical conditions of the average tenement threatened his health. Not only could he die, or go blind, from the alcohol itself but vermin, drawn by the reek of fermenting yeast and sugar, often fell into the mash. When Captain John Stege, one of Chicago's rare honest cops, confiscated one hundred barrels of mash from Little Italy, he found at least one dead rat in every one of them.

The enormous profits from the alcohol cooking allowed them to keep the police in their pockets, but the Gennas could not maintain their power with bribery alone. They also required the support of the political ward bosses, which they gained through violence. During the aldermanic wars of the Nineteenth Ward – often referred to as the "Bloody Ward" – that encompassed Little Italy, thirty men were killed in the streets. They usually died after their killer, using an emotionally sadistic method designed to shatter his victim's nerves, had posted their name to the "Dead Man's Tree," a poplar that grew on Loomis Street that has since been cut down.

The 1921 aldermanic wars, in which the Gennas played a large role, involved an election between Democratic incumbent John Powers and challenger Anthony D'Andrea. The Gennas threw their support behind D'Andrea, a lawyer who turned out to be a defrocked priest and former counterfeiter and bank robber with a prison record. D'Andrea had already twice run for office unsuccessfully, once in 1914 and again in 1916. The second time, he fought a battle against one of Powers' protégés, James Bowler. During the election, one of Powers' men was shot to death in a saloon and the murder was blamed on the Gennas.

The 1921 conflict turned out to be a much deadlier one. Bombs were set off at the homes of both candidates, at a D'Andrea rally and at D'Andrea's election headquarters, injuring five people. Mobsters literally gunned men down in the streets and both candidates required round-the-clock protection. D'Andrea lost the election, but the bloodshed continued. Angelo Genna -- along with "Samoots" Amatuna, Frank Gambino and Johnny Guardino – gunned down Paul Labriola, a municipal court bailiff and Powers supporter, at the corner of Halsted and Congress streets. After Labriola went down with several bullets in him, Genna stood over him and plugged him three more times for good measure before jumping into a waiting automobile and speeding away. Later that same day, a D'Andrea supporter named Harry Raimondi was shot to death in his Taylor Street cigar store.

When a Powers supporter named Nicolo Adamo was murdered, his wife identified Jim Genna as his killer. Another man, Paul Notte, lived long enough to finger Angelo as the one who shot him. Both accusations were later dismissed when Notte died and Mrs. Adamo declined to testify. Only one murder resulted in an arrest and trial when Angelo Genna was charged with Labriola's murder. He went free after the witnesses against him either disappeared or developed what had come to be known as "Chicago amnesia."

In retaliation by the Powers faction, two D'Andrea men, Joe Marino and Johnny Guardino, were struck down. Guardino was shot while standing on a street corner, watching some boys play stickball. At about the same time, a car filled with Powers hoodlums cruised through Little Italy, halted outside a pool room on Taylor Street and emptied shotguns into it.

D'Andrea, who had lost the election, was appalled by the violence and renounced Nineteenth Ward politics. However, this would not be enough to save his life. On the night of May 11, 1921, while his wife and daughters were sleeping, D'Andrea was playing cards in a neighborhood restaurant. While he was out, three men broke into his apartment building

(LEFT) JOHN POWERS AND (RIGHT) ANTHONY D'ANDREA, THE POLITICAL CANDIDATES IN THE ALDERMANIC WARS OF 1921.

at 902 Ashland and entered a vacant apartment that was located on the floor below the D'Andrea place. D'Andrea's bodyguard, Joe Laspisa, dropped off his boss at the apartment a few hours later, watched him climb the stone steps, and then drove away. As D'Andrea approached the front door, two shotgun blasts hit him in the chest. He fell, mortally wounded, but before he died he grabbed his revolver out of his coat and, from the floor of the porch, fired five times through the shattered window. The killers vanished.

Joe Laspisa swore to avenge D'Andrea but he never had a chance – he was gunned down a month later as his car approached the Church of San Filippo Benzi. The angry parish priest posted a sign on the church doors pleading with the community to fight back against the evil that was plaguing the neighborhood. During his sermons, he urged anyone with information about the murders to go to the police but no one was brave enough – or suicidal enough – to do so.

The Genna brothers, with the exception of Tony, were a crude, violent, bloody lot – the stereotype of the Italian criminals that so plagued the honest, hard-working immigrants. To Johnny Torrio, though, their political connections, clout with the police, stable of killers and the fact that their territory had to be crossed during liquor shipments, made them an essential part of his plan to run Chicago's bootleg business.

THE VALLEY GANG

The West Side, between Little Italy and Cicero, was the territory of the Druggan-Lake, or Valley, gang. The original name of the gang came from the area where it was formed, the Valley, which was one of the first large Irish ghettoes in Chicago. It was separated from the red-light district of the Levee by the south branch of the Chicago River. It was bordered by Chicago's once famous water canals and Halsted Street to the west, Fourteenth and Fifteenth streets to the north and south. It was a dreary vista of warehouses and shacks, weather-beaten shanties, overcrowded tenements, empty stores and packed saloons.

In the early 1850s, the Valley was one of the main destinations for Irish immigrants in Chicago, but by 1871, just after the Great Fire destroyed most of the neighborhood, the Irish began to leave the area and were replaced by Jews and Italians. For those Irish that remained, they saw an invisible line being drawn that separated the Irish and Italian sides of the neighborhood. Sidewalk brawls became an almost daily occurrence.

The encroachment of the Italians led to the formation of the Irish Valley Gang. Most of the members were the sons of policemen and low-level politicos whose city hall connections kept the boys out of serious trouble with the law. With that kind of clout, the Valley Gang began to transform itself from a ragtag group of street urchins to a real criminal organization. They began extorting the German and Jewish shop owners for protection money, as well as committing robberies, burglaries and hijackings. Their only real challenge came from the Italians and street wars were a common occurrence. As a result, the Maxwell Street police station saw the highest number of assault and attempted murder cases of any court in the country, outside of the Superior Court in Brooklyn. Only the Valley Gang's political connections – and their work as brutal polling place enforcers -- kept them out of jail.

The first important leaders of the outfit were "Big Heinie" Miller and Jimmy Farley, skilled pickpockets and burglars who ran things into the early 1900s. They were both locked up at Joliet in 1905, together with two other members of the gang, "Tootsie" Bill Hughes and "Cooney the Fox," who police officers of the time called "the smoothest thieves who ever worked the Maxwell Street district."

After the arrest of Miller and Farley, the gang was led by Red Bolton for several years. He also ended his career in prison, serving a life sentence for murder. Bolton was followed by Paddy Ryan, also known as "Paddy the Bear." This red-faced, obese monster was only slightly over five feet tall and weighed more than 250 pounds. He ran a rundown saloon on South Halsted Street and was one of the most feared men in the history of "Bloody Maxwell," as the police district was often called. Ryan was murdered in 1920 by Walter Quinlan, who had taken up with the wife of an imprisoned gangster and was badly beaten for this breach of underworld etiquette. After serving a few years in prison for Ryan's murder, he opened a saloon at Seventeenth and Loomis streets, which became a hangout for local gunmen. During one raid on the saloon, police confiscated a dozen automatic pistols, ten bulletproof vests, and two machine-guns. Quinlan was finally killed by Paddy Ryan's son, who was known as "Paddy the Fox."

The most successful leaders of the Valley Gang were Terry Druggan and Frankie Lake, who took over in 1919. The two men were almost mirror opposites. Both wore horn-rimmed glasses and could have passed for brothers. Lake had been a member of the Chicago Fire Department and was a boyhood member of the gang. He resigned from the department in 1919

FRANKIE LAKE AND TERRY DRUGGAN

to become Druggan's partner. Druggan was an almost comical man. He often played the part of a fool and frequently made fun of himself. This routine was perpetuated, perhaps, to hide his naked ambition and the fact that he was highly intelligent and had a desire to create a territory of the gang that extended far beyond its original borders. He and Lake gained their greatest infamy as beer providers during the Prohibition era. Under their leadership, the gang concentrated its efforts on bootlegging and eventually controlled a string of breweries. Druggan and Lake made millions and they boasted that even the common men who loaded their trucks, "wore silk shirts and rode in Rolls-Royce automobiles."

Druggan was smart enough to be among the first to enter into a lucrative business agreement with Johnny Torrio and was wise enough to pull the Valley Gang off the streets and remodel them after Johnny Torrio's restructured version of Big Jim Colosimo's outfit. With the money that he was making, Druggan bought a magnificent home on Lake Zurich and a winter estate in Florida. He had a swimming pool but he couldn't swim, a tennis court but he didn't play the game, and dairy cattle, which he admitted scared him, in his pastures. He owned a thoroughbred racing stable and raced his horses at Chicago's tracks. One time, when he was ruled off the turf for fixing the race, Druggan pulled his gun on the officials and vowed to kill them all then and there, if they didn't change their ruling. The ruling was quickly changed.

Frankie Lake was Druggan's muscle and best friend. They had grown up together, went into business together and even went to jail together. In 1924, after refusing to answer questions that had been put to them by Judge James Wilkerson of the United States District Court, Druggan and Lake were sentenced to a year in prison on contempt charges.

Several months later, a newspaper reporter called at the county jail to see them and was told that the two men were not available. "They had an appointment downtown and will be back after dinner," he was told. After an investigation, the confused reporter learned that both Druggan and Lake, in return for $20,000 in bribes, had been given extraordinary privileges. While supposedly incarcerated and treated like other prisoners, they actually spent more time in plush downtown restaurants and in their own apartments than they did in jail. They were permitted to come and go as they pleased and the death cell at the jail had been turned into a private office where the gangsters received as many visitors as they liked and even issued orders for criminal activities. On those rare days when they actually stayed in the jail, arising late and having breakfast brought to bed for them, their wives were regular visitors. In fact, on several occasions Druggan had his dentist brought in to do some work.

Later, when the story broke and a reporter asked Druggan to explain his absence from jail, the gangster replied, "Well, you know, it's awfully crowded in there."

Torrio, along with Capone, liked Druggan's style and a mutual respect developed on both sides. Eventually, the Valley Gang was absorbed into the Capone organization.

THE SALTIS-MCERLANE GANG

SLUGGISH AND STUPID, "POLACK" JOE SALTIS HAD A REPUTATION FOR BEING A COWARD. ONLY HIS ASSOCIATION WITH FRANK MCERLANE KEPT HIS BUSINESS FROM BEING TAKEN OVER.

On the Southwest Side, the grim landscape of slaughterhouses, factories and train tracks had been dubbed the "Back of the Yards," a depressing wasteland of rundown homes and buildings that would forever be connected to the nearby stockyards. This bleak area was the domain of the Saltis-McErlane gang.

Saltis, a slow-witted, hulking Hungarian was a saloonkeeper before Prohibition and while he presented an imposing figure, his cowardice had long been known to his underworld colleagues. His ferocity only emerged when he was dealing with someone smaller and weaker than he was. On one occasion, he beat an elderly woman to death after she refused to let him turn her ice cream parlor into a speakeasy. Only his political connections and gangster pals like Frank McErlane kept his business from being taken over by stronger rivals.

Another principal associate was John "Dingbat" O'Berta, a labor racketeer and politician from the Thirteenth Ward. O'Berta was actually of Slavic descent but had fudged his real name of "Oberta" to appeal to the Irish voters of the district. Childhood friends had nicknamed him "Dingbat" after a popular comic strip character of the day but the ruthless mobster was anything but comical. His ambitions ran unchecked. After rivals gunned down labor racketeer "Big Tim" Murphy, O'Berta gained underworld prominence by marrying Murphy's widow, Florence.

Saltis began bringing in beer from Wisconsin at the start of Prohibition and he made enough money to buy one brewery and invest in three others. He also used a percentage of his brewery money to buy a summer home in Wisconsin's Eagle River resort area, a favorite retreat for millionaires in the northern part of the state.

In 1922, he joined forces with killer Frank McErlane, a stocky, hard-muscled man with a taste for alcohol. When he drank, he got crazy, as many unlucky people found out. One night while drinking in Crown Point, Indiana, an equally drunken companion challenged him to show off his skill with a revolver. McErlane picked a stranger at random, an attorney named Thad Fancher, and shot him in the head. He fled the state just one step ahead of the Indiana State Police and fought extradition for a year. When he was finally brought to trail, the state was unable to call its one key witness because his head had been split with an ax. McErlane was acquitted.

McErlane gave Saltis' operation the deadly element that it had been missing and it didn't take long for word to spread that crossing Saltis would incur the wrath of the brutal killer. In addition, the Saltis-McErlane gang was the first in Chicago to adopt what would become the underworld's weapon of choice – the Thompson sub-machine gun. Known as the "Tommy gun," "the chopper" and the "Chicago Typewriter," the weapon had been named for its co-inventor, Brigadier General John T. Thompson, the director of arsenals during World War I. Developed in 1920, it came too late for the war and it was placed on the open market by the New York company, Auto Ordnance. It met with little success with military customers (the Army didn't want to invest in it until World War II) and most law enforcement agencies rejected it as a hazard to innocent bystanders. To General Thompson's dismay, it became very popular with gangsters.

ALTHOUGH HE LOOKED LIKE AN ACCOUNTANT, FRANK MCERLANE (LEFT) WAS KNOWN AS A HARDENED KILLER AND HE PROVIDED THE MUSCLE FOR THE ORGANIZATION. (RIGHT) JOHN "DINGBAT" O'BERTA GAINED PROMINENCE BY MARRYING FLORENCE MURPHY, WIDOW OF SLAIN LABOR RACKETEER "BIG TIM" MURPHY -- A FEW YEARS LATER, SHE WOULD BE A WIDOW AGAIN.

At just over eight pounds, the gun was light enough to be handled by a small boy and it could fire up to 1,000 .45 caliber cartridges per minute. It could penetrate a pine board at five hundred feet and in no time could reduce a heavy automobile to junk. While most cities and states had enacted legislation similar to New York's 1911 Sullivan Law, which made it illegal to carry small, easily concealed firearms, they placed no restrictions on Tommy guns. Anyone could buy as many as he liked by mail order or from sporting goods stores. The seller was only required to register the purchaser's name and address. And if you couldn't buy one, you could steal one from one of the few police or military arsenals that stocked them.

The Tommy gun soon became an indispensable accessory for every self-respecting gangster. Introduced by the Saltis-McErlane gang, the clattering of the machine gun soon became an all-too-familiar background accompaniment to mayhem on the streets of Chicago.

RAGEN'S COLTS

Just southeast of Joe Saltis' territory, between Forty-Second and Sixty-Third streets, was the area run by Ralph Sheldon, a sickly man who had been made frail by tuberculosis. He headed a mob that had evolved from the old Ragen's Colts gang, a mostly Irish bunch from the Stockyards neighborhood. The Colts dated back to the 1890s, when the Ragen's Athletic and Benevolent Association started a baseball team, the Morgan Athletic Club. The star pitcher was a rough and tumble Irish lad named Frank Ragen. By 1902, the club had 160 members and had expanded from baseball alone into soccer, wrestling, football, and other sports. It held an annual fund-raising minstrel show, a picnic and a ball, which citizen's reform groups regularly denounced for its debauchery and drunkeness. The proceeds from the fundraisers, augmented by "donations" from the Democratic Party faithful, paid for a building on South Halsted Street that contained a gym, a ballroom and a pool hall. Frank Ragen began president of the organization in 1908 after a fight broke out over who should head the club during an annual outing in Santa Fe Park. Hundreds of dollars in damage later, Ragen won the presidency and the name of the baseball team was changed to Ragen's Colts, a label which the press and public applied to the general membership in the club.

Many of the Colts held political office, including Ragen, who rose high in the Democratic Party and was

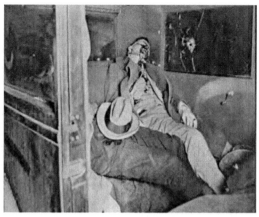

(LEFT) RALPH SHELDON, WHOSE TUBERCULOSIS WOULD EVENTUALLY FORCE HIM TO RETIRE FROM THE CRIMINAL LIFE. (RIGHT) RAGEN'S COLTS MEMBER "DYNAMITE" JOE BROOKS, WHO WAS SHOT IN THE FACE IN THE BACK OF A CAR.

elected city commissioner. His followers insured his election by wrecking polling places and making sure that the balloting went in Ragen's favor. Over a more than twenty-year existence, the Colts gave Chicago many aldermen, county sheriffs, ballplayers and even one mayor, Richard J. Daley, who had allegedly been a Colt.

They also turned out a rogue's gallery of criminals. They included Harry Madigan, the owner of the Pony Inn in Cicero, who racked up eight charges of kidnapping and assault during elections, none of which were ever prosecuted; Joseph "Dynamite" Brooks, a drunken saloon owner who managed his own assault and battery charges; William "Gunner" McPhadden, who committed numerous murders; Danny McFall, an appointed deputy sheriff with the murder of two business competitors on his rap sheet; Hugh "Stubby" McGovern, gambler, larcenist and trigger-man with a record of seven arrests and only two charges – petty fines for carrying a concealed weapon, and Ralph Sheldon, who organized his own splinter gang.

The Colts were notorious racists. They were intent on protecting the white citizens of Chicago against the encroachment of blacks, who they saw as a subhuman threat to white supremacy. On a hot July afternoon in 1919, an African-American boy was swimming off of the South Side beach and crossed into segregated waters. From the lakeshore, a crowd of white swimmers began throwing rocks at him. The boy scrambled onto a float until a carefully hurled rock struck him in the head, knocking him back into the

water. No one came to his assistance and he drowned. The man who threw the fatal rock, George Stauber, was a member of Ragen's Colts.

That night, long-simmering racial tensions on the South Side erupted into violence. In the ensuing riot, members of Ragen's Colts tore through black neighborhoods with guns, bombs and torches, shooting African-Americans on sight. They bombed and burned homes,

RIOTERS ATTACK A FALLEN BLACK MAN ON CHICAGO'S SOUTH SIDE DURING THE 1919 RACE RIOTS. THE RIOTS WERE ALLEGEDLY STARTED BY A MEMBER OF RAGEN'S COLTS.

looted shops and pummelled anyone who tried to stop them. Many black war veterans, armed with their old service revolvers, returned the attack, turning over automobiles and streetcars carrying whites and wrecking white-owned property. Before the terror burned itself out four days later, fourteen African-Americans and twenty whites had been killed and more than 500 people were injured.

Ralph Sheldon's crew emerged from the race riot as the dominant force in the area. He was only 18 years old in 1920 and yet his gang consisted of some of the area's most hardended killers, extortionists and labor racketeers. Like John Torrio, Sheldon maintained his leaderhip with brains, not muscle. He had learned the value of the political fix by the time he was 16, when he escaped a conviction for highway robbery. The fix was so obvious that the trial judge even made a bitter comment about a "miscarriage of justice."

Sheldon was also a devout Catholic and the Colts once assembled a strike force to go to Oklahoma and take on the Ku Klux Klan for their anti-Catholic activities in that state. He was extremely opposed to prostitution, which he saw as immoral, so when Prohibition came along, he vowed to make his crew rich through bootlegging.

TORRIO'S MISTAKE

With all of these forces, Torrio began to put together his master plan for Chicago. These gangs were the only ones, in Torrio's opinion, that had the clout and connections in their respective territories to warrant consideration in his plan.

However, there was one more gang, but in a rare lapse in judgment, Torrio chose to ignore it. Located on the far South Side were the O'Donnell brothers (no relation to the West Side O'Donnells) – Steve, Walter, Tommy, and Ed, who was better known as "Spike." They had been versatile outlaws since boyhood, working as thieves, pickpockets, muggers, labor sluggers and bank robbers. They were largely a mundane lot, with little ambition, but the eldest brother, Ed aka "Spike," had enough intelligence, force of personality and flair that he was able to compensate for his brothers' shortcomings. He was an outwardly cheerful and rakish character, usually sporting plaid suits and jaunty bow ties but he was also a dedicated killer,

ED "SPIKE" O'DONNELL

having been tried twice for murder. He was the brains of the gang and his brothers were merely the muscle. He liked to tell them, "When arguments fail, use a blackjack."

The South Side O'Donnells were a group that Torrio should have reckoned with in his blueprint for citywide organizations between the various gangs. He left them out of his calculations, though, because they were leaderless and drifting at the time. At the start of Prohibition, Spike O'Donnell was doing a five-year sentence at Joliet Penitentiary for the $12,000 daylight robbery of the Stockyard Savings and Trust Bank. Torrio guessed correctly that without Spike, the O'Donnells were a disorganized, floundering crew. Instead of figuring them into his plans, he hired them to work for him at the Four Deuces. They were humiliated into performing odd jobs and errands for Torrio and Capone, secretly building up resentment against them.

Torrio underestimated Spike O'Donnell, who had no intention of serving his entire five-year stretch. His political connections managed to get a dozen letters, asking for his pardon, sent to Governor Len Small from six state senators, five state representatives and a criminal court judge. In early 1920, Torrio had no idea that Spike would be coming home – soon.

6. DIVIDING UP CHICAGO

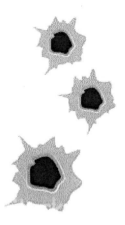

As Johnny Torrio was dividing up Chicago with his plan to supply the city with bootleg liquor, Al Capone was coming into his own in the Windy City. Torrio was pleased with his young friend's business acumen. Capone had opened an antique shop next door to the Four Deuces, which provided him with a cover to carry out their illicit operations. He had business cards printed, presenting himself as "A. Capone, Antique Dealer," but he never tried to sell any of the dusty junk that could be dimly seen though the shop's dirty windows. Anyone who inquired was told that the store was not open that day.

In appreciation of Capone's efforts, Torrio rewarded him with the management of the Four Deuces and a 25-percent share of the profits from all of his brothels. He further promised Capone a 50-percent share of the bootleg business as soon as it started to make a profit. The two men liked and appreciated one another, a trust that went back to their days in New York. They complimented one another, both physically and in their business style, and by their second year working directly together, they had become partners.

RALPH CAPONE

In November 1920, Capone received bad news from New York – his 52-year-old father had died of heart disease. He collapsed in the same Garfield Place poolroom where father and son had often played and died after being carried home.

When Teresa Capone became a widow, Al opened his arms to his entire family, bringing his mother, brothers and sisters to Chicago as quickly as he could – all except for Jim, whose fate was still a mystery to the rest of the family. He fed them, housed them, found jobs for the older boys and, in Italian family tradition, took care of all of their needs. He later had his father's remains exhumed, brought to Chicago and buried in a family plot in Mount Olivet Cemetery.

The first brother to accept the invitation to come to Chicago was Ralph. He was 28 years old at the time and was not lacking in criminal experience. He had had his own brushes with the law, tending bar in a Brooklyn speakeasy and being arrested two times. On the other hand, he had held down more legitimate jobs that Al had, working as a Western Union messenger; in the same book bindery where Al had been employed; as a streetcar conductor; salesman; and a longshoreman.

During World War I, Ralph joined the Marines, but only made it as far as boot camp, where he was sent home for having flat feet. In Chicago, he went to work bartending at the Four Deuces and later, replaced Al as manager. For a time, he shared an apartment with Al and Mae on South Wabash. Charlie and Rocco Fischetti, cousins of the Capones who had also come to Chicago at Al's urging, lived in the same building. They also went to work and rose to a command

CAPONE AND HIS ADORING MOTHER, THERESA.

(RIGHT) THE MODEST CAPONE HOME AT 7244 SOUTH PRAIRIE AVENUE. THE HOUSE STILL STANDS TODAY AS ONE OF THE LAST REMAINING SITES CONNECTED DIRECTLY TO AL CAPONE AND HIS ERA.

level in the Torrio-Capone outfit. Al knew that there was no one that could be more trusted than those connected to him by blood.

Knowing that his mother was coming to Chicago, Capone decided to move out of the apartment where he and his family had been living and build a house. He chose a quiet, tree-shaded lot at 7244 South Prairie Avenue where he built a two-story, 15-room home from red brick. On the outside, it was an unassuming place and one that seemed almost too ordinary for the man who would soon rule Chicago. Inside, though, it had its enhancements. The upstairs parlor had floor to ceiling mirrors and gilded cornices. The bathroom fixtures were imported from Germany and included a seven-foot tub. A steel gate led from an alley at the rear to the basement, which boasted one-foot-thick reinforced concrete walls that were virtually impervious to bullets. The windows were fitted with steel bars that were too close together for a bomb to be thrown inside.

Capone moved into the seven rooms on the first floor with his wife, son, mother and two sisters. Ralph, who had married a woman named Velma Pheasant and had a son and daughter, occupied the eight upstairs rooms. Al enrolled his sister, Mafalda, at the Richards School, a nearby private girl's academy, to which he played Santa Claus for every Christmas thereafter, bringing food and presents to every student and teacher. The two youngest brothers, Mitzi and Matt, also lived at 7244 South Prairie Avenue. Mitzi, a reckless, girl-chasing boy of 18, was barely in Chicago before he was arrested in 1922 for disorderly conduct. Al sent him to Marmion Military School in Aurora, Illinois, then to Pennsylvania's Villanova University. Frank Capone, age 27, also came to Chicago and joined the family.

By 1922, Capone had made a name for himself in the Chicago underworld and was a familiar face to the police department. At the time, however, he was still unknown to the general public and even to the newspapers that regularly reported the activities of the city's gangsters. On the first occasion that Al was mentioned in the news, reporters go his name wrong. The story ran on a morning in early August after Al had been out drinking, whoring and carousing the night before. He was racing his car along North Wabash Avenue with a girl beside him and three men in the back seat. Rounding the corner of East Randolph Street, he crashed into a parked taxi and injured the driver, Fred Krause. He stumbled out of the car in a drunken rage and flashed a deputy sheriff's badge (evidence of his political connections), waving a revolver and threatening to shoot Krause. A conductor on a passing streetcar yelled at Capone to put away his gun.

Al threatened to shoot him, too. His companions fled when a police car pulled up and officers settled things down. An ambulance was summoned to tend to the bleeding cab driver and Al was arrested. According to the news story, "Alfred Caponi" was booked on charges of assault with an automobile, driving while intoxicated and carrying a concealed weapon. Any one of these charges would have landed an ordinary citizen in jail but, as with almost every case filed against him during the next seven years, the charges mysteriously disappeared.

The reporter botched his name this time, but soon, the name "Al Capone" would appear almost daily in every newspaper in the Windy City.

Torrio was finally ready to announce his master plan and to divide up Chicago among the various factions in the city. A large part of his plan involved the brewers that existed in Chicago before Prohibition had gone into effect. Their business options had been limited when Prohibition became law. Simply put, they had three choices about what to do with their breweries. They could convert to the manufacture of legal "near beer," which meant brewing standard beer and then lowering the alcohol content to just one-half percent. Or they could, at considerable financial sacrifice, lease out their breweries or sell them outright. Or they could secretly retain part ownership through an affiliation with gangsters. Under this agreement, the brewers furnished the capital, the technical skills and the management experience while the gangsters, fronting as officers and company directors, paid for police and political protection, fought hijackers and took the legal fall when trouble threatened.

One of the leading brewers in Chicago at the dawn of Prohibition was Joseph Stenson, a beer manufacturer from a wealthy Gold Coast family who chose, to the dismay of his older brothers, to take on Terry Druggan and Frankie Lake as partners. They became involved in his five breweries: the Gambrinus, the Standard, the George Hoffman, the Pfeiffer and the Stege. Early in 1920, Torrio became the fourth partner and with Stenson's backing, obtained control of four other breweries: the West Hammond, the Manhattan, the Best and the Sieben – as well as a few distilleries. Torrio also began working on relationships with smugglers, rum-runners and drivers, all of whom could deliver alcohol to a thirsty Chicago.

While he was establishing these supply lines, Torrio also approached the leaders of the top gangs in the city to present them with his plans. Most of them were already involved in bootlegging in one way or another, in addition to burglary, safecracking, robberies and other violent crimes. However, Torrio pointed out to them that the risks involved in these crimes often did not justify the returns. Bootlegging, on the other hand, could make them millions of dollars at negligible risk and he urged them to concentrate their resources on it. As he saw it, the best way to succeed was through citywide organization, based on each gang holding onto its own territory. Unless a gang already owned or operated its own brewery or distillery, as some did, everyone would buy from the same source. Torrio was prepared to offer all the beer needed for $50 per barrel. In the event of an encroachment into one particular gang's territory, or a hijacking, the injured party could call on other treaty members to join in punitive actions against the offender. Torrio was willing to supervise all transactions between territories and arbitrate any disputes that came up. As the leader of the syndicate, he would control almost 1,000 hardened gunmen.

All of the gang leaders accepted Torrio's plan and with a few of them, he reached secondary agreements. For example, O'Banion's specialty was bringing in whiskey from Canada and cutting it for local distribution, but he also felt that he needed to provide beer for those customers who wanted it. Otherwise, they were going to buy from someone else. Torrio preferred to handle beer, which was the beverage of choice for workingmen in Chicago. The enormous volume that was consumed left a good margin of profit at a relative small price per glass. But Torrio also had to have hard liquor for his suburban roadhouses. So, Torrio and O'Banion put aside their dislike for one another and agreed to exchange commodities.

It wasn't always inventory that Torrio had to trade for. On occasion, he exchanged cash for goodwill.

He had nothing to offer the Gennas but money and protection. Beer did not interest them at all. They really only wanted to control Little Italy's cooking industry and the liquor market it supplied. Torrio bought plenty of product from them, which, in turn, allowed safe passage for his beer trucks through Genna territory.

Unbelievably, Chicago's violent gangland was at peace. Everyone prospered, literally making truckloads of money for the next three years. And then, in the summer of 1923, Spike O'Donnell was released from Joliet Correctional Center.

With Spike's return, the South Side O'Donnells, who had been simmering for years under what they felt was Torrio's contemptuous treatment, decided to revolt. Back up by gunmen imported from New York, notably a bloodthirsty killer named Harry Hasmiller, they began hijacking Torrio's beer trucks and running beer into his territory, as well as territory claimed by the Saltis-McErlane gang. Their best beer salesmen were George "Sport" Bucher and George Meeghan, who used a technique that soon began to be imitated by other gangs. Their method consisted of walking into a speakeasy, looking the owner in the eye and informing him that he was now buying his beer from the O'Donnells – "or else." The added "or else" implied horrible damage to the premises or to the owner himself. The

GEORGE MEEGHAN, O'DONNELL BEER "SALESMAN" AND THUG

warning worked almost every time. If it didn't, the speakeasy owner could count on a beating, a ransacking of his place, or in worst cases, a convenient fire or even death.

By September, the O'Donnell gang had penetrated deep into the South and Southwest Sides. It was the Saltis-McErlane gang, Torrio-Capone allies, who struck the first blow in the "beer wars." On the dark and stormy night of September 7, Bucher and Meeghan, accompanied by Steve, Walter and Tommy O'Donnell and Jerry O'Connor, a Joliet parolee that Spike met inside, paid a second visit to Jacob Geis' speakeasy at 2154 West Fifty-First Street. During their first visit, Geis had not only defied the two O'Donnell men but, with help from his bartender, Nick Gorysko, had thrown them out of the place. On September 7, Steve O'Donnell told Geis that they were giving him one last chance – but Geis still refused to do business with them. He was standing behind the bar, helping Gorysko serve a half dozen customers when he told the interlopers to get out of his place.

Suddenly, the O'Donnell men grabbed Geis and pulled him headfirst across the bar. One of them struck him with a blackjack, fracturing his skull. As blood from his wounded boss sprayed over the bar, Gorysko launched himself at the gangsters. Fists flying, he managed to strike a few blows before he was beaten unconscious. Now angry and out of control, the O'Donnell brothers and their pals stormed five other speakeasies that were getting their beer from Torrio. They broke windows, smashed up furniture and thrashed anyone who got in their way. After creating a path of destruction across the South Side, they ended up at a friendly bar, Joe Klepka's on South Lincoln Street, where Spike O'Donnell joined up with them.

Unknown to the O'Donnells, they had been followed all night by three Saltis-McErlane gunmen, led by Danny McFall. As they stood at the bar drinking in Joe Klepka's place, McFall and the other two men burst through the doors with their guns in hand. According to one of the six other customers who were present in the saloon, McFall ordered the men to put up their hands and he fired a shot over Steve O'Donnell's head. The four brothers and their friends ran for the nearest exits, leaving sluggish Jerry O'Connor behind. McFall managed to snag the man and held him captive, a revolver to his head. McErlane himself then appeared through the doors, carrying a sawed-off shotgun under his gray raincoat. He spoke to McFall and then stepped back outside. Waving his gun in the direction of the doors, he ordered O'Connor to walk out ahead

JERRY O'CONNOR, ANOTHER OF
FRANK MCERLANE'S MANY VICTIMS

of him. The instant they reached the sidewalk, McErlane raised the shotgun and pulled the trigger. O'Connor's head disappeared in an explosion of blood and gore.

Ten nights later, on a stretch of Archer Avenue southwest of Chicago, Bucher and Meeghan were driving two trucks filled with beer, one man following the other. Two men armed with shotguns ran out into the center of the road, stopped them and made them climb out of the cabs. A car approaching from the opposite direction lit up the scene and the holdup men ordered the driver to stop. Terrified, he sped on, never slowing down as buckshot tapped the back of his automobile. From the descriptions the driver later gave to the police, the cops suspected Danny McFall and Frank McErlane were the two gunmen. The following morning, Bucher and Meeghan's bodies were found in a ditch. Their arms had been tied behind their backs and their heads had been blown away by shotgun blasts.

Just after midnight on December 1, on the same roadway, two more O'Donnell truckers, William Egan and Morrie Keane, were driving a load of beer from Joliet to Chicago. They were followed on that cold and miserable night by a second truck that was driven by Martin Brandl. A few miles north of Lemont, two touring cars pulled alongside the trucks and fired a blast with a shotgun, halting both vehicles. Keane and Egan were dragged from the cab, bound hand and foot and thrown into one of the cars. The truck was driven off by two of the hijackers from the touring cars. Brandl was never heard from again.

William Egan was terrified but alert in the back of the car. He would become one of the only men to ever survive a one-way ride. He later recalled:

"Pretty soon the driver [believed to be McErlane gunman Walter Stevens] asks the guy with the shotgun, 'Where you gonna get rid of these guys?' The fat fellow [likely McErlane] laughs and says 'I'll take care of that in a minute.' He was monkeying with his shotgun all the time. Pretty soon he turns around and points the gun at Keane. He didn't say a word just let it go straight at him. Keane got it square on the left side. It kind of turned him over and the fat guy gave him the second barrel in the other side. The guy loads up his gun and gives it to Keane again. Then he turns around to me and says, 'I guess you might as well get yours, too.' With that he shoots me in the side. It hurt like hell so when I see him loading up again, I twist around so he won't hit me in the same place. This time he got me in the leg. Then he gives me the other barrel right in the puss. I slide off the seat. But I guess the fat guy wasn't sure we were through. He let Morrie have it twice more and then he let me have it in the other side. The fat guy scrambled into the rear seat and grabbed Keane. He opens the door and kicks Morrie out into the road. We were doing about 50 from the sound. I figure I'm next so when he drags me over to the door I set myself to jump. He shoves and I light in the ditch by the road. I hit the ground on my shoulders and thought I would never stop rolling. I lost consciousness. When my senses came back, I was lying in a pool of water and ice had formed around me. The sky was red and it was breaking day. I staggered along the road until I saw a light in a farmhouse."

The O'Donnells turned out to be no match for the lethal force that Torrio had created with his syndicate of gangs. The next member of the gang to fall was another beer truck driver, Phil Corrigan, who was shotgunned to death behind the wheel. Walter O'Donnell and the gunman that the boys had imported from New York, Harry Hasmiller, were both shot to death during a running battle with a handful of Saltis-

McErlane shooters. On September 25, 1925, McErlane used a Tommy gun for the first time when he tried to blast Spike O'Donnell to pieces. He was driving past the corner of Sixty-Third and Western Avenue, where Spike was loitering, and let off a flurry of bullets. He kept firing but every shot went wild, shattering glass and chipping off pieces of plaster, brick and masonry. The Tommy gun was such an unfamiliar weapon to the police that they assumed all of the bullet holes in the storefront had been caused by multiple guns.

A month later, near the same intersection, McErlane went after Spike again. He machine-gunned his car and wounded his brother, Tommy, who was in the passenger seat beside him. After this attempt on his life (would-be assassins had

RIDDLED WITH BULLETS, SPIKE O'DONNELL'S CAR WAS LEFT ABANDONED ON THE SIDE OF THE ROAD. AFTER 10 ATTEMPTS ON HIS LIFE, SPIKE LEFT CHICAGO.

gone after him 10 times and wounded him twice), Spike decided to call it quits. He left Chicago and stayed away for two years. "Life to me is just one bullet after another," he told a reporter on his way out of the city, "I've been shot at and missed so often that I've a notion to hire out as a professional target."

McErlane and the other members of the syndicate had not only beaten the South Side O'Donnells but had managed to beat the law, as well. McErlane, who could account for at least five deaths among the O'Donnells, was charged with the murder of Morrie Keane and was held briefly under a kind of house arrest at the Hotel Sherman by order of State's Attorney Robert E. Crowe. Without warning, he was unconditionally released. Public pressure came to bear on Crowe and he was forced to seek a grand jury indictment against McErlane. Delay after delay, caused by months of legal manipulations, eventually saw the indictment dismissed. Crowe also obtained indictments against McErlane and Danny McFall for the slayings of Bucher and Meeghan, but they were also dismissed. A third indictment also named McFall as the killer of Jerry O'Connor but while he was out on bail, McFall vanished.

During several of the shooting and violent incidents with the O'Donnells, Capone was rumored to be on the scene with his gun in hand. None of the eyewitnesses would ever testify against him under oath. Even when the surviving members of the gang were brought face-to-face with him at police headquarters and asked if they could connect him to the killings, they refused to speak. Capone, of course, denied any involvement in the destruction of the South Side O'Donnells. "I'm only a second-hand furniture dealer," he reportedly told the police.

But that was a story that he wouldn't be able to stick with for much longer.

7. THE BATTLE FOR CICERO

The conquest of Cicero, the peaceful western suburb of Chicago, which was started by Torrio and completed by Capone, was begun out of necessity and was accomplished in Torrio's usual style – without shedding a single drop of blood.

Torrio and Capone first had to work things out with the West Side O'Donnells – Klondike, Myles and Bernard – who not only held firm ground in the area around Madison Street and Chicago Avenue but were entrenched in Cicero and connected to the town's political backroom dealer, Eddie Vogel. The town's president (a title that was the same as a mayor), Joseph Z. Klenha, took orders from Vogel, from the O'Donnells and from Eddie Tancl, a former prizefighter who had retired after killing a man in the ring and had opened a saloon in Cicero called the Hawthorne Park Café.

Cicero, while politically corrupt, was relatively crime-free in those days. It was a suburb of Chicago, with a population of about 60,000 people, mostly first- and second-generation Slavic immigrants. They were industrious, hard-working people who generally worked in the nearby factories or for Western Electric, the area's largest employer. They liked beer and didn't mind breaking the law to get it. There were few other vices in Cicero, though. There were no brothels and gambling was limited to slot machines, whose owners gave a cut of their profits to Vogel.

Torrio had a clever plan to "invade" Cicero. He started the first phase in October 1923 by moving several dozen prostitutes into a house that he had rented on Roosevelt Road. As he expected, the local police raided the place and locked up the girls. Torrio opened another brothel at Ogden and Fifty-Second with the same result. Without protest, he closed down both houses. He had no clout in Cicero, but he did have officials on his payroll in Cook County, like Sheriff Peter B. Hoffman. Two days after the Ogden Avenue raid, Hoffman – at Torrio's suggestion – sent a squad of deputies into Cicero to impound every slot machine they could find. Eddie Vogel got the point: if Torrio couldn't have whorehouses in Cicero, then no one was going to have slot machines, either.

The result of this exercise was a treaty between the parties concerned.

WESTERN ELECTRIC, CICERO'S LARGEST EMPLOYER

Vogel recovered the slot machines with assurances that the sheriff's department would not bother them again. The O'Donnells got an exclusive beer franchise in several sections of Cicero and Torrio reaffirmed their dominance of the West Loop. But what Torrio really wanted from the deal was not -- contrary to what Vogel believed -- free reign to run prostitutes in the city. He already made so much money from the brothels that he had that he didn't need to stretch them out into Cicero. He had bigger stakes in mind. When he agreed that he would not import any more prostitutes into the city, he was granted permission to sell beer anywhere in Cicero that was not part of the O'Donnells' territory. He could also run gambling houses there and establish a base of operations.

CICERO GANGSTER, EDDIE TANCL

The new treaty angered Eddie Tancl, who hated Torrio, and he refused to have any part in the negotiations. He now announced that he would buy his beer anywhere that he chose and his friendship with the O'Donnells, who had been supplying him, turned cool. When they tried to sell him some barrels of "needle beer" (low alcohol "near beer" to which raw alcohol had been added), he broke off contact with them altogether. Torrio and Klondike O'Donnell ordered him out of Cicero – and Tancl laughed in their faces. More trouble would be coming from Tancl in the near future.

The question that some might ask was this: if Torrio was making so much money with his operations in Chicago, why would he need to set up a new base in the suburb of Cicero? The move was not really made by choice. Reform was coming to Chicago and Torrio, always looking to the future, was haunted by what he saw coming. The abuses that took place during Big Bill Thompson's time in office were so flagrant that it seemed impossible that he would have a chance for re-election. Millions of dollars had vanished and scandals had erupted with political appointees and city hall insiders. Thompson's campaign manager, Fred Lundin, was indicted, along with 23 co-conspirators, for misappropriating over one million dollars in funds intended for the public schools. Lundin managed to stay out of jail but the public was enraged. Thompson, knowing when he was beat, withdrew his candidacy from the 1923 primary.

The mayor's office went to a Democrat, Judge William E. Dever, who chose Morgan Collins to be his chief of police. Dever had won the office on a reform platform, which sent a shiver of fear through Chicago's underworld. After winning the office, Dever told Collins, "There's a dry law on the nation's books. This town will immediately become dry. Tell your captains I will break every police official in whose districts I hear of a drop of liquor being sold." Collins tried hard to enforce Prohibition in Chicago. With his encouragement, the police went so far as to invade private homes and arrest people for the possession of even a single bottle of liquor, a crusade that, not surprisingly, turned the public against him. Chicago wanted its booze. As Capone would later famously say, "I'm just trying to give the people what they want."

While Torrio was planning for the worst, he still made every effort to try and make the new system work as smoothly as the old one had. Through an intermediary, he offered Chief Collins $100,000 a month not to interfere in the syndicate's activities. Collins responded to the attempted bribe by padlocking the Four Deuces. Torrio later offered him $1,000 a day to merely overlook the movement of 250 or so barrels of beer. Collins again refused and stepped up his attack on Torrio-Capone activities. He harassed the operators of Torrio's breweries, brothels and gambling parlors and his men arrested more than 100 of his gunmen and soldiers. By the end of the year, gambling had ceased to be a major source of income for the Chicago underworld. Collins and the new administration had done too much damage.

(LEFT) NEW CHICAGO MAYOR WILLIAM DEVER AND HIS CHIEF OF POLICE, MORGAN COLLINS. A RARE THING IN CHICAGO IN THE 1920S -- AN HONEST COP AND AN HONEST POLITICIAN. THEIR ATTEMPTS AT GENUINE REFORM DROVE TORRIO AND CAPONE INTO CICERO.

Torrio knew that his plan to make inroads into Cicero had been the right choice. As long as Dever occupied the mayor's office, they would need a safe haven that was beyond his reach. While most of their Chicago establishments continued to thrive – for no reformer could ever purge the corrupt elements from the ranks of the Chicago police department altogether – serious damage had been done. Torrio and Capone chose to maintain homes in Chicago and spent most of their leisure time there, but Cicero became their center of operations during Dever's time in office. The men who worked with them in Cicero had become the core of the syndicate operation and included Ralph and Frank Capone; the Capone cousins, the Fischettis; the Guziks; Louis and Joseph La Cave; Pete Penovich; Jimmy Mondi; Tony "Mops" Volpi; Peter Payette; Louis Consentino; Frankie Pope; and Frank "The Enforcer" Nitti. In addition, Dion O'Banion had become a close member of the operation, working in the gambling and brewery end of the business.

In the fall of 1923, Torrio decided to take a vacation and he departed for Europe with his wife and mother. He carried more than one million dollars in cash and negotiable securities with him overseas and he opened accounts in several foreign banks. He also purchased a seaside villa in Naples for his mother,

THE HAWTHORNE INN, THE TORRIO-CAPONE HEADQUARTERS IN CICERO.

staffed it with servants and filled a bank account for her that would allow her to live out the rest of her days in great comfort.

Capone was left behind to handle business matters and in his friend's absence, he chose the Hawthorne Inn at 4833 Twenty-Second Street as his Cicero headquarters. The brown-brick hotel stood two stories high and had white tiles set into the upper façade. The lobby was crowded with four green columns, which supported the ceiling, and stuffed big-game heads lined the walls. Capone had bulletproof, steel shutters added to every window and he placed armed gunmen at every entrance. He took over the hotel's second floor and he and his men often used the suites located there when they spent the night outside of the city. Liquor, women and plenty of cocaine (years later, in prison, Capone was found to have a hole in his septum from too much cocaine use) were almost always available on the premises.

Torrio returned from Europe just in time for the spring 1924 elections. This would turn out to be a critical time for the Torrio-Capone outfit. A Democrat reform ticket was threatening the Klenha faction that had run the town for three terms. Worried that similar problems like those occurring in Chicago under Mayor Dever might infect Cicero, Eddie Vogel came to Capone and Torrio with an attractive proposition – if they ensured a re-election victory of Mayor Klenha, they could count on immunity from the law for any enterprise that they undertook in Cicero, with the exception of prostitution. This was a challenge that called for violence over diplomacy, which made it a job for Capone and his brother Frank, a man who although quiet on the surface, had a taste for blood. Capone borrowed about 200 soldiers from their Chicago allies to make sure the election went their way. The opposition, despite their claims of reform, was not opposed to gangster support either and they manage to rally a group of small-time beer wholesalers to their cause. These men were eager to take over Torrio-Capone territory for themselves and pledged their own muscle to the election.

The first casualty in the Cicero election war was the Democratic candidate for town clerk, William K. Pflaum. On the night before the elections, March 31, Capone men broke into his office, wrecked the place and then beat him up. When the polls opened the following morning, black cars carrying heavily armed Capone gunmen cruised through town, spreading terror everywhere they went. They so far outnumbered the thugs hired by the opposition that there was never any real danger from them. Cicero residents known to favor Democrats were slugged and voters were blatantly intimidated. Those standing in line at the polls were approached and asked how they intended to vote. If the reply wasn't a satisfactory one, the menacing hoodlum would snatch the ballot out of the would-be voter's hand, mark it himself and then hand it back, glowering nearby until it was dropped into the ballot box. Defiant voters were beaten, honest poll watchers and election officials were kidnapped and held captive until the polls closed. A Democratic campaign worker named Michael Gavin was shot in both legs and then dumped in the basement of a Chicago hotel with eight other defiant Democrats. Thugs snatched an election clerk, Joseph Price, beat him up and then held him prisoner at Harry Madigan's Pony Inn until voting was finished for the day. A policeman was blackjacked. Two men were shot dead in the street near the Hawthorne Inn and two others were killed in Eddie Tancl's saloon.

Word of the violence in Cicero reached the ears of Cook County Judge Edmund K. Jarecki, who immediately went to Mayor Dever's office and demanded that the city of Chicago send its police force to restore order in Cicero. Dever pointed out that Cicero had its own police force and that Chicago officers had no jurisdiction there. However, he did point out that there was nothing to stop Judge Jarecki from deputizing citizens to keep the peace in Cicero and that Chicago policeman could certainly be part of the detail if he wanted them to be. Jarecki contacted the Chicago police chief who appointed a special squad of seventy officers to "protect the workers of Western Electric from gunfire in the streets of Cicero." Before departing, this hastily assembled riot squad met at Chicago's Lawndale police station, where they were issued shotguns. There were a few irregularities with this brigade of officers. All of the cops were in

plainclothes and they rode in black, unmarked sedans – the same kind of cars in which Capone's men were stalking the streets of the city.

In many accounts, the violence that led to the death of Frank Capone occurred as he and his brother Al, and his cousin, Charlie Fischetti, were intimidating voters on the street with drawn revolvers. This would have made Frank's death understandable, perhaps even justified, but another account of his death was reported by newspaper publisher Robert St. John – and it told a very different story.

Robert St. John had no love for the Capones. In the fall of 1923, as the Torrio-Capone syndicate began making inroads into Cicero, the idealistic, 21-year-old journalist decided that Cicero needed a newspaper that would stand up to the encroaching power of the gang. His weekly *Cicero Tribune* began publishing exposés of criminal activity and attacking the alliance between the mobsters and city hall. He had soon had a circulation of over 10,000 readers.

Capone responded to the new paper by targeting its supporters and advertisers who found taxmen and city inspectors on their doorsteps. Of course, all of those problems went away when the advertisers started giving their money to the mob-controlled *Cicero Life* instead. St. John hung on, though, continuing to defy the mob while his bribed and threatened reporters quit and his advertisers defected to the rival newspaper.

St. John continued to be a nuisance to Capone for the next two years, writing editorials about mob activities and stirring up public resentment of the gangsters. In 1925, he featured a story about a brothel that Capone had opened on the outskirts of Cicero and the local residents were incensed. One morning, an arsonist hired by the Cicero Citizen's Association burned the place down. Capone knew that the damage could be blamed on St. John and he had no choice but to make an example out of him. Murder was too risky since St. John had become such a public figure. Capone tried intimidation instead. A message was sent to the journalist that spelled out the fact that Al and Ralph Capone were very angry with him. Recklessly, St. John sent a letter back. He was angry too – "angry that the whole lot of them had not yet decided to get out of Cicero."

Two days later, as St. John was walking to work, a black car halted beside him and four men jumped out. He dropped to the ground and curled into a ball with his arms covering his head, but before he closed his eyes, he recognized Ralph Capone among them. Using the butt end of a gun, a blackjack and a bar of soap in the end of the woolen sock, Capone's men beat St. John until he was unconscious. Two policemen stood nearby, watching the assault. St. John was left bleeding on the sidewalk and the four assailants drove away.

On the same day, St. John's brother, Archer, who worked for a newspaper in Berwyn, was kidnapped, held in a remote hotel and then later released in a wooded area in Western Illinois. The police failed to investigate either crime. Robert St. John spent a week in the hospital recovering from the beating. When he was discharged, he tried to pay the bill but the hospital refused to accept his money. He was told that a well-dressed man had paid the entire amount in cash. "He didn't give his name," St. John was told, "Just said he was a friend of yours."

St. John refused to back down from his print attacks on the mob. He also went down to the police station and demanded that the police issue warrants of the arrest of Ralph Capone and the other men who beat him up. A friend in the police department gave him a warning. "Al likes you. He likes all newspapermen. But he likes Ralph better. So, take it easy, kid." St. John just shook his head and promised to be back at the police station the next morning to swear out the warrants.

When St. John went to the police station the next day, he found Al Capone arriving at the same time. He was shocked when he was left alone in an office with him. Capone smiled and put out his hand, telling St. John how glad that he was to meet him. He apologized for what had happened to him, swearing that he had given orders for the young newspaperman not to be touched. Unfortunately, the men had been drunk and forgot. "Sure, I got a racket," Capone told him. "Everybody does. Name me a guy that ain't got a racket. Most guys hurt people. I don't hurt nobody. Only them that get in my way. I give away a lot of dough. Maybe I don't support no college or build no libraries, but I give it to the people who need it, direct." Capone expressed again his dismay that St. John had been injured and offered to pay for his time, his lost work and his injuries. He had already paid his hospital bill, but he wanted to help some more. As Capone began peeling $100 bills of a roll in his pocket, St. John angrily left the room, slamming the door behind him.

Capone wasn't able to charm the newspaperman but he did shut him down. Soon after the meeting, he bought out the other investors in the *Tribune* and St. John became an employee of the gangster that he was trying to put out of business. With no other choice, he left the Chicago area and took a job with a small paper in Vermont. He later became a successful foreign correspondent and never returned to the streets of Cicero.

Robert St. John's dislike of the Capone organization made him an avid observer on election day in Cicero. From his vantage point across the street from the Western Electric Plant, on the border between Chicago and Cicero, he watched the police squad roll into town, driving in a single line of black sedans at about 50 miles per hour. Just then, he noticed a well-dressed man leave a building on the Cicero side of the street. At first, he thought the man was a store owner or businessman but then he realized that it was Frank Capone, who had been trying to negotiate a lease on the building out of which he had just walked. At the same time, the driver of the lead police car also recognized Frank.

The car suddenly screeched to a halt with the sedans behind it following suit, almost causing a chain collision. St. John later wrote that it was hard to imagine what was going through Frank's mind at that instant: "He heard the screaming of brakes, turned quickly, saw thirty or forty men in ordinary street clothes leaping from a long line of seven-passenger touring cars... he reached with his right hand for his right rear trouser pocket."

Before Frank could identify the men in front of him, or get off a shot, the police officers opened fire and he was struck repeatedly. The bullets forced him back several steps. Concealed behind their cars, and never identifying themselves as policemen, the squad opened up with shotguns and continued to fire into Frank's body until their guns were empty.

Robert St. John rushed to the scene. He later wrote, "When we rolled over his corpse, his hand was still on his revolver. For the first time, I understood the newspaper cliché

FRANK CAPONE -- ALWAYS NATTILY-DRESSED, EVEN ON HIS WAY TO JAIL.

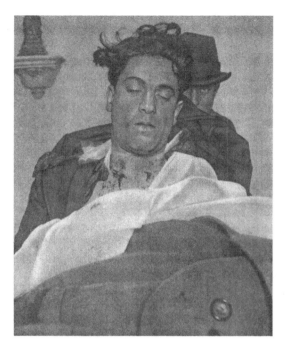

FRANK CAPONE AT THE MORGUE.

about a body 'riddled with bullets.' No one ever determined how many shots were fired, but a sizable percentage of the Chicago detectives, seeing a Capone reach for his gun, had acted in a manner generally described by coroner's juries with the expression 'homicide committed in self-defense.'"

This is what St. John wrote, but the scene that he described – and his own private feelings – said something else. The inquest that followed, along with many later accounts of the day, stated that Frank had lured the police into a gun battle and forced them to shoot him in self-defense. However, the number of bullets in Frank's body and the fact that his own gun was unfired, belied these claims. There was no way that Frank could have known that the men in the black sedans were police officers. They were in plainclothes, riding in unmarked cars, and never identified themselves. For all he knew, he was about to be ambushed by rival mobsters. Robert St. John always felt somewhat responsible for Frank's brutal death. It has been his newspaper, after all, that had run the countless exposés that led to the death of a man who, though far from blameless, did not deserve to be gunned down in the street.

When Al Capone heard the news of his brother's death, he turned white with fury. He and his brother Ralph went to the Cicero morgue to identify the body. He was stunned by the loss of his beloved brother and even Capone could not believe how reckless and dangerous the Chicago police had been. Frank's corpse was soon taken to the Cook County Morgue and was laid out on a slab to be photographed by Chicago reporters. Because of this, Frank became the first of the Capones to have his photograph appear in the Chicago newspapers.

Before he began mourning his brother, Capone demanded vengeance in Cicero. It was still early afternoon and the polls were still open. All across town, Capone cohorts continued to kidnap election officials and steal ballot boxes. When the votes were counted that night, the election – despite the reign of terror carried out by Capone – was surprisingly close. Klenha won by just over 1,000 votes and the rest of the Republican ticket won by similar margins. After the smoke cleared, it was realized that Capone had won the battle for Cicero – at the cost of his brother's life.

This was a higher price than even Al Capone wanted to pay.

Eddie Vogel kept his side of the bargain and on May 1, Torrio and Capone opened their first Cicero gambling parlor, the Hawthorne Smoke Shop, next door to the Hawthorne Inn. It was managed by Frankie Pope and was primarily a floating handbook that sometimes moved around to other locations. From time to time, it was raided by the police for appearance's sake but they always gave ample warning before they arrived so that everything incriminating could be moved to another location.

The unobstructed move into Cicero was a cause for celebration for the syndicate, but Capone was still mourning his brother. Frank's funeral had been a somber affair. Dion O'Banion had come through in fine form for the event, buying out his wholesalers and working around the clock to make the extravagant wreathes and arrangements that were purchased in Frank's memory. Tens of thousands of dollars were spent on the affair and the services eclipsed even the splendor of Big Jim Colosimo's spectacular sendoff. The coffin was satin-lined and silver-plated and the magnificence of the floral arrangements was unlike anything that had been seen in Chicago before. By noon on the day of the funeral, the Capone home had been filled with flowers and even more of them were heaped on the front porch and the lawn. Finally, lack of space made it necessary to hang wreathes and baskets on the trees and lamp posts along the street. In Cicero, as a sign of respect to the slain man, nearly all of the saloon owners closed their blinds and locked their doors for two hours. Frank was buried in the family plot in

EDDIE TANCL'S SALOON, THE HAWTHORNE HEIGHTS INN

Mount Olivet Cemetery. Al Capone attended the funeral unshaven, a gangland mourning custom.

A despondent Capone was cheered by the continued success in Cicero. The number of gambling establishments in town grew to 161 and all sold liquor and beer, operating 24 hours a day. Many of them were owned outright by Torrio and Capone and their gunmen were on hand to watch over things and protect the proprietors – and their money – from thieves. They took a cut of between 25 and 50 percent of the gross. The majority of these places, as well as Cicero's 123 saloons, bought their beer from the Torrio breweries.

The only continuing problem in Cicero was Eddie Tancl. He defied both Torrio and the O'Donnells, buying his beer wherever he wanted to. Early one Sunday morning, Myles O'Donnell and a friend, John Doherty, came into Tancl's saloon after an all-night bender and ordered breakfast. At a table across the room sat Tancl, his wife, head bartender, Leo Klimas, and his star entertainment, Mayme McClain. Only one waiter, Martin Simet, was working after a long, very busy night. After the two men finished eating, Simet brought them their bill--- which was just the excuse they had been looking for. O'Donnell began to loudly complain that Simet had overcharged them. He jumped out of his chair and grabbed the waiter by the front of his shirt.

Tancl came over to the table just as O'Donnell threw a punch at Simet. The former prizefighter stepped between the two men and O'Donnell shoved him out of the way. Tancl snapped. The dislike that had been brewing for months between the saloon owner and the O'Donnells caused both men to explode. They pulled their guns and fired at the same time, wounding each other in the chest. Doherty snatched his own gun and joined the fray, firing wildly. Simet and Klimas rushed at him and tried to take the weapon away. O'Donnell, who had fallen but was not out of the fight, fired and hit Klimas, sending him crashing into the bar. He was dead before he slumped to the floor.

O'Donnell and Tancl, both bleeding badly, continued firing at each other until their guns were empty. O'Donnell had been hit four times but managed to stumble out into the street, followed by Doherty. They ran in opposite directions. Tancl, although mortally wounded, grabbed another gun from behind the bar and went after O'Donnell, determined to finish him off. As he burst through the front doors of the bar, he fired madly at the fleeing figure, only stopping when the revolver clicked on an empty chamber. With a cry of rage, he hurled the gun after him. This effort sapped the last of his energy and he fell down into the street.

A short distance away, O'Donnell also fell. Tancl tried to crawl to the other man but he collapsed into the dust. He was dying and he knew it. When Simet came running outside, Tancl choked out his final words. "Get him," he said. "He got me." Following his boss' last orders, Simet kicked O'Donnell until the man stopped moving. He left him in the street for dead.

Jim Doherty, gravely wounded, dragged himself to the hospital. The police brought in O'Donnell and after several weeks, he managed to recover from his wounds. They were both prosecuted by Assistant State's Attorney William McSwiggin, but without success.

Stories of violence in Cicero made the rounds and tales of the kind of brutality that occurred in Eddie Tancl's saloon gave the city a sordid reputation. Mayor Klenha, worried about the bad image his town was receiving, claimed that Cicero's ugly reputation was greatly exaggerated. It was, he insisted, no worse than Chicago – who could tell when one left Chicago and entered Cicero? A Chicago reporter answered that question for him: "If you smell gunpowder, you're in Cicero."

Friday, May 8, 1924 was a cloudy, cool day in Chicago. It was just five weeks after Frank's funeral and at the corner of Twenty-Second and Wabash, near the Four Deuces, Capone's friend, Jake "Greasy Thumb" Guzik, encountered a small-time hoodlum named Joe Howard. At 28, Howard still lived with his mother above her small grocery store and worked part-time as a bank robber and hijacker. Without warning, Howard, who may have been drunk, lurched in Guzik's direction and asked him for a loan. Guzik turned him down and walked on. Suddenly, Howard chased after him, slapped him across the face and called him a "dirty little kike."

JAKE GUZIK, LATER IN LIFE. HE WAS THE MONEY MAN FOR CAPONE'S ORGANIZATION AND WAS ONE OF THE FEW MEN THAT CAPONE TRULY TRUSTED.

It was an insult that would get him killed.

Jake Guzik was the oldest of the Guzik brothers and a man that Capone often referred to as "the only friend I really trust." Their friendship dated back to the early days at the Four Deuces when Guzik, an old hand at running brothels, joined up with the Torrio outfit. More than a decade older than Capone, the pudgy, unassuming man resembled a businessman rather than a gangster. He once complained, "I don't know why they call me a hoodlum. I never carried a gun in my life." He rarely swore and he never used violence. He was an accountant who used his skills to the betterment of the brothel, then later, to the bootlegging business. He became the accounts manager and the number-three man in the Torrio-Capone syndicate and set things up to run as an actual business. When Mayor Dever's police closed down the Four Deuces, he set up a new headquarters two blocks away at 2146 South Michigan Avenue and hung out a shingle that read "A. Brown, M.D.". The place was arranged to look like a doctor's office but on shelves in the back were row after row of sample liquor bottles. Retailers who wanted to place large orders could sample the wares and even have them analyzed by a chemist. In this way, the syndicate gained a reputation for having quality merchandise.

The rest of the "doctor's office" was used to accommodate Guzik, his clerical staff, and the records of the outfit's transactions in six different areas. One group of ledgers listed hundreds of wealthy individuals, hotels and restaurants that bought wholesale quantities of liquor. A second set of ledgers listed all of the speakeasies in Chicago that were being supplied. A third detailed the channels through which smuggled liquor came into the country from Canada and the Caribbean. The fourth outlined the corporate structure of the breweries the outfit owned or controlled. The fifth contained the assets and incomes of the brothels, and the sixth named police and Prohibition agents who were regularly receiving payoffs.

THE BUILDING AT 2146 SOUTH MICHIGAN AVENUE, WHERE GUZIK'S "DOCTOR'S OFFICE" WAS LOCATED AND WHERE HE KEPT ALL OF THE BOOKS FOR THE MOB.

The syndicate faced near catastrophe in the spring of 1924 when a police raid on the office, ordered by Mayor Dever, allowed the incriminating ledgers to fall into the hands of the police. The raid had been led by Detective Sergeant Edward Birmingham and Guzik offered him $5,000 to give back the ledgers and keep silent about them. The detective reported the offer to his superiors and Dever was sure that he finally had the evidence to shut down Capone and Torrio's operation. His celebration turned out to be short-lived. Before either the state's attorney or any federal agency could get a look at the incriminating ledgers, a municipal judge, Howard Hayes, returned them to Torrio, stating that they were outside the scope of the police search warrant. The ledgers vanished soon after.

After Guzik's confrontation with Joe Howard, the accountant immediately went to Capone and told him about the insult. The unprovoked attack on his friend gave Capone an excuse to track down Howard. The small-time punk had previously been overheard saying how easy it was to hijack beer trucks, including Torrio's, and Capone decided to teach him a lesson. He found Howard at Heinie Jacob's saloon on South Wabash, chatting with the owner. Two regular customers, a garage mechanic named George Bilton and a carpenter named David Runselbeck, were at the bar drinking beer. As Capone came through the door, Howard turned to him with an outstretched hand and greeted him by name. Capone ignored the hand and with a menacing snarl, grabbed the man by the shoulders and demanded to know why he had struck Guzik. Howard shook off his hands and spat at him.

"Go back to your girls, you dago pimp," he snapped.

Capone pulled out a gun and emptied it into Howard's face.

The police were summoned and after questioning the men present, whose accounts of the slaying more or less agreed, Chief of Detectives Michael Hughes told reporters, "I'm certain it was Capone" and issued a general order for his arrest. The next day, readers of the *Chicago Tribune* saw the first photograph of a face that would become as familiar to them as that of President Calvin Coolidge or any Hollywood star. The newspaper, however, still didn't get his name right – "Tony (Scarface) Capone, also known as Al Brown, who killed Joe Howard..." the caption read.

During the hours between the murder and the inquest, two of the witnesses developed cases of "Chicago Amnesia," that pesky condition that seemed to affect so many witnesses to mob-related crimes. Heine Jacobs testified that he never actually saw the shooting, having gone into the back room to take a telephone call just before it occurred, and Runselbeck claimed that he would not be able to identify the

CHIEF OF DETECTIVES MICHAEL HUGHES

killer. George Bilton had disappeared without a trace.

Jacobs and Runselbeck were held as accessories after the fact, in hopes the charge would get them to talk, and the inquest was postponed for two weeks. Capone had gone underground after the murder and was still missing so the inquest was adjourned again. Then, on June 11, he strolled into a police station and said that he had heard he was wanted and wondered why. He was taken to the Criminal Courts Building, where he was filled in on the charges against him by William H. McSwiggin, an eager young state's attorney who, thanks to his record, was often referred to as the "Hanging Prosecutor." He questioned Capone for hours and got nothing. Capone maintained that he knew nothing about the murder of Joe Howard and that he knew no one named Torrio or Guzik. He was, he insisted, a reputable businessman who dealt in antiques.

The third and final session of the inquest took place on July 22. Jacobs and Runselbeck, terrified and visibly shaking, could add nothing to their earlier testimony. The verdict in the case stated that Joe Howard was killed by "one or more unknown, white male persons."

As they promised before the election, Torrio and Capone brought no more prostitutes to Cicero. Instead, they opened brothels in nearby communities like Stickney, Berwyn and Oak Park. Soon, the syndicate had 22 bordellos operating in the Chicago suburbs, bringing in an annual gross of more than ten million dollars.

The mob so thoroughly infiltrated one village on the edge of Cicero called Forest View that it sarcastically became known as "Caponeville." Forest View was originally a farm community with a population of fewer than 300 people. It wasn't even incorporated until an attorney named Joseph W. Nosek spent several pleasant days there conferring with a client about an impending case. As a war veteran and an official in the American Legion, he told several of his friends and fellow legionnaires about the place, and they decided to support Nosek in his plan to officially start a town. Papers of incorporation were issued in 1924. At the first village meeting, Nosek was elected police magistrate and his brother, John, was voted president of the village board. For the chief of police, they chose William "Porky" Dillon, who claimed to be a former serviceman. The enthusiastic villagers even managed to get free materials from Cook County to pave the streets.

Soon after the meeting, Chief Dillon informed Nosek that Al and Ralph Capone wanted to build a hotel and social club in Forest View. Nosek saw no harm in it. He believed that it would improve the village – but he had no idea who the Capones were.

Once the "hotel" was built, Nosek was appalled by the thugs and prostitutes that had moved into his village. He ordered Dillon to get rid of them. The following day, Nosek ran into Ralph Capone, who told him that if he ever spoke another word against him or his brother, they would throw him into the village drainage canal. Nosek, thinking that Ralph was joking, replied: "If I go into the canal, you'll go with me."

In the early morning hours, two armed gunmen broke into Nosek's house and dragged him to the village hall. Seven other men were waiting there. They told Nosek that they intended to kill him. He was kicked and beaten over the head with gun butts until he was a crumpled, bloody mass on the floor. He begged for his life and he was only spared because he agreed to leave Forest View. He later recalled, "I

THE SMALL FARMING COMMUNITY OF FOREST VIEW, ILLINOIS WAS INVADED BY THE CAPONE GANG AND NEWSPAPER REPORTERS STARTING CALLING THE PLACE "CAPONEVILLE". AT LEFT IS A BUILDING BELIEVED TO BE THE MAPLE INN (BETTER KNOWN AS THE STOCKADE) AND RIGHT IS A CAPONE BREWERY. THE STOCKADE WAS LATER BURNED TO THE GROUND BY ARSONIST REFORMERS.

moved. Others were forced to move... Eighteen or twenty of the respectable men in our village were slugged and beaten and driven away."

At the next election, all of the winning candidates for president of the village board, trustees and police magistrate were Capone's men. Porky Dillon continued on as chief of police. In truth, he was no military veteran but an ex-convict who had been pardoned by Governor Small.

Torrio and Capone then proceeded to build their largest brothel yet, the Maple Inn, which was better known as the Stockade. It offered sixty girls in its stable, but it was much more than just a whorehouse. It also served as a hideout, a suburban headquarters and an ammunition dump. The wood frame and stone structure was hidden along a country back road. It contained a maze of secret passages and chambers installed behind walls, under floors and above the ceilings. The largest chamber was used as a hiding place for the girls in case a raid ever took place. Fugitive gangsters could hide out in a room secreted under the eaves and lined with corkboard so that it was soundproof. Anyone hiding there could communicate through a secret speaking tube and receive food and water by dumbwaiter. Other passages in the house allowed a view of customers in the bar or at the gambling tables through eyes that were cut out of wall paintings. There were even hidden safes with sliding panels that concealed guns, ammo and explosives.

Capone's men overran the town, much to the dismay of the former inhabitants. Nosek complained, "All of the beautiful ideals that my associates in the Legion and I had have been swept away. The streets that we built with so much arduous effort but with happiness and hope are now little more than thoroughfares for the automobiles of gunmen, booze runners and disorderly women."

Just like the streets of Chicago....

8. DEATH IN A FLOWER SHOP

"Oh, to hell with them Sicilians!"

It was an offhand remark that was repeated with smirks among the members of Dion O'Banion's North Side gang, but overheard by others, it became a deadly insult. It was a quip that would eventually mark a man for death.

For three years, O'Banion had remained in the good graces of John Torrio and Al Capone. In fact, after the death of Frank Capone in April 1924, he had even prospered because of that uneasy friendship. Capone had not forgotten the extravagance with which O'Banion had prepared the arrangements for his brother's funeral and he maintained a grudging fondness for the North Side gangster that likely kept the man alive longer than he deserved to be. O'Banion's business flourished, not just the flower shop, but bootlegging, which was netting him almost a million dollars a year. He supplemented his income with daring hijackings that netted him high-quality whiskey, pulled off trucks by members of his eccentric gang. On one occasion, he raided a warehouse that contained almost 2,000 barrels of liquor and replaced the booze with water as a joke. In spite of all this, he wasn't happy. Officially, he was allied with Torrio and Capone, which offered him protection from rival bootleggers and the numerous freelancers that lurked about Chicago, but even though he had contributed men to act as muscle during the Cicero election, he felt slighted, used and unappreciated.

To improve O'Banion's mood, Torrio offered him a small piece of the action in Cicero, a beer territory that added up to less than $20,000 a month – walking-around money by the standards of the Torrio organization, but it was still something. O'Banion took it and ran with it. He owed his talent for making money to the fact that he was a little bit crazy and he proved this once again by encouraging speakeasies to move to Cicero. Torrio and Capone were impressed and more than a little resentful. Capone complained about giving O'Banion the territory to begin with and urged Torrio to take it back. But ever the peacemaker, Torrio proposed that O'Banion kick back a percentage of his new business in exchange for a percentage of the outfit's income from prostitution. The deal was typically Torrio, linking possible adversaries in a mutually beneficial enterprise. But O'Banion, like many Irish-Catholic racketeers, hated prostitution. It was a filthy business they believed better left to the Italians and the Jews. During his time as leader of the North Side, not a single bordello could be found in Chicago's Gold Coast neighborhood. He refused Torrio's deal.

O'Banion tolerated Torrio and Capone but he outright despised their closest allies, the "Terrible Gennas." The Gennas sold their homemade poison for just $3 a barrel, which was half the price of O'Banion's high-class whiskey. Each of their stills produced as much as 350 gallons of the wretched high-proof stuff each week with ingredients that cost less than $1 a gallon. When the Gennas began selling their whiskey in O'Banion's territory on the North Side, he implored Torrio to send the Sicilians back to their own neighborhood on the West Side. Torrio stalled for time. He knew how dangerous the Gennas were – heavily armed, entrenched in Sicilian blood oaths and connected to the police – and he didn't want to get involved in the dispute. So, O'Banion dared to do what no sane bootlegger would do and hijacked a truck that carried $30,000 of the Gennas' liquor. The Sicilians were infuriated but with Torrio acting as a peacekeeper, the animosity between O'Banion and the Gennas stopped short of bloodshed.

Even though the situation was close to boiling over, O'Banion made matters even worse by developing his own private relationship with the police. Capone complained, "He was spoiling it for everybody. Where we had been playing a copper a couple of hundred dollars, he's slip them a thousand. He spoiled them." In return for his money, O'Banion received information that he planned to use against his bootlegging partners in a complicated scheme that proved just how clever – and reckless – he could be.

O'BANION'S TALENT FOR MAKING MONEY CAME FROM THE FACT THAT HE WAS A LITTLE BIT CRAZY AND USED IT TO HIS ADVANTAGE.

Six weeks after the funeral of Frank Capone, and days after the murder of Joe Howard, O'Banion paid a visit to the Hawthorne Inn in Cicero. He met with Torrio and Capone and stunned them with the news that he planned to retire from bootlegging. He was tired of dealing with the Gennas, he explained, and wanted to leave the dangerous life in Chicago and settle down in Colorado. Although they tried not to show it, Torrio and Capone were thrilled by the news and were even happier when O'Banion named his price. The three men jointly owned the Sieben Brewery and O'Banion offered to sell his share for half a million dollars. He even volunteered to transport the last shipment of beer as partners; it was scheduled to go out on May 19, 1924. Torrio and Capone immediately agreed to his terms and saw to it that O'Banion received his payment in full.

Unknown to Torrio and Capone, O'Banion's offer to sell his share of the Sieben Brewery was nothing more than an elaborate ruse. Prior to the meeting, he had learned through his police contacts that the brewery was going to be raided by the police on the night of May 19. Normally, a brewery raid was of little concern in Chicago. It usually just meant that a precinct captain had not been paid off, or wanted more money, and it was easy to avoid if the right amount of cash ended up in the right pocket. But this raid was different. This time, federal authorities under orders from the U.S. Attorney were running the operation with Mayor Dever's full approval. Since Torrio already had a prior federal conviction for violating Prohibition laws in 1923, a second conviction would lead to a large fine and a mandatory jail sentence.

On the night of May 19, the raid on the brewery occurred just as O'Banion knew it would. Torrio and O'Banion were supervising the loading of the trucks that would take the beer to speakeasies all over Chicago when the police broke in and arrested everyone in the place. Torrio was detained, as was O'Banion, so that he could maintain the ruse that he knew nothing about the raid. Only Capone managed to avoid arrest since he was not present at the brewery that night. Once Torrio was delivered to the federal authorities, he realized that O'Banion had betrayed and humiliated him. Seething, he refused to post bond for O'Banion, as he routinely did for his other partners and employees. Torrio himself was soon free on bail, but he was later convicted of owning a brewery and was sentenced to nine months in jail and a $5,000 fine – all thanks to Dion O'Banion.

After the raid and Torrio's arrest, O'Banion's days were numbered. Strangely, he seemed completely oblivious to the fact. He worked each day at his flower shop, cheerfully greeting his customers and spent

SIEBEN'S BREWERY WAS ONLY SUPPOSED TO BE A TOKEN TO APPEASE O'BANION BUT WHEN HE STARTED MAKING MONEY WITH IT, TORRIO WANTED IT BACK. O'BANION GAVE IT TO HIM -- ON THE SAME DAY HE KNEW IT WAS GOING TO BE RAIDED BY THE COPS.

his evenings at home or having dinner with his friends. Months passed and O'Banion had no idea that several of his old bootlegging partners were plotting his demise. Only Torrio hesitated to have him killed. He knew that O'Banion's death would spark all-out war in Chicago. However, after the brewery raid, even the cautious Torrio was leaning toward O'Banion's murder.

On November 3, O'Banion and Hymie Weiss arrived at The Ship, a Capone-run gambling joint in Cicero, to divide up profits with his partners. Business proceeded as usual until Capone mentioned that Angelo Genna had racked up $30,000 in gambling debts that had never been paid. In the interest of preserving the peace, Capone suggested that they forgive the debt. O'Banion adamantly refused. He went straight to a telephone, called Genna, and demanded that he pay the debt within a week's time. Capone and Torrio were shocked at O'Banion's rash behavior. Capone and Torrio were doing all they could to keep the murderous Gennas happy, but they could not control the reckless O'Banion – and were not sure they really wanted to. As they left the gambling den that day, Weiss cautioned O'Banion to stop antagonizing the Gennas and Torrio. But O'Banion, in a typically rebellious mood, waved away his friend's words. "Oh, to hell with them Sicilians," he said.

THE SHIP, CAPONE'S GAMBLING JOINT IN CICERO, WHERE O'BANION MADE HIS SLUR AGAINST THE GENNAS -- AND MARKED HIMSELF FOR DEATH.

This bold statement soon became a refrain among O'Banion's men and among many other Chicago bootleggers, most of whom felt the same way but had never been brave enough to say it out loud – to hell with the Sicilians. To the Gennas and other Italian mobsters, though, such words were the worst kind of insult and together with Torrio and Capone, the Gennas put the final touches on their plan to assassinate O'Banion. The murder would be carried out the old-fashioned way, which meant O'Banion would be killed face-to-face, at his place of business, in the middle of the day, and everyone in Chicago would know who was responsible and why it had been done.

To carry out such a public assassination, the Torrio-Capone organization required the blessing of Mike Merlo, the president of the powerful Unione Siciliane. Merlo was opposed to the idea of eliminating O'Banion, however. The murder was bad for business, he told them, and as long as he was in office, O'Banion would not be killed. Torrio took the news calmly for he knew that Merlo was suffering from end stage cancer and would not be around to protect O'Banion for long. He would be patient, knowing the time for action would come. He didn't have long to wait – Merlo died on November 8.

Initially, Merlo's death was a windfall for O'Banion, who promptly sold over $100,000 in flower arrangements to the mourners, including a spectacular floral effigy of the deceased that stood twelve feet high. Capone himself purchased $8,000 worth of flowers. O'Banion also received unusual order, so small that he almost overlooked it. Jim Genna, one of his sworn enemies, visited the store and ordered a

MIKE MERLO, PRESIDENT OF THE UNIONE SICILIANE. HIS DEATH MADE O'BANION'S MURDER EVEN EASIER TO CARRY OUT.

wreath for Merlo's funeral. He gave O'Banion $750 to pay for the arrangement and told him that some boys would be by to pick it up on Monday morning. He left the shop quietly, barely speaking, but he was there long enough to put together a mental blueprint of the place – just in case he had need to visit it again.

The selection of Mike Merlo's successor as president of the Unione Siciliane brought Frankie Yale back to Chicago. As the head of the powerful New York branch of the organization, Yale had considerable influence over who took over the corresponding post in Chicago. He conferred with Torrio and Capone and the three men decided to appoint Angelo Genna to the position. As the new president of the Unione Siciliane – and a man who had been recently humiliated over a gambling debt by O'Banion and wanted to see him dead – he had no objection to the immediate elimination of the North Side bootlegger. This finally put into motion the most highly publicized and significant gangland slaying in Prohibition-era Chicago – the murder that would make Chicago a city at war.

On Monday, November 10, 1924, two days after the death of Mike Merlo, O'Banion left his apartment and went straight to Schofield's flower shop on North State Street. There was still much to do in preparation for Merlo's funeral and he spent most of the morning working on large orders for the event. He worked alongside three of his employees, surrounded by plants and flowers of every description. Late in the morning, the telephone rang and the caller asked if O'Banion had the Genna wreath ready to be picked up. O'Banion replied that it could be picked up at noon.

At five minutes past the hour, a blue Jewett sedan parked in front of the flower shop. The driver remained at the wheel, the motor idling, and the passenger door standing open. Gregory Summers, an 11-year old junior traffic officer who was guiding some children across the street near Holy Name Cathedral, saw three men get out of the car. "Two of them were dark and looked like foreigners. The other man had a light complexion," he later said. The three men passed him and entered the flower shop.

O'Banion was in the back, working on a flower arrangement, but the porter, an African-American man named William Crutchfield, was sweeping up flower petals and looked up to see the men enter the shop. He assumed they were racketeers, like many of the men that O'Banion did business with. He didn't recognize the men, but it was obvious that his boss did, which is likely why O'Banion never drew any of the three guns that he habitually kept hidden on his body. O'Banion, who was dressed in a long white smock and holding a pair of florist's shears in his left hand, came out from behind the counter and extended his right hand in greeting. He said to them, "Hello, boys. You want Merlo's flowers?"

The three men walked abreast and approached O'Banion with smiles on their faces. The man in the center – either Frankie Yale or Mike Genna, depending on which version of the events you believe –

INSIDE OF SCHOFIELD'S FLOWER SHOP AT THE SITE WHERE O'BANION WAS SHOT TO DEATH.

(RIGHT) A CROWD GATHERED ON STATE STREET OUTSIDE OF THE FLOWER SHOP WHEN WORD SPREAD THAT O'BANION HAD BEEN ASSASSINATED INSIDE.

reached out his own hand. The two men beside him were almost definitely John Scalise and Albert Anselmi. They were shorter and stockier, with dark complexions, and would kill anyone on the orders of whoever their boss happened to be at the time.

Crutchfield heard the man in the middle reply, "Yes, for Merlo's flowers." He then stepped closer to O'Banion, grabbed his hand in greeting and pulled him close. The two men at his sides moved around him and drew pistols. Then, at close range, the center man rammed his own pistol into O'Banion's stomach and, holding his arm in a vice-like grip, opened fire. The other two men also fired their weapons, the bullets ripping into O'Banion. Two slugs struck him in the right side of the chest, two hit him in the throat and one passed through each side of his face. The shots were fired at such close range that powder burns were found around each wound. From that point on, this up close and personal method of murder became known as the "Chicago Handshake."

The leader of the North Side gang fell, having died on his feet, into a display of geraniums. O'Banion's pistols were unfired, not even drawn. The three men fled from the store, jumped into the blue sedan and, as young traffic patrol Gregory Summers watched in amazement, sped away.

With the death of O'Banion, the Torrio-Capone syndicate had eliminated the most unpredictable and dangerous bootlegger in the city. They had also ingratiated themselves with the Gennas and set the wheels in motion to take over O'Banion's wealthy North Side territory. O'Banion's funeral, for the South Side outfit, was not an occasion for mourning, but a time for celebration. Torrio and Capone were glad to see him go and were happy to contribute to his send-off. But it wouldn't be easy. The Catholic Church, under the authority of Cardinal Mundelein, refused to permit a funeral mass for O'Banion to be held at Holy Name, the cathedral across the street from the flower shop and the place where the young O'Banion had served as an altar boy. Mundelein also forbade him to be buried in consecrated ground. But Torrio and Capone refused to let this dampen the festivities. They were intent on throwing O'Banion the most lavish gangster funeral that Chicago had ever seen.

For the next three days, O'Banion "lay in state" (in the words of the *Chicago Tribune*) at the funeral home of John Sbarbaro, a man with a curious double life. Not only did he own gangland's mortuary of choice, but he also worked as an assistant state's attorney. In fact, he worked with William McSwiggin, the young "hanging prosecutor" who had been so intent on indicting Capone for the murder of Joe Howard only six months earlier. Sbarbaro personified the Chicago connection between criminals and politicians, a phenomenon that so often thwarted the prosecution of even the most blatant crimes.

THE CROWD OUTSIDE OF THE SBARBARO FUNERAL HOME, WHERE DOZENS OF GANGSTERS WERE PREPARED FOR BURIAL.

Sbarbaro's funeral home was located at 708 North Wells Street, where O'Banion was placed in a $10,000 casket made from silver and bronze. He was surrounded by candles and, of course, flowers. A gold plaque above his head read "Dion O'Banion, 1892-1924." At the age of 32, he was probably five years past his prime by gangland standards and considering his reckless behavior, it was probably a miracle that he lived as long as he had. As musicians from the Chicago Symphony Orchestra played solemn music in the background, mourners filed past the coffin to pay their respects to the fallen mobster. "Why? Oh, why?" O'Banion's widow sobbed, clinging to the arm of her father-in-law. Louis Alterie and Hymie Weiss were reported to "cry as women might" and many other wise guys "had handkerchiefs to their eyes." The pallbearers included Weiss; George Moran; Vincent Drucci; Alterie; Frank Gusenberg, a gunman in O'Banion's employ, and Maxie Eisen, a labor racketeer and the president of the Kosher Meat Peddler's Association.

The funeral procession was so large that it became the subject of national fascination. It extended for a mile and included three bands and a police escort dispatched by Capone from the village of Stickney. Chief Collins had issued an order that prevented Chicago police from joining the parade or an embarrassingly large contingent of city police officers would have most assuredly been involved. More than two dozen cars were required to transport floral tributes from the funeral home to the cemetery, including a large basket of roses that bore the ironic message: "From Al."

For blocks in every direction, from the street, from the windows of office buildings, and from rooftops, thousands watched the cortege forming. It reached gigantic proportions – 10,000 people walked behind the hearse and when they reached Mount Carmel Cemetery, they joined another 10,000 mourners assembled at the gravesite. Mounted police had to clear a path through the mob so that the motorcade could advance. Every trolley car to the area near Mount Carmel was packed with curiosity-seekers.

A grave was dug for O'Banion in a section of unconsecrated ground. This area, reserved for lapsed or excommunicated Catholics, was as close to holy ground as could be found. At the grave, Father Patrick Malloy, who had known and liked O'Banion since he was a boy, delivered a short eulogy. Cardinal Mundelein had forbidden a funeral service, but Malloy defied him just enough to at least offer words of comfort and prayers. Five months later, Viola O'Banion managed to have her husband's remains disinterred and reburied in consecrated ground. Although this was brought to the attention of Cardinal Mundelein, he

VIOLA O'BANION, AFTER HER HUSBAND'S DEATH

did not have the body removed. A stone obelisk bearing O'Banion's name stands in the cemetery today, a short distance from some of his rival gangsters and a few feet from a mausoleum that contains the remains of a bishop and two archbishops. The irony of this turn of events led Police Captain John Stege to remark, "Strange, isn't it? A murderer and he's buried side by side with good men of the church."

Capone and Torrio were in attendance at the cemetery, although they knew that O'Banion's friends saw past the elaborate floral arrangements and empty words of grief and knew exactly who was responsible for his death. A reporter came up to Hymie Weiss and asked him who he thought was responsible for O'Banion's murder. Was it Al Capone? Weiss mockingly recoiled. "Blame Capone?" he asked, his voice dripping with sarcasm, "Why Al's a real pal. He was Dion's best friend, too." Passions ran so high that all mourners were ordered to check their weapons until the funeral was over. It was likely a good thing. Capone and Torrio spent a long, uncomfortable afternoon being glared at across O'Banion's grave by Weiss, Drucci and Moran.

Louis Alterie's rage was only kept in check until the day after the funeral. He threw down the gauntlet in a newspaper interview. "I have no idea who killed Deany," he told a reporter, "but I would die smiling if only I had the chance to meet the guys who did, any time, any place they mention and I would get at least two or three of them before they got me. If I knew who killed Deany, I'd shoot it out with the gang of killers before the sun rose in the morning and some of us, maybe all of us, would be lying on slabs in the undertaker's place." As he had during the funeral, Alterie proposed a shoot-out at the corner of State and Madison streets, but no gangster advertised his guilt by taking him up on the challenge.

Alterie's newspaper comments angered Mayor Dever. "Are we still abiding by the code of the Dark Ages?" he thundered in his own interview. "Or is this Chicago a unit of the American commonwealth? One day we have this O'Banion slain as a result of a perfectly executed plot of assassination. It is followed by this amazing demonstration. In the meanwhile, his followers and their rivals openly boast of what they will do in retaliation. They seek to fight it out in the street. There is no thought of the law or the people who support the law."

As for the law, it certainly didn't have any respect for Dion O'Banion. Relieved that another racketeer was out of the way, the police didn't try too hard to catch his killers. The half-hearted investigation went nowhere. As a matter of routine, they questioned John Torrio, Al Capone and the Gennas, all of whom claimed to revere O'Banion. They were deeply grieved by his death, they said, and pointed to the large and expensive floral arrangements they purchased as proof. Frankie Yale was also questioned but he claimed to be in town only to attend the funeral of Mike Merlo. He had nothing to do with the death of O'Banion, he said. After making a statement to the police, he returned by train to New York.

After the inquest, the Cook County Coroner made a note in the margin of the court record: "Slayers not apprehended. John Scalise, Albert Anselmi and Frank Yale suspected, but never brought to trial." Officially, the murder of Dion O'Banion was marked with one word – unsolved.

O'Banion's men had no doubts about who had carried out the assassination, though. They knew that Torrio, Capone and the Gennas were behind it and as Hymie Weiss assumed the leadership of the North Side gang, he swore out an oath of vengeance.

The streets of Chicago were about to run red with blood.

9. WAR IN THE WINDY CITY

The assassination of Dion O'Banion turned out to be John Torrio's last great achievement in Chicago. He left the city soon after the funeral and embarked, with his wife, Ann, on an extensive tour of vacation spots in the South and the Caribbean. They visited Hot Springs, Arkansas (a favorite gangland recreation spot of the era), New Orleans, Havana, the Bahamas, Palm Beach and St. Petersburg – never realizing that they were staying just one step ahead of gunmen that had been dispatched by Hymie Weiss to kill Torrio whenever they got the chance. To Weiss' regret, they never caught up with him, always arriving a day or two late, or perhaps missing them only by a few hours.

Torrio's hastily arranged pleasure trip caused him to miss what turned out to be the Chicago underworld's social event of the season: a Genna wedding. On January 10, 1925, Angela Genna married leading Chicago attorney Henry Spignola's sister, Lucille. An invitation to the wedding reception was published in newspapers, inviting the entire city to the Ashland Auditorium, and more than 3,000 people packed into the venue. It turned out to be a grand celebration, centered around a massive wedding cake that took six men to carry into the auditorium. The party went on all night with Al Capone in attendance. Rumor had it that assassins were following him everywhere he went. If this was true, they chose not to strike until two days later.

On January 12, Capone and two bodyguards were driven by his chauffeur, Sylvester Barton, to a restaurant at State and Fifty-Fifth streets. When they reached the restaurant, Capone got out of the car, leaving the two bodyguards behind. The door had just closed behind him when a long black car cruised slowly by. Inside were Hymie Weiss, Vincent Drucci and George Moran, all clutching shotguns and automatics. As they rolled up next to Capone's car, they opened fire, raking it from front to back with their weapons. A policeman later said, "They let it have everything but the kitchen stove." The bodyguards managed to come out of the hail of bullets unscathed but Sylvester Barton, the driver, was hit once in the back.

The close call prompted Capone to place a special order with General Motors – a $30,000 custom-built limousine that weighed over seven tons. It had a steel, armor-plated body, a steel-hooded gas tank, bulletproof windows, a gun compartment behind the rear seat and a removable back window that allowed occupants to open fire unimpeded on pursuing vehicles. Capone began using the car regularly, even when traveling short distances. He knew that he was an easy target walking down the sidewalk. When he had to cross a street – or even a hotel lobby – a cluster of bodyguards surrounded him, walking two and three deep on every side. In the nightclubs that he patronized, no strangers were allowed to sit at adjacent tables. At the opera, bodyguards took the seats on every side. In his office, as a precaution against an assassin who might somehow slip past his guards, he used a swivel chair with a high, armor-plated back.

He rarely kept an appointment at the agreed upon time and place, always sending a messenger ahead to make a last-minute change. Ironically, despite all these precautions, no life insurance company would sell him a policy, as he found out when he applied for one in 1925.

While Barton the chauffeur was recovering from his wound, Capone used Tommy Cuiringione, alias Rossi, as his driver. He proved to be a chauffeur and bodyguard of exceptional loyalty. Not long after he started driving the boss, some of Weiss' men kidnapped him and tried to force him to tell them where they might ambush Capone. One morning, a month later, two boys were walking a horse through some woods southwest of Chicago and stopped at a cistern to water the animal. The horse backed away and refused to drink. That afternoon, the boys mentioned the odd incident to a police officer they knew. He instructed the boys to take him to the cistern. He looked inside and hauled out what remained of Tommy Cuiringione. He had been beaten and burned with cigarettes and then shot five times in the head. His killers had tried to hide the body by wiring his wrists and ankles to a concrete block and dropping him in the cistern. Capone never forgot the fact that Tommy never talked.

Torrio and his wife returned to Chicago in the mid January. After being free for seven months on bail, Torrio and eleven co-defendants now had to stand trial in the Sieben Brewery case. He was almost happy to be inside a courtroom because he knew that it was a safe place to hide from Weiss' gunmen. Torrio was shaken by the latest attempt to kill Capone and he was looking for a place to find refuge. Where would be the safest? In federal prison, he realized. On January 23, Torrio appeared before Federal Judge Adam Cliffe and entered a guilty plea in his case. He would be safely behind bars and by the time he got out, Capone would have dealt with Hymie Weiss.

Before passing sentence, Cliffe offered Torrio five days during which time he could settle his affairs. He took his wife shopping on Michigan Avenue on January 24. His car was in the shop for repairs, so he borrowed a Lincoln sedan from Jake Guzik, along with his driver, Robert Barton, Sylvester's brother. It was almost dusk when the automobile, packed with shopping bags and parcels, turned onto Clyde Avenue on Chicago's South Side. It stopped in front of 7011, where the Torrios occupied a third-floor apartment. Neither Barton nor the Torrios noticed the black Cadillac with no license plates that was parked at the corner of Clyde and Seventieth streets.

TORRIO'S CAR WAS RIDDLED WITH BULLETS DURING THE ASSASSINATION ATTEMPT.

Barton opened the rear door of the sedan and helped the Torrios gather up their bags. Ann Torrio went ahead along the short sidewalk that led to the front door in the center of the apartment building. The Cadillac slowly moved forward. As she pushed the door open, backing inside since her hands were full, the Cadillac stopped across the street, directly alongside the sedan. Ann could see what appeared to be four men inside the car – and all of them were holding guns! She started to scream as Torrio stepped out of the car and onto the sidewalk. It was too late. She could only watch helplessly as two men, later determined to be George Moran and Hymie Weiss, jumped from the car with automatics drawn and ran toward her husband. The first man (Moran) fired two shots and Torrio fell to the ground, his jaw broken by one bullet and the other in his chest. As he twisted on the sidewalk, Weiss shot him in the right arm and the groin. At the same time, the two men who were still in the Cadillac, Vincent Drucci and Frank Gusenberg, opened fire with shotguns at the sedan, shattering windows and tearing open holes in the metal. A bullet hit Barton in the right leg below the knee.

Moran bent over Torrio and held his automatic to the fallen man's temple, planning to deliver the final shot, but the clip was empty. Before he could reload, Drucci began honking the horn of the Cadillac, signaling frantically that they needed to leave. Moran and Weiss ran to the car and they sped away.

Somehow, Torrio managed to crawl toward the apartment building and his wife, who was still screaming, dragged him inside. A neighbor, Mrs. James Putnam, witnessed the shooting and called the nearby Woodlawn police station. An ambulance arrived and Torrio was raced to Jackson Park Hospital.

Barton, ignoring his leg wound, got into the sedan and sped off toward Seventy-First Street. He passed a car driven by retired detective sergeant, Thomas Conley, who, spotting the sedan filled with bullet holes, gave chase. He confronted Barton in a drugstore as he was limping out of a telephone booth. The bleeding man refused to tell Conley what was going on. He pushed past him, got back into the car and drove off again. After traveling halfway across the city, he was finally forced to pull over by a patrol car, taken to a local station house, and then the hospital. The person that Barton had telephoned, the police believed, was Al Capone.

Newspaper reporters managed to get to Torrio at the hospital and began badgering the badly wounded, but still conscious, mobster with questions. He spoke with difficulty because of his shattered jaw but managed to say, "Sure, I know all four men, but I'll never tell their names." And he never did.

The police found a neighbor who was willing to talk, though. The 17-year-old son of the apartment building's janitor, Peter Veesaert, had been standing in the doorway of the building at the time of the attack. He was shown some photographs that were taken by the police during Dion O'Banion's funeral and he pointed out George Moran as the first man who shot Torrio. Bravely, he insisted that his identification was correct when he was brought face-to-face with Moran after he was arrested. "You're the man," Peter said. The police wanted to hold Moran until they could establish some evidence in support of the boy's identification but Judge William Lindsay released him under $5,000 bail. He was never indicted for the crime.

Capone made it to Jackson Park Hospital soon after the ambulance arrived. He was in tears when he learned that his friend's condition was critical. He not only refused to leave Torrio's bedside but he insisted that Torrio be given an inner room on the top floor. Two policemen stood on guard outside of Torrio's door but Capone also placed four of his own bodyguards in the corridor. It turned out that these precautions were necessary. During the night, hospital staff reported three carloads of armed men circling the building. The police were notified and eventually the cars drove off.

Despite the seriousness of his wounds, Torrio recovered quickly. In less than three weeks, he was discharged from the hospital. He left by way of a hidden fire escape, surrounded by bodyguards. That same day, February 9, with his jaw and face bandaged and hidden behind a scarf, he appeared again before Judge Cliffe. He was ordered to pay a $5,000 fine and sentenced to spend nine months at the Lake County

STILL RECOVERING FROM HIS WOUNDS, TORRIO SHOWED UP IN COURT WITH A SCARF COVERING HIS LOWER FACE AND NECK.

Jail in Waukegan, Illinois.

Aware of the danger that Torrio was in, the warden of the jail fitted the windows of Torrio's cell with bulletproof, mesh-steel blinds and assigned two deputy wardens to patrol the corridor outside. Other additions to the cell had nothing to do with Torrio's safety. The little chamber was cozily outfitted with throw rugs, an easy chair, framed pictures and a down mattress for the bunk. This was not unheard-of treatment for rich, well-connected prisoners – especially in Chicago.

The warden also allowed Torrio to hold business conferences at the jail and in March, a month after his incarceration; he met with Capone and his attorneys. The treaties between the gangs that Torrio had created and worked so hard to enforce were now wrecked beyond recovery. There was no hope of peace in the Chicago underworld and Torrio had no stomach for war. So, he announced to Capone and his lawyers that he planned to retire from Chicago and divest himself of all of his interests in the city. With no demands, payments or conditions, he turned everything over to Capone: the brothels, the breweries, the speakeasies and the gambling houses, which together produced annual revenue in the tens of millions of dollars.

Capone was literally the crowned the king of the Chicago underworld and he became the most powerful man in the city – at only 25 years old. But his new empire did not come cheap. With the syndicate crumbling, it was all in danger of coming apart. To secure it again, and continue producing wealth, Capone had to win back, overthrow or destroy every major gang in Chicago.

The near miss on John Torrio was the next battle in what became the longest, bloodiest gang war in Chicago history. It went beyond just Hymie Weiss' thirst for revenge – control of the entire Chicago underworld was at stake.

After Torrio's attempted murder, and Capone's takeover of the syndicate, the gangs began to realign themselves, mostly according to ethnic ties. The Irish, Polish and Jewish gangsters mostly rallied behind O'Banion's successor. The West Side O'Donnells, for example, and later the Saltis-McErlane gangs, once allies of Torrio, went over to Weiss. The Italians and the Sicilians, notably the Gennas, stayed with Capone, as did Druggan and Lake. Some of the lesser gangs, like Ralph Sheldon's boys and a few independent crews, shifted back and forth with the changing fortunes of the war.

Trying to follow the example set by Torrio, Capone forged a large, disciplined criminal organization. At the top, his number two man was Jake Guzik, acting as business manager. Frank Nitti had risen from gunman to treasurer and he also served as Capone's chief link with the Unione Siciliane and later with the national crime syndicate created in New York. Al's brother, Ralph, became the organization's director of liquor sales. He acquired the nickname "Bottles" during this time because of his persuasiveness with bar owners who were reluctant to stock Capone merchandise. All of the Capone brothers, except for Matt and the missing James, worked for the organization at one time or another but Ralph was the only one who achieved a position of importance.

Capone's captains included Charlie Fischetti and Lawrence "Dago" Mangano, who supervised the distribution of liquor, and Frank Pope, who managed the Hawthorne Smoke Shop, off-track horse betting and other gambling enterprises. Peter Penovich took care of the gambling houses and the floating card games and casinos. From the gambling houses that Capone did not own outright, he made sure that all of them kicked up a share of profits to the boss. Hymie "Loud Mouth" Levine oversaw Capone's collections and Mike de Pike Heitler, and Harry Guzik oversaw all of the whorehouses. Capone's *consigliere* (Italian for counselor) was Tony Lombardo, a cool-headed Sicilian seven years his senior who could always be counted on for worthwhile advice. Lombardo also owned a wholesale grocery company in Little Italy. Perhaps the most important "behind-the-scenes" man in Capone's outfit was Louis Cowan. Every member of the organization carried a card with his name on it and a phone number to call in case of arrest. The number was to a pay booth in a Cicero drugstore at Twenty-Fifth Street and Fifty-Second Avenue. When the telephone rang, the druggist would go to the door and beckon to Cowan, a small, frail man who owned the

CAPONE "FAMILY" MEMBERS: (LEFT TO RIGHT) FRANK NITTI; CHARLIE FISCHETTI; LAWRENCE "DAGO" MANGANO; HYMIE "LOUD MOUTH" LEVINE

(LEFT TO RIGHT) PHIL D' ANDREA; WILLIAM "THREE-FINGERED" WHITE; SAMUEL "GOLF BAG" HUNT; MURRAY "THE CAMEL" HUMPHREYS

newsstand outside. A green sedan was always parked on the street nearby. Cowan would hurry to the phone, listen intently, then get into the car and drive quickly to whatever police station he was needed at. Cowan was the organization's chief bondsman, a position that should have gotten him out of selling newspapers. However, he had worked that same newsstand since he was a boy and didn't have the heart to leave it behind. Working for Capone, it doubled as his office. Capone trusted Cowan to such a degree that he placed several apartment buildings that he owned in the man's name. Whenever Cowan went to bail out one of the men who had been arrested, he offered the apartment buildings up for security.

Capone also had scores of soldiers working for him in the lower ranks. They were sluggers, gunmen, killers and bombers who were used to break labor strikes or blow up competitors who didn't heed warnings or speakeasies that didn't want to do business. He also had a number of bodyguards. Phil D' Andrea, who became Capone's favorite bodyguard, was a crack shot who could split a quarter in mid-air. William "Three-Fingered" White was an equally good shot, but with his left hand, his right hand having been smashed by a brick when he was a boy. As sensitive about the damage to his hand as Capone was about his facial scars, White always wore gloves in public and stuffed cotton into the empty fingers. Another favorite Capone gunman was Samuel "Golf Bag" Hunt, who kept a shotgun concealed in a golf bag that he carried around with him. Once, when a cop opened the bag, he explained that he liked to shoot pheasants on the golf course.

JACK "MACHINE GUN" MCGURN

A number of Capone's young recruits eventually rose quite high in the organization. Antonio Accardo, known as "Joe Batters," and Felice De Lucia, better known as Paul "The Waiter" Ricca, both had long criminal histories before joining up with Capone. Ricca had murdered two men in his native Naples before fleeing to Chicago with counterfeit immigration papers. They were joined in the Capone outfit by Sam Giancana, who was rejected for military service because he had psychopathic tendencies, and by Murray "The Camel" Humphreys, who almost always sported a camel hair overcoat and made an early name for himself by pulling off a long series of robberies for which he was never arrested. All of them would have important roles in the Chicago outfit after Capone was eventually sent to prison.

But Capone valued none of these men more highly than he did his favorite gunman, "Machine Gun" Jack McGurn. James Vincenzo De Mora, or Jack McGurn as he later became known, was born in Chicago's Little Italy in 1904. He grew up as a clean-cut kid from the slums who excelled in school and was an excellent boxer. A promoter managed to get him into the ranks of professional fighters and at the man's suggestion James adopted the ring name of "Jack McGurn." It was his prowess in the ring, and his lightning-fast punches, that earned him the nickname of "Machine Gun," not his skill with a Tommy gun.

McGurn seemed to have a promising career ahead of him until his father, Angelo De Mora, a grocer with a store on Halsted Street, ran into trouble working for the Genna brothers. As a grocer, Angelo De Mora sold sugar to the Gennas for their liquor still operations, a relatively safe enterprise until some of his competitors shot Angelo to death in front of his store on January 8, 1923.

McGurn never got back into the ring. He was only 19 years old, but had a mother and siblings to take care of. He picked up a gun and started working for Al Capone, who regarded him as his most trustworthy enforcer. He was given the most dangerous and grisly assignments and within a few years, "Machine Gun" Jack McGurn was the most feared of Capone's killers. McGurn relished his work, especially when any of his targets worked for the Gennas. He learned that one of the Gennas had scornfully referred to his late father as small-time "nickel and dimer." So, after any of the Genna men were killed, McGurn pressed a nickel into each of their palms, his sign of contempt and a trademark that would be forever linked to his murders.

When not working for Capone, McGurn frequented Chicago's hottest jazz spots and managed to become part owner of several of them through intimidation and violence. By the time he was 23, McGurn owned pieces of at least five nightclubs and managed a number of other lucrative properties. His favorite nightspot was the famed Green Mill on Chicago's North Side. Capone gave him a 25 percent share in its ownership in exchange for his loyalty. This became his usual hangout and he could often be found sipping liquor in one of the green-plush upholstered booths.

The Green Mill opened in 1907 as Pop Morse's Roadhouse and from the very beginning, was a favorite hangout for show business people in Chicago. In those days, actors from the North Side's Essanay Studios made the roadhouse a second home. One of the most popular stars to frequent the place was "Bronco Bill" Anderson, the star of dozens of silent Westerns from Essanay. Anderson often rode his horse to Pop Morse's and the obliging proprietor even installed a hitching post that Anderson's horse shared with those of other cowboy stars like Wallace Beery and William S. Hart. Back then, even screen greats like Charlie Chaplin stopped in occasionally for a drink.

Around 1910, the Chamales Brothers purchased the club from the original owners. They installed a huge, green windmill on the roof and re-named the place the Green Mill Gardens. The choice of the name "Green Mill" was inspired by the infamous Moulin Rouge in Paris (Moulin Rouge is French for "Red Mill") but green was chosen so that it would not be confused with any of the red light districts in Chicago. The new owners added outdoor dancing and live entertainment in the enlarged sunken gardens and also added a rhumba room next door. Tom Chamales later went on to construct the Riviera Theater, located around the corner from the Green Mill. He and his brother leased the Green Mill to Henry Van Horne and it soon began to attract the best – and worst – of Chicago's the late-night denizens.

THE GREEN MILL IN THE 1920S. THE CLUB IS STILL OPERATING TODAY AND OFFERS ONE OF THE ONLY GANGSTER NIGHT SPOTS THAT STILL EXISTS IN THE CITY.

By the time that Prohibition arrived, the Green Mill had become known as the most jumping spot on the North Side. Jazz fans flocked to the club to savor this new and evolving musical art form, which had been born in the South but had been re-created in Chicago after World War I. The jazz crowd ignored the laws against alcohol and hid their bootleg whiskey in hip flasks, which they eagerly sipped at the Green Mill. The club helped to launch the careers of singers who went on to become legends, among them Helen Morgan, Anita O'Day, and Billie Holliday. It also offered an endless procession of swinging jazz combos and vaudevillians who dropped in to jam or just to relax between sets at other clubs.

In the middle 1920s, Van Horne gave up his interest in the place and the Chamales Brothers leased the club to Al Capone. Capone enjoyed hanging out at the club, listening to the music and drinking with friends. He had McGurn install a trap door behind the bar that offered access to tunnels under the building, just in case the place was raided by the police or attacked by rival gangsters.

McGurn was fiercely loyal to the Green Mill and in 1927, he became enraged when the club's star attraction, singer and comedian Joe E. Lewis, refused to renew his contract, stating that he was going to work for a rival club. Lewis opened to a packed house at the New Rendezvous the next night. Days later, McGurn took Lewis aside as he was about to enter his hotel, the New Commonwealth. McGurn had two friends with him and all three of them had their hands shoved in their pockets. McGurn told Lewis that they missed him at the club and that "the old Mill's a morgue without you." Lewis assured him that he would find another headliner and when McGurn told him that he had made his point and needed to come back, Lewis refused. He bravely turned his back on the killer and walked away.

On November 27, three of McGurn's men stormed into Lewis' hotel suite, beat him and then cut his throat almost from ear to ear. The comedian survived the attack, managed to recover his singing voice and continued with his career. Capone, unhappy with McGurn's actions, but unable to rebuke one of his best men, was said to have advanced Lewis $10,000 so that the performer could get back on his feet. Capone asked him, "Why the hell didn't you come to me when you had your trouble? I'd have straightened things out." Lewis probably asked himself the same question.

Although they kept their individual identities, several smaller gangs were absorbed into the Capone syndicate. The most important were the Guilfoyle Gang and the Circus Gang. Martin Guilfoyle, whose followers included Matt Kolb, a Republican politician, and Al Winge, an ex-police lieutenant, controlled liquor and gambling along West North Avenue. The Circus Gang, made up mostly of gunmen and labor racketeers, took its name from its headquarters, the Circus Café at 1857 West North Avenue. The gang's founder was John "Screwy" Moore, better known as Clyde Maddox. Located in the western part of the North Side, the two gangs served to balance that side of the city against Hymie Weiss.

Capone also co-opted some of the gunman from the smaller gangs, along with their techniques, often with bloody results. He had been following with interest the exploits of Frank McErlane and his Tommy gun. After his failure to take out Spike O'Donnell, McErlane had used the gun on other enemies with better results. Firing the weapon from a speeding car that was going past the Ragen Athletic Club, Ralph Sheldon's hangout, he had slaughtered Charles Kelly, who happened to be standing outside and seriously injured a Sheldon gang member inside. In an attempt to kill two beer runners from a rival gang, he had used the gun to rip apart a South Side saloon. He wounded the beer runners, but failed to kill anyone inside. Amazed by McErlane's weaponry (although probably not by his aim) Capone equipped his own arsenal with Tommy guns. Peter von Frantzius, a timid little man who owned Sports, Inc. at 608 Diversey Parkway, became Capone's chief weapons supplier.

Some of the organization's greatest power came from its associates who held political office, like Johnny Patton, the mayor of Burnham. As virtually a member of the gang, Patton kept the village open for vice. His chief of police tended bar at the Arrowhead Inn, in which Capone owned a controlling interest, and several town officials worked there, as well. During periods when Prohibition agents were keeping too close of a watch on Chicago breweries for them to produce anything other than near beer, the Arrowhead Inn became an important source for the real thing. Capone's trucks would haul barrels of legal beverage from Chicago to Burnham. They were followed by Capone's brother Mimi, driving a Ford couple and accompanied by armed guards who watched for hijackers. When they arrived, the barrels would be unloaded, a hole drilled in the top and a mixture of ginger ale and alcohol added to each one. This raised the alcohol content of the near beer and the spiked stuff could be sold for much more.

As Capone was building his empire, he still had problems to contend with, notably the previously mentioned newspaper publisher Robert St. John, but also Reverend Henry C. Hoover and his West Suburban Citizen's Association. Hoover had succeeded in making himself somewhat of a celebrity in Chicago; even those who disagreed with him didn't dare to criticize a man of the cloth. The newspapers liked him because he made good copy. He liked to be quoted and he made things simple: good versus evil. The papers began calling him the "Raiding Pastor" and the name stuck. He called a lot of attention to

COOK COUNTY SHERIFF PETER HOFFMAN

Capone's operations in Stickney and Cicero and generated negative publicity for outfit operations by being the first to proclaim Capone king of the Chicago rackets.

On May 16, 1925, having badgered a reluctant Sheriff Hoffman into taking action against the Hawthorne Smoke Shop, the minister accompanied a token force of sheriff's deputies on a raid of the gambling parlor. They were followed by some of the most militant members of the reverend's association. While they scattered throughout the building, armed with search warrants, Chester Bragg, a Berwyn real estate broker, stood guard at the door. Thousands of people gathered in the street to watch the show.

A few minutes after the start of the raid, Capone, who had spent the night at the Hawthorne Inn next door, elbowed his way through the crowd. It had been a late night and while almost noon, Capone was still unshaven and wearing silk pajamas and a robe. Bragg, who had no idea who Capone was, refused to let him in the door. "What do you think this is? A party?" Bragg demanded when Capone tried to shove his way inside.

"It ought to be my party!" Capone snapped and then, without thinking, added, "I own the place!"

Bragg stepped aside and mockingly bowed as he let Capone inside.

David Morgan, a machinist from Western Springs, went upstairs with Capone to the main room, where about 150 customers had been gambling. Under the direction of Reverend Hoover and a police lieutenant attached to the sheriff's staff, the raiders were dismantling roulette wheels and crap tables and preparing to load them into trucks waiting outside.

"This is the last raid you'll ever pull," Capone reportedly said to Hoover.

"Who is this man?" the indignant reverend asked.

Capone replied with his favorite alias. "I'm Al Brown, if that's good enough for you."

Hoover replied. "I thought it was someone like that, more powerful than the president of the United States."

Capone went into the back room, took the money and betting slips from the cash box and stuffed them into the pockets of his robe. He ordered his bookkeeper, Leslie Shumway, to remove the contents of the downstairs safe but it was too late – the raiders had already emptied it. One of the reverend's raiders was a magistrate and he filled out warrants charging Capone and eight of his employees with violations of anti-gambling laws. Capone returned to the Hawthorne Inn and came back a short time later shaved, powdered and elegantly dressed. He drew Hoover aside and asked him if they might come to an understanding – perhaps he could withdraw from Stickney if the minister would leave his Cicero operations alone.

Hoover dismissed him with disgust. "Mr. Capone, the only understanding that you and I can have is that you must obey the law or get out of the western suburbs."

Capone's men didn't allow the raiders to leave the scene without some reminders of their visit. Chester Bragg's nose was broken with a blackjack and David Morgan was knocked to the ground and kicked in the face. Between the raid and the trial that was held over the charges filed that day, they and their fellow vigilantes were often threatened. One night, four men waited for Morgan in his garage, shot him and left him for dead. He recovered, but spent a month in the hospital. After that, the Citizen's Association decided not to participate in any more raids. None of them testified at the trial and even though there was enough evidence to convict the defendants, Judge Dreher dismissed the case. Bragg wrote him a scathing letter of condemnation and the judge turned it over to friends in the Cicero town hall and suggested they muzzle troublemakers like Bragg.

The Hawthorne Smoke Shop stayed closed less than one day. About a half hour after the raiders departed, new gambling equipment and cash reserves arrived. By nightfall, it was operating at full strength once again.

10. THE END OF THE "TERRIBLE" GENNAS

ANGELO GENNA

Angelo Genna had long been considered the toughest and most brutal of the Genna brothers. It was Angelo who created the brothers' first "Black Hand" extortion schemes and essentially launched them into a life of crime. When he married Lucille Spignola, a member of one of the city's wealthiest and most prominent Italian families, the Gennas achieved society status in the city. Their wedding turned out to be one of the largest in Chicago history. After the wedding, the newlyweds moved into the fashionable Hotel Belmont, near the lake. They were hunting for houses, but couldn't have been happier in a neighborhood that was then occupied by leading Chicagoans like former Mayor Thompson, who lived directly across the street. Like his brother Tony, Angelo loved the opera and loved to play host to local and visiting performers, all of whom were delighted to accept his hospitality.

In May 1925, Angelo and Lucille found a home they liked in suburban Oak Park and began making plans to move in. On the morning of May 25, Angelo set out in his roadster coupe to pay for the new house in cash. He drove south from Belmont harbor on Sheridan Road and then turned southwest on Ogden Avenue, which at that time extended all of the way to Lincoln Park. As he approached Hudson Avenue, a large black touring car carrying four "characteristically 'unknown' assailants," as the *Chicago Tribune* described them, sped up next to Genna's car. The passengers fired a dozen shotgun bullets into Angelo Genna's car, causing him to lose control and crash into a lamppost. As his attackers gunned the engine and escaped, Angelo began to lose consciousness.

Genna was rushed the hospital. As he lay on his deathbed, Police Sergeant Roy Hessler pleaded with him to name the men who attacked him. "You're going to die, Angelo," he said, softly. "Tell us who bumped you off."

But Genna just shrugged his shoulders and closed his eyes. He died a short time later, never revealing the names of the men in the black touring car. The police suspected that Frank Gusenberg was the driver and the men with the guns in the back seat were Weiss, Moran and Drucci. But as the newspaper said – "You'll know who murdered Angelo when the next big guy in the neighborhood is murdered."

The next "big guys" to be killed, though, weren't gangster rivals – they were members of the Genna family.

Angelo's funeral, like his wedding, was one of the grandest in the city's history. Cardinal Mundelein refused to allow him a church funeral and so he was buried at Mount Carmel Cemetery in unconsecrated ground, steps away from the resting place of Dion O'Banion. Thousands of dollars were spent on

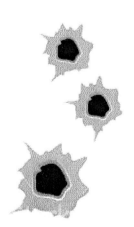

floral tributes and Al Capone sent an eight-foot-tall arrangement of lilies. Torrio, from his comfortable cell in Lake County, sent a huge vase of pink and white carnations. At the graveside, which saw thousands in attendance, a quartet of police officers from the Gennas' local Maxwell Street station frisked everyone for weapons.

MIKE GENNA

On June 13, less than three weeks later, Mike Genna joined his brother in death.

The occasion of his murder turned out to be a complicated double-cross that was played out on the city's South Side. The principals were four members of the Genna gang – Mike Genna, Samoots Amatuna, John Scalise and Albert Anselmi – and the same three men believed to have killed Angelo on May 25, Weiss, Moran and Drucci. A few days earlier, the North Side gang members had approached Amatuna and promised him a payoff if he would deliver Scalise and Anselmi (believed to have killed O'Banion) into their hands. They wanted them brought to the corner of Sangamon and Congress streets at 9:00 a.m. on June 13. Weiss, Moran and Drucci would then drive past and gun them down. Amatuna pretended to accept the offer, then told Scalise and Anselmi about it. Angry, they told Mike Genna, who put together a double-cross.

That morning, Moran and Drucci were waiting in their car at the corner (Weiss had other business), confident that two of their sworn enemies would soon be dead. Suddenly, a large black car raced past them and shotguns were fired from the windows. Glass shattered and pellets pounded into Moran and Drucci's car. Both men were wounded but managed to return fire. They roared off in pursuit of the black car but their own vehicle was too badly damaged to give much of a chase. They abandoned it on Congress Street and then collapsed on the sidewalk in pools of blood. Both men ended up in the hospital where they recuperated for weeks.

Meanwhile, the shooters in the other car were speeding south on Western Avenue. At Forty-Seventh Street, they passed by a northbound detective squad car that was driven by Harold Olson. His commander, Michael Conway, was in the car, along with detectives William Sweeney and Charles Walsh. Recognizing Mike Genna at the wheel of the other car, Conway ordered Olson to turn around and go after the speeding sedan. The detectives were in a foul mood. Three of their fellow officers had been murdered by gangsters the previous week and it's likely they were looking for a little payback. The Gennas hadn't been involved in the police officer's murders but at that point any gangsters would do.

ALONG SOUTH WESTERN AVENUE IN THE 1920S

With its siren clanging, the squad car spun around and chased after Gennas' car, reaching speeds of up to 70 miles an hour. At Fifty-Ninth Street, a truck pulled out into the avenue, forcing Genna to slam on the brakes and swerve, crashing into a telephone pole. Unhurt, the mobsters jumped out of the car with shotguns in hand. The squad car screeched to a halt a few feet away and the detectives scrambled out, their revolvers drawn.

"Why didn't you stop?" Conway demanded. "Didn't you hear our gong?"

In reply, the gangsters raised their weapons and fired. Conway went down with a

DETECTIVE SHOEMAKER AND THE "CURSE OF THE GREEN CHAIR"

The years of Prohibition were a boom time for the Chicago underworld and created not only fortunes from ill-gotten gains, but a number of curious legends, as well. One of the strangest tales – which became known to underworld figures all over the city – was the "Green Chair Curse," also referred to sinisterly as the "Undertaker's Friend." The curse was named after a green leather chair found in the office of William "Shoes" Shoemaker, who became Chicago's Chief of Detectives in 1924. Several of the city's top gangsters were hauled into Shoemaker's office for questioning and ordered to sit in the green chair. Strangely, many of them died violent deaths a short time later. This could hardly be that surprising, given the death rate during the gang wars in Chicago, but the newspapers quickly seized on the story and a belief in the "curse" of the chair began to grow. Shoemaker, probably delighted with the attention, stated that he was now keeping track of the criminals who sat in the chair and later died violently. When the inevitable later occurred, he would put an "X" next to the gangster's name. These men included the Genna brothers (Angelo, Tony and Mike), Porky Lavenuto, Mop Head Russo, Samoots Amatuna, Tony Lombardo, Antonio "the Cavalier" Spano – and John Scalise and Albert Anselmi. Legend had it other well-known gangsters, including Al Capone, absolutely refused to sit in the chair.

When Shoemaker retired in 1934, there were 35 names in his notebook and 34 of them were marked with an X. Only one criminal, Red Holden, was still among the living and he was doing time in Alcatraz for train robbery. "My prediction still stands," Shoemaker told reporters upon his retirement. "He'll die a violent death. Maybe it'll happen in prison. Maybe he'll have to wait until he gets out. But, mark my words, it'll happen."

But Holden managed to outlive Shoemaker. The detective died four years later and the green chair was passed on to Captain John Warren, who had been Shoemaker's aide. He continued to seat an occasional hoodlum in it, perhaps hoping to "scare them straight" with the eerie legend. By the time that Warren died in September 1953, the chair's death rate stood at 56 out of 57 men. Only Red Holden was still alive.

Holden was released from Alcatraz in 1948 and afterwards was involved in several shoot-outs, all of which he survived. Then, he was convicted on murder charges and was sent to prison for a 25-year sentence. He died in the infirmary of Illinois' Statesville Prison on December 18, 1953. According to the newspapers, he was smiling contentedly when he passed -- because he had beaten the green chair!

Holden's death revived the legend and a search began for the mysterious green chair. No one knew what became of it after Captain Warren had died. Finally, it discovered that the chair had been destroyed. It was traced to the Chicago Avenue police station, where it had been stored in the cellar after the death of Captain Warren. When it was found to be infested with cockroaches, it was broken apart and burned in the station's furnace. This happened shortly before Red Holden had died in his hospital bed.

Otherwise, some claimed, he would have never escaped the curse.

load of buckshot in the chest. Walsh and Olson were also shot. Sweeny, the youngest officer, crouched behind the squad car and began firing over the hood.

At that time, South Western Avenue was largely an industrial area, filled with factories. Soon, hundreds of workers began pouring out into the street to watch the action. Factory whistles blew out a warning and riot calls began coming into the switchboard of the local police station. The gangsters fled but Sweeney bravely followed, a revolver gripped in each hand. The gangsters ran across a vacant lot and Scalise and Anselmi ducked into an alley. Genna ran on alone and then turned to face the advancing detective. He raised his shotgun and pulled the trigger – but both barrels were empty. He threw down the gun and ran toward a house beyond the empty lot. Sweeney fired, hitting Genna in the upper leg, but he kept going. He fell down near the house, smashed a basement window and dragged himself inside. When Sweeney and two other policemen found him, he was sitting on the basement floor, blood gushing from a severed artery. An ambulance was summoned and he was rushed to Bridewell Hospital. As they were traveling, a guard leaned over to adjust the stretcher and Genna kicked him in the face. "Take that, you son of a bitch," he choked out. He bled to death in the ambulance before they made it to the hospital.

Scalise and Anselmi managed to escape from the scene but – unbelievably – decided to go into a dry goods store on Fifty-Ninth Street to replace the hats they had lost while running away. The police were still swarming over the area, but the gangsters thought little of going into the store. The proprietor, Edward Issigson, was immediately suspicious of the pair. He had heard the gunshots and sirens and knew that something had happened nearby. When the two bedraggled men came into the shop, their clothing torn and dirty, speaking in a foreign tongue, he refused to sell them anything. The two gangsters retreated from the shop and seeing a streetcar coming to a stop at the corner, they ran for it. At the same time, another police car came roaring down Western Avenue. Issigson hailed it and pointed at the two men, who he was now convinced had something to do with the guns and excitement. The streetcar was just starting to move when the police pulled Scalise and Anselmi off the rear platform.

They were taken to the central detective bureau and grilled by Chief of Detectives William Shoemaker, who questioned them through an interpreter. They were charged with first-degree murder for the slaying of the detectives. In a radio broadcast, State's Attorney Crowe asserted, "These men will go straight to the gallows." He assigned Assistant State's Attorney McSwiggin, the young "hanging prosecutor," to the case.

Capone shed no tears over the deaths of Angelo and Mike Genna. Although their role in the syndicate had been indispensable to Torrio's master plan, their greed, treachery and bloodlust had made them problematic allies. In addition, they also blocked Capone's control of Little Italy and its booming alcohol-cooking industry. The Gennas had also made too much of their prestige from the presidency of the Unione Siciliane, gained after Mike Merlo's death. Since Capone was not a Sicilian, he could not qualify for membership in the organization but he did have plans to dominate it by installing his own officers in key positions. The Gennas had been in the way. Angelo had taken over the president's chair but Capone wanted his *consigliere,* Tony Lombardo, in the top spot. For this reason, he had no regrets over the destruction of the clan – in fact, he contributed to it.

According to an informer in Little Italy, Mike Genna was doomed that day, no matter how things turned out. The source told the police that Scalise and Anselmi had secretly defected to Capone and had accepted a contract from him to kill Genna. As Mike drove them down Western Avenue after the attempted hit on Moran and Drucci, he was actually being taken on a "one-way ride" by Scalise and Anselmi – and by Al Capone.

Tony Genna was the next to die.

On July 8, a member of the Genna gang, Giuseppe Nerone, known as "Il Cavaliere," telephoned Tony. Nerone had been unhappy with his position in the Genna organization for some time. He felt that the brothers didn't appreciate his talents and was likely thinking that by killing off the rest of the Gennas, he could get a bigger piece of Little Italy for himself. Nerone told Genna that he had important information for him and wanted to meet him in front of Cutilla's grocery store on Grand Avenue at 10:30 a.m. When Genna arrived, the two men greeted one another and then Tony was given a version of the "Chicago Handshake." As Nerone embraced Genna in greeting, an unknown associate stepped out of a doorway and fired five shots into Genna's back.

Dying in the County Hospital, Genna whispered to his mistress, Gladys Bagwell, a name that sounded like "Cavallaro." The police searched for a nonexistent Italian by that name instead of Nerone the Cavalier and by the time they realized their mistake, Nerone has been shot to death in a North Side barbershop. Detectives believed that Nerone was coaxed into killing his boss and then taken out to get him out of the way. But who talked him into it? The cops were divided – some suspecting Vincent Drucci and others Al Capone.

Tony was buried next to Angelo in Mount Carmel Cemetery. One of the mourners, noting the proximity of Dion O'Banion's grave, quipped, "When Judgment Day comes and them three graves are opened, there'll be hell to pay in this cemetery!"

The surviving Gennas fled Chicago in panic. Jim returned to his native Sicily and Sam and Pete went into hiding outside of the city. Jim was later arrested for theft and spent two years in prison. All three brothers eventually returned to Chicago, but their power had been broken. They lived out the rest of their days in obscurity, importing cheese and olive oil.

To Capone's annoyance, his man, Tony Lombardo, failed to gain the presidency of the Unione Siciliane. With the Gennas vanquished, Samoots Amatuna rallied the remnants of their gang behind him and with two armed gunmen, strode into the organization's headquarters and claimed the coveted office for himself. The Sicilian's blood was up after the murders of the Gennas and even Capone knew better than to get in the way.

CAPONE'S CONSIGLIERE TONY LOMBARDO, WHO WOULD TRY FOR YEARS TO OBTAIN THE PRESIDENCY OF THE UNIONE SICILIANE -- BUT WHEN HE DID GET IT, IT WAS LITERALLY A JOB THAT KILLED HIM!

But there was better news on other fronts. The road to the gallows that had been promised by Scalise and Anselmi turned out to be a twisting and turning one. Three months went by with no trial. Meanwhile, Capone, the Unione Siciliane and the last members of the Genna gang (who never suspected that the defendants planned to kill one of their bosses) worked together to raise a defense fund for the two jailed gunmen. Under the personal direction of President Amatuna, collectors shook down immigrant families in Little Italy, coercing them into giving up money for attorneys' fees – and likely a little for the collector's pockets. With blackmail and blackjacks, they had soon raised a fund of more than $50,000.

Scalise and Anselmi finally went on trial for the murder of Detective Olson on October 5. Six days later, while jury selection was taking place, Detective Sweeney, the state's star witness, who, like every other witness in the case had been receiving threats through the mail all summer, was killed by a bomb. In addition, so many members of the pool were threatened that it took weeks to seat a jury. Two of the jurors who were finally selected had to have round-the-clock police protection.

The prosecution presented a clear-cut case. Numerous eyewitnesses to the shooting on Western Avenue identified Scalise and Anselmi as the perpetrators. The defendant's attorney,

Michael J. Ahern, who worked for Capone and other top-ranking gang leaders, never attempted to refute the evidence against his clients. Instead, he offered a justification for killing police officers. He told the jury, "If a policeman detains you, even for a moment, against your will, you are not guilty of murder, but only manslaughter. If the policeman uses force of arms, you may kill him in self-defense and emerge from the law unscathed."

The defendants grinned when the jury returned a verdict of manslaughter and fixed their penalty at 14 years in prison. The cry of outrage from the police and the public forced the presiding Judge William V. Brothers to announce that the defendants would be returned to his courtroom without delay to face charges in the murder of Detective Walsh. Three months passed.

Meanwhile, in late October, John Torrio was released from the Lake County Jail. Three automobiles filled with bodyguards provided by Capone, waited for him at the gates and spirited him away to Gary, Indiana. There, he boarded a train to New York, where his wife met him, and from there they sailed to Italy.

In preparation for Scalise and Anselmi's second trial, fund-raising efforts in Little Italy were doubled – although Samoots Amatuna was no longer around to organize them. A few weeks earlier, Hymie Weiss and the West Side O'Donnells had joined forces to prevent Amatuna's main goal, which was the reconstruction of the Genna gang under his leadership. On the evening of November 13, before taking his fiancée, Rose Pecorara, to the opera, he stopped at a Cicero barbershop for a shave and a manicure. Two men followed him inside, walked up to his chair and pulled revolvers from their coats. Amatuna jumped to his feet and tried to scramble for cover behind the barber chair, but it was too late. Both men opened fire and Amatuna was hit four times. On his deathbed at Jefferson Park Hospital, Amatuna asked a priest to marry him and Rose, but he died just before the ceremony began.

TWO BARBERSHOP SHOOTINGS IN A MATTER OF MONTHS PROMPTED PROPRIETORS OF SHOPS THAT CATERED TO CHICAGO GANGSTERS TO BEGIN KEEPING THEIR CHAIRS FACING THE DOOR AT ALL TIMES. IN ADDITION, IT BECAME A RULE TO NEVER COVER A PATRON'S FACE WITH A TOWEL -- JUST IN CASE.

Although the police were never able to make any arrests in the slaying of Samoots Amatuna, the identity of the killers was common knowledge in the underworld – Vincent Drucci and Jim Doherty, who had been with Myles O'Donnell during the murder of Eddie Tancl.

Three days after Amatuna's funeral, the two gunmen who had helped him to take over the Unione Siciliane, Eddie Zion and Bummy Goldstein, were also murdered. Zion was ambushed and killed on the street and Goldstein was gunned down in a drugstore. His assassin had brazenly stolen a shotgun from a police car parked outside to carry out the deed.

These deaths cleared the way for Tony Lombardo's accession to the presidency of the Unione Siciliane, giving Capone complete control of the Chicago branch of the organization.

Before 1925 came to an end, Capone saw more bloodshed – but not in Chicago.

On occasion, members of the Capone family returned to Brooklyn. Capone's mother especially loved to visit her old neighborhood and when she did, Frankie Yale or Lucky Luciano always provided her with a car, driver and ample protection. In late December, though, Al and Mae Capone traveled to Brooklyn because their son was very ill. At the age of seven, Sonny had developed a deep mastoid infection, which required dangerous surgery. The mastoid bone controls hearing and balance. Wanting the best care for his only child, Capone sought out highly qualified doctors in New York to perform it. The operation was performed

RICHARD "PEG-LEG" LONERGAN, IRISH MOBSTER

on Christmas Eve and while Sonny survived, he was left partially deaf and had to wear a hearing aid.

After the operation, the Capones were sent home to get some sleep and they spent the holiday evening and the next day with Mae's family. The following night, December 26, a friend dropped by and asked Al to go with him for a glass of beer. According to his version of the events, "My wife told me to go; it'd do me good. And we were no sooner there than the door opens and six fellows come in and start shooting. My friend had put me on the spot. In the excitement, two of them were killed and one of the fellows was shot in the leg. And I spent the Christmas holidays in jail."

As it turned out, Capone's version of the events may not have been completely accurate. It is believed that the murders were actually planned in advance as a service to old associates and in defense of local Italian gang interests. The "friend's place" was the Adonis Social Club, a hangout from Capone's younger days. When Al arrived, the place was infested with Irishmen, including the leader of Brooklyn's Irish rackets, Richard "Peg-Leg" Lonergan, the scourge of the Italian mob. He was accompanied by other members of his gang, including Aaron Harms, Cornelius "Needles" Ferry, James Hart, "Ragtime Joe" Howard, and Patrick "Happy" Maloney.

For as long as Capone could remember, Irish gangsters had controlled the Brooklyn docks. Lately, though, the Italians had been challenging the Irish monopoly, creating violence and chaos that resulted in a handful of murders. Lonegran's presence in the Adonis Social Club, an Italian stronghold, was added provocation and he aggravated the situation by referring despairingly to the regular customers and the staff as "dagos" and "ginzos." When a couple of Irish girls came in with Italian escorts, he chased them away and told them to "come back with white men."

Capone arrived at the club around 2:00 a.m. with several companions, including Frank Galluccio, the now- forgiven man who had inflicted Capone's facial scars years before. Besides the Irish, there were about 10 other people in the place, all Italians, as well as the staff, which included owners "Fury" Agoglia and Jack Stabile, bartender Tony Desso, and waiters and bouncers George Carozza, Frank Piazza and Ralph Damato. Capone and his friends took a table at the back of the room and moments later, the lights went out.

Immediately, the sound and flash of gunshots filled the air. Bullets began to fly about the room. Chairs and tables were overturned, glasses shattered, and in the darkness and chaos, screaming customers fled out the front door, leaving hats, coats and belongings behind. No one had any idea what was going on — they just knew that they wanted out of the club.

A short time later, Patrolman Richard Morano of the Fifth Avenue police station passed by the club on his early morning rounds. It was dark and silent. In the gutter near the entrance, he spotted the body of Aaron Harms. The back of his head had been blown away. Using his flashlight, Officer Morano followed a trail of blood into the club. Cornelius Ferry and Richard Lonergan, both shot through the head, were lying in front of the piano. Another patrolman found James Hart a few blocks away, crawling along the sidewalk. He had been shot in the thigh and both legs and was taken to Cumberland Street Hospital.

After rounding up everyone who had been at the Adonis Social Club that night, and getting vague and contradictory stories from all of them, the police arrested the owners, their four employees and Al Capone, who was still so little known outside of Chicago that a local newspaper mistook him for a "club doorman." All seven suspects were arraigned in Homicide Court and were held without bail pending Hart's recovery, since his testimony was the only thing that could assure a conviction. But Hart not only refused to testify, he claimed that he had never set foot in the Adonis Social Club that night. He had been wounded in the street, insisted to police, apparently by stray bullets from a passing car.

The court released the prisoners on bond and later dismissed the case altogether.

Capone arrived back in Chicago around the same time that new fundraising efforts were being kicked off on behalf of Scalise and Anselmi for their next trial. Extortion efforts were being run by Orazio "The Scourge" Tropea and his crew. When Tropea found that contributors for the first fund were reluctant to kick in again, he decided on some harsher measures. Henry Spignola, the brother-in-law of the late Angelo Genna, had already paid $10,000 toward the first defense, and he rejected another demand for the same amount. Tropea feigned understanding and invited him to dinner to patch things up between them. He chose Amato's Restaurant on South Halsted Street and Spignola accepted his invitation on the night of January 10. After an elaborate meal, Spignola left the restaurant for home just after 9:00 p.m. Two men, waiting in a car across the street, slaughtered him with shotgun blasts as he walked out the door.

Two brothers, Agostino and Antonio Morici, macaroni manufactures and purveyors of yeast and sugar to Little Italy's liquor distillers, had also paid into the first defense fund. After refusing to pay any more, they were forced to hire bodyguards to protect them from Tropea and his crew. Unfortunately, the bodyguards weren't with them on the cold, wintry night of January 27 when they drove home to the Lakeside Place house that they had bought from the fugitive Jim Genna. Members of Tropea's crew overtook them on the road and opened fire on their car. Both brothers were killed and their sedan careened off the road and crashed into a billboard.

The friends and family of the two men were quick to retaliate. When it came to Tropea, though, there was little need for them to seek revenge. When fellow gangsters learned that Tropea was skimming a much larger piece of the fund for himself that was originally thought, they took care of matters themselves. On February 15, Tropea was cut down by two shotgun blasts as he was walking along South Halsted, thus ending his career.

His crew was wiped out soon after. Nine days later, one of his top men, Vito Bascone, was found in a ditch in Stickney. He had been shot once between the eyes and the index fingers on each of his hands had been shot off. These defense wounds were believed to have occurred when he raised his hands for mercy just before the fatal gunshot to his head. At the bottom of a nearby stone quarry was found the car that had opened fire on the Morici brothers. It belonged to Ecola "The Eagle" Baldelli, another of Tropea's men. Baldelli's body turned up that same night in a smoldering ash heap in a North Side alley. He had been beaten, stabbed and finally shot. Another gunman, Tony Finalli, died of shotgun wounds on March 7. Felipe Gnolfo survived three attempts on his life but was killed during the fourth try in 1930. This brought the number of killings connected to the Scalise-Anselmi fundraising efforts to eight.

The second trial began on February 7 and the same difficulties were encountered while trying to seat a jury. Out of 246 people called, all but four of them managed to excuse themselves. One of them, Orval W. Payne, leveled with the judge: "It wouldn't be healthy to bring in a verdict of guilty. Pressure is brought to bear on our families. I'd have to carry a gun for the rest of my life."

The trial eventually got under way and the defendants managed to win an acquittal. This was mostly due to the two defense witnesses who swore that the detectives fired at Mike Genna before he fired at them. In May, Scalise and Anselmi were sent to Joliet Correctional Center to start the fourteen-year sentence that had been handed down by Judge Brothers in the first trial.

But Chicago had not heard the last of the two bloodthirsty gangsters.

11. DEATH OF THE "HANGING PROSECUTOR"

On the same day that Bascone and Baldelli's bodies were discovered, Vice President Charles G. Dawes presented a petition to Congress that demanded a federal investigation of the lawlessness that was occurring in Chicago. Dawes had been pressured into passing along the petition by the Better Government Association of Chicago and Cook County, a reform group that targeted not only the lawbreakers in the region, but pointed specific fingers at the "alien element" – the immigrants that it felt were responsible for the bootlegging, kidnapping and assassinations. In addition to its borderline racist charges, the petition also listed breweries that were operating in violation of Prohibition laws and bombings perpetrated during 1925. The group also complained about the crooked police officers on the Mafia payroll and the public officials that are "in secret alliance with underworld assassins, gunmen, rum-runners, bootleggers, thugs, ballot box stuffers and repeaters."

The harshest political corruption accusations were hurled at the state's attorney, Robert Emmett Crowe. Few officeholders had promised so much during their campaigns and delivered so little after getting elected. Crowe was first

ROBERT E. CROWE

elected as part of Big Bill Thompson's Republican slate in 1921. When he took office, he manfully told the police, "You bring 'em in and I'll prosecute 'em." The cases he actually prosecuted were greatly outnumbered by the hundreds of indictments that were filed and then never followed up on. For instance, he had successfully prosecuted Fred Lundin, mainly to hurt the Thompson clique that he had broken from, but he never acted on the indictments of the other 39 members of the Board of Education who stole money from public coffers.

During Crowe's first two terms in office, the number of murders in Cook County almost doubled, an increase he attributed (rightfully so) to Prohibition. Out of 349 victims, 215 were gangsters killed in the beer wars. Yet despite the size of Crowe's staff – 70 assistant state's attorneys and scores of investigators, the largest staff in the history of the office – it obtained only 128 convictions for murder, none involving gangsters, and only eight killers went to the gallows. There were also 369 bombings during that time and not a single conviction. Felony charges were at an all-time low and hundreds of cases were either reduced to lesser offenses or dropped altogether. The state's attorney's office was in shambles and blame would only be laid at the feet of Robert Crowe.

Crowe was born in Peoria, Illinois, in 1879. For three years after graduating from Yale Law School, he practiced privately in Chicago at the firm of Moran, Mayer & Meyer. He married Candida Cuneo, daughter of an Italian merchant who founded Chicago's oldest wholesale firm. He entered politics at the age of 30 as an assistant state's attorney on the staff of John E.W. Wayman, a Republican politician aligned with the vice lords of the Levee District. In 1914, Crowe went to work for Mayor Carter Harrison, Jr. and served as an assistant city corporation counsel. He then spent a year as a Cook County circuit court judge. In 1919, he was named chief justice of the Criminal Courts, the youngest man to ever hold the position. By then he had joined the Thompson faction, which two years later carried him to the post of state's attorney.

Crowe was an often-unlikable man with a heavy brow, small, sharp nose, small eyes obscured by thick glasses, and a thin mouth that was often set in a thin line of disapproval. He craved power and loved to extol his own virtues, limited as they might have been. He was known for making wild claims and proclamations – "Give me plenty of judges so I can try the killer while the blood of his victim is still warm!" was one of his best known.

Crowe's tenure in office was not without merit, though. He transformed the office of the state's attorney, expanding its scope of operations and recruiting young, ambitious law school graduates. He managed to enlarge the budget of his office to hire more prosecutors and succeeded in getting 1,000 policemen added to the city's force.

He recognized the folly of Prohibition and knew the Volstead Act could not be enforced. He contended that 80 percent of Cook County was wet and that included most judges and jurors. "I'll tell you something," Crowe confided in one of his speeches, "the town is wet and the county is wet, and nobody can dry them up. They holler about Sheriff Hoffman permitting the county to run wide open. Well, it is wide open. But for every dive in the county there are two in the city, and everybody in Chicago knows it except [Mayor] Dever. Why don't I get busy and stop it? For the simple reason that I am running a law office, not a police station. If Chicago wants things cleaned up, let somebody bring the law violators in here and I'll send them to the penitentiary. But I will not be both arresting officer and prosecutor."

Among Crowe's major court victories (as he often reminded the public) was the destruction of a statewide auto-theft ring. He also assigned one of his top assistants, Charles Gorman, to the prosecution of Fred "Frenchy" Mader, president of the Building Trades Council. Using bombs and threats of strikes, Mader had been extorting Chicago construction firms for 10 percent of the costs whenever they put up a new building. Despite the fact that jurors and witnesses were both intimidated and bribed, Mader and 49 members of his gang were convicted. They never served a day in jail, however – Governor Small pardoned them all. Crowe blamed Small for his low conviction rate. "He lets them out as fast as we put them in," he griped.

The petition that was presented to Congress raked Crowe over the coals and accused him on consorting with criminals, namely the Gennas. The recriminations were still flying when a murder occurred that would lead to the most damaging disclosure yet about the complicity between public officials and gangsters.

The murder also raised a lot of questions.

What had an assistant state's attorney been doing driving around Cicero with four notorious gangsters?

And what had he been doing drinking bootleg beer with them, when only months before he had been trying – or so it seemed — to send two of them to the gallows?

At the age of only 26, William McSwiggin was one of the toughest, smartest and most dedicated prosecutors on Robert Crowe's staff. The previous year he had won convictions in nine capital cases. Handsome, dapper and witty, McSwiggin had grown up in Chicago's West Side Irish neighborhood and was

"HANGING PROSECUTOR" WILLIAM MCSWIGGIN

a close friend of future gangsters like the O'Donnells and Jim Doherty. He was a policeman's son, like Doherty, and the only boy among five children born to Sergeant Anthony McSwiggin, who became a Chicago cop in 1881. He attended De Paul Academy, then De Paul University and finally graduated from the university's law school. He worked his way through school as a salesman, a movie usher, dance hall bouncer, truck driver and a special agent for the American Railway Express Company. He graduated from law school with such high honors that Crowe specifically recruited him for his staff.

But academics were not all that impressed Crowe about his young protégé. As a popular Thirteenth Ward Republican, McSwiggin had garnered votes for the state's attorney in 1920 and again in 1924. And so had his friends, the O'Donnells. Politics brought him into contact with Al Capone, who often spoke of him warmly as "my friend, Bill McSwiggin." A bachelor, McSwiggin lived with his parents and four sisters at 4946 West Washington Boulevard. His father constantly hounded him to cut ties with the O'Donnells and other disreputable friends from his younger days but the younger McSwiggin saw nothing wrong with going to parties with them, drinking and playing cards with his old pals.

The sequence of events that led to McSwiggin's death (and subsequently to months of grand jury hearings and special investigations) began on April 17 at the Hawthorne Inn in Cicero. McSwiggin went there to meet with Al Capone and although Capone later confirmed that the meeting had taken place, he never revealed the reason for it. Police Sergeant McSwiggin, who claimed to know what had occurred between his son and Capone would only shake his head and say, "If I told, I'd blow the lid off Chicago. This case is loaded with dynamite. It's dangerous to talk about."

On the evening of April 27, McSwiggin was eating supper at his parent's home when Red Duffy dropped by. Leaving his meal unfinished, McSwiggin left with him, telling his family that he was going to play cards in Berwyn. They climbed into Jim Doherty's car and Doherty, who McSwiggin had unsuccessfully tried to prosecute for the murder of Eddie Tancl, was driving. Doherty's co-defendant in the same case, Miles O'Donnell was in the back seat with his brother, Klondike. The men in the car had spent a long day intimidating election officials. In the recent Republican primaries, the Crowe slate had defeated the ticket that was endorsed by Senator Deneen, who demanded a recount. The O'Donnells, Duffy and Doherty had spent the day at the County Building in Chicago, wearing badges that identified them as ballot watchers for Crowe's faction. The recount confirmed the Crowe victory (and four investigations into voter fraud failed to reverse it). As they left the County Building, Klondike O'Donnell stated that they should go out to Cicero for a beer. He knew it was good, he told his companions, because he had delivered it himself. A man who worked for Capone happened to overhear the remark and he telephoned the Hawthorne Inn and passed along a message that the O'Donnells were going to be in town. Before driving out to Cicero, the gangsters stopped to pick up their old pal, McSwiggin.

Many wondered why McSwiggin would have gone along with them that night. The Crowe office claimed that he was a valiant, hardworking prosecutor who accompanied the gangsters only to gather material for upcoming cases, including the second Scalise-Anselmi trial. According to the O'Donnells, McSwiggin had asked for their help in recovering some stolen bulletproof vests for a friend named Arthur Dunlap. The anti-

Crowe faction stated that McSwiggin, like his boss, was corrupt and pointed to his conduct in the first Scalise-Anselmi trial as proof, claiming that he had steered the jury away from the kind of punishment that the killers deserved. More likely, McSwiggin probably committed no offense other than having a poor choice in friends. Clan loyalties among the Irish were just as fierce as those among the Italians of Chicago. In many cases, gangsters and politicians maintained lifelong friendships, despite the difference in what they did for a living. McSwiggin's father had often told him that hanging around with his old friends from the neighborhood was bound to get him in trouble – and this time, he was right.

John Doherty only drove a few blocks before the engine of the car began sputtering and acting strangely. He left the car at a West Side garage for repairs and the five men moved over to Klondike O'Donnell's new Lincoln sedan. A sixth man then joined the group, Edward Hanley, a former police officer. He drove and they barhopped around Cicero for about two hours, drinking beer in several saloons. Their last stop was Harry Madigan's Pony Inn at 5613 West Roosevelt Road. The white, two-story building stood on a weedy lot about a mile from Capone's Hawthorne Inn.

By late April, the relationship between the O'Donnells and the Capone gang, once stalwart allies, had deteriorated almost to the point of open warfare. The Irishmen had gotten bold with their encroachments into Capone's territory. They had been selling beer to Cicero saloon owners for $10 less than what Capone was charging and Harry Madigan had convinced many saloonkeepers to do business with the O'Donnells. Capone was enraged and when he heard that night that the O'Donnells were in town, he decided to teach them a lesson.

Capone assembled a crew of gunmen, all armed with Tommy guns, and instructed them to deploy five cars to look for the O'Donnells. Soon, a lookout reported that O'Donnell's Lincoln was parked in front of the Pony Inn. The Capone cars were sent to the scene and at about 8:30 p.m., the Irishmen emerged from the bar, drunk on beer, and walked across the street to the Lincoln. They opened the doors and started to get

MCSWIGGIN'S BODY WAS FOUND ALONGSIDE A LONELY ROAD OUTSIDE OF BERWYN, WHERE IT HAD BEEN DUMPED BY HIS LIFELONG FRIENDS.

inside when the five Capone cars suddenly roared past. An eyewitness who lived above the saloon said that she saw a car speeding away "with what looked like a telephone receiver sticking out the rear window and spitting fire." Hundreds of bullets slammed into the Lincoln and into the twitching bodies of three of the Irishmen.

Duffy, Doherty and McSwiggin all suffered terrible wounds, but Hanley and the O'Donnells managed to crouch flat on the pavement behind the sedan, causing the bullets to fly over their heads. As the Capone cars vanished into the darkness, the brothers scrambled over to their blood-soaked friends. McSwiggin, with slugs in his back and neck, was twisting in agony on the sidewalk. Both of Doherty's legs had been shattered. The O'Donnells knew that they would be grilled by the police if they took the survivors to the hospital, so they loaded them into the bullet-ridden car and drove them to Klondike's home on Parkside Avenue. Duffy, who they believed was beyond help, was left propped up against a tree near the spot where the attack had occurred.

When they reached the house, it was decided that they would call a doctor they could trust. Unfortunately, both men bled to death before medical help arrived. Leaving Doherty's body in the car, the O'Donnells carried McSwiggin's corpse into the house. They emptied his pockets, cut off any identifying marks in his clothes and then took him back out to the car. With one brother following behind the other, they drove to Berwyn, found a lonely stretch of road, and dumped the bodies of their boyhood chums. They continued on to Oak Park, where they abandoned the battered sedan. That task accomplished, they disappeared soon after and were not seen or heard from again for a month. Capone also vanished during this time and was not seen in Chicago until three months later.

Duffy was found first, propped against the tree. Amazingly, he was still alive when a motorist picked him up alongside Roosevelt Road and drove him to the hospital. He died the next morning and in his pockets, the police found a list of sixty Cicero saloons and speakeasies, many of them with a pencil checkmark next to them. The list mysteriously disappeared, turning up later in the coroner's office with all of the checkmarks erased. No one admitted to knowing just what the checkmarks might have meant.

A motorist happened upon the bodies of Doherty and McSwiggin that same night at about 10:00 p.m. The Berwyn police brought them to the morgue and assumed they were the bodies of two more gangsters who had died violent deaths. However, around midnight, a Chicago reporter on the crime beat identified one of the bodies as that of State's Attorney Crowe's star prosecutor, William McSwiggin.

The headlines that appeared in the next day's papers stunned Chicago. Most had grown complacent to the more than two hundred lives that had been claimed by the beer wars. "They only kill each other – good riddance," was the attitude most often expressed when it came to gangsters gunning each other down in the streets. But the murder of an assistant state's attorney stunned the city.

Crowe spouted off his usual rhetoric, promising to take the war to the gangsters. He ordered his detectives to arrest every hoodlum in sight. He had Sheriff Hoffman deputize one hundred city detectives for county duty and, placing them under the command of Chief Shoemaker and Deputy Chief Stege, sent them out into the suburbs to raid speakeasies, gambling dens and brothels. He headed the Cicero raiding party himself and offered a $5,000 reward for the arrest of McSwiggin's killers out of his own pocket. But not everyone was convinced that Crowe could be taken seriously. His political enemies came out of the woodwork and began working to prove that his office was corrupt, along with his murdered prosecutor.

Crowe fought back by petitioning Judge William Brothers to set up a special grand jury to look into the murder. Brothers, a part of Crowe's political faction, went along with it. While Crowe could not actually direct the grand jury, he had no intention of relinquishing control of the investigation and allowing the jury to truly delve into the connection between crime and politics in Cook County. Instead, he called upon Attorney General Oscar Carlstrom, another reliable party hack, to direct the jury so that he could dictate its moves from behind the scenes. No evidence that Carlstrom ever presented led to an indictment.

Meanwhile, the Cook County Coroner, Oscar Wolff, as well-known for being inept as for being connected to mobsters, set up his own special jury to sit in on the McSwiggin inquest. As the hearings bumbled along, Wolff made the grand gesture of bringing in a special prosecutor from Terre Haute, Indiana, named Joseph Roach to take part in the inquest. Roach had recently made headlines by sending

COOK COUNTY CORONER OSCAR WOLFF

a number of Indiana gangsters to prison. Roach arrived in Chicago amid great fanfare but was never allowed to demonstrate the investigative skills that had made him famous in Terre Haute. Almost immediately, Wolff adjourned the inquest. It was reconvened twice more in the next two years but no verdict was ever reached.

The only thing that Wolff actually achieved was to assemble dossiers on about thirty gangsters whom he accused of murder and referred them to Attorney General Carlstrom. Unbelievably, Carlstrom ignored most of the material. His jury did vote a few indictments but none of them were related to the McSwiggin case and none of them ever went to trial. When he finally got around to the McSwiggin murder, the witnesses included more than two hundred Cicero saloon owners, and while they offered no information about the murder, they did tell the jury a great deal about the sources of their illegal liquor. This information could have been helpful to federal investigators, who were then looking into bootlegging in Cicero, but Carlstrom never bothered to give it to them.

Cynical newspaper reporters were quick to see the waste of time that the grand jury investigations had become. A week after the McSwiggin murder, the *Chicago Tribune* noted: "The police have no more actual evidence as to the motives of the shooting and the identity of the killer than they did when it happened." The grand jury eventually stated that the crime was impossible to solve, thanks to "silence and the sealed lips of gangsters."

The dead man's father made his own statements to the press. "I thought my life's work was over," he said, "but it's just begun. I'll never rest until I've killed by boy's slayers or seen then hanged. That's all I have to live for now."

Sergeant McSwiggin undertook an investigation of his own, trying to cajole witnesses and informants to give testimony against Capone. None of them dared. Eventually, he named the four men whom he believed killed his son – Capone, Frank Rio, Frank Diamond and a Cicero bootlegger named Bob McCullough. The lookouts that he believed tracked down the O'Donnells were Eddie Moore and Willie Heeney. McSwiggin wouldn't reveal where he had gotten this information – he claimed an oath of secrecy prevented it. With no evidence to back up the claims, the police were powerless to do anything about them.

Crowe's deputies did inflict serious damage on Capone's suburban operations during this time, making it became the lowest point of the crime boss' career. Capone owned or controlled 25 of the 33 resorts that the raiders overran, smashing gambling dens, destroying roulette wheels, crap tables and slot machines,

POLICE CAPTAIN, THEN DEPUTY CHIEF, JOHN STEGE

cutting open beer barrels and drums of liquor, breaking bottles, arresting prostitutes and hauling away safes filled with cash. They partially wrecked Capone's largest brothel, the Stockade. The next night, residents of Forest View completed the destruction. They set fire to the place and when the local fire brigade arrived, they just stood back and watched it burn to the ground.

"Why don't you do something?" one of Capone's men asked.

"Can't spare the water," a fireman laconically replied.

Deputy Chief Stege laughed when he heard about the incident. He declined to investigate the arson.

The raids became an interesting topic to the federal grand jury that was sitting in Cicero, and on May 27, the jury indicted members of both the Capone and O'Donnell gangs, including Al and Ralph Capone, Charlie Fischetti, Peter Payette, the three O'Donnells and Harry Madigan. The charge was conspiracy to violate the Volstead Act.

Capone was still a fugitive at the time and the search for him took Chicago detectives to New York, into the woods of Northern Michigan and to Courderay, Wisconsin, where he had recently acquired a country estate that he had outfitted with a lookout tower near the main house that had placements for machine guns. No trace was found of him anywhere.

The O'Donnells were captured in Chicago or they surrendered – the circumstances were never made clear – on the same day they were indicted. Chief Shoemaker took them directly to the state's attorney's office rather than to police headquarters. This change from normal procedure made some suspicious that the brothers had been arrested according to a prearranged plan and given plenty of time to fabricate stories and concoct alibis. They refused to testify before the grand jury until threatened with jail for contempt of court. Soon after, they created their own version of events for the night of April 27, mentioning the stolen bulletproof vests for the first time. They claimed that they were not with McSwiggin when he was killed. He was taken to Klondike O'Donnell's house after he was shot, but they would not say who brought him there. They also denied knowing how his body, along with that of Doherty, ended up sprawled on a road outside of Berwyn.

The state authorities took no further action against the O'Donnells and the federal charges against them for liquor violations were left hanging for two years, and then quietly dropped.

Illinois law limited the length a special grand jury could be convened to one month. If an investigation was going to be continued, then another jury had to be sworn in. The Carlstrom jury was disbanded on June 4. In its final report, it absolved McSwiggin of any wrongdoing and accepted the story of the stolen bulletproof vests, even going as far as to swallow Crowe's statement that McSwiggin's evening with gangsters had been a "social ride." The jurors surmised, probably correctly, that his killers likely had no knowledge of the prosecutor's identity. The report also made a point to praise the state's attorney and condemn his political detractors. Newspaper reporters, and the general public, were dismayed at the poor performance of the special jury.

To try and smooth things over, Crowe petitioned Chief Justice Thomas J. Lynch of the Criminal Courts to empanel a second special grand jury. It was needed, he said, to investigate voter fraud during the recent primaries and to look deeper into the McSwiggin case. In this way, Crowe managed to sidetrack and confuse another special jury by giving it too much to do. This jury made no more progress than the first. A third special grand jury followed.

On July 28, toward the end of the third jury's equally useless existence, Al Capone – for whom secret arrest warrants had been issued – surfaced in Indiana. He notified Crowe that he was ready to surrender. As he waited for Crowe's chief investigator, Pat Roche, to pick him up at the Illinois state line, he spoke to reporters and assured them that he planned to prove himself innocent of the erroneous charges that were being leveled against him. To a suburban reporter, whose paper had speculated that Capone killed McSwiggin by mistake, thinking that he was Hymie Weiss, he said: "Of course, I didn't kill him. Why should I? I liked the kid. Only the day

FORMER POLICE DETECTIVE TURNED CHIEF INVESTIGATOR FOR PROSECUTOR CROWE, PAT ROCHE (FAR RIGHT)

before he was up to my place and when he went home I gave him a bottle of scotch for his old man."

Why, then, did Capone flee from Chicago after the prosecutor was killed? He feared, he said, that the police would shoot him on sight. "The police have told a lot of stories," Capone said. "They shoved a lot of murders over on me. They did it because they couldn't find the men who did the jobs and I looked like an easy goat. They said I was sore at McSwiggin because he prosecuted Anselmi and Scalise for killing two policemen. But that made no difference. He told me he was going to give them the rope if he could and that was all right with me."

Capone then added a single statement that would bring great embarrassment to State's Attorney Crowe: "I paid McSwiggin. I paid him plenty and I got what I was paying for."

Capone was taken back to Chicago and when he arrived at the Federal Building, he found more reporters waiting for him. As usual, he couldn't wait to make a statement that painted himself in the best light possible. "I'm no squawker," he told the newsmen, "but I'll tell what I know about this case. All I ask is a chance to prove that I had nothing to do with the killing of my friend, Bill McSwiggin. Just ten days before he was killed I talked with him. There were friends of mine with me. If I had wanted to kill him, we could have done it then. But we didn't want to. We never wanted to. I liked him. He was a fine young fellow.

Doherty and Duffy were my friends, too. I wasn't out to get them. Why, I used to lend Doherty money. Big-hearted Al I was, just helping out a friend. I wasn't in the beer racket and didn't care where they sold. Just a few days before that shooting, my brother Ralph and Doherty and the O'Donnells were at a party together."

Capone appeared before Justice Lynch and an assistant state's attorney named George E. Gorman withdrew the murder complaint against him. He stated in court that the complaint had been made by Chief of Detectives Shoemaker with only cursory information. The numerous investigations had revealed no clear link between Capone and the murders. Justice Lynch dismissed the case and Capone sauntered out of the courtroom with a broad smile on his face.

In early August, a fourth special grand jury was impaneled to look into voter fraud and the McSwiggin case but it was also quickly distracted by another issue. On August 6, according to eyewitnesses, Joe Saltis and his chauffeur, Frank "Lefty" Koncil, shot to death a member of the Sheldon gang named John "Mitters" Foley because he had been selling beer in the Saltis-McErlane gang territory. The jury stopped their original inquiries to indict the pair.

The fourth jury's only other accomplishment was to return indictments against forty election officials in the Forty-Second Ward. The State Supreme Court later quashed all of them. Their investigation into the McSwiggin case went nowhere. Crowe took the witness stand to testify and claimed that his assistant had been killed by gunmen imported from either New York or Detroit. He never said where he had come by this information.

A fifth special grand jury was put together a short time later. Judge Lynch, when considering the action, was told that two new clues and two new witnesses had been found but that it was "necessary to keep the names of the witnesses secret. The moment any of the witnesses learn that they are wanted, they disappear, or are even killed." Judge Lynch granted the request but on the condition that the jury confine itself to investigating the McSwiggin case. It adjourned on the first day, pending the presentation of the new evidence. But neither the new clues nor the new witnesses ever materialized.

A sixth special grand jury brought the investigation to an embarrassing close in October. The murder of William McSwiggin had now grown cold. Officially, it has never been solved. The only thing the investigation into the case ever revealed was that the government of Chicago and Cook County were helpless when pitted against the forces of organized crime.

12. BLOOD IN THE STREETS.

VINCENT DRUCCI KEPT A SUITE AT THE CONGRESS HOTEL ON SOUTH MICHIGAN AVENUE. IT WAS A POPULAR SPOT FOR GANGSTERS, EVEN THOSE FROM OPPOSING SIDES IN CHICAGO'S BEER WARS. CAPONE OFTEN PLAYED POKER IN A PRIVATE ROOM ON AN UPPER FLOOR. THE CONGRESS IS CONSIDERED ONE OF THE MOST HAUNTED LOCATIONS IN CHICAGO TODAY.

Hymie Weiss was a man motivated by revenge. Since the murder of his friend Dion O'Banion, he had been head of the North Side gang that O'Banion had founded. However, Weiss seemed less interested in making money and more concerned with wrecking the operations of Capone and his allies – and wiping them out. Weiss and his men had wounded John Torrio and caused him to flee Chicago. They had attacked Capone twice, killed Angelo Genna, and wounded and murdered dozens of enemy gunmen.

But Capone retaliated next. He marked Weiss and Vincent Drucci for death and assigned gunman Louis Barko to carry out the murders on August 10, 1926. The event became known as the "Battle of Michigan Avenue."

Drucci had a suite at the Congress Hotel, four blocks north of the Standard Oil Building at Ninth Street and Michigan Avenue. On the morning of August 10, following a late breakfast in Drucci's eighth floor suite, Weiss and Drucci walked toward the Standard Oil Building, where they were supposed to meet with Morris Eller, a Sanitary District Trustee, and John Sbarbaro, owner of gangland's favorite funeral home. Eller was the mobbed-up boss of the Twentieth Ward and a cheap racketeer who offered a presentable face as a politician. Drucci was carrying $13,500 in cash in his pockets, which was allegedly a down payment on a piece of real estate, but was more likely bribe money for the North Side gang's Twentieth Ward sponsors.

As Drucci and Weiss were about to pass through the neo-Italian Renaissance doors of the building, Louis Barko and three other men jumped out of a car on the east side of Michigan Avenue and opened fire on them. Windows shattered and bullets chipped the stone walls as Drucci scrambled for cover behind parked cars. Weiss managed to get into the lobby of the building, shaken but unhurt.

Drucci pulled out his own gun and returned fire before jumping onto the running board of an automobile driven by C.C. Bassett, a startled motorist who had been trapped in the crossfire. Drucci's

escape was interrupted by the arrival of the police, who dragged him off the car. The attackers ran back to their car and when one of them fell behind, the others drove off without him. The affair turned out to be bloodless and it was over in less than two minutes. The police officers on the scene recognized Barko as one of Capone's gunmen and assumed this was an attempted mob hit. However, Drucci denied it. When questioned by the police at the South Clark Street station, he claimed that he didn't know Barko and dismissed the whole thing as an attempted robbery. "It was a stick-up, that's all," he told the cops. "They were after my roll."

Hymie Weiss' mother, Mary, posted the necessary bond and freed her son's friend from behind bars.

Their luck continued five days later. On August 15, Drucci and Weiss were driving south on Michigan Avenue and as they passed the Standard Oil Building, a car that had been trailing close behind them suddenly raced ahead, swerved to the right and rammed them. The men in the other car opened fire and bullets smashed all of their windows. Drucci and Weiss ducked down and scrambled out of the passenger side of the sedan. As they ran for the shelter of the closest building, they fired back over their shoulders with their own handguns. Miraculously, once again, no innocent bystanders were killed in the attack. As bullets slammed into the attacker's car, they roared away down Michigan Avenue.

It was incidents like this that caused Charles "Lucky" Luciano, after visiting Chicago, to remark, "It's a real goddamn crazy place! Nobody's safe in the streets."

Soon after, Weiss and George Moran led a hasty assault on the Four Deuces at 2222 South Wabash. Capone somehow escaped unhurt but his driver, Tony Ross, died behind the wheel.

A week later, on September 20, 1926, Weiss pulled one of his craziest stunts yet. He sent a caravan of automobiles, each carrying a trio of machine gunners, to Capone's Cicero headquarters, the Hawthorne Inn.

Capone was having lunch with one of his bodyguards, Frank Rio, in the rear of the Hawthorne Inn's restaurant, facing the windows that looked out on Twenty-Second Street. The diner was packed, with every seat taken by excited race fans who were on their way to a big event at the nearby Hawthorne Race Track. Capone and Rio had just finished eating and were sipping their coffee when they heard the roaring engine of a car and the familiar clatter of a Tommy gun from the street outside. A dark sedan raced past the window and vanished down the street. They hurried to the door with the other startled patrons to see what was going on. Strangely, no glass had been shattered and there were no bullet chips in the stone front of the hotel. Had the men in the car completely missed the hotel, or....?

Suddenly, Frank Rio grabbed hold of Capone, shoved him back into the restaurant and flung his body on top of his surprised boss. The whole thing had been a ruse, he realized, an attempt to draw Capone out into the open. As the two men tumbled to the floor, the rattling of machine guns once again was heard from outside. Bullets streaked over their heads, shattering glass, splintering woodwork and slamming into the plaster walls. Ten sedans cruised past the hotel in single line. Gun barrels were pointed out all of the windows, spitting fire and lead. The cars took their time. As each one came abreast of the hotel, it stopped and sprayed the front of the building, right to left, up and down.

Louis Barko, who ran into the restaurant during the initial volley of fire, was hit in the shoulder. He fell to the floor, blood soaking through his jacket, his gun in hand. The cars parked outside at the curb, most of them belonging to civilians, were torn apart by the hail of bullets. Clyde Freeman, a race fan had driven all the way from Louisiana with his wife and five-year-old son. The family was still in their car when the guns opened up. A bullet ripped through Freeman's hat. Another creased his son's knee. Flying bits of glass from the shattered windshield cut Mrs. Freeman's arm and gashed her right eye. When the last carload of attackers stopped in front of the hotel, a man in a khaki shirt and overalls got out with a Tommy gun in his hands. He walked calmly up to the entrance and emptied the entire drum cartridge into the doorway. When the mechanism clicked on an empty chamber, he walked back to his car and climbed inside. The

CAPONE BODYGUARD, FRANK RIO

motorcade then slowly drove off down Twenty-Second Street, returning to Chicago.

The assault had left the restaurant, hotel lobby and the nearby storefronts in ruins. Unbelievably, only Barko and the Freemans had been injured. Capone was shaken but remarkably calm. He was said to have been more in awe of the ferocity of the Tommy guns than worried about the danger to his life. When he learned that Mrs. Freeman's injured eye would require surgery, he insisted on paying the hospital bill, which came to over $10,000. He also paid for the damage to the storefronts around the Hawthorne Inn.

Chief of Detectives Shoemaker, who was certain he knew the identity of the gunmen who carried out the attack, summoned Barko to a line-up at the police station. He put him in front of Weiss, Drucci, Moran, Frank Gusenberg and his brothers, Pete and Henry, and asked him if he could identify any of the men. Barko smirked and swore that he had never seen any of them in his life.

On October 4, Capone made a curious move. It was one that would have pleased his old mentor John Torrio, but was uncharacteristic of the more hot-headed Capone: he proposed a peace talk. Weiss agreed to a meeting at the Morrison Hotel, but Capone himself did not attend. He sent Tony Lombardo in his place and, to placate his enemy, he authorized Lombardo to offer Weiss exclusive sales rights to all of the beer territory in Chicago north of Madison Street, an outrageously handsome concession.

But Weiss wouldn't have it. His thirst for revenge overrode his business interests. The only price that he would accept for peace was the deaths of Scalise and Anselmi, the men responsible for O'Banion's murder. Lombardo telephoned Capone for instructions. When he gave Capone's answer – "I wouldn't do that to a yellow dog" --- Weiss stormed out of the hotel in a fury.

Capone realized that there was no negotiating with Weiss. With this realization, the man's days were numbered. Weiss had been a thorn in his side for too long.

October 11, 1926 was a day like any other in downtown Chicago. Workday crowds and shoppers shuffled up and down the pavement and automobiles moved back and forth on the busy streets.

Across State Street from Holy Name Cathedral, at 738 North State Street, was the old flower shop that had been run by Dion O'Banion, and now operated solely by John Schofield. Hymie Weiss continued to maintain an office on the second floor.

Next door, at 740 North State Street, was a three-story rooming house that was kept by Mrs. Anna Rotariu. The house had an unusual literary connection. The property belonged to a prolific crime writer named Harry Stephen Keeler. Although little-known today, Keeler was a prolific author of more than fifty books, including *Sing Sing Nights*, the *Voice of the Seven Sparrows* and *The Mysterious Mr. Wong*, which was turned into a motion picture starring Bela Lugosi. He was born and raised in the house on State Street and wrote several of his thrillers there, moving away after he was married in 1919.

Early in October, a young man who called himself Oscar Lundin, or Langdon, rented rooms from Mrs. Rotariu. He wanted a room on the second floor, facing State Street, but all of the front rooms were occupied so he agreed to take one in the rear until something in front opened up, as one did on October 8. It was a small, rather dismal room furnished only with two straight-backed wooden chairs, an old oak dresser, a brass bed, a tin food locker, a gas ring and a shelf that held a few mismatched cups, cracked plates and tarnished cutlery. In spite of this, Lundin appeared to be delighted with the room.

On the same day that Lundin moved into his new quarters, a pretty blond woman, who gave her name as Mrs. Theodore Schultz of Mitchell, South Dakota, rented a front room on the third floor of an apartment building at 1 Superior Street, which ran at a right angle to State Street, south of the flower shop. Lundin's windows offered an unobstructed view of the east side of State Street from Holy Name Cathedral to the corner, while Mrs. Schulz's windows overlooked both the front and rear entrances of the flower shop. Anyone approaching or leaving the immediate area in any direction had to pass within range of one or the other 's windows.

IN EARLY OCTOBER, HYMIE WEISS WAS ATTENDING THE MURDER TRIAL OF JOE SALTIS AND LEFTY KONCIL, TWO FORMER CAPONE ALLIES THAT HAD DEFECTED TO WEISS AND THE O'BANION GANG.

Lundin occupied his new room for only one day. After paying a week's rent in advance, he vanished. Two men, who had visited him during his short stay, moved into the room. Mrs. Rotariu described them as an older man who wore a gray overcoat and fedora, and a younger man who wore a dark suit and light cap. Mrs. Schultz of Mitchell, South Dakota, also vanished after paying a weeks' rent. Two men also moved into her room. The landlord later said that they looked like Italians.

During that week in early October, Hymie Weiss spent most of his time at the Criminal Courts Building, four blocks from his headquarters above the flower shop. He was watching the jury selection in the trial of Joe Saltis and Lefty Koncil for the murder of Mitters Foley. The trial held special interest for Weiss, as evidenced by the list of officials and witnesses that was later found in his office safe. These documents would give substance to the rumor that he had paid out more than $100,000 to guarantee an acquittal in the case.

When court recessed for the day on October 11, Weiss left the building with four friends – his driver Sam Peller, a bodyguard and part-time beer runner, Patrick "Paddy" Murray, a Twentieth Ward politician

THE TWO BUILDINGS USED BY WEISS' ASSASSINS -- THE WINDOWS OF THE APARTMENTS WHERE THE SHOOTERS WAITED ARE MARKED WITH WHITE "X"'S IN BOTH PHOTOGRAPHS.

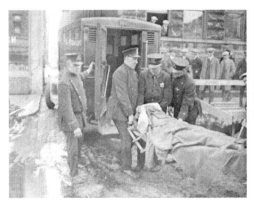 

(LEFT) SAM PELLER'S BODY IS TAKEN AWAY BY THE POLICE. (RIGHT) PATRICK "PADDY" MURRAY IN REPOSE.

and private investigator named Benny Jacobs, and William O'Brien, one of Chicago's top criminal attorneys, who was leading the Saltis-Koncil defense team.

At about 4:00 p.m., Peller parked Weiss' Cadillac coupe in front of Holy Name Cathedral, across from the flower shop, and the five men started across State Street. The two men in Mrs. Rotariu's rooming house had been waiting for two days with their chairs drawn up to the windows, guns in hand. Dozens of cigarette butts littered the floor. The two men in the side-street apartment had also been keeping watch since October 9, smoking and drinking wine, but now saw they were no longer needed. As they hurried out of the apartment, they left behind a shotgun and two bottles of wine.

As the five men reached the center of the street, the deafening sound of rattling Tommy guns pierced the air. Pedestrians scattered as bullets poured out of the windows of the rooming house. Weiss died instantly but Patrick Murray was hit ten times and survived long enough to be pronounced dead at Henrotin Hospital without regaining consciousness. Peller, hit fifteen times, fell dead in the street. O'Brien, with bullets in his arm, thigh and abdomen, dragged himself to the curb. The first policeman on the scene found him begging people in the growing crowd to take him to a doctor. Jacobs was hit once in the leg, and managed to drag himself to safety. The bullets that killed Hymie Weiss tore away portions of the inscription on the church's cornerstone and left bullet holes as a graphic reminder of the event. The church tried to have them removed years later but the chips and marks remain. They can still be seen on the corner of the cathedral today.

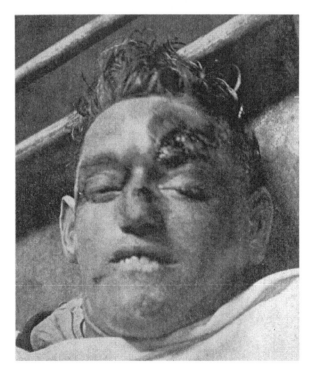

A GRUESOME PHOTOGRAPH OF HYMIE WEISS IN THE MORGUE.

Meanwhile, the assassins fled their third-floor lair, ran down a back staircase, exited the building through a ground-floor window into an alley and disappeared into the crowd. A discarded Tommy gun was found atop a dog kennel in an alley off Dearborn Street but it couldn't be traced back to the killers. On a bed in the rented room the police found a fedora with a label a label from a store in Cicero near the Hawthorne Inn. No record of the owner was ever found.

Although one has to wonder how hard the police actually looked for it. Chief Morgan Collins issued a gruff statement: "I don't want to encourage the business, but if somebody has to be killed, it's a good thing the gangsters are murdering themselves off. It saves trouble for the police."

While Weiss was being prepared for burial at the Sbarbaro Funeral Home, Capone was holding a press conference at the Hawthorne Inn. "That was butchery," he lamented over the course of several interviews as he handed out drinks and cigars to the reporters. "Hymie was a good kid. He could have got out long ago, taken his and been alive today. When we were in business together in the old days, I got to know him well and used to go often to his room for a friendly visit. Torrio and me made Weiss and O'Banion. When they broke away and went into business for themselves, that was all right with us... But then they began to get nasty. We sent 'em word to stay in their own backyard. But they had the swelled heads and thought they were bigger than we were. Then O'Banion got killed. Right after Torrio was shot – and Torrio knew who shot him – I had a talk with Weiss. 'What do you want to do, get yourself killed before you're thirty?' I said to him. 'You better get yourself some sense while there are a few of us left alive.' He could still have got along with me. But he wouldn't listen to me. Forty times I tried to arrange things so we'd have peace and life would be worth living. Who wants to be tagged around night and day by guards? I don't, for one. There was, and there is, plenty of business for us all and competition needn't be a matter of murder, anyway. But Weiss couldn't be told anything. I suppose you couldn't have told him a week ago that he'd be dead today. There are some reasonable fellows in his outfit, and if they want peace I'm for it now, as I have always been."

One of the reporters asked if Al had any idea who might have killed Hymie Weiss. He shook his head sadly. "I'm sorry Hymie was killed, but I didn't have anything to do with it. I phoned the detective bureau that I'd come in if they wanted me, but they told me they didn't want me. I knew I'd be blamed for it. There's enough business for all of us without killing each other like animals in the street. I don't want to end up in a gutter punctured by machine gun slugs, so why should I kill Weiss?"

The question brought a grunt of disgust from Chief of Detectives Shoemaker when he read the interview in the newspaper. He had his own statement for reporters, one much more succinct than Capone's. "He knows why," Shoemaker said, "and so does everyone else. He had them killed."

Chief Collins agreed. When he was asked why Capone was not arrested for the crime, he replied: "It's a waste of time to arrest him. He's been in before on other murder charges. He always has his alibi."

Hymie Weiss' funeral was a sad affair, not only for his friends, but in comparison to other gangster funerals. A group of his boyhood classmates from St. Malachy's School served as his pallbearers and with the last rites of the church denied to him, he was buried in unconsecrated ground at Mt. Carmel Cemetery, not far from the resting place of his friend, Dion O'Banion. The floral tributes fell far below the usual gangland standards and the only underworld figures in attendance were Vincent Drucci and George Moran, who now ran the gang together, and Max Eisen, the fish and meat market racketeer.

Al Capone was upset.

Some disturbing information had come to light after the death of Hymie Weiss – information that suggested that he had traitors in his midst. He had assumed that Joe Saltis and Frank McErlane were still his allies. The more than 200 saloons that they operated with Dingbat O'Berta had been a major outlet for his beer and whiskey. But it was revealed from the lists of state's witnesses and jury members found in Weiss' possession that his supposed allies had secretly entered into a pact with his enemies. Further investigation by Capone also revealed that Saltis had planned to turn over the supply end of the saloon business to Weiss and the North Side gang.

Capone was angry and usually such a betrayal would have demanded a bloody reprisal. This time, though, Capone, in his eagerness to restore peace among Chicago's gangs and reestablish the territories that Torrio had originally created, decided to overlook it for the moment. But he let the word slip out that he knew what had been going on. He knew this might make his former allies both cautious and nervous at the same time.

The plan succeeded. The suggestion of a new peace treaty came from Joe Saltis. Terrified of what Capone might do now that his arrangements with Weiss had been brought to light, he turned to Dingbat O'Berta for advice. O'Berta consulted Max Eisen, whom the underworld respected as a man of wisdom and experience. It was Eisen's opinion that Saltis' continued good health depended on a general cease-fire, which Eisen offered to try and arrange. He went to first to see Capone's *consigliere,* Tony Lombardo, and asked him to feel out his boss in regards to the situation. Lombardo called Eisen the next day and said that Capone definitely wanted peace. Arrangements were made at the office of Billy Skidmore, ward heeler, court fixer and gambler, for a truce meeting to take place in a suite at the Hotel Sherman, just steps away from both City Hall and police headquarters.

The gang leaders came, as agreed, unarmed and without bodyguards. The Capone delegates included Capone, his brother Ralph, Tony Lombardo, Jake Guzik and Ed Vogel from Cicero. From the North Side came Drucci, Moran, Jack Zuta, who handled their gambling operations, and Frank Foster, an importer of Canadian whiskey. Myles and Klondike O'Donnell were also present, as were Billy Skidmore and Christian "Barney" Bertche, another prominent gambler. While loosely affiliated with the North Side gang, Skidmore and Bertche each ran independent operations. Ralph Sheldon was the only member of his gang on hand and Max Eisen represented the Saltis-McErlane-O'Berta interests.

There was little effort made to keep the meeting a secret. A detective from police headquarters across the street sat in as an observer and reporters, although excluded from the actual meeting, waited in the corridor outside the suite and were kept apprised of all developments. Eisen opened the meeting by appealing to everyone's common sense, explaining how foolish they looked killing each other off. Capone then dominated the meeting and proposed a five-point peace treaty that hearkened back to Torrio's days of power.

1. A general amnesty was to go into effect, ending all previous feuds and grievances.
2. Violence would not be used to settle problems between gangs; arbitration would be used instead.
3. There would be an end to "ribbing," essentially a tool of psychological warfare that spread malicious gossip with the intention of causing friction between rival gangs and gang members.
4. No more stealing customers or encroaching on other gangs' territories.
5. The head of each gang would punish violations committed by his own gang members.

According to the new alignment of territories, the North Side gang would withdraw from all sectors they had invaded after O'Banion's death and confine their activities to the (lucrative) Forty-Second and Forty-Third Wards. There they would have an exclusive franchise on the sale of beer and liquor, as well as gambling. This was no hardship to the gang since this was a heavily populated business and residential area that stretched east to west from Lake Michigan to the Chicago River and north and south from Belden Avenue to Wacker Drive. The Saltis-McErlane gang and the Sheldon gang divided equally the Southwest Side of Chicago, an area about three miles square, lying between the lake and the river. Skidmore and Bertche would operate their gambling houses as before, but now under Capone's jurisdiction. The O'Donnells were under a probation of sorts and they were not assigned any territory to speak of. In view of their various grievances against Capone, he wanted to make sure they adhered to the terms of the treaty before giving them any more territory than they already had. This new division left Capone nearly all of Chicago below Madison Street, a domain that contained almost 20,000 speakeasies and only he and his top men knew how many roadhouses, gambling dens and brothels.

Capone told reporters later that the new treaty had come about because no real business was being done. "We're making a shooting gallery out of a great business," he complained, "and nobody's profiting from it." There was plenty of beer business for everyone, so why kill each other over it? He also added that one of the main reasons for his new attitude was paternal love. "I wanted to stop all that because I couldn't stand hearing my little kid ask why I didn't stay home. I had been living at the Hawthorne Inn for fourteen months. He's been sick for three years – mastoid infection and operations – and I've got to take care of him and his mother. If it wasn't [sic] for him, I'd have said: 'To hell with you fellows! We'll shoot it out.' But I couldn't say that, knowing it might mean they'd bring me home some night punctured by machine gun fire. And I couldn't see why those fellows would want to die that way either."

Everyone at the conference accepted the terms of the new treaty with little argument. They shook hands and made peace and promised that if anything happened between them, they would talk about it instead of shooting. The meeting left the hotel and adjourned to Bella Napoli Café for a peace celebration. It became a night of ghastly revelry or, as one reporter called it, "a feast of ghouls." Arm in arm, back-slapping and howling with laughter, former enemies recalled how they had tried to murder one another. They chuckled over captives they had tortured and they boasted of old murders to the friends of their victims. As wine flowed, the conversation turned maudlin. There were expressions of remorse, pleas for forgiveness, sentimental tears and oaths of eternal friendship.

The violence was over, they all swore – but one has to wonder how many of those present knew that the promises would never last?

On November 7, Hymie Weiss' last plans came to posthumous fruition. The jury acquitted Joe Saltis and Lefty Koncil, which meant that the money got into the right hands whether Weiss was dead or not. "I expected a different verdict on the evidence presented," said presiding Judge Harry B. Miller in an outrageous understatement. The prosecutor in the case was a bit more blunt. "A number of unusual and significant circumstances arose both prior to and during the prosecution of the trial," he said. "Prior to the trial, two of the state's important witnesses disappeared, the immediate members of their family either refusing or being unable to give any information or clue as to their whereabouts." He also mentioned the discovery of the witness lists in Hymie Weiss' safe and their obvious implication. He concluded, "In addition to these significant facts, certain of the state's witnesses testified to having been threatened with violence in the event they testified against the defendants, and having been approached with offers of bribery for either withholding their testimony or testifying falsely."

In another example of the blurring between Chicago politics and crime, Christmas came one day early for two of the most notorious inmates at Joliet Correctional Center – Scalise and Anselmi. On December 24, the Illinois Surpreme Court granted the two killers – who had served seven months of their fourteen-year sentence – a new trial on their lawyer's pleas that if they were guilty of murder, the sentence was "but a mockery of justice" and if guilty of only manslaughter, "an injustice." They were released on bail awaiting a third trial.

They returned to a Chicago underworld that was unnervingly peaceful. "Just like the old days," Capone boasted to a reporter. "They [the O'Banion gang] stay on the North Side and I stay in Cicero and if we meet on the street, we say 'hello' and shake hands. Better, ain't it?"

13. THE RETURN OF "BIG BILL"

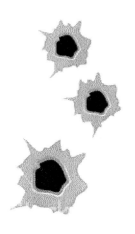

In the fall of 1926, the "best friend" of Chicago gangsters returned to politics and got his name added to the Republican mayoral primary ballot. William "Big Bill" Thompson was back from political exile, although he had never managed to disappear completely from the public eye after his defeat by reform candidate Dever in 1923. That same summer, he had made headlines with a fairly typical Thompson antic – a planned yachting expedition to the South Seas to photograph mudskippers, a fish that can live on land for long periods, jump as high as three feet and climb trees. The idea had been presented to Thompson by a press agent for the cypress wood industry, whose clients were happy to construct a boat for the expedition, which was christened *Big Bill*. The craft boasted a cypress figurehead that had been carved in the likeness of the corpulent former mayor. Thompson gained the additional support of the Fish Fans Club, which he had founded the year before to "urge and encourage the propagation of fish in American waters." In early July, the *Big Bill*, carrying an assortment of politicians, businessmen, beer-swilling clowns and assorted cronies, sailed down the Chicago River and into Lake Michigan, cheered on by thousands of people who lined the shore. The boat never left American waters and Thompson abandoned the trip about halfway to New Orleans. The man was a walking punch-line, but people loved him.

After arriving home, he began to slowly rebuild his political capital, heartened by the fact that Chicago was not a city that wanted reform as badly as the current mayor wanted to offer it. He campaigned for Governor Small's re-election and made peace overtures to State's Attorney Crowe, who accepted them, despite his earlier statement that "any man interested in protecting gambling and vice I refuse to travel along with, politically or otherwise."

Thompson was back on the ballot for the 1926 Republican primary, running against Edward R. Litsinger, a member of Senator Deneen's faction, and Dr. John Dill Robertson, a former health commissioner and a defector from the Thompson ranks. His opponents inspired him to spout some of his most classic rhetoric. Reacting to their accusations that he colluded with criminals, Thompson fired back:

"Litsinger is dry and Robertson is so dry that he never even takes a bath. The Doc used to boast that he hadn't taken a bath in years... The Doc is slinging mud. I'm not descending to personalities, but you should watch Doc Robertson eat in restaurants – eggs in his whiskers, soup on his vest. It's enough to turn your stomach! Imagine anyone thinking of electing a mayor with a name like John Dill Pickle Robertson! I'm not a mudslinger but the papers have been saying things about me that I can't let pass. And Ed Litsinger's been making statements about me. I've told you and I'll tell you again that he's the biggest liar that was ever a candidate for mayor. And you know what else? He plays handball in the semi-nude! That's right, with only a little pair of pants on. I know one thing. You won't find Bill Thompson having his picture taken in the semi-nude!"

Believe it or not, the Republican majority ate it up and chose Thompson by the widest margin of votes ever recorded in a Chicago

EDWARD R. LITSINGER

Republican primary. This was done to the disgust of the *Chicago Tribune,* which griped, "Thompson is a buffoon in a tommyrot factory."

At the campaign rallies that followed, the crowds chanted an anthem that was penned by a former vaudeville tune writer name Milton Weil. It celebrated one of the two major planks in the Thompson platform:

> *America first and last and always!*
> *Our hearts are loyal. Our faith is strong.*
> *American first and last and always!*
> *Our shrine and homeland, tho' right or wrong.*
> *United we stand for God and country,*
> *At no one's command we'll ever be.*
> *America first and last and always!*
> *Sweet land of freedom and liberty.*

Wrapping himself in an American flag, Thompson shouted back to his audiences, "This is the issue! What was good enough for George Washington is good enough for Bill Thompson! I want to make the King of England keep his snoot out of America! American first, and last, and always! If you want to keep the American flag from bowing down before King George of England, I'm your man. If you want to invite King George and help his friends, I'm not. America first! The American who says 'America second' speaks the tongue of Benedict Arnold and Aaron Burr."

At this point, the mystified reader may be trying to recall the problems that the United States was having with Great Britain in the late 1920s and the possible threat of invasion that Chicago faced from our allies across the Atlantic. If you are unaware of these issues, you're not alone. Somehow, though, Thompson managed to turn his dislike for the English into a major plank in his campaign platform – insinuating that the king and his minions were somehow influencing the education of Chicago school

THOMPSON PULLED OUT ALL STOPS FOR THE CAMPAIGN. (LEFT) DRESSED AS AN AVIATOR FOR A BARNSTORMING APPEARANCE AND (ABOVE) AS A COWBOY ON THE STREETS OF DOWNTOWN CHICAGO.

students. He claimed that the history books used in Chicago schools were partial to the English and he attacked Dever's school superintendent, William McAndrew, and promised to fire him if he was elected. "Read these histories for yourselves," Thompson urged his followers. "The ideals you were taught to revere, the great Americans you were taught to cherish as examples of self-sacrificing devotion to human liberty, are subtly sneered at and placed in a false light, so that your children may blush with shame when studying the history of the country. These men and others falsified facts to glorify England and vilify America. When I went out of office, Washington fell out and the King of England fell in... and McAndrew is his lackey. Didn't he refuse to let our schoolchildren contribute pennies to preserve Old Ironsides? You know why? Because Old Ironsides kicked the hell out of every British ship she met and the King of England wouldn't like to have us preserve that ship. So he gave orders to his stooge, this McAndrew, and our children were not permitted to solicit pennies and preserve a priceless heritage. It's up to us, the red-blooded men and women of Chicago, to stand fast until this city is rid of the pro-British rats who are poisoning our wells of historical truth."

It's likely that Al Capone felt this plank in Thompson's platform was as ridiculous as most people did, but the second issue enlisted his wholehearted enthusiasm. "I'm wetter than the middle of the Atlantic Ocean," Thompson loudly bragged, in open violation of Prohibition. "When I'm elected, we'll not only re-open places these people [the Dever administration] have closed, but we'll have 10,000 new ones."

That prospect was so attractive to Capone that he contributed $260,000 to Thompson's campaign fund and applied every form of bribery and terrorism imaginable on his behalf. While Capone was credited in the campaign with inventing the famous tongue-in-cheek slogan, "Vote early and vote often," the phrase first appeared in 1859 in a letter about American voting practices that was reprinted in *The Times* of London. While its humor would have appealed to both Thompson and Capone, and later, to longtime Chicago Mayor Richard J. Daley, none of them actually coined the phrase.

In late 1926, Capone was temporarily distracted from the hijinks of Thompson's campaign by the resumption of gang warfare in the city. Hilary Clements, a beer runner who worked for Ralph Sheldon, had been selling his beer to saloons inside the Saltis-McErlane territory. Instead of using arbitration to deal with

CAPONE FRIEND, THEODORE "THE GREEK" ANTON, WHO RAN CAPONE'S FAVORITE RESTAURANT AT THE HAWTHORNE INN.

POLICE DETECTIVES LOOK OVER THE SPOT WHERE ANTON'S BODY WAS FOUND, ENCASED IN QUICKLIME.

this breach of the Hotel Sherman treaty, as he was supposed to do, Saltis simply ordered Clements killed. On December 30, a shotgun blast to the man's face ended a peace that had lasted for seventy days. Sheldon complained to Capone, who reluctantly agreed that stringent disciplinary measures had to be taken if the treaty was going to be preserved. As a result, Lefty Koncil and another Saltis gunman, Charlie "Big Hayes" Hubacek, were killed on March 11. The North Side O'Banion men, meanwhile, restless under the restraints that had been imposed on them by the treaty and unable to reconcile themselves to Capone being the top boss in the city, took advantage of the moment by renewing their attacks against him. They struck first at a man that had nothing to do with organized crime, but one whom Capone treasured as a friend.

Theodore "The Greek" Anton ran a popular restaurant upstairs from the Hawthorne Smoke Shop in Cicero. He adored Capone and never tired of telling people what a good man, faithful friend and generous benefactor he was. As an instance of the gangster's kindheartedness, he liked to recall an incident with a newsboy who came into the restaurant one winter night, his body frozen with the cold. "How many papers you got left, kid?" Capone asked him. "About fifty," the discouraged boy replied. Capone gave him $20, and instructed, "Throw them on the floor and then run along home to your mother."

On the night of January 26, 1927, Capone was eating a late dinner in Anton's restaurant. Anton got up from the booth where the two men were chatting and went to the entrance to greet some customers. He never came back to Capone's table. O'Banion gunmen, waiting outside, pulled him into their car and drove away. When Capone found out what happened, he burst into tears and sat in the booth for the rest of the night, weeping inconsolably. Anton's body was later found encased in quicklime. He had been tortured and shot.

In March, Capone took a short trip to Hot Springs, Arkansas. Vincent Drucci, who somehow learned of the vacation, followed him there and made an attempt on his life. He fired a shotgun from a passing car, but missed.

As election day, April 5, drew closer, Capone's suite at the Hotel Metropole became a secret annex to the Thompson campaign headquarters on the sixteenth floor of the Hotel Sherman. Messages and money passed between the two suites, as did the players in the whole farce, from union men to outright gangsters. Jack Zuta, who ran a string of

DEPUTY CHIEF JOHN STEGE LOOKS OVER THE REVOLVER THAT WAS USED TO KILL VINCENT DRUCCI.

POLICE DETECTIVES GATHER AROUND THE CAR IN WHICH DRUCCI WAS SHOT TO DEATH.

whorehouses for Capone was also a member of the William Hale Thompson Republican Club, and contributed $50,000 to the campaign fund. On election day, Capone, working the telephone, issued orders to enforcers scattered throughout the city, directing shootings, beatings and kidnappings – anything to ensure that Thompson won the election.

The first act of violence was not one that was planned by Capone, but it's likely that he was pleased by it. O'Banion's men, like most gangsters in Chicago, were firmly behind Thompson and his wide-open policy. On the day before the election, a group of them, led by Vincent Drucci, broke into the offices of the Forty-Second Ward's Alderman Dorsey R. Crowe, a backer of Mayor Dever, with plans for mayhem. Crowe was out, so they beat up his secretary, knocked over filing cabinets and broke windows. The police caught up with Drucci that same afternoon. Drucci became enraged when one of them, Detective Dan Healy, laid hands on him. From the back of the squad car, Drucci lurched forward, swearing revenge, and tried to

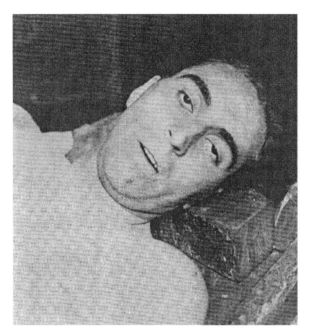

DRUCCI ON THE SLAB AT THE MORGUE

get hold of Healy's gun. The detective managed to wrestle it it away from him, rammed the revolver into Drucci's side and pulled the trigger four times.

"Murder?" Chief of Detectives Shoemaker barked when a lawyer retained by Drucci's widow demanded an investigation. "We're having a medal struck for Healy." Any charges of wrongdoing disappeared and the police managed to rid Capone of one of his deadliest – and most reckless – enemies.

Drucci, like his friends, was buried in unconsecrated ground at Mount Carmel Cemetery. Although he was denied the last rites of the church, he was accorded military honors by the American Legion, to which he belonged, having served in World War I. A squad of uniformed Legionnaires fired off a salute over his flag-draped coffin and a bugler blew taps. Capone, who sent one of the showiest floral offerings on display, put in an appearance at the graveside.

Mayor Dever's chief of police knew that election day violence was inevitable but did what he could to prevent it by assigning more than 5,000 men to special duties. A police detail guarded every polling place, while detectives in squad cars, outfitted with Tommy guns and tear gas, patrolled the nearby streets. The day turned out to be exceptionally peaceful – for a Chicago election, that is. Only two bombs were thrown, both of them at Forty-Second Ward Democratic clubs, only two election officials beaten and kidnapped and only a few dozen Dever supporters prevented from voting by men with guns. Only one polling booth and private home were shot up.

Thompson easily carried the election, winning by more than 83,000 votes. In the ballroom of the Hotel Sherman that night, he jumped up onto a chair and waving a ten-gallon hat, roared in a drunken voice, "I thank you one and all. I thank you. Tell 'em, cowboys! Tell 'em! I told you I'd ride 'em high and wide!"

Thompson's return to City Hall brought about another era of bloodshed, corruption and violence and it made an earlier Chicago seem like a place of peaceful law and order. His first appointments set the tone of the administration. For chief of police, he brought Michael Hughes back from obscurity in the highway patrol department. As a cousin of State's Attorney Crowe, Hughes had resigned as chief of detectives during Dever's term after he was reprimanded for attending a banquet in honor of Dion O'Banion. For city comptroller, Thompson chose his former chief of police, Charles Fitzmorris, who once publicly admitted: "Sixty percent of my police are in the bootleg business." For city sealer, the official in charge of weights and measures, he appointed Daniel Serritella, who was Capone's agent on the city council. Dr. Arnold Kegel, the Thompson's family physician became the new health commissioner.

Soon after the election, a *Daily News* reporter asked Deputy Police Commissioner William P. Russell how it was that numbers racketeers were operating openly in the city. Russell replied, "Mayor Thompson was elected on the open town platform, I assume that the people knew what they wanted when they voted for him. I haven't had any order from downtown to interfere in the policy racket and until I get such orders, you can bet that I'm going to keep my hands off. Personally, I don't propose to get mixed up in any jam that will send me to the sticks. If the downtown authorities want this part of the city closed up, the downtown authorities will have to issue an order. I'm certainly not going to attempt it on my own." No such order ever came but Russell's way of thinking earned him many admirers among the "downtown authorities." He eventually succeeded Hughes as the chief of police.

Within a month after the election, Capone had expanded his headquarters at the Hotel Metropole to fifty rooms. He moved back into Chicago, reserving the Hawthorne Inn in Cicero as a secondary base of operations, and set to work enlarging his empire. With the reformers finally out of office, Capone was ready and willing to get back to business. The Metropole was the perfect location from which to do it. The hotel was a landmark in Chicago's First Ward and, being convenient to both City Hall and the Police Department, it was very accessible to the steady stream of administrators, cops and politicians who were easily bought and paid for. It was a convenient spot for corrupt police officers to drop in and collect their second paycheck, the one from Capone. They earned rewards for such services as escorting liquor shipments, warning of raids that were about to be staged to pacify the public reform movement and furnishing Capone's gunmen with officially stamped cards that read: "To the Police Department – You will extend the courtesies of the department to the bearer." Crimes committed by Capone's men were either ignored or entered in the records as "unsolved." Capone estimated that he paid as much as thirty million dollars a year to police officials in various small towns and the city. His own payroll listed roughly half of the entire Chicago Police Department.

In addition to the cops, the hotel swarmed with politicians, city inspectors and other officials who always had their hands out. Capone welcomed them, not only with cash but also with a speakeasy in the lobby that was operated by a ward boss, and with obliging women who roamed the hotel. He had free reign to do pretty much whatever he wanted. The hotel management opened a private saloon for Capone and his men on the upper floors and gave them storage space in the basement for their own private stock of wines and liquors.

HOTEL METROPOLE -- CAPONE MOVES BACK INTO CHICAGO

Mobsters kept their favorite girls in suites and several rooms were turned over to gambling. Capone himself was a compulsive – and unlucky – gambler and seldom staked less than $1,000 on a roll of the dice or a spin of the roulette wheel. At the horses and dog tracks he never backed his choice to place, only to win. Because of his heavy gambling losses and his extravagant lifestyle, he never accumulated a great fortune – but he certainly had one to spend.

In May, Capone was chosen to be part of the welcoming committee for the Italian flier Commander Francesco de Pinedo, who was circling the globe as Mussolini's goodwill ambassador. He landed his hydroplane on Lake Michigan and came ashore at Grant Park to meet the committee. This group consisted of the Italian consul Italo Canini; Ugo Galli, the president of the city's *Fascisti*; Collector of Customs Anthony Czarnecki; officers from the Sixth Air Corps; Mayor Thompson's personal representative, Judge Bernard Barasa; and Al Capone. Capone was among the first to shake de Pinedo's hand when he stepped ashore. Some Chicagoans questioned the addition of Capone to the welcoming committee – which essentially represented the people of Chicago. The police lamely replied that they were expecting an anti-Fascist demonstration and hoped the presence of Capone could prevent it turning into a riot. The expected "riot" never happened and the few demonstrators who showed up were orderly.

In June, the third trial of Scalise and Anselmi, to whom Capone had been giving money and legal assistance since they had killed Detectives Walsh and Olson two years before, finally began. The familiar problem of seating a jury – more than 100 people got themselves excused – delayed the trial more than a week. Scalise took the witness stand on June 22 and admitted that he had fired a single bullet at the detectives. The burden of his attorney's summation was that his clients had acted in self-defense against "unwarranted police aggression." The jury bought this preposterous argument and voted not guilty.

"There's nothing more to be done," Detective Walsh's widow told reporters. "My husband and his friend were killed by these men who now have a crowd waiting to shake their hand. I give up."

Capone threw a banquet to celebrate the acquittal. Vintage champagne, imported from Canada at $20 per bottle, flowed freely as toast after toast was offered to the jury who allowed the guests of honor to go free. More than 100 celebrants jammed the dining room, elbow to elbow with the elite of the Little Italy underworld. The life of the party was an arrogant, strutting Sicilian gunman, a crony of Scalise and Anselmi, named Giuseppe Giunta, who was nicknamed "Hop Toad" because of his nimbleness on the dance floor. The party reached a climax in a mock battle with whooping guests using popping champagne corks for missiles.

As a grinning Capone looked out over the drenched and drunken scene, he could hardly have imagined that three of his guests – Hop Toad Giunta, Scalise and Anselmi – would soon join in a conspiracy to destroy him.

14. "KILL CAPONE!"

JOE AIELLO

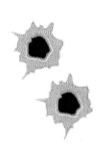

Trouble had been brewing, so to speak, among the liquor stills of Little Italy for some time. The Gennas had been replaced by a ruthless boss named Joseph Aiello, who, along with his eight brothers and innumerable cousins, easily took over the territory. Aiello was a squat, distasteful man with ruthless ambitions. He lived lavishly in a three-story mansion, but its regal appointments were all for show. What appeared to be leather-bound books lining the walls of the library were actually hollow imitations, hiding a store of arms and explosives. Aiello was violent and bloodthirsty, much like the Gennas before him but in his case, he hated Al Capone.

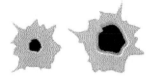

When the antipathy started is unknown, but dislike turned to hatred when Tony Lombardo, with Capone's backing, attained the coveted presidency of the Unione Siciliane. Joe Aiello had been the runner-up. For years, Aiello and Lombardo had been profitably associated both as powers in the Unione Siciliane and in the cheese import, bakery, brokerage commission, liquor cooking and other businesses. Political contention within the Unione damaged the relationship and it was wounded beyond recovery when Lombardo won the presidential election. Bent upon eliminating Lombardo and Capone, Aiello formed an alliance with the North Side O'Banion men, now captained by George Moran, and with West Side gangs under Billy Skidmore and Barney Bertsche.

Aiello put out the word that he was offering $50,000 to anyone who killed Capone. Between the spring and fall of 1927, four free-lance, out-of-town gunmen came to Chicago – Tony Torchio from New York, Tony Russo and Vincent Spicuzza from St. Louis and Sam Valente from Cleveland. None of these killers lasted long after they showed up in Chicago. Each of them was found shot to death with a nickel clutched in his hand – the signature of Jack McGurn. During the same period, four local Aiello men were also gunned down and a fifth was killed, tied up, stuffed in a sack and left in a ditch. McGurn, along with another Capone gunman, Orchell De Grazio, were arrested after they were identified as being seen near the ditch. With no other evidence, they were released.

Bullets didn't seem to work, so Aiello tried poison. Knowing that Capone frequented Joe Esposito's Bella Napoli Café, he offered the chef $35,000 if he would lace the mobster's minestrone with prussic acid. The chef agreed and then gave up the plot to Capone.

Faced with eleven unsolved gang murders in less than six months, the new chief of detectives, William O'Connor, felt he should make some sort of gesture

NEW CHIEF OF DETECTIVES WILLIAM O'CONNOR ENCOURAGED THE MEN OF THE NEWLY FORMED ARMORED CAR UNIT TO GO OUT AND HUNT DOWN GANGSTERS ON THE STREET -- AND SHOOT TO KILL IF POSSIBLE!

to reassure the public. He announced that he was organizing a special armored car unit that would be tasked with wiping out gangsters. He stated that he needed volunteers from within the ranks of the police department who had fought overseas during the war and knew how to handle a machine gun. After his squad was formed, he issued an order of amazing irresponsibility: "Men, the war is on. We've got to show that society and the police department, and not a bunch of dirty rats, are running this town. It is the wish of the people of Chicago that you hunt these criminals down and kill them without mercy. Your cars are equipped with machine guns and you will meet the enemies of society on equal terms. See to it that they don't have you pushing up daisies. Shoot first and shoot to kill. If you kill a notorious feudist, you will get a handsome reward and win promotion. If you meet a car containing bandits, pursue them and fire. When I arrive on the scene, my hopes will be fulfilled if you have shot off the top of the car and killed everyone inside of it."

Chief O'Connor did not say what he wanted the men to do if their machine gun forays onto the streets of Chicago managed to mow down any innocent bystanders.

On November 22, an anonymous tip led some of O'Connor's detectives to an apartment building that rented flats by the week. It was located directly across the street from Tony Lombardo's house at 442 West Washington Boulevard, north of Cicero. The detectives found an array of machine guns trained on the Lombardo house, where Tony lived with his wife and two small children. The apartment was deserted but another lead took the cops to 7002 North Western Avenue, where they found a hidden supply of dynamite. The missing occupant of the place left behind a key to the Rex Hotel, which was farther north on Ashland Avenue. Making their third call of the day, detectives broke in on Angelo Lo Mantio, a young gunman from Milwaukee, along with Joe Aiello and two of his cousins. The whole lot was rounded up and they were immediately taken to the detective bureau. Lo Mantio quickly broke under questioning and confessed that Aiello had brought him to Chicago to kill Capone and Lombardo. He was supposed to gun down Lombardo at his home and then kill Capone from ambush on South Clark Street. Capone often stopped into a cigar store at 311 South Clark, which was across the street from the Hotel Atlantic. Lo Mantio had a high-powered rifle waiting in the window of Room 302.

One of the cops on Capone's payroll placed a call and informed the mobster that Lo Mantio and Aiello had been taken to the detective bureau lockup. Within an hour of the cell door clanging shut behind them, several taxi cabs pulled up in front of the station and a number of men got out. A policeman who glanced out the window first mistook them for detectives bringing suspects into the thirteen-story building for questioning, but none of them came inside. The men scattered instead, some to the street corners and others to side streets, vanishing into alleys and doorways. A few moments later, three of the men started toward the bureau's main entrance. One of them dipped into his coat and shifted an automatic from a holster into a side pocket. As the startled policeman recognized Louis "Little New York" Campagna, an ugly bruiser whom Capone had recently added to his corps of bodyguards, the cop realized that Capone had sent his men to kill Aiello. They had surrounded the building and were about to lay siege to it. His warning cry sent a dozen detectives out into the street. They seized the trio, which had almost reached the front door, disarmed and handcuffed them, and hustled them into the lockup. They were placed in the cell next to Aiello. A detective who spoke and understood Sicilian had himself placed in a cell nearby, posing as a prisoner so that he could spy on whatever happened between the Capone gunmen and Aiello.

Campagna strolled into the cell as if he owned it and leaned on the bars between his cell and the one where Aiello was incarcerated. "You're dead, friend, you're dead," he hissed in Sicilian. "You won't get up to the end of the street still walking."

Aiello, his bluster vanished after hearing the other man's words, replied in a quavering voice. "Can't we settle this? Give me fourteen days and I'll sell my stores, my house and everything and quit Chicago for good. Can't we settle it? Think of my wife and baby."

Campagna sneered at him. "You dirty rat! You've broken faith with us twice now. You started this. We'll finish it."

Hours later, Aiello's attorney managed to get his client released but Aiello refused to leave the station. He knew that Capone's men were waiting for him outside, watching for him to set foot in the street. Aiello went to Chief O'Connor and begged him for protection. O'Connor, wary of the newspaper reporters that had gathered at the bureau when word spread about what was going on, gave him a sarcastic response. "Sure," he laughed, "I'll give you police protection

LOUIS "LITTLE NEW YORK" CAMPAGNA

– all the way to New York and onto a boat. The sooner you go, the better. You can't bring your feud ideas here and get away with it, so you'd better start back. You'll get no police protection around Chicago from me." But O'Connor relented when Aiello's wife and small son arrive at the bureau, brought there by his lawyer. He either starting feeling sorry for Aiello, or received a generous pay-off, no one knows for sure. Regardless, he allowed a pair of policemen to escort the family to a taxi.

With his brothers, Tony and Dominic, Aiello left Chicago that night. They went to Trenton, New Jersey, and, except for a couple of secret visits back to Chicago, stayed there for almost two years. But they never backed down on their plans to kill Al Capone.

Capone couldn't have cared less, or at least that's how he acted. After Aiello fled the city, he spoke to reporters, "When I was told that Joey Aiello wanted to make peace, but that he wanted fourteen days to settle his affairs, I was ready to agree. I'm willing to talk to anybody, anyplace, to bring about a settlement. I don't want no trouble. I don't want bloodshed. But I'm going to protect myself. When someone strikes at me, I will strike back."

He reminded the reporters, "I'm the boss. I'm going to continue to run things. They've been putting the roscoe [gun] on me for a good many years and I'm still healthy and happy. Don't let anyone kid you into thinking that I can be run out of town. I haven't run yet and I'm not going to. When we get through with this mob, there won't be any opposition and I'll still be doing business."

But what Capone failed to take into consideration was Mayor Thompson's thirst for power.

When word reached Chicago that President Calvin Coolidge didn't plan to run for re-election in 1928, "Big Bill" Thompson, emboldened by his Chicago, mob-bought popularity, saw no reason why he shouldn't make a run for the White House. He was, unfortunately, starting to believe his own press. With a conglomeration of publicity agents, drinking buddies and various hangers-on, he set out in the fall of 1927 on a cross-country train tour to see how the rest of the nation, outside of Chicago, reacted to him. At each station, his press agents touted him as the founder of the America First movement and distributed leaflets and buttons while a quartet sang the tuneless "America First and Last and Always" from the rear platform of the train. Newspaper publisher William Randolph Hearst welcomed Thompson at his California ranch, likely knowing a good story when he saw one. When the mayor returned to Chicago, State's Attorney Crowe, now firmly set up in the Thompson camp, issued a proclamation: "He is a great American. He has done more for Chicago than anything that has happened in my lifetime. And he has, by this trip, reduced the prejudice that has existed in some localities, created by unfair critics of Chicago." Some suggested that Thompson had only managed to show those "localities" that Chicago was not only corrupt, but stupid, too. Only a city with no morals, or filled with idiots, could have elected such a buffoon as its mayor.

With aims toward the highest political office in the land, Thompson didn't have to be smart to know that Capone was a liability to his campaign. The mobster's conspicuous presence

CAPONE LOVED GIVING PRESS CONFERENCES AND TREATED THE REPORTERS LIKE THE FRIENDS AND ADMIRERS THAT SO MANY OF THEM WERE.

in the city, especially with his ties to the mayor's office, would certainly become known all over the country. So, with a few words to Chief of Police Hughes, the official treatment of the gang leader changed from indulgence to harassment. His gunmen began to be arrested on trumped-up charges, his breweries, brothels and gambling dens were repeatedly raided and Capone himself was followed everywhere by marked police vehicles.

Eventually, Capone grew tired of the treatment. On December 5, he held a press conference at the Hotel Metropole and announced that he was leaving Chicago for St. Petersburg, Florida. "Let the worthy citizens of Chicago get their liquor the best way that they can," he said. "I'm sick of the job. It's a thankless one and full of grief."

He was being forced into exile, he told the reporters, by misunderstanding and injustice – all because he was giving the public what it wanted. "I violate the Prohibition law, sure. Who doesn't? The only difference is that I take more chances that the man who drinks a cocktail before dinner and a flock of highballs after it. But he's just as much a violator as I am."

Even though he had bought and paid for dozens of them over the years, he couldn't help but express his distaste for corrupt politicians. "There's one thing worse than a crook and that's a crooked man in a big political job. A man who pretends he's enforcing the law and is really making dough out of someone breaking it, a self-respecting hoodlum hasn't any use for that kind of fellow – he buys them like he'd buy any other article necessary to his trade, but he hates them in his heart."

Capone couldn't stop talking and the reporters ate it up, egging him on and acting like the mobster's biggest fans. Most of them had benefited from writing about Capone in one way or another, whether it was from free drinks, free entry to one of his clubs, or merely from getting a good story. Capone was always encouraged by the press' interest in him. He continued talking, even though he knew as well as the reporters did that much of his statements were outright lies. "I have never been convicted of a crime not have I ever directed anyone else to commit a crime. I have never had anything to do with a vice resort. I don't pose as a plaster saint, but I never killed anyone. I never stuck up a man in my life. Neither did any of my agents ever rob anybody or burglarize any homes while they worked for me. They might have pulled plenty of jobs before they came with me or after they left me, but not while they were in my outfit," he said.

Capone was not a criminal, he stated, he was a humanitarian for his fellow Chicagoans. "I've been spending the best years of my life as a public benefactor. I've given people the light pleasures, shown them a good time. All I get is abuse – the existence of a hunted man. I'm called a killer. Ninety percent of the people of Cook County drink and gamble and my offense has been to furnish them with those amusements. Whatever else they may say, my booze has been good and my games have been on the square. Public service is my motto."

Poor, misunderstood Capone was packing up and leaving town, he told the admiring representatives of the press. He was sick of being treated poorly and he didn't know when he would return to Chicago, if ever. He added sarcastically, "I guess murder will stop now. There won't be any more booze. You won't be able to find a crap game even, let alone a roulette wheel or a faro game. I guess Mike Hughes won't need his 3,000 extra cops, after all. The coppers won't have to lay all the gang murders on me now. Maybe they'll find a new hero for the headlines. It would be a shame, wouldn't it, if while I was away they'd forget about me and find a new gangland chief?"

Capone shook his head and smiled ironically. He waved a hand to the reporters and left with only a few more words, "I leave with gratitude to my friends who have stood by me through this unjust ordeal and forgiveness to my enemies. I wish them all a Merry Christmas and a Happy New Year."

Capone's trip was supposed to take him to Florida, but at the last minute, he changed his itinerary and went to Los Angeles with his wife, their son, and two bodyguards. Rumor had it that he went to the West Coast to look into the possibility of expansion. Los Angeles had traditionally been largely free of organized crime. There was plenty of drinking, gambling and girls, especially with the Hollywood movie colony in full swing, but for the most part, there was no one in charge of really running things. Capone hoped to change all that, but when he arrived in Los Angeles, he got a big surprise. There was little organized crime in L.A. because it simply wasn't tolerated by the cops, who were as brutal and hardened as the most violent lawbreakers.

Capone registered at the Hotel Biltmore under his favorite alias, Al Brown, but was recognized and news of his visit was plastered on the front pages of the local newspapers. Barely twenty-four hours after

NOTORIOUSLY CAMERA SHY MAE CAPONE USUALLY STAYED IN THE BACKGROUND OF HER HUSBAND'S LIFE. SHE LOVED AL DEARLY BUT LATER TOLD HER SON THAT HIS FATHER BROKE HER HEART.

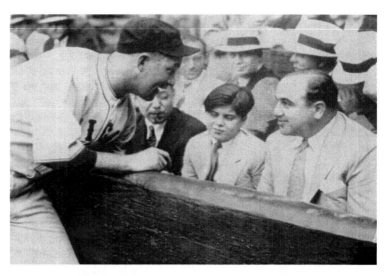

AL WITH SONNY AT A BASEBALL GAME. THE SHY, WITHDRAWN AND HEARING-IMPAIRED BOY WOULD LIVE IN HIS FATHER'S SHADOW THROUGHOUT HIS ENTIRE LIFE.

the Capones arrived, they were kicked out of the Biltmore. Soon after, he was visited by a contingent of local police officers, who frankly told him that he was not welcome in the city. The Los Angeles chief of police gave him twelve hours to get out of town.

He planned to go back to Chicago, despite the fact that in the Windy City, Chief Hughes told the press: "The police drove Capone out of Chicago. He cannot come back." But shortly before climbing onto an eastbound Santa Fe train on December 13, he defiantly stated, "I'm a property owner and a taxpayer in Chicago. I can certainly return to my own home."

At Chillicothe, Illinois, a reporter from the *Herald-Examiner* boarded the train and rode in Capone's private drawing room as far as Joliet. He found the gang boss was feeling depressed. "It's pretty tough," Capone said, "when a citizen with an unblemished record must be hounded from his home by the very policemen whose salaries are paid, at least in part, from the victim's pocket. You might say that every policeman in Chicago gets some of his bread and butter from the taxes I pay. And yet they want to throw me in jail for nothing when I seek to visit my own home and see my wife and little son. I am feeling very bad, very bad. I don't know what all the fuss is about. How would you feel if the police, paid to protect you acted towards you like they do towards me?"

Readers could practically hear the violins playing at this point but Capone's next words were defiant.

"I'm going back to Chicago. Nobody can stop me. I've got a right to be there. They can't throw me out of Chicago unless they shoot me in the head. I've never done anything wrong. Nobody can ever say that I did anything wrong. They arrest me. They search me. They lock me up. They charge me with all the crimes there are when they get me into court. The only charge they can book against me is disorderly conduct, and the judge dismisses even that because there isn't any evidence to support it. The police know they haven't got one black mark against my name and yet they publicly announce that they won't let me live in my own home. What kind of justice is that? Well, I've been the goat for a long time. It's got to stop sometime and it might as well be now. I've got my back to the wall. I'm going to fight."

Capone knew the police would be waiting for him at the train station in Chicago, so he telephoned ahead and instructed his brother, Ralph, to meet him with a car in Joliet. But the Joliet police were also waiting. Ralph and the three gunmen that he brought with him had been careless. They showed up at the station in Joliet on December 16, an hour before the Santa Fe train pulled in. They hung around the depot and a policeman on duty noticed the bulges in their coats. He took them to the station house and they were charged with carrying concealed weapons. When Capone and his bodyguards stepped off the train, Joliet's Chief of Police John Corcoran was waiting to greet them. "You're Al Capone," he said.

"Pleased to meet you," Capone replied genially. As Corcoran relieved him of two revolvers, Capone suggested, "You may want some ammunition, too. These are no good to me now," he said as he handed over two cartridge clips.

Mae and Sonny Capone were allowed to continue on the train to Chicago, but Al was taken to the police station. He was lodged in a cell with two dirty, tattered derelicts. "Pay their fine and take them away," he imperiously told the warden. "They bother me." He authorized the jail officials to deduct the men's fines from the wad of cash totaling almost $3,000 that was in his pocket when he was arrested.

Capone didn't remain behind bars for long. That afternoon, two of his attorneys and about 25 gunmen, arrived from Chicago and posted bond for Al, Ralph, and the bodyguards. That evening, Capone slipped quietly into the city, where he dined with Jake Guzik in a local restaurant and then retired early to his Prairie Avenue home. He was in bed asleep at the same time that Chief Hughes was betting a reporter the price of a new hat that Capone wouldn't dare show his face in Chicago.

"My orders still stand," Hughes said. "He's to be taken to jail every time he shows himself."

This state of affairs only lasted for a short time. As soon as it became apparent to "Big Bill" Thompson that he didn't stand a chance of winning a presidential election, he lost interest in harassing Capone. Even so, he refused to admit that he had been deterred from running. "I don't want to be president," Thompson said in a face-saving speech. "I'm a peace-loving man and I'm afraid if I were president I'd plunge this country into war, for I'd say 'Go to Hell!' to any foreign nation that attempted to dictate the number of ships we could build or that tried to flood in propaganda as is being done now."

Chicago reverted back to its status as a "wide-open town" and Capone was soon more in favor than he had been before. By the time he stood trial in Joliet on December 22, he had recovered his customary bravado. When Circuit Court Judge Fred A. Adams commented, after imposing fines and court costs on him for $1580.80, "I hope this will be a lesson to you not to carry deadly weapons," Capone retorted, "Yes, judge, it will teach me not to carry deadly weapons – in Joliet." He handed over $1,600 to the court clerk and waved away the change the man offered him. "Keep it, "he said, "or give it to the Salvation Army Santa Claus on the corner and tell him it's a Christmas present from Al Capone."

If there was any lesson that Capone learned from the pressure applied in Chicago – and the unwelcome reception he received in Los Angeles – it was that he needed a second home to which he could retreat whenever a change in Chicago's political climate forced him to do so. He had found a safe haven in Cicero during the Dever administration and he realized that his next new place could be both a sanctuary and a winter retreat in the sun. Attempts to seek out such a location produced no offers of hospitality. To set foot in St. Petersburg, New Orleans, the Bahamas or Cuba, he learned, was to risk arrest and expulsion.

Then, during the last days of 1927, he headed to Miami.

Capone was joined in Miami by his wife and son. They spent the winter together in a furnished bungalow at the beach, paying $2,500 for the season. The absent owner, a Mrs. Sterns, had listed the property with a real estate agent and was appalled when she learned that her tenant, "Al Brown," was actually Al Capone. She spent anxious weeks wondering what kind of damage would be done to the house and was pleasantly surprised to find that it suffered none. The Capones not only left the place in perfect condition, but they left behind several extra sets of china and silverware that they purchased for parties. A letter from Mae Capone urged the owner to accept them as gifts. In the cellar, Mrs. Sterns also found several unopened cases of wine, to which she was also invited to help herself. The only unpleasant surprise was a telephone bill for $780 for calls to Chicago. Soon after it arrived in the mail, a gleaming Cadillac pulled into her driveway and a slim, pretty young woman with shoulder-length blond hair got out. "I'm Mrs. Capone," she said. She apologized for the telephone bill, which had slipped her mind, and offered to pay it without further delay. When Mrs. Sterns told her about the charges, Mae gave her a $1,000 bill. She told the surprised landlady not to worry about the difference. She feared that a few things might have gotten broken during her family's stay and the extra money should cover any damage that was done.

In addition to the bungalow, Capone also rented a suite on the top floor of the nine-story Hotel Ponce de Leon in downtown Miami that was used for both business and pleasure. He was befriended by the hotel's 24-year-old owner, Parker Henderson, Jr., whose late father had been the mayor of Miami. Henderson's tastes ran to prizefights,

MIAMI IN THE 1920S

horse and dog races and the company of celebrities, no matter what their claim to fame. He was thrilled to be able to slap Capone on the back, shoot craps with him and share a few drinks while boldly addressing his new pal as "Snorky." He couldn't do enough for his tenant and Capone rewarded him, as he did many people who pleased him, with a diamond-studded belt buckle.

When Capone needed cash, Henderson was happy to enlist himself in a scheme that was designed to confuse any law enforcement officials who were curious about the mobster's finances. From Chicago, an associate would send a Western Union money transfer to "Albert Costa," an alias that had been created for the purpose. Henderson would then go down to the Western Union office, sign for the transfer with disguised handwriting, cash it, and then deliver the money to Capone. Between January and April 1928, he collected more than $30,000 for him in this way.

The city of Miami had mixed feelings about Capone's presence in town. Publicly, nearly everyone was alarmed by it, but privately, many local businessmen hated to see his money being spent somewhere else. The economy of southern Florida was still hurting from the collapse of the post-war land boom. Around Miami and South Beach, the damage from the hurricane of September 1926 was still being felt. Over $100 million in damage had been done and more than 50,000 people had been left homeless by the storm. For Miami's mayor, John Newton Lummus, Jr., the conflict of interest caused by Capone's presence was acutely painful. In his official capacity as mayor, he could hardly ignore the complaints raised by the city council, not the mention those from the *Miami Daily News*, which clamored for Capone to be kicked out of town. At the same time, as vice-president of the real estate firm Lummus & Young, he desperately wanted to sell Capone a house.

Capone, shrewdly aware of the fact that a desire for profits would prevail in his case, made a public show of candor. He requested a meeting with Miami's chief of police, Leslie Quigg, to be followed by a press conference. "Let's lay the cards on the table," he told Quigg. "You know who I am and where I come from. I just want to ask a question: do I stay or must I get out?" He added that he had no intention of operating a gambling house or any other illegal enterprise in Miami.

Quigg shrugged. "You can stay as long as you behave yourself."

"I'll stay as long as I'm treated like a human being," Capone shot back.

At his press conference, he told reporters that he was at their service. "I've been hounded and pushed around for days. It began when somebody heard I was in town. All I have to say is that I'm orderly. Talk about Chicago gang stuff is just bunk." He launched into heavy praise of the city of Miami, calling it the "sunny Italy of the New World." If he was permitted, he said, he hoped to open a restaurant, and if invited, he would join the Rotary Club.

Two days later, under combined pressure of the city council and the newspaper, the mayor and City Manager C.A. Henshaw called a press conference of their own. After a talk with Capone at City Hall, Mayor Lummus told reporters, "Mr. Capone was one of the fairest men I have ever been in conference with. He was not ordered to leave Miami Beach, but he decided it would be to the best interests of all concerned if he left. It was a mutual agreement."

The city manager also spoke, "There was no argument or threat. Our conference was made up simply of statements of fact on both sides and Mr. Capone announced that he was leaving immediately."

Publicly, Capone left Miami but out of sight of the newspapers and the politicians, he stayed on – with full knowledge of the mayor. He continued to divide his time between the rented bungalow and the Ponce de Leon, often visiting the racetrack at Hialeah and the local nightclubs. He took up golf and tennis but was terrible at both games. Like so many men used to always getting their way, he hated to lose and occasionally, in the midst of a tantrum, would break his racket or fling his clubs across the golf course in disgust.

Henderson and Mayor Lummus worked behind the scenes with real estate companies and helped Capone look into buying a winter home. He eventually found a place that he liked on Palm Island, a man-made sliver of prime real estate in Biscayne Bay that was located midway between the mainland and the beach. The house at 93 Palm Avenue was built in 1922 by the St. Louis brewer Clarence M. Busch. At the time when Capone first looked at it, it was owned by a Miami man named James Popham. The house was not as special as legend has made it out to be. It was a two-story Spanish-style structure with a flat, green-tiled roof, shaded by twelve royal palm trees. Located in the center of a large lot, it had fourteen rooms and a long, glass-enclosed sun porch. A gatehouse, which spanned the gravel driveway, contained three rooms. Mosaic-paved patios and walks rimmed both buildings and a dock on the north side could accommodate three or four boats. As far as Miami palaces went, it was only an average dwelling.

The asking price for the house was $40,000. Capone gave Henderson $2,000 down as a binder and not long after, added another $8,000, making the first of four annual payments. He wasn't asked to pay interest. Henderson took title to the property and deeded it to Mae Capone. When the *Daily News* exposed the transaction, both Capone and Lummus came under heavy attack. An indignant citizens' group demanded the mayor's resignation. At the insistence of the city council, a five-man police detail began following Capone everywhere he went.

It was a development that the crime boss couldn't be bothered with, though. Just as he was in the process of taking possession of the Palm Island house, political developments in Chicago urgently required his presence back in the Windy City.

THE CAPONE HOUSE ON PALM ISLAND IN FLORIDA

"Big Bill" Thompson's first year back in office had been a disaster as far as political observers were concerned. Discontent about his incompetence and about corruption in City Hall was spreading, especially with the city of Chicago almost $300 million in debt. Primary elections for state and county offices were set for April, but election violence began in January, ten weeks before anyone went to the polls. The election came to be known as Chicago's "Pineapple Primary," with "pineapple" being a slang term for hand grenade. It became the most violent political period in the city's history.

On the evening of January 27, the homes of Thompson-appointed city controller, Charles C. Fitzmorris, and of Dr. William H. Reid, the commissioner of public service, were bombed within a half-hour of one another. "This is a direct challenge from the lawless," a stunned Thompson told reporters, "When the fight is over, the challengers will be sorry."

(LEFT) JOE ESPOSITO AND HIS FAMILY IN A CHICAGO RESTAURANT

(ABOVE) HIS CHILDREN WERE WATCHING HIM WALK HOME THROUGH THE WINDOW WHEN ESPOSITO WAS SHOT DOWN OUTSIDE THE FRONT DOOR.

His warning was ignored and on February 11, another bomb damaged the home of State's Attorney Crowe's brother-in-law and secretary, Lawrence Cuneo. A week later, a fourth bomb exploded in the Sbarbaro funeral parlor, where so many gangsters had been prepared for burial over the years. Thanks to an endorsement from Thompson, Sbarbaro was now a municipal court judge.

Senator Deneen's choice to replace Crowe as state's attorney was Judge John A. Swanson, and the senator's friend, Joe Esposito, had promised to help by running again for Republican ward committeeman. On the morning of March 21, with the primary three weeks away, Esposito received a telephone threat, warning him to get out of town or be killed. Later that same morning, two Capone gunmen dropped into the Bella Napoli Café and repeated the warning. Esposito's associates begged him to heed the threats, but he told them that he had to keep his word to the senator. Later that evening, he left the Esposito National Republican Club and started the short walk home, flanked by his bodyguards, brothers Ralph and Joe Varschetti. His wife, Carmella, and their three children were watching for him from a front window. As he came within sight of his family, a car carrying three men roared up on him from behind. As the car veered up next to him, the men inside opened fire on Esposito with two double-barreled shotguns and a revolver. The weapons were tossed out into the street and the car vanished around the corner. The Varschettis had thrown themselves to the sidewalk in time but Esposito was badly hit. He lay dying, blood pooling around him. Carmela rushed to his side, shrieking that she would kill the men in the car. But despite the promise of vengeance, neither the widow nor the bodyguards identified the killers and failed to furnish a single clue. Like so many other gangland slayings, the murder of "Diamond Joe" Esposito was never solved.

Senator Deneen was one of the horde of politicians who attended Esposito's funeral. The next day, a bundle of dynamite wrecked the front of his three-story Chicago home. Later that same night, Judge Swanson, while turning his car into his driveway, narrowly escaped the full blast of a bomb that was hurled from a passing vehicle. Deneen brayed the obvious: "The criminal element is trying to dominate Chicago by setting up a dictatorship in politics. The 'pineapple' industry grew up under his administration."

Mayor Thompson and State's Attorney Crowe figuratively fired back. "I am satisfied," Crowe said, "that the bombings were done by leaders in the Deneen forces to discredit Mayor Thompson and myself. They realize they are hopelessly defeated and in a desperate attempt to overcome their tide of defeat, they are resorting to dangerous tactics." This accusation was so cynical that it alienated many of the supporters that had been in the Crowe camp. The Chicago Crime Commission, until then partial to Crowe, issued an open letter to voters, denouncing him as "inefficient and unworthy of his great responsibility to maintain law and order in Cook County."

Fearing more bombs at the primary polls, a federal marshal asked the U.S. Attorney General to commission more than five hundred marshals for special duty. President Coolidge was urged to withdraw Marines from Nicaragua, where they were fighting anti-American guerillas, and put them on the streets of Chicago. Both requests were denied.

As the primary drew nearer, the violence on the streets of Chicago became national, then international, news. Correspondents from all over the country and from Europe were assigned to Chicago

SENATOR CHARLES DENEEN, WHO LATER WENT ON TO BECOME ILLINOIS' GOVERNOR.

as if they were covering a war. They were not disappointed. Thompson took to the campaign trail for Judge Barasa, his favorite for the Cook County Board of Review. He was battling an old foe, Edward R. Litsinger. Appealing to working class men in the enemy's district, Thompson addressed them during a meeting that was held a week before the primary. "Litsinger was brought up back of the gashouse [the local neighborhood], but it wasn't good enough for him, so he moved up to the North Side and left his poor old mother behind..." The meeting broke up in chaos when Litsinger's sister jumped to her feet, shouting, "You're a liar! My mother died long before my brother moved!"

The next night, Litsinger went on the attack at the Olympic Theater. Thompson, he said, was a "low-down hound," a "befuddled beast" who "should be tarred and feathered and ridden out of town." He was a "man with the carcass of a rhinoceros and the brains of a baboon." Litsinger then held an envelope over his head, using an old trick. "I have affidavits here relating to the life of the big baboon," he said. "Shall I read them?" The audience cheered him on but Litsinger shook his head. "No, that old German mother of mine this man has struck at through me is looking down on me from above and may God strike me speechless if I ever descend to Thompson's level." Then, he went ahead and descended to the mayor's level, taking another swipe at him. "You know the Three Musketeers? They are Big Bill, Len Small [Illinois governor] and Frank L. Smith [the Thompson senate candidate]. The right way to pronounce it is 'three-must-get-theirs...'"

On Easter Sunday, two days before the primary, the entire clergy of Chicago – Catholic, Protestant and Jewish alike – spoke out against the Small-Thompson faction. "We have a governor who ought to be in the penitentiary," they said. "Ours is a government of bombs and bums."

On April 10, the Tuesday of the primary, party hacks on both sides, with the entrenched Thompson machine in the majority, began employing the strategies that had been perfected through years of Cook County electoral hijinks. Before the polling booths opened, ballot boxes were stuffed with bundles of ballots that had already been marked in favor of their faction. Those who had managed to get themselves appointed as election officials padded the registration lists with fictional names under which fraudulent voters could vote. They inserted the names of unregistered voters, submitted by ward bosses, who had verified them from pre-election pledge cards. They registered vagrants whose votes had been purchased for a few dollars, assigning them fake names and addresses. Even the dead were able to vote in Chicago!

As the voting got under way, Capone's men, packing bombs and guns and far outnumbering the thugs that had been enlisted by the Deneen faction, cruised the streets around the polling places in cars bearing America First stickers. Capone himself had returned from Florida to personally direct the troops. With threats of mayhem, they drove away voters who they believed were favoring the opposition. A few skirmishes broke out with Deneen supporters but with more men in the field, the Capone camp easily maintained control. They terrorized honest election officials into keeping away from their posts and if intimidation failed, they dragged them away and held them captive until the polls closed. Polling judges were then forced to appoint a last- minute substitute and gunmen made sure that only Thompson supporters were available.

There were five kinds of fraudulent Chicago voters. There was the "stringer," who voted according to a relay system. The first man in the string entered the polling booth with two ballots, a blank one furnished by the clerk and a second that was pre-marked. After dropping the marked ballot into the box, he slipped the blank one to the next man in the string, who repeated the process and so on down the line. A "floater" was recruited from the city's transients and he voted frequently throughout the day. Gangsters usually drove him by car to precinct after precinct. The "stinger" was an armed "floater," prepared to shoot any poll watcher who might try and expose him. The ward bosses had gone as far as to actually house some of the bums in their ward during the thirty days before the election, which was required by the residency law. These bums were often called "mattress voters." The "repeater" voter voted as many as one hundred times in the same precinct while using different names and addresses. One repeater gave a different name, but used the same address sixteen times. In a grand jury investigation that took place after the primary, the address turned out to be a riding stable. A newspaperman smirked that, "every horse voted."

After all of the fraud carried out during the voting process was over, a whole new set of dodges occurred during the counting of ballots. Corrupt officials disqualified ballots that were hostile to their cause by secretly marking them twice – inserting X's in boxes that had been left empty. They transferred the totals on the tally sheets to the credit of their candidates, substituted bogus tally sheets, and made up their own totals. Thousands of anti-Crowe votes were destroyed altogether. To discourage any accusations of cheating, gunmen menacingly paced the rooms where the counting was talking place.

Of course, none of these ploys could have succeeded without help from the police – which they offered in the form of their absence from the scene. The precinct captains, obeying orders from the local ward bosses (and in many cases directly from Capone) with promises of demotions or rewards, assigned their men to duties that took them far away from the polls. Without any sort of police protection, polling officials who were reluctant to go along with the fraud that was taking place had no choice but to comply.

The Pineapple Primary ended in murder. Octavius Granaday, an African-American attorney, had challenged the candidacy of Morris Eller, Thompson's pick for the Republican committeeman of the Twentieth Ward. This was the first time that a black man had dared to demand political equality in the Twentieth Ward and the powers that be didn't stand for it. How many votes he managed to get that day didn't matter in the end. Shortly after the polls closed, Granaday was standing outside chatting with friends, when a shot from a passing car barely missed him. Granaday jumped into his car and fled, but the other car turned and followed him. Shotguns blasted and Granaday crashed into a tree. An easy target in the headlights of his pursuers, he was literally torn to pieces by a dozen slugs. Eventually, four policemen and three mobsters stood trial for his murder. All were acquitted.

Not surprisingly, predictions had already been made that the Thompson-Crowe faction would easily carry the day. As the best-organized, most powerful party machine in Chicago history, it had never lost a primary. Through patronage, it controlled practically every state, county, and city office and in addition to its militant gangland arm, it could muster up to 100,000 campaign volunteers. But what the forecasters failed to see coming was the boomerang effect of the violence leading up to the primary. Chicagoans who had seldom worried about voting in a primary were jolted out of their disinterest by the bombs, the shootings and the mayor's cynical statements. "Sure, we have crime here," Thompson nonchalantly conceded after the bombings of the Deneen and Swanson homes. "We will always have crime. Chicago is just like any other big city. You can get a man's arm broken for so much, a leg for so much, or beaten up for just so much. Just like New York, excepting we print our crime and they don't." People were angry. Should Chicago's mayor have such a blasé attitude toward crime on the city streets? And most of all, should he be so closely connected to a man like Al Capone?

The answer to both questions was a resounding no. The voter turnout on April 10 far exceeded even the most optimistic estimates. Almost 800,000 people turned out at the polls and not even fraud and terrorism could save a single Thompson candidate. Governor Small and State's Attorney Crowe sank under a wave of disgust and revulsion. Although Thompson himself had three more years to serve as mayor, his political career was shattered beyond repair that day. The primary returns, as well as a judicial inquiry into his conduct and the barbs of a hostile press, left him with little energy for continued combat as his party prepared to meet the Democrats in the fall elections. He was broken both mentally and physically. Drinking heavily, he retreated to his country house for the summer, leaving City Hall in the hands of Acting Mayor Samuel Ettleson.

Capone didn't stay in Chicago long after the election. He returned to Florida and began making improvements to his new house on Palm Island. Some of the best architects, landscape designers, masons and carpenters in Dade County were kept busy for months. A concrete wall was erected around the estate and heavy oak portals were hung behind the iron gates at the entrance, shutting off the view of the compound. A house phone was installed at the gate so that visitors could be announced. Of course, none of them were admitted until an armed guard, stationed behind the oak portals, had inspected them. The largest swimming pool in the area was installed between the house and the bay and was outfitted with one of the first filter systems to allow for both fresh and salt water. On the bay side of the yard, a two-story bathhouse in the shape of a Venetian loggia was built. A rock pool, with borders planted with lush foliage, was dug and stocked with rare tropical fish, which Al and Sonny fed with bread crusts from the kitchen.

The house was extensively remodeled and lavishly furnished. The living room was stuffed with massive, over-upholstered furniture and the central adornment was a life-size oil painting of the Capones. The

CAPONE BEGAN SPENDING MORE AND MORE TIME IN FLORIDA, FAR FROM THE CHILLY WEATHER -- AND FLYING BULLETS -- IN CHICAGO.

master bedroom at the rear of the house offered a sweeping view of the pool, the bathhouse and the bay. Capone slept in an immense four-poster bed, at the foot of which stood a wooden chest that he kept filled with cash. Capone didn't trust banks. In the bathroom, he had a massive shower installed with seven extra shower heads jutting from all sides. The improvements to the interior of the house alone cost over $100,000.

For fishing and cruising, Capone purchased several watercrafts, including a Baby Gar speedboat, which he named the *Sonny and Ralphie*, and a 32-foot cabin cruiser called the *Arrow*. When his Chicago pals visited him, he liked to pack hampers full of salami sandwiches and beer and charter a seaplane to fly them to Bimini.

There was no question about it; Capone was now living the good life, seemingly far away from the trouble in Chicago and the violence that he was accustomed to. Soon, though, he would reach a regretful decision that would end the life of an old friend and early patron – and have bloody repercussions.

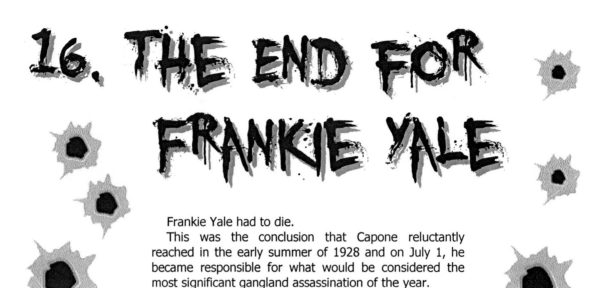

16. THE END FOR FRANKIE YALE

Frankie Yale had to die.

This was the conclusion that Capone reluctantly reached in the early summer of 1928 and on July 1, he became responsible for what would be considered the most significant gangland assassination of the year.

Yale, a Brooklyn gangster who had once employed Capone as a barroom bouncer, had started out as a member of a gang in the Five Points neighborhood with John Torrio. Yale had supplied Capone with liquor for years and on several occasions, had come to Chicago to perform assassinations. However, the goodwill between Yale and Capone eventually evaporated.

One of the causes of the falling out had to do with the Unione Siciliane, or the Italo-American National Union, as it was now called. When the murder of Angelo Genna opened up the presidency of the Chicago chapter, Yale, as the national president, had failed to help pick a successor. Wanting the retain the goodwill of both Capone and the North Side gang, he had refrained from coming out in favor of either contender for the position: Capone's Tony Lombardo or Joe Aiello, who O'Banion's men wanted to see in the spot. Upon Capone's insistence, he did not oppose Lombardo, but at the same time, he quietly encouraged Aiello's hopes of later gaining the presidency. It really didn't matter to Yale who ran the Chicago branch of the Unione, as long as he still received a share of the profits from the various rackets, which made it odd that he failed to support the candidate of his old ally, Capone. After Lombardo took over the position, Capone retaliated against Yale and the Brooklyn gangster's share dwindled to mere token payments. Yale fought back by bringing Aiello to New York during his troubles with Capone after Aiello promised to restore his customary tribute if Lombardo was overthrown.

This was enough to anger Capone, but Yale had taken things even further in their dealings over liquor. Since 1926, Capone had been expanding his bootlegging operations on a national scale. Through a network of multi-state alliances – including Abe Bernstein's Purple Gang in Detroit, Egan's Rats in St. Louis, "Boo Boo" Hoff in Philadelphia and others – Capone managed to obtain the highest quality liquor that was brought in at lake and coastal points from Canada, Cuba and the Bahamas and he marketed it all over the Midwest. Yale, who supervised arrivals on Long Island, had shipped regular consignments to Chicago by truck. However, starting in the spring of 1927, many of the trucks were hijacked before they even left Brooklyn. To hijack liquor and then sell it

FRANKIE YALE

was a common double-cross in those days and Capone was suspicious. He sent a gunman named James Finesy de Amato to Brooklyn to serve as a spy. He was killed less than a month after he arrived, but not before he sent a message back to Capone to let him know that his suspicions about Yale were correct. Soon after, Frank Yale received an ominous anonymous message: "Someday you'll get an answer to de Amato."

During the last week of June 1928, Capone met at the Ponce de Leon in Miami with several associates, including Charlie Fischetti, Jake Guzik and Dan Serritella. A few days earlier, he asked his always-obliging young friend Henderson to pick up a few guns for him and Henderson purchased a dozen assorted weapons from a Miami pawnshop. On June 28, six Capone men boarded the Southland Express train for Chicago. At Knoxville, Tennessee, four of them got off the train, bought a used Nash sedan from a local car lot for $1,050 and drove it to New York.

On the afternoon of Sunday July 1, Frank Yale, wearing a light gray summer suit and a Panama hat, was drinking in a Borough Park speakeasy when the bartender called him to the telephone. Whatever he heard over the receiver caused him to slam down the phone and run to his car, which was parked nearby. A few minutes later, on Forty-Fourth Street, a black sedan roared up next to him and crowded him to the curb. Guns opened up from the sedan and bullets from several weapons – shotguns, revolvers and a Tommy gun – nailed him to the front seat of his car. Blood flew and Yale's body jerked back and forth from the violence of the shots. Yale's murder went down in infamy as the first assassination by Tommy gun in New York history.

The killers abandoned the black Nash – and their assortment of weapons – on Thirty-Sixth Street between Second and Third avenues. The serial numbers on two .45 revolvers led the police to Capone's pal Parker Henderson, who was brought to New York for questioning. He had, he admitted in front of a grand jury, bought the guns for Al Capone but he insisted that after he delivered them, he never saw them again. The Tommy gun, meanwhile, was traced to Peter von Frantizius' Chicago sporting goods store. New York's Police Commissioner, Grover Whalen, was clearly upset when the grand jury adjourned without indicting anyone. "In my opinion," he told reporters, "there was enough evidence to not only get an indictment, but a conviction, as well."

Frankie Yale's funeral turned out to be the most spectacular send-off in New York gangland history.

Yale's death would soon be avenged. His murder set off a string of killings back in Chicago. Two months later, the Aiello forces, restored to full strength in Little Italy, staged a daylight street shooting as payback for Frankie Yale. It happened not far from the Italo-American National Union offices, located in the Hartford Building at 8 South Dearborn Street. Tony Lombardo spent nearly every afternoon there in his eleventh-floor office, a fact of which his killers were very aware. On the afternoon of September 7, just as he was finishing work, he received a telephone call from Peter Rizzito, a North Side merchant, which kept him at

FRANKIE YALE WAS FORCED OFF THE ROAD AND SLAUGHTERED. HIS SPECTACULAR ASSASSINATION MARKED THE FIRST TIME THAT A TOMMY GUN WAS USED TO CARRY OUT A MURDER IN NEW YORK CITY.

TONY LOMBARDO WAS SHOT TO DEATH IN BROAD DAYLIGHT IN BUSY DOWNTOWN CHICAGO.

his desk for another fifteen minutes. According to rumors that circulated later, Rizzito was an ally of Aiello who had only called Lombardo to delay his departure and give gunmen time to set up a trap for him on the street below.

Lombardo finally left the office at 4:30 p.m. He departed in the company of two bodyguards, Joseph Ferraro and Joseph Lolordo, whose older brother, Pasquale, was a Unione politician. They turned onto Madison Street, working their way through the busy afternoon crowds of shoppers, office workers and business people. As they passed a restaurant about halfway down the block, Lolordo heard a voice behind them say, "Here he is."

The words were followed by four thundering pistol shots.

Lombardo's head exploded and he was thrown forward, slamming onto the sidewalk. Ferraro fell beside him, two bullets in his back. Before Lolordo could even react, he saw two men running in opposite directions, one wearing a dark suit and the other a gray one. He pulled his own gun from its holster and started off in pursuit of the man in the gray suit. Before he could manage more than a few steps, he was solidly pinned by a police officer and his pistol was wrestled away from him. The killers escaped and Lombardo's murder was never solved.

Ferraro was badly wounded and at his hospital bedside, Assistant State's Attorney Samuel Hoffman asked him to name the killers. Ferraro refused. "You're going to die," Hoffman told him coldly but Ferraro wouldn't rat anyone out. He died two days later, never revealing the identities of the men who shot Lombardo and himself. Lolordo also refused to name names. Although he had seen the killers clearly and had begged the patrolman who disarmed him to let him pursue them, he insisted at the coroner's inquest that he had seen nothing.

Tony Lombardo was the fourth Unione Siciliane president to be assassinated since political terrorists shot Anthony D'Andrea in 1921. He was not the last. Over the course of the next three years, the office proved lethal to every incumbent, as well as to several candidates. So, why would anyone want the job? The benefits were apparently too tempting to pass up. Under Unione control, the liquor-cooking industry had grown to include the majority of Chicago's Italian immigrant households. Over 2,500 home stills bubbled away, producing the raw materials for a multi-million dollar bootleg market. Every Unione president received a huge taste of the profits, which made the job just about irresistible.

There was another scramble for the job after the murder of Tony Lombardo. Pasquale Lolordo beat

Peter Rizzito for the position and took office on September 14. Rizzito died a short time later, gunned down in front of his Milton Street store, near an area of Chicago that had been dubbed "Death Corner" during the days of the Black Hand. No one knows who ordered his death – Capone or Joe Aiello – but his slaying was never solved. Later that same week, Capone gunmen launched a Tommy gun attack on Aiello headquarters, wounding Tony Aiello and one of his men. More attacks and counter-attacks followed, killing four Aiello men and two Capone gunmen.

PASQUALE LOLORDO HELD THE PRESIDENCY OF THE UNIONE SICILIANE FOR JUST FIVE MONTHS BEFORE HE WAS SHOT TO DEATH IN HIS OWN HOME.

Pasquale Lolordo lasted just five months as the Unione Siciliane president. Under the mistaken impression that he and Aiello could be friends, Lolordo invited Joe and two of his brothers to his apartment on North Avenue for a drink. They gunned him down while his glass was raised in a toast. His wife, Aleina, hearing gunfire in the next room, rushed in to see the Aiellos finishing him off as he lay on the floor. Angry and grieving, she identified Joe Aiello as one of the killers from a photograph that the police showed her, but once she was herself again, she fell silent and refused to name names.

Finally, Joe Aiello won the presidency of the Unione Siciliane and he held it for almost a year. Then, on the evening of October 23, 1930, as he was leaving a friend's house at 15 North Kolmar Avenue, he was gunned down in the crossfire of two machine gun positions that had been set up in flats rented ten days earlier – a well-tested Capone tactic.

It had taken a while, but Capone finally had his revenge on the man who tried to kill him.

17. CHICAGO RACKETS

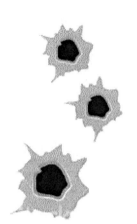

In the summer of 1928, Capone decided to pack up and move his headquarters from the Metropole to the Lexington Hotel, which was located diagonally across the street. The Lexington had once ranked among the best of the city's hotels, playing host to scores of esteemed visitors, including President Grover Cleveland, who had once addressed Chicagoans from a balcony that opened off the grand ballroom. While its glory had faded somewhat by the time that Capone moved in, it was still imposing with its bay windows and turreted corners and a lofty main entrance that opened off South Michigan Avenue through to Wabash, its lobby rising a full story to a shopping gallery.

Capone and his entourage occupied the entire fourth floor (and a good part of the third floor) of the ten-story hotel. Their assorted women were kept in rooms that were scattered throughout the place. When Capone wished to dine in his six-room suite, the food and wine were brought to him on rolling tables from a fourth-floor kitchen that the management had installed for his exclusive use. His private chef, who lived next door to the kitchen, tasted everything before Capone ate or drank it; a precaution that had been implemented after Aiello had tried to have the boss poisoned.

To ensure that no one knew when he was coming or going, Capone devised an escape route that required not only the cooperation of the Lexington's management but that of the owners of the adjacent office building, as well. Accompanied by a half-dozen bodyguards, he would ride the freight elevator to the second floor and enter a maids' locker room. Behind a full-length mirror, hinged at one side, was a door that had been cut to Capone's specifications. He could swing the door aside, step through into the office building next door and then walk down two flights of stairs to a side door where a car and driver would be waiting. The secret door was not discovered for several decades. In the late 1960s, the owner of the hotel (which had been re-named the New Michigan) spotted a door that led from the hotel to nowhere when the office building next door was torn down. An elderly porter, who had worked at the Lexington since Capone's day, explained what it had been used for. Additional escape routes and tunnels (which are surprisingly common under the streets of Chicago) were also used.

THE LEXINGTON HOTEL

On rare occasions, Mae Capone shared her husband's hotel suite, but she almost never accompanied him to the theater, to nightclubs or to the racetrack. Few members of the gang ever got to

GERALDO RIVERA AND THE LAST GASP OF THE LEXINGTON HOTEL ✋

In 1986, television reporter and talk show host Geraldo Rivera took a national television audience into what was then one of the last remaining landmarks of the Chicago crime era and the reign of Al Capone ---- the old Lexington Hotel at the corner of Michigan Avenue and Twenty-Second Street. Rivera was in search of lost treasure, a fortune that Capone had allegedly left behind in secret vaults in the hotel's basement. Earlier in the 1980s, a construction company owned by a local woman had investigated the possibility of restoring the hotel, which was by then a shadow of its former grandeur. As the construction workers explored the building, they discovered a shooting gallery that had been used by Capone's cronies for target practice and dozens of secret passages and stairways, including the one behind Capone's medicine chest that led to his mistress's quarters. Some passages led to hidden tunnels that connected taverns and whorehouses on the Levee and to the immediate west. The tunnels had been designed to provide elaborate escape routes from police raids and attacks by rivals.

This led to more interest in the hotel and soon researcher Harold Rubin came to the crumbling old building and began a search of the premises. In addition to recovering many priceless artifacts from the hotel's glory days, Rubin stumbled across one of the great secrets of the place when exploring the escape tunnels. It was said that Capone had vaults in the lower levels of the Lexington where he had stashed some of his loot. These vaults were so well hidden that even Capone's closest accomplices were not aware of them. Rubin's discoveries led to a newspaper article in the *Chicago Tribune* but his extensive research would be overshadowed by Geraldo Rivera, who brashly stated that if the secret money vaults could be found, he would discover them --- and would do so on national television.

Capone had been gone from the hotel for many years. He was sent to prison in 1930 and the remnants of Capone's gang abandoned the Lexington in 1932. After that, the hotel changed ownership several times as the state of the place declined with the surrounding neighborhood. It was re-named the New Michigan Hotel in the 1950s but soon after became a bordello, a transient hotel and finally, a crumbling eyesore. By the 1980s -- and the arrival of Geraldo Rivera -- it was scheduled for demolition. But the Lexington had one final act left in its old bones.

On the night of April 21, 1986, Rivera broadcast live in a two-hour special from the deserted and echoing empty hotel. The place had already been picked clean by vandals and souvenir hunters, but Rivera was convinced that secrets from the past still remained inside and the show was hyped accordingly with tantalizing guesses about whether stacks of greenbacks and bodies of dead gangsters were hidden inside the secret chamber. In the basement, a crew blasted away a 7,000-pound concrete wall that was believed to be hiding a secret compartment containing thousands, perhaps millions, of dollars. The Internal Revenue Service had agents on hand to claim their share of the loot. When the smoke cleared, to Rivera's chagrin only debris, including a few empty bottles and an old sign were found. The fortune, if it had ever been there at all, had long since been spirited away.

After Geraldo tried and failed to upstage everyone in Chicago who had researched Capone for years, the person who actually discovered the location of the vault, Harold Rubin, got the last laugh. He worked for the production company that produced one of the most-watched television specials ever and was interviewed on CBS television on the night of Geraldo's blunder. To this day, no one has ever done as much research into the history of the Lexington and Rubin stands as the man who discovered the old place's greatest secrets -- whether the vaults were empty or not. The Lexington Hotel finally "gave up the ghost" and was torn down in November 1995. Another chapter in the history of Chicago crime had been closed for good.

know her. In the tradition of the old Italian dons, gangsters' wives were usually kept away from the business end of things and Mae stayed at either the Prairie Avenue house or at the Florida house on Palm Island. Gang members usually kept girlfriends stashed away in apartments and hotel suites. At the time he moved to the Lexington, Capone was seeing a young Greek girl whom he had salvaged from one of his suburban brothels. He installed her in a two-room suite at the Lexington.

When Capone, his family, or a member of the gang needed medical attention, they consulted Dr. David V. Owens, who was also an investor in the Hawthorne Kennel Club. In this way, he was well rewarded for his treatment of illnesses and bullet wounds, as well as for his silence. When Capone's girlfriend came to him one day complaining of a genital sore, Owens diagnosed syphilis and began a series of arsphenamine injections. The drug, also called Salvarsan, was developed in the 1910s to treat syphilis. Owens urged Capone to take a Wassermann test, which checked a person's blood or spinal fluid for infections, but Capone was so terrified of needles that even the thought of one piercing his skin horrified him. Neither the doctor's assurance of negligible pain nor his graphic description of the devastating death untreated syphilis could bring would persuade him to do it.

Capone insisted that he felt fine – there was nothing the matter with him, he said.

Capone had been at the Lexington for just three months when he received a very curious visitor – Frank Loesch, illustrious president of the Chicago Crime Commission. Loesch came to Capone seeking his help during the fall 1928 elections. He reminded him of the "Pineapple Primary" earlier that year and the death and violence that had been meted out by professional terrorists, many of them Capone gangsters. The homes of candidates had been bombed, party workers killed and voters intimidated and through it all, the police did not intervene. What could Capone do to see that nothing like this happened again?

Capone listened carefully to Loesch's appeal before he replied, "I'll give you a square deal if you don't ask too much of me."

Loesch was upset by the arrogance of the man's reply. He was coming to the gangster on behalf of all Chicago voters, whether Democrat or Republican, in fear that the April primary had been nothing more than a bloody preview of what the city could expect in November. He managed to stifle his anger, though. "Now

FRANK LOESCH

look here, Capone," Loesch said, "will you help me by keeping your damned cutthroats and hoodlums from interfering with the polling booths?"

Capone must have been amused by the old lawyer's moxie. "Sure," he replied, "I'll give them the word because they're all dagos up there, but what about the Saltis gang of micks on the West Side? They'll have to be handled different. Do you want me to give them the works, too?"

Loesch told him that it would be greatly appreciated.

Capone answered. "All right, I'll have the cops send over squad cars the night before the election and jug all the hoodlums and keep 'em in the cooler until the polls close."

Capone kept his word. He gave orders to the Chicago police department and the cops obeyed. On the eve of the election, they spread throughout the city, rounding up and disarming scores of known gangsters. On election day, seventy police cars cruised the polling area and votes were cast without a hitch. Years later, Loesch said, "It turned out to be the squarest and most successful election in forty years. There was not one complaint, not one election fraud and no threat of trouble all day."

The November 1928 elections turned out to be one of the most amazing displays of power by an outlaw before or since. But why did he do it? It seems that by giving into Loesch's demands, Capone acted against his own best interests. An honest election was bound to fill county offices with anti-Thompson men who would gladly crush Capone if they could. There is no doubt that vanity played a huge role in his decision. He must have been deeply gratified to have the head of the Chicago Crime Commission come to him, hat in hand, to ask for his help. Capone craved gratitude and admiration, no matter where it came from, and continually sought out appreciation with shows of civic spirit or charitable donations. His gifts to his followers, his huge tips to working class people -- $5 to newsboys, $20 to hatcheck girls, $100 to waiters – his donations of food, coal and clothing to the poor, were all widely publicized.

"There's a lot of people in Chicago that have got me pegged as one of those bloodthirsty mobsters that you read about in storybooks," Capone once complained, "the kind that tortures his victims, cuts off their ears, puts out their eyes with a red-hot poker and grins while he's doing it. Now get me right. I'm not posing as a model for youth. I've had to do a lot of things that I don't like to do. But I'm not as black as I'm painted. I'm human. I've got a heart in me. I'll go as deep in my pocket as any man to help a guy that needs help. I can't stand to see anybody hungry or cold or helpless. Many a poor family in Chicago thinks I'm Santa Claus. If I've given a cent to the poor in this man's town, I'll bet I've given a million dollars. Yes, a million. I don't take any credit to myself for being charitable and I'm just saying this to show that I'm not the worst man in the world."

And there were many in this era who agreed that Capone was not the monster that some of the newspapers and the politicians made him out to be. Those who were recipients of his generosity – no matter the real reason behind it – called Capone a "swell guy" and a "wonderful person who took from the rich and gave to the poor." A man who lived near the site of the Four Deuces called Capone and his men "fine boys." Capone later opened soup kitchens for the hungry and gave away thousands of dollars at the onset of the Depression. Of course, none of this changed the fact that he was able to do these things because he broke the Prohibition laws, took millions from gambling tables and made a fortune from the broken and abused bodies of the women who staffed his brothels. Generous or not, he was still a violent and sometimes monstrous criminal.

Capone may have offered help to Frank Loesch out of vanity, but his vanity was not so blind that it placed him in any real peril. The Thompson political machine was already doomed and Capone knew it. He really had little concern as to how the majority voted. Two different administrations had risen and fallen during the time he was in Chicago and neither had seriously hampered his operations. Under both of them, the outfit had weathered reformers, raids, police shakedowns and grand jury investigations. Mayors, city and county officials had come and gone and his operation had remained intact. It was easy for him to help out Loesch. What did he have to fear from those who took office next? This was Chicago – where corruption was king.

In the national elections that year, Herbert Hoover defeated Al Smith. It was a close race in Chicago with Hoover defeating his opponent by just a little over 20,000 votes. Soon after his victory, the President-elect was invited to Miami by his friend, chain store magnate J.C. Penney. The Penney estate on Belle Isle was not far from Palm Island, a short distance that gave rise to a larger-than-life legend.

According to the story, the sounds of revelry of the partygoers at the Capone estate, which included loud music, gunfire, laughter and screeching women, disturbed Hoover's sleep and kept him awake most of the night. The next morning, when he learned who owned the nearby home from which the disturbance emanated, he allegedly vowed then and there to crush Capone.

Was the story true? It's unlikely, since another similar story has it that Hoover was miffed because the newsmen in Miami paid more attention to Capone than they did to him, on one occasion turning away from

him in a hotel lobby when the gangster came through the front doors.

The real reason behind Hoover's vow to bring down Capone, which he made during his early days in office, remains unclear, but he did order an all-out attack against the gang boss. For the first time, Capone would no longer be facing just law enforcement officials from Chicago or Cook County. It was now the federal government who wanted to get him.

Capone continued to run his gambling and prostitution operations but liquor still made up the bulk of his profits. However, he knew this couldn't last. He knew that he needed to diversify, a lesson that he learned from John Torrio, who foresaw that Prohibition would only go on for so long. Capone went into other businesses, some of which were entirely legitimate. One of them was the New Orleans Pinball Machine Co., in which he invested as a partner. He also acquired a 25 percent interest in his favorite nightclub, Midnight Frolics, where he turned up a few nights each week, always surrounded by bodyguards, to stamp his feet to the music of Austin Mack and his Century Serenaders and drink whiskey out of a teacup. He seldom brought women with him and he never, ever danced.

But Capone's most profitable alternative to bootlegging was racketeering. A racketeer was defined as the boss of a supposedly legitimate business operation (like a labor union). Using violence and intimidation, he then organizes the union or he pushes a group of businessmen into a "protective association." After that, he proceeds to collect fees and dues, imposes fines, regulates prices and hours of work and turns the outfit into a profit-making entity. A worker or merchant who does not join or refuses to stay in the union and pay tribute, is bombed, beaten or intimidated into changing his mind.

Racketeering in Chicago involved most consumer goods and services and for this reason, prices went up on almost everything, from meat to laundry services and even milk, under the mob's control. In fact, the story of the mob and milk in Chicago is an interesting tale in itself.

By the late 1920s, Capone was working hard to legitimize his business. When he was indicted in 1931, he guessed that he would end up spending about two years in prison and by the time he got out, Prohibition would have been repealed. When he was released, he hoped to be the owner of an established retail dairy business, competing for the sale of milk to families all over the Chicago area. Capone was well aware what a moneymaker the sale of milk could be and he wanted to get in on the action. It would be a real, legitimate business – no matter how he managed to get it started.

In the late spring of 1931, just after Capone was indicted, two of his representatives came to call on Steve Sumner, business agent for Teamsters Local 753 of the Milk Wagon Drivers Union. Sumner later identified them as Murray Humphreys and Frank Diamond, also known as Frank Maritote, whose brother, John, was married to Capone's sister, Mafalda.

Sumner said that Humphreys and Diamond asked for his help in starting Meadowmoor Dairies. They wanted to make sure that Capone wouldn't have any union trouble when he started the dairy – and they wanted Sumner to buy into the business. Sumner refused. Humphreys then gave him an alternative – he would offer him $100,000 to walk away from his job as the union's business agent and Humphreys would take over the position. Sumner again refused and the two men left. Soon after, Sumner ordered sheet metal to be affixed to the union headquarters, making it bulletproof. After turning the place into a fort, he armed his driver, installed bulletproof glass in his car and hired bodyguards for his home and office. But as it turned out, Sumner was never bothered again.

Instead, Humphreys went after Robert G. Ritchie, the Teamsters Local 753 president. He was kidnapped in December 1931 and Sumner had to pay a $50,000 ransom to get him released. Interestingly, when Meadowmoor Dairies, Inc. was started in February 1932, it was chartered with a capital of $50,000. In another twist, Humphreys was later accused by the IRS of withholding taxes on the ransom money. He pled guilty and paid the taxes on the money.

Four years later, in November of 1936, Cook County State's Attorney Investigator, Tubbo Gilbert, was indicted for helping the Teamsters fix milk retail prices in Chicago. By that time, the union was little more than an extension of the Chicago mob. The scandal involved Dr. Herman Bundesen of the Chicago Board of Health, as well as officials of Local 753 of the Milk Wagon Drivers Union. The indictment claimed that they had conspired to fix the amount of milk delivered in the city to squeeze the smaller distributors out of the business, leaving only Meadowmoor Dairies. In spite of massive amount of evidence, the case went nowhere. The state's attorney refused to prosecute and Gilbert was allowed to resign.

The men who had established Meadowmoor were used to getting their own way and when the smoke from the case cleared, the dairy was permanently established in the Chicago market. It operated at 1334 South Peoria Street in the "Back of the Yards" neighborhood and oddly enough, Meadowmoor's entry into the fresh milk market was said to be one of the best things that ever happened to the health of the people in the Chicago area. The new competition, in the depths of the Depression, forced the old established dairies to lower their fresh milk prices to become more affordable to families whose incomes had been reduced.

Not only that, but Meadowmoor also forced the city to finally come up with a legal definition for Grade A Milk. Capone adherents in the city council fought for the definition of Grade A Milk, insisting that no fresh milk of lesser quality should be offered for sale in the city. According to their plan, milk could not be offered as "fresh" unless it was sold within 72 hours of leaving the cow. The date by which milk was to be sold had to be clearly stamped on the container, where the consumer could read it. In those days, dated milk did not exist and customers had to depend on the dairy's word as to whether or not their milk was fresh. Needless to say, it frequently wasn't.

Although this plan was promoted with the consumer in mind, Humphreys was really trying to drive most of his competitors out of the market. In many cases, it worked. The old, established dairies fought the change, calling it unnecessary and probably unconstitutional. The newspapers covered the story with irony. Usually, it was bankers, merchants and store owners who were portrayed as the protectors of the people, while the forces of the underworld were seen as destroyers of public health. When it came to milk, though, their roles were apparently reversed.

In the end, the Capone forces won and the children of Chicago were granted the protection of freshness dated milk, a practice now required of all meat, fish, and dairy distributors across the country.

Dealing with the rackets in Chicago rarely had such a happy ending as the one involving milk. The rackets became so prevalent that a special rackets court was established with jurisdiction over the most frequently committed offenses. These included destruction of property and injury of persons by explosives, making or selling of explosives, throwing stench bombs, malicious mischief to houses, collecting penalty payments, entering premises to intimidate, kidnapping for ransom, mayhem, and intimidation of workers.

During the 1920s, more than two hundred different rackets flourished in Chicago under names like Concrete Road; Concrete Block; Sewer and Water Pipe Maker's and Layer's Union, Local 381; Soda Dispensers and Table Girl Brotherhood; Bread, Cracker, Yeast and Pie Wagon Driver's Union, and scores of others. The members of the Midwest Garage Owner's Association each paid organizer, David Albin, $1 a month for each car serviced. In one month, boys working for Albin slashed 50,000 tires on cars belonging to customers at garages that didn't belong to the association.

Simon J. Gorman, a former Ragen's Colts gang member, became the top man in Chicago's laundry rackets. With his partner, Johnny Hand, he organized the Chicago Wet and Dry Laundry Owner's Association, and bullied enough businesses into joining that he was netting at least $1,000 per week. Gorman had powerful connections at City Hall and he used them to cause trouble for operations that refused to join up with him. They often found themselves closed down after inspectors condemned their boilers or their establishments. Usually, they found it easier to join the association rather than fight the system. Johnny Hand later ended up being gunned down in a vacant lot behind the Hawthorne Inn, but Gorman went on to dominate the Laundry Owners, Linen Supply, Hand Laundry and Laundry Service associations, often imposing tributes for as much as ten percent of a store's gross.

The Kosher Meat Peddlers Association used poison to persuade delicatessens to join up with them. Bottles of it were often hurled into the stores, contaminating everything in the place. The Beauty Parlors' Protective Association came after uncooperative prospects in two stages – first, a little black powder was ignited on the ledge of a rear window and if that didn't work, a stick of dynamite was tossed down the center of the shop. For a time, few sporting events could be held in Chicago without injuries unless the promoters hired members of the Theater Ticket Taker's and Usher's Union at $5 per man. Since the union's labor pool mostly consisted of young boys who were happy to take tickets and work as ushers for free, as long as they got to watch the game, the profit margins for the union were exceptionally large. The Electric Sign Club found it easy to extort payments of as much as $2,000 from theater owners after thugs from the union flooded one theater with gasoline and set it on fire. The Janitor's Union worked alongside the Milk Wagon Driver's Union to victimize the owners of apartment buildings. The milk drivers refused to deliver to buildings that did not employ extra janitors, while the janitors would not stay on the job unless the tenants bought their milk from designated suppliers. The Elevator Operators obtained an assessment of $1,000 from each of 25 skyscrapers in the Loop on pain of suspending service with no warning, leaving hundreds of people stranded on the top floors.

In late 1928, the State's Attorney's office compiled a list of 91 Chicago unions and associations that had fallen under the grasp of racketeers. They affected nearly every small business in the city and a good many big ones, including fruit dealers, photo developers, junk dealers, candy store clerks, wagon owners and drivers, City Hall clerks, steamfitters and plumbers, theater workers, bakers, barbers, soda pop peddlers, ice cream dealers, garbage haulers, window cleaners, street sweepers, auto mechanics, electrical workers, clothing workers, musicians, dentists, florists, carpet layers, undertakers, and many more. Virtually the entire city was affected in some way by infiltration from the mob.

Gradually, Capone (or one of his associates) came to control the majority of the Chicago rackets. As he was in the liquor business, he was a force to be reckoned with when it came to racketeering – even though he briefly found himself on the other side of the fence when he had the chance to protect a business from the rackets in 1928. Not surprisingly, though, his "protection" led to his own control of the racket's target a short time later.

The Master Cleaners' and Dyers' Association was a monster when it came to rackets. It not only skimmed two percent from the gross earnings of every member wholesale plant, but also collected $220 in fees each year from every retail shop that received clothing from the plants and from every trucker who delivered to them. A favorite method of its terrorists for forcing independents to join up was the "exploding suit." Flammable chemicals would be sewn into the seams of a suit and then it would be sent for cleaning at the plant that was refusing to join the association. When heat was applied, the suit would explode. When detectives from the state's attorney's office asked the association's business agent, Sam Rubin, who had never worked as a cleaner or dyer, how he was qualified for the position, he proudly replied, "I'm a good convincer."

In the spring of 1928, the association announced that prices were going to increase citywide. The price would change for the pressing of men's suits from $1 to $1.75 and from $2 to $2.75 for women's dresses. Morris Becker, an independent owner of a chain of retail stores as well as a wholesale plant, refused to go along with the increase. Soon after, his foreman introduced him to Sam Rubin, who menacingly told him that he would raise his prices – or else. Becker laughed and replied that the Constitution guaranteed him the right to life, liberty and the full pursuit of happiness. In other words, he could do whatever he wanted.

"To hell with the Constitution," Rubin snarled, "I'm a damned sight bigger than the Constitution."

Three days later, a dynamite blast partially wrecked Becker's main plant. This was followed by a visit from another association officer, a man named Abrams. Becker refused to speak to him other than to tell him that he was determined to stick by his prices that were already set

"If you do, Becker, you're going to be bumped off," Abrams warned him.

By this time, Becker was infuriated with the situation and filed a complaint with the State's Attorney's office. Fifteen officers from the association, including Sam Rubin, were indicted. They were defended by Clarence Darrow, best known for defending thrill killers Leopold and Loeb and for arguing on the side of evolution in the famous Scopes "Monkey Trial." The only prosecution witnesses to show up for the trial were Becker and his son, Theodore. When they asked the prosecutor trying the case what had become of the others, he replied: "Go out and get your own witnesses. I'm a prosecutor, not a process server." The racketeers were all acquitted.

Since the law could not protect him, Becker turned to Al Capone. The result was a newly incorporated chain, the Sanitary Cleaning Shops, with Capone, Jake Guzik and Louis Cowan sharing a $25,000 equity. The first Sanitary Cleaning Shop opened near Capone's Prairie Avenue home. "I have no need of the state's attorney, the police or the association now," said Becker, in a statement that angered all of them. "I now have the best protection in the world."

"Capone Wars on Racketeers" was the headline over a *Chicago Daily Journal* story that scorned the authorities, adding "Independent Cleaners Boast Gangsters Will Protect Where Police Failed." The consumers were the ones who really came out ahead. The Sanitary Cleaning Shops maintained the old prices so the association had no choice but to do the same. When Capone was later asked to give his occupation, he liked to say, "I'm in the cleaning business."

Becker never had any reason to regret his decision to go into business with Capone. He was given all of the protection that he could ever need and often liked to say, "You know Mr. Capone, and so does the Master Cleaners' and Dyers' Association." Two years later, Becker came to terms with the association and Capone dropped out of the business, mostly because it never made him the money that he originally thought it would.

One venture that did make Capone a lot of money was dog racing, mostly thanks to his association with a man named Edward Joseph O'Hare – a man who would eventually contribute to the fall of Al Capone.

O'Hare was born and raised in the tough Kerry-Patch neighborhood of St. Louis and lucked into a fortune through dog racing. The inventor of the mechanical rabbit for dog racing was a St. Louis promoter named Oliver P. Smith. He first tested the device with greyhounds in 1909 and spent the next decade developing it. After he filed for a patent, he formed a partnership with sharp, young St. Louis attorney Eddie O'Hare. For the right to install a mechanical rabbit dog track, the owners paid Smith and O'Hare a percentage of the gate. Smith died in 1927 and under an arrangement with his widow, O'Hare obtained the patent rights for the metal rabbit. He became a major player in the racing world and an overnight millionaire.

He started his own dog track in Madison, Illinois, across the river from St. Louis, and founded the Madison Kennel Club. The money poured in until a series of police raids forced him to shut down. A Cook County judge, Harry Fisher, meanwhile, had come to the aid of the Capone outfit by declaring dog tracks

(LEFT) A RARE PHOTOGRAPH OF EDDIE O'HARE.

(RIGHT) THE MECHANICAL RABBIT IN WHICH O'HARE HELD THE PATENT. THE DEVICE WOULD MAKE HIM VERY RICH AND IN GREAT DEMAND BY THE GANGSTERS WHO RAN MOST OF THE DOG TRACKS.

O'HARE DID EVERYTHING THAT HE COULD TO KEEP HIS PERSONAL AND BUSINESS LIFE SEPARATE FROM THE MEN THAT HE HAD TO DEAL WITH. UNFORTUNATELY, HE BECAME HOPELESSLY ENTANGLED IN THEIR AFFAIRS.

legal and preventing the police from raiding them. The judge's brother, Louis Fisher, was the lawyer representing the dog track owners. The Illinois Supreme Court eventually overruled him, but for a time, Capone prospered with dog racing at the Hawthorne Kennel Club, located on the outskirts of Cicero.

Arriving in Chicago in the 1920s, O'Hare opened the Lawndale Kennel Club and was set out to make a fortune. His track was uncomfortably close to Capone's but O'Hare had something that everyone else wanted: the mechanical rabbit. He let it be known that should anyone attempt to harm him or put him out of business, he would withhold the rights to the rabbit in Cook County. If he couldn't operate there, no one could.

Capone knew that O'Hare was making huge profits and was not obligated to pay a percentage of the gate for the use of the rabbit. He didn't want to put O'Hare out of business, but he did decide to cut himself into the profits. When he suggested that O'Hare merge his Lawndale Kennel Club with the Hawthorne Kennel Club, O'Hare readily agreed.

Unlike the later closely supervised legal sport, the dog racing of the 1920s was easy to fix, much to the dismay of innocent bettors. For example, if eight greyhounds were run, seven of them could be overfed or made to run an additional mile before the race, leaving the eighth dog as the almost guaranteed winner.

O'Hare despised the men with whom he had to work almost as much as he loved the money he was making. However, he believed that there was plenty of money to be made working with mobsters, as long as he didn't associate with them personally. "You will run no risk," he once said, "if you don't associate personally with them. Keep it on a business basis and there's nothing to fear."

But O'Hare had his own brushes with the law in his past. At the outset of Prohibition, the authorities permitted a liquor wholesaler named George Remus to store about $200,000 worth of whiskey in the same building where O'Hare had his law office. Remus had to put up a $100,000 bond as surety that he would not remove a single bottle without government sanction. Nevertheless, by 1923, all of the liquor had found its way into the bootleg markets of Chicago, New York, and other cities, even though Remus never saw a cent of profit. Enraged, he filed charges and caused indictments to be filed against 22 men, including Eddie O'Hare. The lawyer was sentenced to a year in jail and fined $500, but won a reversal on appeal when Remus withdrew his original testimony. O'Hare, it was later learned, offered to pay Remus to drop the charges against him.

O'Hare quickly made a name for himself in Chicago and earned the nickname of "Artful Eddie." He was a well-mannered, cultivated and handsome man. A strong athlete, he rode, boxed, swam, and played golf.

He never smoked and never drank hard liquor. Married young, he fathered two girls and a boy. His son, Edward H. O'Hare, nicknamed "Butch", was 12 when his father first met Al Capone. O'Hare idolized the boy and more than anything, he wanted a great career and wonderful life for his son.

O'Hare made many friends in high places. His association with Judge Eugene J. Holland of the rackets courts managed to keep more than 12,000 defendants whom he represented from serving serious prison time. Holland dismissed all but 28 of those arrested and charged with violations of gambling statutes. O'Hare thereby gained a reputation as a well-connected man to know.

Meanwhile, he was making a fortune with the dog racing track. The public was mad about the sport and grandstands could not be constructed quickly enough to hold the increasing crowds. The weekly net ran as high as $50,000. O'Hare acted as both manager and counsel, a double function that he handled with such skill that the Syndicate later entrusted him with other dog tracks in Florida and Massachusetts. O'Hare had planned to keep himself socially above Capone and his mobsters, but he became hopelessly entangled in their affairs.

Unbeknownst to his mob friends, Eddie O'Hare became a secret government informant. He risked his life to provide information for the IRS about Capone's business dealings. He put his life and his business on the line for one reason – his son.

As 1928 came to an end, Capone was working hard to expand into more diversified fields. He kept remembering the advice that had been given to him by his friend and mentor, John Torri: Prohibition was not going to last forever. True, gambling and prostitution would always be profitable but only legitimate enterprises could bring in the kind of money that illegal liquor did. It was time to open new markets and new businesses.

But even as Capone tried to do this, he found the same old challengers continuing to hamper his efforts. The North Side gang, now led by George Moran, was just as relentless as it had been under the leadership of O'Banion, Weiss and Drucci. On the highway between Detroit and Chicago, they hijacked trucks of liquor that had been shipped to Capone by the Purple Gang. They bombed saloons that exclusively sold his beer. They had assisted Joe Aiello when he had reclaimed the liquor stills of Little Italy. There were rumors that Moran had helped plan, and perhaps took a direct hand in, the murder of Pasquale Lolordo. The North Side gang had attempted twice to kill Capone's favorite gunman, Jack McGurn. The second time, the Gusenberg brothers had caught up with him in a telephone booth at the Hotel McCormick and emptied a Tommy gun through the glass. Major surgery and a long recovery in the hospital saved his life. The gang even started their own dog racing tracks. Moran opened a track in Southern Illinois while his business manager, Adam Heyer, opened the Fairview Kennel Club in Cicero, not far from Capone's Hawthorne Kennel Club – which was set on fire during a terrorist attack. In late 1928, Moran became entrenched with the Master Cleaners' and Dyers' Association, a blatant challenge to Capone. He managed to get control of an independent plant, the Central Cleaning Company, and installed two of his men, Willie Marks and Al Weinshank, as vice-presidents. In short, Moran took every opportunity to provoke Capone, both on the streets and in the newspapers.

In December 1928, Capone left for Miami, arriving in time to spend the holidays in the balmy weather of south Florida. In early February, Jack McGurn, arrived from Chicago for a short visit. After his departure, Capone spoke (as telephone records would later show) at length every day with Jake Guzik, who lived at Chicago's Congress Hotel. The telephone conversations between the two men stopped on February 11. Then, a single call was placed to Palm Island three days later.

That call came on February 14 – St. Valentine's Day.

18. A VALENTINE FOR BUGS MORAN

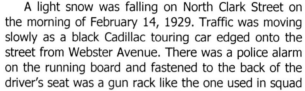

A light snow was falling on North Clark Street on the morning of February 14, 1929. Traffic was moving slowly as a black Cadillac touring car edged onto the street from Webster Avenue. There was a police alarm on the running board and fastened to the back of the driver's seat was a gun rack like the one used in squad cars. The driver of the Cadillac had on horn-rimmed glasses and was a wearing a policeman's uniform, which included a cap with a brass star. A man sitting next to him in the passenger's seat also had on a police uniform. The three men in the back seat were wearing civilian clothes.

As the Cadillac turned the corner onto Clark Street, a truck sideswiped it, forcing it to stop. The truck driver, Elmer Lewis, horrified at having hit what he assumed was a police car, scrambled out of his cab and, filled with remorse and nervous fear, hurried toward the Cadillac. The blue-uniformed man behind the wheel smiled at him, a gap showing where one of his upper front teeth was missing, and waved, reassuring him that no real damage had been done and that he could return to his truck as if nothing had happened. Baffled but relieved, Lewis watched the car drive on for about half a block, then stop in front of a combination garage and warehouse belonging to a shipping and packing company at 2122 North Clark Street. Four men got out of the car and went inside.

POLICE CAR OF 1929

Meanwhile, North Side gang leader George "Bugs" Moran was also on his way to the same garage. The night before, a hijacker had called Moran and offered him a truckload of whiskey from Detroit that could be his for $57 per case. Moran had told him to deliver the shipment around 10:30 a.m. to the North Clark Street garage, which was used as a distribution point for the gang. He told the hijacker that he would have men on hand to help unload the truck.

Moran had been suffering from a head cold and got a late start for the rendezvous. With a gambler friend, Ted Newberry, he left his Parkway Hotel apartment, not far from the garage, a little after 10:30

a.m. The temperature was a biting 15 degrees and a bone-chilling wind was blowing from the west. Hunched against the cold, Moran and Newberry took a shortcut through an alley behind the garage. Willie Marks, one of the gang's specialists in business racketeering, was also running late. He arrived by trolley car at almost the same time.

The garage was a one-story building, constructed from red brick. It was 60 feet wide and 120 feet long, sandwiched between two four-story buildings. Both the plate-glass window in front and the glass-paneled door to the right of it had been painted black to hide the garage's interior. A white placard with black lettering was placed in the lower part of the window. It read:

THE SMC CARTAGE CO. AS IT LOOKED AT THE TIME OF THE MASSACRE

S-M-C CARTAGE CO.   SHIPPING -- PACKING   PHONE DIVERSEY 1471   LONG DISTANCE HAULING

Behind the window, running the width of the building, was a narrow office that was separated from the warehouse by a wooden partition. The warehouse had a concrete floor and brick walls. The original whitewash that had covered the brick walls had turned grimy and yellow with age. Tall, wide doors at the rear opened on the loading area in the alley behind the building.

On the morning of February 14, three empty trucks were parked in the garage. A fourth was jacked up in the center of the floor and lying under it, wearing oil-spattered coveralls and repairing a wheel, was Johnny May, a 35-year-old failed safecracker that Moran hired as a mechanic for $50 a week. May lived in an apartment at 1249 West Madison Street with his wife, Hattie, their six children, and a German shepherd named Highball. The dog was tied by his leash to the axle of the truck that May was fixing. May had brought some scraps of meat for him in a paper bag.

Six other men were in the warehouse that morning, gathered around a coffee pot that percolated on a hot plate. They wore their hats and overcoats, shivering in the unheated building.

The men included the Gusenberg brothers, Frank and Pete, who had a long day ahead of them. As soon as the hijacked liquor was delivered, they were supposed to drive two empty trucks to Detroit to pick up some smuggled Canadian whiskey. Pete "Goosey" Gusenberg was a 40-year-old career criminal who first started showing up in police files in 1902. He spent several years in the Joliet Correctional Center, earning his parole in 1911, only to end up in Leavenworth in 1923, sentenced along with "Big Tim" Murphy and others after the Dearborn Station mail robbery. After his release, he became a gunman for Moran. Pete was married to Myrtle Gorman. As far as she knew, her husband was a salesman.

Frank Gusenberg was four years younger than his brother. Despite having a police record that dated back to 1909, his only prison sentence was for ninety days in Bridewell for disorderly conduct. Frank was a bigamist, married to two women -- Lucille and Ruth -- at the same time. His double life was unbeknownst

VICTIMS OF THE
ST. VALENTINE'S
DAY MASSACRE!

(LEFT TO RIGHT) FRANK GUSENBERG; PETE GUSENBERG; AL WEINSHANK, WHO IT WAS BELIEVED WAS MISTAKEN FOR GEORGE MORAN BY LOOKOUTS ACROSS THE STREET ON THE MORNING OF THE MASSACRE.

to them, as well as the fact that his alleged career as a salesman was a front for robbery and burglary.

Adam Heyer was also present that morning. A business college graduate and certified accountant before doing prison time for embezzlement, he handled all of the gang's finances and also managed the Fairview Kennel Club, the North Side gang's dog-racing enterprise. Little else is known about Heyer. Even his wife of seven months, Mame, did not know his birth date, although he was believed to be around 40 years old.

Al "Gorilla" Weinshank (or Weinshenker), the newest member of the gang, had helped Moran muscle into the cleaning and dyeing rackets and was the owner of a club called the Alcazar. Heavyset and round-faced, he bore a resemblance to Moran, which was enhanced on February 14 by the fact that both men happened to be wearing tan fedoras and gray overcoats. It is believed that he may have been mistaken for Moran by a lookout that morning.

The sixth man was Albert Kachellek, who was better known as James Clark, an alias that he had adopted to spare his mother grief over his frequent brushes with the law. Clark was 42 years old and had first been arrested in 1905 for robbery. He spent the next nine years in and out of the Pontiac Reformatory and Joliet Penitentiary. With a string of murders under his belt, he was known as Moran's chief gunmen, often wreaking havoc alongside the Gusenbergs. Oddly, newspaper reports after the massacre identified

JOHN MAY'S DOG, HIGHBALL

Clark as George Moran's brother-in-law. This mistake was hotly denied by his sister, Mrs. Marie Neubauer, at the coroner's inquest but writers copying previous writers have kept the error alive over the years.

The seventh man in the garage that day was the anomaly of the group. His name was Reinhart Schwimmer and he was an optometrist (although today he would be considered an optician since he had no formal training in conducting eye examinations or treating eye ailments). Schwimmer was 29 and spent most of his time with gangsters. He had started associating with members of the North Side gang after his divorce in 1923. He spent much of his time in the company of O'Banion, Weiss and Drucci, to the detriment of his legitimate business. Even after marrying a rich widow, he couldn't stay away from his underworld pals. He liked to pretend that he was

(LEFT TO RIGHT) MECHANIC JOHN MAY, WHO WAS IN THE WRONG PLACE AT THE WRONG TIME THAT MORNING. HE HAD BEEN KEEPING A PROMISE TO HIS WIFE TO GIVE UP A LIFE OF CRIME; ADAM HEYER; JAMES CLARK.

NO PHOTOGRAPHS OF OPTOMETRIST REINHARDT SCHWIMMER SEEM TO BE IN EXISTENCE TODAY.

AD FOR REINHARDT SCHWIMMER'S OPTOMETRY SERVICE IN THE CHICAGO TELEPHONE BOOK FOR 1929

in the bootlegging business and often told friends that he could have people killed if he wanted to. After his second wife divorced him in 1928, he moved into the Parkway Hotel and befriended George Moran. Schwimmer was considered part of the gang, although he never got involved in crime – he simply liked the rush of being in the company of gangsters. On the morning of February 14, he had dropped into the garage, as he frequently did on the way to work, to see what the gang was up to. He had stayed behind to chat – a decision that he wouldn't live long enough to regret.

Elmer Lewis, the truck driver, was not the only person to see the Cadillac stop at the SMC Cartage Company and the four men go inside, the pair in uniform leading the way. On the second floor of the rooming house next door, the landlady, Jeanette Landesman, was ironing a shirt when she heard the car and the truck collide at the corner. She went to the window to take a look and then saw the Cadillac stop in front of the warehouse. Mrs. Landesman also saw four men go into the building.

When Moran and Newberry saw the Cadillac parked out front, they assumed that a police raid or a shakedown was taking place and hurried down the street to a coffee shop. They decided to wait things out and drink coffee until the cops left. Willie Marks, approaching from the south, reached the same conclusion. He ducked into a doorway and avoided the garage altogether.

On the second floor of the rooming house, Mrs. Landesman heard a peculiar banging sound outside, almost like someone furiously beating a drum. The sound lasted for more than a minute and then it was followed by two thunderous blasts, like two cars backfiring. The silence that followed was broken by the plaintive sound of a howling dog. Disturbed, Mrs. Landesman went back to the window and looked out at the snowy, windy street. Her friend across the way, Josephine Morin, looked out of her third-floor window at the same time and they both saw the same four men reappear. The first two, in civilian clothes, had their hands raised. The two men behind them, wearing police uniforms, held guns to their backs and prodded them toward the car. It was a police raid and two men had been arrested, the two women assumed; the fifth man driving the car must have been a plainclothes detective. They climbed into the Cadillac and drove

away, continuing south on Clark Street and turning right onto Ogden Avenue.

Next door in the garage, the dog continued to howl mournfully and Mrs. Landesman's uneasiness grew. Finally, she asked one of her tenants, a man named C.L. McAllister, to see what was going on next door and find out why the dog was howling. He went next door to the warehouse but he didn't stay inside for long. His face was a ghostly pale when he hurried back up the steps into the rooming house. "The place is full of dead men," he cried.

We will never know for certain what took place inside of the SMC Cartage Co. on the cold morning of February 14, 1929. Only one man survived the initial slaughter and he never talked. However, historians and crime enthusiasts have spent many years trying to put together the pieces of one of the greatest (technically) unsolved crimes in history.

Here's what most think happened that day:

The massacre was set in motion by a telephone call from a rooming house across the street from the garage, signaling the killers that everything was in place for an assault on the North Side gang. It is believed that Weinshank was mistaken for George Moran, who had not actually arrived.

At 10:30 a.m., a Cadillac touring car, painted and outfitted to look like a police car, pulled up in front of the warehouse and four men got out, two of them dressed in police uniforms and two in plain clothes. A fifth man, also in plain clothes, stayed behind the wheel of the car.

 The Moran gang members inside were likely puzzled when the two uniformed officers walked into the

A CROWD GATHERED IN FRONT OF THE SMC CARTAGE CO. IN HOPES OF GETTING A GLIMPSE THROUGH THE PAINTED WINDOWS AT WHAT WAS GOING ON INSIDE. IRONICALLY, THIS PHOTO WAS TAKEN FROM ALMOST THE EXACT SAME VANTAGE POINT THAT THE LOOKOUT HAD IN THE DAYS BEFORE THE MASSACRE.

garage. Protection money was undoubtedly being paid to avoid problems from the police but the gangsters probably assumed that it was a raid being carried out to appease the reformers. It was likely that they would be out of jail

(LEFT) THE POLICE TAKE AWAY THE VICTIMS OF THE MASSACRE THROUGH THE LOADING DOORS IN BACK OF THE BUILDING.

almost as quickly as they were taken in. The uniformed men took weapons from five of the men in the garage. Reinhart Schwimmer was unarmed and so was Johnny May, who was pulled from under the truck protesting that he was only a mechanic and not part of the gang. He was a failed criminal and had promised his wife that he would stay on the straight and narrow. As he had promised her, he carried a St. Christopher medal in his back pocket. The experience was probably only mildly annoying at that point. Schwimmer would most likely have been thrilled to be arrested. Now he would be able to prove to his friends that he really did have gangster connections!

After removing the weapons from the North Side men, the police signaled the two men in plain clothes who were waiting on the other side of the front office partition. The two men walked into the warehouse, Thompson machine guns in their hands. The North Side men were then herded up against the wall and shot to death. Only one of them survived – Frank Gusenberg. With fourteen slugs in his body, he managed to crawl about twenty feet from the rear wall. The others were dead where they had fallen at the foot of the wall, Clark on his face, Weinshank, Heyer, May and Schwimmer on their backs. Pete Gusenberg had died kneeling; his upper body slumped against a chair. Schwimmer was still wearing his hat and Weinshank's tan fedora rested on his chest. Where the seven men had been standing against the wall, the bricks were now splashed with blood. Darker crimson stains ran across the oily floor. Highball, howling and snapping, pulled at his leash, trying in vain to get to the executioners.

The murders had been carried out with precision. The Tommy guns were swung back and forth three times, first at the level of the victim's heads, then their chests, and finally at their stomachs. The victims were

SERGEANT TOM LOFTUS WAS THE FIRST COP ON THE SCENE THAT MORNING. HE KNEW FRANK GUSENBERG AND TRIED TO GET HIM TO TALK.

literally blown to pieces. Some of the corpses on the floor were only held together by bits of gristle, flesh and bone. In spite of this, signs of life must have still flickered in Johnny May and James Clark after the machine gun fire, for they had also been blasted with shotguns at such close range that their faces had almost been obliterated.

Then, spreading leaving pools of blood, seventy shell casings and the mutilated bodies of seven men behind, the plainclothes killers walked out with the phony cops, pretending that they are being arrested. The driver was still waiting for them behind the wheel of the car outside.

After the discovery of the massacre, the police were summoned and the investigation began. It wasn't long before crowds began to gather in front and in back of 2122 North Clark Street, all hoping to get a look at the dead bodies inside.

When the police arrived, Sergeant Tom Loftus was the first on the scene. Oddly, a detective named Clarence J. Sweeney would later place himself at the scene and would also claim that he was at the side of Frank Gusenberg when he died from his wounds in the hospital three hours later. Sweeny kept the myth going over the years, involving himself more and more in the story, but Loftus was actually the first policeman to arrive and he questioned Gusenberg before the ambulance got there. Frank had managed to crawl almost twenty feet, leaving a bloody trail behind him, before collapsing on the floor.

Loftus asked him: "Do you know me, Frank?"
Gusenberg: "Yes, you are Tom Loftus."
Loftus: "Who did it or what happened?"
Gusenberg: "I won't talk."
Loftus: "You're in bad shape."
Gusenberg: "Pete is here, too."

Loftus then asked him if they had been lined up against the wall and Gusenberg again told him that he wasn't going to talk. Gusenberg's legendary statements of "Nobody shot me" and "I ain't no copper" turned out to be fabrications of Detective Sweeney and the newspapers. Sweeney claimed to be at Frank's bedside, yet Loftus detailed Officer James Mikes to be near Gusenberg at all times with no mention of Sweeney ever being there.

Loftus visited Gusenberg at Alexian Brothers Hospital and tried to question him again. Once more, Frank refused to talk. Before he died, though, Loftus asked him if the killers wore police uniforms and this time Frank whispered "Yes" before he finally succumbed to his wounds.

One newspaper quote that was printed correctly came from George Moran. When he learned of the massacre that he had escaped by only a few minutes, he told reporters: "Only Capone kills like that."

"ONLY CAPONE KILLS GUYS LIKE THAT", GEORGE MORAN TOLD THE NEWSPAPERS.

News of the massacre quickly spread throughout the city and across the country – even to as far away as Miami, where Al Capone was conveniently hosting guests who were in town for the impending world championship fight between Jack Sharkey and "Young" Stribling. Capone had invited more than one hundred guests to his place on Palm Island, including sportswriters, gamblers, show business people, racketeers, and politicians. Capone was a boxing enthusiast and bet on Sharkey to win the title. He frequently visited his training camp and was photographed by news cameramen standing proudly between Sharkey and Bill Cunningham, a sportscaster and former All-American center.

On the night of February 14, Capone hosted an elaborate party at his estate. They feasted on a lavish buffet and drank champagne that was served by a half dozen of Capone's bodyguards. Mae Capone stayed quietly in the background, seeing to everything that anyone needed. When it came to be Sonny's bedtime, his father took him by the hand and led him from group to group to say goodnight. The small boy with the hearing aid, a shy, withdrawn little figure with huge eyes and a bashful smile, was a sharp contrast to his bombastic father.

Jack Kofoed, sports editor for the *New York Post*, brought his wife, Marie, to the party. As the humid night wore on, she decided to cool off in the swimming pool. She retired to the Venetian bathhouse carrying her bathing suit and she saw, in the corner of the ladies' dressing room, what appeared to be a crate covered with a canvas drop cloth. She sat down on it to remove her shoes and quickly jumped up with a cry of pain. Something had poked her in the leg. She lifted the cloth and saw that the open crate was filled with shotguns, revolvers and Tommy guns.

The guests at the party that night whispered among themselves about the Chicago massacre that was being reported in the evening papers and on radio broadcasts. Tact prevented them from speaking about it too loudly. Capone never mentioned it at all.

The next morning, when additional details had been published, among them Moran's comment about the massacre, Jack Kofoed called on his party host. "Al, I feel silly asking you this," he said, "but my boss wants me to. Al, did you have anything to do with it?"

"Jack," Capone said, bending a serious gaze on his friend, "the only man who kills like that is Bugs Moran."

In the minds of many Chicagoans, the St. Valentine's Day Massacre was the final blow to the city's already-bloody reputation. Mortified and angry, the Chicago Association of Commerce (which had founded the Chicago Crime Commission in 1919) posted a reward of $50,000 for the arrest and conviction of the killers. Finally having had enough of the mobsters in their midst, the angry public collected another $10,000 for the reward. The city council and the state's attorney's office each added $20,000, bringing the total to $100,000, the biggest price ever put on the heads of gangsters.

But no agency wanted a swifter solution to the case than the police department because many people believed just what the killers wanted them to believe: that police officers had carried out the murders. This was the kind of reputation that the Chicago Police Department had earned by the end of the 1920s – a corrupt, scandal-ridden, lawbreaking organization. Even the local Prohibition administrator, Frederick D. Silloway, spoke out against the department. "The murderers were not gangsters," he said. "They were Chicago policemen. I believe the killing was the aftermath to the hijacking of five hundred cases of whiskey belonging to the Moran gang by five policemen six weeks ago on Indianapolis Boulevard. I expect to have the names of these five policemen in a short time. It is my theory that in trying to recover the liquor the Moran gang threatened to expose the policemen and the massacre was to prevent the exposure."

Russell, by that time police commissioner, was likely unsure about what illegal activities many of his men were involved in, joined in: "If it is true that coppers did this, I'd just as soon convict coppers as anybody else." Chief of Detectives John Egan added, "I'll arrest them myself, toss them by the throat into a cell, and do my best to send them to the gallows."

The next day, Silloway retracted the accusation that he made against the department, claiming that he had been misquoted. To ease tensions with the police, his bosses in Washington transferred him to

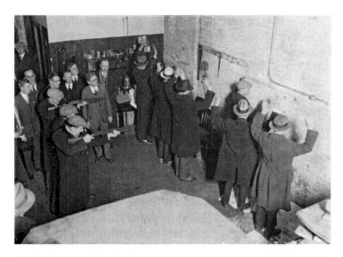

POLICE OFFICERS RE-ENACT THEIR VERSION OF THE MASSACRE EVENTS FOR NEWSPAPER REPORTERS DURING THE INVESTIGATION THAT FOLLOWS.

another district. By then, however, the damage was done and suspicions lingered for many years.

The investigation proceeded under John Egan, the state's attorney's staff and Cook County Coroner Dr. Herman N. Bundeson, each working different angles of the case. Egan and his men searched the SMC Cartage Company warehouse and recovered the empty .45-caliber machine-gun cartridges.

Assistant State's Attorney Walker Butler and his detectives canvassed the neighborhood and found two corroborating stories at 2119 and 2125 North Clark Street, rooming houses run by Mrs. Michael Doody and Minnie Arvidson. Ten days before the massacre, three young men showed up, looking for rooms to rent along North Clark Street. Mrs. Doody was able to accommodate two of them and Mrs. Arvidson took in the third. They said that they were cab drivers who worked the night shift and they insisted on rooms in the front, overlooking Clark Street. The three men rarely left their rooms. When either landlady went in to clean, the tenant was almost always at the window, looking outside. All three of them vanished on the morning of the massacre. Butler suspected that the Purple Gang was somehow involved in the murders and he showed the landladies photographs of sixteen members. They identified three of them as the mysterious lodgers. But when questioned, at Butler's request, by the Detroit police, all three of the men produced unshakable alibis, people who swore that they had been nowhere near Chicago.

On February 22, a fire broke out in a garage behind a house at 1723 North Wood Street, about three miles west of the crime scene. The firemen who answered the call discovered a black Cadillac touring car that had been partially demolished by an acetylene torch, axes and hacksaws. The torch, it was believed, had accidentally started the blaze and the men wrecking the vehicle had fled before its destruction was complete. Egan examined the remains of the Cadillac and the still-legible engine number allowed him to trace the car to Cook County Commissioner Frank Wilson, who had sold it to an auto dealership on Irving Park Road. The car dealer stated that he had then sold the car in December to a man identifying himself as "James Morton of Los Angeles."

From the owner of the Wood Street property, a neighborhood grocer, Egan learned that a

THE CHOPPED-UP AND BURNED REMAINS OF THE CAR THAT WERE FOUND IN THE NORTH WOOD STREET GARAGE -- JUST AROUND THE CORNER FROM THE HEADQUARTERS OF CAPONE ALLIES, THE CIRCUS GANG.

man who gave his name as "Frank Rogers" had rented the garage on February 7. He gave his address as 1859 West North Avenue, which was right around the corner. The house was now deserted but, significantly, it adjoined the Circus Café, the headquarters of Claude Maddox and the Circus Gang, whose ties to Capone, the Purple Gang and Egan's Rats of St. Louis were well known. Even more significant was the fact that one of Maddox's gang members, "Tough" Tony Capezio, had recently been badly burned in a fire. It has been suggested that Capezio had been cutting up the car to get rid of evidence and had accidentally started the fire by using the acetylene torch too close to a can of gasoline. The police could never prove it, however.

EVEN THOUGH BOTH WOULD PLAY AN ACTIVE ROLE IN THE LATER OPERATIONS OF THE OUTFIT, NEITHER TONY ACCARDO (ABOVE) OR SAM GIANCANA TOOK PART IN THE MASSACRE. BOTH WERE LOWLY TRIGGERMEN IN 1929. ACCARDO WAS A MEMBER OF THE CIRCUS GANG WHO BECAME A BODYGUARD FOR CAPONE A SHORT TIME AFTER THE EVENTS OF FEBRUARY 1929. IT IS BELIEVED THAT HE HELPED DISPOSE OF EVIDENCE FROM THE MASSACRE, EARNING CAPONE'S TRUST.

Another member of the Circus Gang at the time was Tony Accardo, who, according to a police theory formed later, helped plan the massacre. Soon after, he became a Capone gunman and was often seen seated in the lobby of the Lexington Hotel with a Tommy gun across his knees. Most likely, however, Accardo was not directly involved in the murders. He was a small-time member of the gang in those days and was likely tasked with disposing of evidence with Capezio and others.

Unable to pin anything on Maddox and his men, the police continued searching for the elusive "James Morton" and "Frank Rogers" but no trace of them were ever found. As for George Moran, he refused to disclose anything about the hijacker who had telephoned him on the night before the massacre, other than that he had known him for a long time and planned to "pay him back" for his treachery.

The police only had theories, but they developed one that they believed was accurate:

Al Capone knew about the massacre and had requested it, leaving the planning to others. Jack McGurn certainly took part in the planning, as did Jake Guzik, who spoke frequently with Capone from the Congress Hotel. The plan that was conceived called for two men who could persuade their victims to surrender their weapons without a fight, which was the reason behind the police uniforms. These men had to be total strangers to the Moran men, which meant that they had to be imported (likely by Maddox) from either Detroit or St. Louis. They were kept hidden until needed and then provided with the phony police car.

The function of the three Clark Street lodgers was to watch for Moran in exactly the same way that earlier Capone gang ambushes had been carried out. The killers were then informed by telephone when Moran entered the warehouse. What saved Moran's life was his resemblance to Al Weinshank. Believing that Moran had already arrived, the lookouts gave the word to the killers.

The collision with the truck on Clark Street suggested the route that the killers took – north along Wood Street for a mile to Webster Avenue, then east for two miles on Webster to Clark, which would have taken about fifteen minutes. The men wearing civilian clothes probably waited in the garage's front office while their uniformed companions relieved the Moran gang of their weapons. After that, they emerged with Tommy guns and ordered the seven men to face the wall. Even though the killers may have realized by then that Moran was not there, they didn't dare let the others live since it's possible that they recognized the men in civilian clothing. The killers then staged their final scene to confuse any witnesses as they reappeared on the street posing as policemen after a raid with their prisoners.

The investigators may have figured out the methods of the massacre, but debate raged as to the reasons behind it and just who might have been involved – debate that continues to this day.

Crime historians have named the most likely suspects (even though they number more than the actual number of killers – everyone has their own opinion) as:

FRED "KILLER" BURKE

FRED "KILLER" BURKE

Fred Burke, who was born Thomas Camp on a farm near Mapleton, Kansas, in 1893, was an armed robber and contract killer who was responsible for many crimes during the Prohibition era. He first ran afoul of the law at the age of 17 after being duped into participating in a land fraud scheme by a traveling salesman who had befriended his family. Fleeing his home in disgrace, he ended up in Kansas City and became involved with the underworld. By 1915, he was in St. Louis and joined up with the infamous Egan's Rats.

Under an indictment for forgery, Burke (as he had become known) enlisted in the military at the start of World War I. He served as a tank sergeant in France. After returning home, he was arrested in Michigan for fraud and sentenced to a year in prison, followed by another year behind bars in Missouri for his earlier forgery case.

In early 1922, he rejoined Egan's Rats, along with his best friends, fellow St. Louisians and war veterans Gus Winkler, Bob Carey and Raymond "Crane Neck" Nugent. Burke and his pals were suspected of robbing a St. Louis distillery of $80,000 worth of whiskey in April 1923. During the robbery, Burke disguised himself as a police officer to fool the security guards. He also plotted and carried out the robbery of the United Railways office, the city's streetcar provider, on July 3, 1923. The heist netted $38,000.

After the Egan's Rats gang fell into disarray with the imprisonment of its leadership in 1924, Burke and his friends moved to Detroit, where they began committing robberies in the region and carrying out contract murders for the Purple Gang. Burke was suspected of introducing the Tommy gun to Detroit's underworld in March 1927 when he used on to kill three rival gangsters who were suspected of killing his friend, Johnny Reid.

By the summer of 1927, the relationship between Burke's crew and the Purple Gang had cooled. Burke accused gang boss Joe Bernstein of killing his friend Ted Werner in New Orleans on April 16 and the gang claimed that Burke was kidnapping Purple Gang associates for ransom. The feud turned bloody on July 21 when Burke was accused of machine-gunning a number of gang members as they exited a bar on Oakland Avenue. Three men were wounded and one, Henry Kaplan, was killed. Joe and Abe Bernstein sent word that they wanted to iron out a peace treaty with Burke and Gus Winkler at a downtown Detroit hotel but Burke sent Raymond Shocker in his place – who was almost killed in an ambush.

After the falling out with the Purple Gang, Burke moved his crew to Chicago, where they joined up with Capone's organization. Burke and Winkler, especially, grew close to the Chicago crime boss, who referred to them fondly as his "American Boys."

Over time, Fred Burke and his crew were suspected of robbing banks and armored cars in St. Louis, Louisville, New Jersey, Wisconsin, Michigan, Indiana, Los Angeles and Ohio. The Ohio job, on April 16, 1928, resulted in the murder of a Toledo police officer. Burke and his partners were also linked by ballistic evidence and informants to the murder of Brooklyn mob boss Frankie Yale in July 1928.

The Burke crew became the leading suspects in the St. Valentine's Day Massacre and Burke was even named publicly as a suspect by the Chicago Police in the weeks after the murders. Burke has never been "officially" linked to the massacre but he was convincingly fingered by Byron "Monty" Bolton in 1935.

Bolton was an expert machine-gunner in the U.S. Navy before turning to a life of crime and kidnapping and stated that the planning for the massacre was carried out at a resort owned by Fred Goetz on Cranberry Lake, six miles north of Couderay, Wisconsin, in October or November of 1928. Capone was present, as was Gus Winkler, Burke, Goetz, Louis "Little New York" Campagna and William Pacelli, a North Side politician who was later elected to the Illinois state senate. Bolton also involved Claude Maddox in the plot. Bolton himself claimed to be one of the lookout men on Clark Street, a claim that seems backed up by the fact that a medicine bottle and a letter, both with his name on them, were found in one of the rooming houses during the neighborhood canvass. Bolton claimed that Burke and Fred Goetz were the men disguised as police officers during the massacre and Maddox, Carey and Winkler were the shooters in plain clothes.

Bolton was under arrest in St. Paul, Minnesota, for the ransom kidnapping of Edward Bremer, along with members of the Barker Gang, when he made the confession. Informed of his statement, Chicago police captains John Stege and William Shoemaker, probably the most honest crime fighters in the city during the Prohibition era, believed Bolton. "The first suspect I sent for was Maddox," Shoemaker said. "I felt sure he was one of the executioners but I could not prove it. I had to let him go." Lieutenant Otto Erlanger of the homicide bureau added that he thought Bolton's story was "true in every word."

Bolton's claims were later corroborated by Gus Winkler's widow, Georgette. Bank robber and Barker Gang member Alvin Karpis later endorsed Bolton's story to Capone biographer John Kobler.

But not everyone was convinced. FBI director J. Edgar Hoover, who had Bolton in custody on the federal kidnapping charge, dismissed his claims. He stated that the massacre was a "Chicago matter for the local police to resolve." Claude Maddox was brought in for another round of questioning in 1935 but he was let go. Nothing was done to follow up on the story and as the press lost interest, it faded away and was mostly forgotten.

As for Fred Burke, his downfall came after he hit a motorist in St. Joseph, Michigan, on December 14, 1929. Burke had been drinking and tried to flee the scene. A police patrolman named Charles Skelly overtook him and forced him to the curb. As Skelly jumped onto the car's running board, Burke shot him three times and sped away. Skelly died at the hospital and Burke's car was found on U.S. Highway 12, cracked up against a telephone pole. The registration papers in the glove compartment bore the name "Fred Dane" and listed an address on the outskirts of St. Joseph. When police raided the bungalow, they found a bulletproof vest, bonds recently stolen from a Wisconsin bank, two Thompson submachine guns, pistols, and thousands of rounds of ammunition. Ballistics tests conducted by nationally renowned expert Calvin Goddard revealed that both of Burke's Tommy guns had been used in the St. Valentine's Day massacre; the

THE ARSENAL FOUND INSIDE OF BURKE'S HOME INCLUDED TWO TOMMY GUNS THAT WERE USED IN THE ST. VALENTINE'S DAY MASSACRE AND ONE THAT HAD BEEN USED TO KILL FRANKIE YALE.

same tests showed that one of them had been used to murder Frankie Yale, as well.

Burke became America's most wanted man but he didn't stay on the run for long. He managed to elude the police for just over a year, until he was arrested at a farm near Green City, Missouri, on March 26, 1931. The Chicago authorities wanted him for his possible role in the massacre but Michigan refused to surrender him, preferring to try him for the murder of Patrolman Skelly. He was sentenced to life imprisonment at the Michigan State Penitentiary and died there of heart disease at the age of 47.

Fred "Killer" Burke is the only man who has been tied by evidence to the massacre, but he certainly didn't act alone and the list of his possible accomplices is a long one.

FRED SAMUEL GOETZ

Goetz, also known as "Shotgun" George Zeigler, was a long-time mobster who was also believed to have been involved in the massacre. Born in Chicago, the son of German immigrants, he was stationed at Langley Field, Virginia, during World War I and served as a pilot in the U.S. Army's aviation branch, where he rose to the rank of second lieutenant. After graduating from the University of Illinois, in 1922, Goetz worked as a lifeguard at Clarendon Beach until he was charged with sexually assaulting seven-year-old Jean Lanbert, after luring her into an alley with a promise of candy. Goetz denied the charges and jumped bail on June 10, 1925. Four months later, Roger Bessner implicated Goetz in the failed robbery of Dr. Henry R. Gross, in which the family driver was killed.

During the next several years, Goetz would become associates with underworld figures such as Joseph "Yellow Kid" Weil and Morris Klineman, as well as participating in several armed robberies, including the robbery of $352,000 from the Farmers and Merchants Bank, in Jefferson, Wisconsin, with Fred Burke, Gus Winkler and others, in 1929. His connections with Burke and his crew possibly led to his inclusion in the massacre hit squad. According to Byron Bolton, he was one of the men dressed as police officers.

After the massacre, Goetz left Chicago and began bootlegging operations in Kansas City, Missouri before becoming associated with the Barker Gang. He later participated in several bank robberies with Alvin Karpis, Fred and Doc Barker and took part in the kidnapping of St. Paul millionaire Edward Bremer in 1933. Goetz was the gang member who collected the ransom and released Bremer.

Goetz was killed on March 20, 1934. He had returned to Chicago and was murdered in a drive-by shooting outside of a closed Cicero restaurant, the Minerva. The murder remains unsolved, although a number of his former associates, including the Barker Gang, had reasons to kill him. Alvin Karpis believed that Outfit boss Frank Nitti ordered the murder.

ROBERT CAREY

Born in St. Louis, Carey joined the Egan's Rats gang when he was in his early twenties. By 1917, he had become close friends with Fred Burke and after serving in the Army during World War I, continued on as a low-level associate in Egan's Rats. At this time, while Burke was serving prison time, Carey became associated with a Cincinnati gunman called Raymond "Crane Neck" Nugent. Both men were suspected of robbing a Cincinnati bank messenger in December 1921 and trying to fence the bonds through the Egan's Rats.

Carey was known for being exceptionally smart but he was also an alcoholic who took great risks and became violent when he drank. In spite of this, he was the mastermind behind the St. Louis distillery robbery and Fred Burke's policeman disguise in 1923.

After the collapse of Egan's Rats in 1924, Carey went with Burke to Detroit and was arrested in March for the robbery of the John Kay jewelry store. While Carey was suspected of being part of the crew, only Isador Londe was convicted of the crime and received a 10- to 20-year sentence.

Cary continued to run with Burke and his crew through the 1920s. He was specifically charged by the Detroit authorities for the murder of two freelance gunmen, James Ellis and Leroy Snyder, on March 16, 1927, after he caught them cheating at poker. On April 16, 1928, Carey, along with Winkler, Goetz, Nugent and Charlie Fitzgerald, took part in an American Express armored car robbery in Toledo, Ohio. The robbers made off with $200,000 and a Toledo cop named George Zientara ended up dead.

Even though he was never publicly named as a suspect, Carey was sought by the Chicago police after the St. Valentine's Day Massacre. Nothing could be pinned on him, although Byron Bolton did name him as one of the men involved.

With most of his closest associates locked up or dead by early 1932, Carey left Chicago for the East Coast. He and his girlfriend, Rose, ended up in Baltimore, where they began blackmailing well-to-do businessmen and politicians. The marks would bed Rose and Bob would discreetly take pictures. This operation had dead-ended by summer and they moved north to New York. Carey, now using the alias of Sanborn, rented a flat on 104th Street and started a high-quality counterfeiting racket. Despite his newfound success, Carey was drinking heavily – with fatal results. According to NYPD reports, on the night of July 29, 1932, a drunken Carey went berserk and shot Rose to death, after which he turned the gun on himself.

RAY "CRANE NECK" NUGENT

Ray Nugent was born in Cincinnati around 1895 and came to St. Louis during the heyday of Egan's Rats. He managed to talk himself into the gang's good graces and became friends with fellow war veteran Bob Carey. Nugent was heavily built, with a strong jaw, muscular shoulders and no neck to speak of. For reasons that no one can fathom (except, perhaps, irony), he was nicknamed "Crane Neck." Although no one actually called him that, the moniker followed him on police records for the rest of his life. Ray also sometimes used the alias "Gander." He and Carey shared similar voracious appetites for booze and violence.

Nugent also became closely associated with other suspected massacre gunmen like Burke, Winkler and Goetz and took part in the distillery robbery in April 1923. When the remnants of the gang left St. Louis for Detroit in 1924, Nugent went with them. He was involved in a number of robberies with elements of Burke's crew, including a home invasion on Halloween night 1926. Nugent, Carey and another crew member named Tony Ortell broke into the home of real estate broker Edward Loveley and made off with about $40,000 in diamonds, furs, and antiques. Carey and Nugent, identified from mug shots, dumped the loot and fled west to Los Angeles, where they were arrested on suspicion of robbing a jeweler. Both were extradited to Detroit to stand trial for the Loveley caper but the charges didn't stick.

In the spring of 1927, Nugent, Carey and Gus Winkler kidnapped popular Detroit gambler Mert Wertheimer with plans to bring in a six-figure ransom. They drove him to Chicago and kept him in a North Side apartment on Grace Street. It turned out that Wertheimer was not only protected by the Purple Gang but was also a good friend of Al Capone. Winkler and his wife, Georgette, had just moved into the Leland Hotel when Winkler was contacted by an emissary of Capone, who wanted to have a meeting.

Knowing that Wertheimer was stashed only a couple of blocks away, Winkler nervously told Carey and Nugent that Capone wanted to meet with them. Not surprisingly, they had no interest in accepting an invitation to their own murder and wanted nothing more than to get out of Chicago as soon as possible. Winkler talked them into coming with him to the meeting and, hoping to make a good impression on the crime boss, cleaned up his partners and gave them a crash course in manners.

In May 1927, the three men met with Capone at the Hawthorne Inn in Cicero. Capone was his often-charming self and explained to his guests how the kidnapping racket was no place for talented men. He suggested that they get into a real business. Winkler enjoyed the evening chatting with Capone but, to his dismay, both Nugent and Carey drank too much and began talking loudly and laughing. Surprisingly, Capone ignored their antics and generously offered the three men some cash to replace the ransom that they were going to lose by releasing Wertheimer. Winkler declined but his pals eagerly snatched up the money. Shaking his head, he was pleased about how the evening had gone but less than thrilled with the behavior of Nugent and Carey.

Mert Wertheimer was immediately released and Carey and Winkler settled in Chicago. Nugent went back to Ohio where his wife, Julia, was living with their two children. His partners began hanging around Capone, hoping to ingratiate themselves with the mob boss and his men. Capone began calling the crew his "American Boys" and after the almost disastrous robbery in Toledo, he gathered them all back to Chicago.

Nugent became one of the leading suspects in the massacre, mostly because of the company that he kept and the fact that he was dangerously violent. Many believe that he was one of the plainclothes killers, who machine-gunned the North Side gang members to death.

After the massacre, Nugent remained a low-level member of the Capone gang. In April 1930, he was arrested for drunk driving with Ralph Capone in the Miami area. About a year later, Nugent disappeared. Rumor had it that he had become a liability to the Outfit and had been taken out into the Everglades and fed to the alligators. Whatever happened, he was never again seen. In 1951, his wife filed a petition in Cincinnati to have him legally declared dead so that she could claim his pension as the widow of a World War I veteran.

GUS WINKLER

GUS WINKLER

Born August Henry Winkeler in St. Louis in 1901, Winkler was a member of the St. Louis-based Cuckoo Gang during his teenage years. After a stint as an Army ambulance driver in World War I, Winkler joined up with the Egan's Rats before moving to Detroit with Burke and the other remnants of the gang in 1924.

Working with the Purple Gang until 1927, he and Burke were often hired out for freelance work and began their own crime spree holding up banks, armored cars, and mail trucks. After moving to Chicago, Winkler and the others began working almost exclusively for Al Capone and are believed to have been directly involved in the massacre. It is widely believed that Winkler was the fifth man in the murder team, the one waiting behind the wheel of the black Cadillac while the others murdered the North Side gang members.

Winkler and Burke's crew broke up during the fallout from the St. Valentine's Day Massacre, and Winkler was suspected of planning and later taking part in the robbery of two million dollars from a bank in Lincoln, Nebraska in September 1930. However, he gave evidence against his partners and returned his share of the loot in exchange for clemency, damaging his reputation in the underworld. In spite of this, he was able to carve out a lucrative position in the rackets of Chicago's North Side, mostly based on the close friendship that he had maintained with Capone.

Upon Capone's 1931 imprisonment, Winkler was surrounded by gangsters who didn't trust him, in particular Frank Nitti. However, he still remained a force in post-Capone Chicago, controlling rackets on the North Side independent from the Outfit.

In June 1933, a close friend of Winkler's, Verne Miller, was accused of helping gun down three policemen and a federal agent in an attempt to free bank robber Frank Nash during the Kansas City Massacre. Winkler, who was trying to sever ties with the violent end of the business so that he could concentrate on his gambling and nightclub operations, was seen going into the Banker's Building office of

Melvin Purvis, the head of the FBI's Chicago field office, likely to give him a tip on where to find Miller. The fact that Winkler seemed to be getting cozy with the cops again – once a snitch, always a snitch, in the standard underworld credo – was too much for Frank Nitti to handle.

At 1:40 p.m. on October 9, 1933, as Winkler was going into the beer distribution office of Charles Weber at 1414 North Roscoe Avenue, a green delivery truck cruised by and its occupants opened fire with shotguns. Winkler was hit with 72 shotgun pellets and succumbed to his wounds a half-hour after arriving at a local hospital. He managed to gasp out the Lord's Prayer before he died. His murder remains officially unsolved.

CLAUDE MADDOX

"Screwy" Claude Maddox was born John Edward Moore in St. Louis in 1897. Little is known about him prior to his founding of the Circus Gang, which had a beer and booze concession on the western edge of Dion O'Banion's territory during Prohibition. His headquarters, the Circus Café, was a dive bar on North Avenue and would figure prominently in the theories regarding the massacre. Maddox was a former member of Egan's Rats and for this reason, he welcomed Burke and his crew to the city and likely offered them assistance covering things up after the massacre. If Byron Bolton's story is to be believed, Maddox also took part in planning and carrying out the murders.

After the black Cadillac touring car that had been driven by the massacre killers was found in the burning garage on Wood Street, the police traced the renter of the garage, "Frank Rogers," to an address that adjoined the Circus Café. The bar was jointly owned by Maddox and "Tough Tony" Capezio, who had recently suffered burns. Detectives were excited about what they saw as a new lead, connecting the massacre to the Circus Gang. In addition, the address given by "Frank Rogers" was also directly across from the apartment of the late Patsy Lolordo and had apparently been used as an indoor shooting range. The café itself had been recently closed and was being stripped of its fixtures, but at the address listed by "Rogers," police found guns and overcoats flung down in such as way that seemed to indicate that the occupants had fled in a hurry as soon as the garage caught on fire.

Maddox had very basic living quarters at the café, but he had given his home address as 1642 Warren Avenue on the West Side. He had a reputation as a Capone man, his territory offering a safe place between the Aiellos in Little Italy and Moran on the North Side. Members of the Circus Gang included gunmen like Jack McGurn, Tony Accardo, Rocco de Grazia and assorted hoods from the "Patch," an area of fluctuating boundaries on the West Side that comprised nearly a dozen different European immigrant communities. It was also a hangout for Maddox's St. Louis friends, Al Capone's so-called "American Boys."

Maddox was almost immediately suspected as being part of the massacre, but the cops could never make anything stick. After Byron Bolton's 1935 confession, he was picked up once again but investigators had to let him go since Hoover and the FBI refused to cooperate with the Chicago police.

Maddox stayed involved with the Outfit after Capone went to prison and his effectiveness in union racketeering spared him the fate of Gus Winkler when Frank Nitti began cleaning house in the early 1930s. Those skills, along with his partnership in a semi-legal gambling equipment firm, allowed him to rise high in the mob before his death in 1958. Maddox quietly passed away at his Riverside, Illinois, home – one of the few men connected to the massacre who did not die a violent death.

The theories about who was involved in the St. Valentine's Day Massacre are as numerous as the theories as to why the massacre took place. There have been scores of theories put forth by crime historians over the years and just about any of them can make sense if they are presented in just the right way. Many of them are preposterous and impossible and others seem to make a cunning bit of sense. Logically, the massacre was ordered by Capone (but planned by his henchmen) in an effort to eliminate

George Moran and bring an end to the harassment by the North Side gang once and for all.

There were a number of reasons why Capone would want Moran and his gang out of the way, not the least of which was the constant hijacking of Capone's liquor trucks and the undercutting of his business interests in the city. It could have also been retribution for the murders of Tony Lombardo and Pasqual Lolordo, Capone's presidents of the Unione Siciliane. Moran's backing of Joe Aiello would have also increased Capone's hatred for the man. Capone was also being hampered by Moran in his takeover of the Cleaners' and Dyers' Association, which was a powerful racket into which Capone wanted to expand. There was also the matter of revenge for the attempted murder of Jack McGurn by the Gusenbergs, something that likely figured into McGurn's thoughts as he helped plan the massacre.

The massacre was a simple, cold-bloodedly efficient assassination that was meant to kill George Moran and break the back of the North Side gang, opening up its territories and operations to Al Capone. While the identities of the killers will most likely always remain a mystery – the reason behind the massacre has never seemed very puzzling.

In spite of this, many writers feel the need to try and shock the public with alternate theories or bizarre twists that really don't seem to be backed up by the historical evidence. For instance, one claim was that the men were not gathered at the garage that day to await a liquor shipment, but to discuss the presence of a traitor in their midst and take action against him. It was suggested that Moran would not have come to the warehouse for a mere liquor shipment. However, this angle does not hold up when one takes into account the fact that Moran was a "hands-on" gang manager who often took delivery of shipments. In addition, he was supposed to be there because his presence had been specifically requested by a hijacker whom he knew and trusted. Moran railed against this man so often in the newspapers after the massacre that it's unlikely that he didn't exist. It's also unlikely that Reinhart Schwimmer – essentially a "gangster groupie" – would have been allowed to hang around the garage that day if such an important meeting was going to be taking place.

Perhaps the most ridiculous theory is one that received some attention in recent years. It asserted that Capone had nothing to do with the massacre at all – that it was a revenge killing by a low-level gunman who was looking to avenge his cousin. The theory was based one of the hundreds of crackpot letters that were received by the police and the FBI after the massacre. This particular letter had been sent by Frank Farrell in January 1935. Farrell, who had a patronage job in the state highway department, wrote about his connection to William Davern, Jr., a former fireman who was shot in a gangster hangout called the C&O Cabaret and Restaurant at 509 North Clark Street. Davern died a month later from his wounds – but not before allegedly getting some startling information. According to Farrell's letter, William "Three-Fingered Jack" White, who was a cousin of Davern, told Davern (who was visiting him at the county jail) that Davern had been shot by one of the Gusenbergs. In retaliation for Davern's shooting, White lured the Gusenbergs to the garage at 2122 North Clark Street and then killed them, along with everyone else inside. Farrell waited several years and then sent the information in a letter to the FBI.

While an interesting story, the tale in the letter has a number of fatal flaws. Despite a 2010 book that touted it as the "solution" to the massacre mystery, most historians dismissed the letter (which was easily accessible in the files of the case) because it has no credibility. One of the biggest problems with the letter theory is that it does not explain how Fred Burke ended up with the Tommy guns that were used in the massacre (one of which had killed Frankie Yale in 1928). It also doesn't explain the need for Byron Bolton as a lookout (remember that physical evidence placed him at the scene), or why Claude Maddox and his gang disposed of the car involved, or most of the other known facts in the case.

The letter also confuses names and basic details of the case, such as how people are related to one another. For example, Davern's mother was not the sister of Jack White's father. Davern's mother, born Anna Gillespie, was the sister of White's mother, Mary Gillespie.

Another problem is that, according to the Chicago Police Department, the leading suspect in the fatal shooting of William "Billy" Davern was Jack McGurn. This means that if one of the Gusenberg brothers, or some other North Side gang member, did not shoot Davern, then White would have no reason to kill them in revenge. According to a newspaper account, Davern was likely involved in the March 1928 attempt on McGurn's life.

It should also be noted that Davern was so serious after being shot that he lingered in the hospital until he died in December 1928, fighting for his life the entire time. It is highly unlikely that he could have gone to the Cook County Jail so that White could tell him that he had been shot by one of the Gusenbergs.

This brings us to the most important problem of all: according to newspaper and police reports, Jack White was in the Cook County Jail when the St. Valentine's Day Massacre took place. White was sent to jail in 1926, without bond, for his part in the murder of a police officer. He was not released until July 1929, when his conviction was overturned, months after the massacre took place. Therefore, White couldn't have been out of jail killing anyone on February 14, 1929.

How this theory has gained attention in recent times is more puzzling than trying to pin down who carried the Tommy guns into the SMC Cartage building that day. Cook County Coroner Herman Bundeson, who Farrell contacted before writing to J. Edgar Hoover, probably dismissed Farrell's letter as nonsense as soon as he checked the jail records. He rejected the letter as a fraud and so should anyone with a genuine interest in the case.

While Fred "Killer" Burke became a leading suspect in the massacre, he was far from the only one. Almost immediately after the murders, the Chicago police began "rounding up the usual suspects" and one of the first arrested was Jack McGurn. The warrant sworn out for McGurn's arrest was based on the testimony of a young man named George Brichet who happened to be walking down Clark Street in front of the warehouse on February 14. As he was passing by, he saw the five killers enter and he heard one of them say "C'mon, mac." He picked out McGurn's photograph from a police rogue's gallery and said that he recognized him. Many historians have questioned the identification, although they don't doubt that Brichet heard what the man said correctly. In those days, "mac" was a casual way for someone to address a man, like "pal," or "buddy." It didn't necessarily have to be someone's actual name. Brichet heard it and repeated it to the cops, who saw it as a perfect excuse to roust McGurn, whom they felt was undoubtedly tied into the massacre somehow.

When the police showed up for McGurn, they found him at the Hotel Stevens with a blonde woman named Louise Rolfe. He was indicted for seven murders and his bail was set at $50,000. He raised that amount using a hotel that he owned that was valued at over one million dollars as collateral. McGurn said he was with Miss Rolfe when the killings took place, causing newspapermen to dub her "the Blonde Alibi." He swore that he had never left her side at the Hotel Stevens between 9:00 p.m. on February 13 and 3:00 p.m. on February 14. The state's attorney had him indicted for perjury but before McGurn could be tried on that charge, he married Louise Rolfe. A wife cannot be forced to testify against her husband.

As the investigation into the massacre dragged on, McGurn's lawyer began calling for his client to be brought to trial. Under Illinois law, if the accused demanded to be tried at four separate terms of court and the state was not prepared to prosecute him, the state had to dismiss the case. Between the spring and winter of 1929, McGurn made four demands for a trial. None of them were met and on December 2, he walked out of the courtroom a free man. By then, the authorities had revised their version of his role in the massacre and concluded that although he did not take part in the murders, he definitely had a role in their planning. They had no evidence of this, however, and McGurn was never charged with anything relating to the crime.

Later, he and Louise were convicted of conspiring to violate the Mann Act, which prohibited interstate transport of women for "immoral purposes" when they were visiting Capone in Florida. The convictions were later overturned by the U.S. Supreme Court.

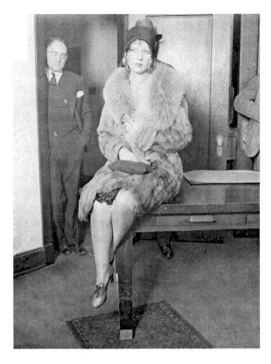

MCGURN IN COURT WITH LOUISE ROLFE

(LEFT) LOUISE ROLFE, THE BOMBSHELL THAT REPORTERS DUBBED THE "BLONDE ALIBI". MCGURN LATER MARRIED HER SO THAT SHE DIDN'T HAVE TO TESTIFY AGAINST HIM IN COURT.

McGurn was not the only one arrested and indicted for having a possible role in the massacre.

During Coroner Bundeson's inquest, he summoned every gun dealer in Cook County that he could find, including Peter von Frantzius, the reputed weapons source for all of Chicago gangland. He admitted that he had recently sold six Tommy guns to a man named Frank H. Thompson, who was allegedly acting as a buyer for the Mexican consul general, whose government wanted the weapons to help put down revolutionaries. The police knew that Thompson was an ex-convict, a safecracker, a hijacker and lately, an arms dealer. He was then wanted for attempting to machine-gun his wife and her lover in his hometown of Kirkland, Illinois.

Thompson surrendered to Bundeson. He admitted that he had purchased the guns but claimed that he had sold them to James "Bozo" Shupe, who was killed soon after. Shupe, detectives knew, was a close associate of Capone gunmen Scalise, Anselmi and Joseph Giunta, the current, Capone-backed president of the Unione Siciliane. With these thin connections, the police arrested the three Sicilians, mostly on the basis that if Capone had ordered something violent and bloody to be carried out, these men were probably involved. Giunta, with no actual evidence against him, was immediately released, but new witnesses placed Scalise and Anselmi in the fake police car. They were indicted and then released after posting a $50,000 bond.

Unfortunately, they didn't live long enough to ever stand trial for the massacre murders.

Two days after Scalise, Anselmi and Giunta were arrested, the state's attorney added four more names to the list of alleged assassins, bringing the total to seven, instead of five. The first was Joseph Lolordo, a natural suspect since his brother had been murdered in a plot likely engineered by Moran. During World War I, he had served with a detachment of machine-gunners and many believed he had been behind the actual murders. He had since disappeared. Another suspect was Frank Rio, a Capone bodyguard and gunman.

The disclosure of the third and fourth names followed eyewitness testimony furnished by prominent Chicagoan H. Wallace Caldwell, president of the board of education. Caldwell had been one of the witnesses to the accident on Clark Street between the truck and the Cadillac. As he glanced over, he happened to see that the driver in the police uniform was missing an upper front tooth. This distinguishing mark fit Fred "Killer" Burke and soon after, he became one of the most wanted criminals in the country.

The other indictment issued was for "James Ray," alleged to be a constant companion of Burke. James Ray may have been an alias used by Gus Winkler or Ray Nugent, but a mug shot of Ray that was published in the March 6, 1929 edition of the *Chicago Tribune* shows a large, square-jawed man with hard eyes and thinning hair. "James Ray" was neither Winkler, Nugent, nor anyone else known to be in the Burke crew. His identity remains a mystery.

So, who really carried out the St. Valentine's Day Massacre? Thanks to the ballistics evidence that tied Fred Burke to the crime, it seems likely that he and his former Egan's Rats companions performed the hit at the behest of Al Capone. But for whatever reasons – indifference, corruption, or lack of hard evidence – the murders were never officially solved.

The St. Valentine's Day Massacre marked the end of any significant gang opposition to Capone, but it was also the event that finally began the decline of Capone's criminal empire. The massacre had simply taken things too far and the authorities – once content to let gangsters kill gangsters – and even Capone's once-adoring public, were ready to put an end to the bootleg wars. The massacre started a wave of reform that would eventually send Capone out of power for good.

RISE AND FALL OF 2122 NORTH CLARK STREET

Chicago, in its own way, memorialized the warehouse on Clark Street where the massacre took place. It became a tourist attraction and the newspapers even printed the photos of the corpses upside-down so that readers would not have to turn their papers around to identify the bodies.

Right after the massacre, the SMC Cartage Company was temporarily boarded up. The building had been leased by Moran gang associate Adam Heyer but was owned by Frank C. Brusky, who moved his own trucking firm (Brusky Overland Movers) into the space in 1930. When he did, he renovated the building, installed two more windows and added space for storage on the second floor.

During the renovations, Brusky discovered a trap door in the corrugated ceiling of the garage, directly above the spot where the Moran gangsters were killed. The door led to a concrete chamber nestled against the second floor wall that was undetectable from below. The chamber contained funnels, a stool, an alcohol hydrometer, a crate that could contain a five-gallon bottle of liquor and a block and tackle system that could lower the crate to the floor of the garage. Brusky called the police, who searched the premises again. They first believed the secret room to be torture chamber (like the one in the basement of the Four Deuces), but Police Captain Thomas Condon concluded that it was merely an alcohol cache.

By 1935, the building was occupied by Red Ball Movers, Inc., a moving company that also did telephone directory pick-

THE FORMER SMC CARTAGE CO. WAS BOARDED UP FOR A TIME, IT'S PREVIOUS INCARNATION OBLITERATED BY PAINTED OVER SIGNS.

THE BUILDING IN THE 1950S, WHEN IT WAS THE WERNER'S STORAGE COMPANY.

(RIGHT) THE INFAMOUS WALL WHERE THE MASSACRE TOOK PACE DURING THE TIME WHEN THE BUILDING WAS OWNED BY THE WERNERS. THEY WERE FREQUENTLY HARASSED BY PEOPLE WANTING TO TAKE A LOOK AT THE WALL.

ups and exchanges each year. In 1936, it was purchased by Anaconda Van Lines, which was owned by Samuel J. McArthur.

In 1949, the building was taken over by Charles and Alma Werner, who turned it into a moving, packing, shipping and storage office for antique furniture. At the time, they had no idea of the buildings' bloody past. They soon found that tourists, curiosity-seekers and crime buffs visited the place much more often than customers, all of them asking to see the infamous wall in back. Depending on her mood, Mrs. Werner either turned them away or allowed them to take a look. She once stated that she wished she and her husband had never bought the building. The Werners were later bought out by the city of Chicago, who wanted the place torn down and replaced with apartments for the elderly.

In 1967, the building was demolished. However, the bricks from the bullet-pocked rear wall were preserved and purchased by a Canadian businessman named George Patey. The bricks were packed and shipped across the border and then put together as the main attraction for a traveling crime show that was displayed at shopping centers, museums and galleries. The show was only a moderate success so, in 1971, Patey opened a Roaring Twenties themed nightclub called the Banjo Palace and rebuilt the wall, for some strange reason, in the men's restroom. Three nights a week, women were allowed to peek inside at this macabre attraction. To make matters even more bizarre, a sheet of clear acrylic was placed in front of the wall so that patrons could urinate and try and hit targets that were painted on the glass. The club closed down in 1976 and the 417 bricks that made up the back wall were placed in storage until 1997.

Patey tried offering the wall for sale, along with a written account of the massacre but had trouble selling the entire wall in one piece. Patey, along with a friend named Guy Whitford (who contacted me about the wall in 2002) tried to sell the single piece for some time, without success. The original lot came with a diagram that explained how to restore the wall to its original form. The bricks were even numbered to facilitate reassembly. They remained on the market for several years, but there were no buyers. Eventually, Patey broke up the set and began selling them one brick at a time for $1,000 each. Patey died in December 2004, by which time he had sold most of the bricks. According to legend, he even sold some of the bricks more than once!

The stories say that some buyers returned their bricks soon after purchasing them. It seemed that anyone who bought one was suddenly stricken with bad luck in the form of illness, financial ruin, divorce and even death. According to the stories, the bricks had somehow been infested with the powerful negative energy of the massacre. This story has been dismissed as a "journalistic embellishment," but there are many who maintain that it's

GEORGE PATEY WITH THE BRICKS FROM THE MASSACRE WALL

the truth. These same people insist that Patey's 417 bricks were not the only surviving bricks from the warehouse.

In recent years, other bricks have emerged that are said to have come from the wall, or at least from the building itself. These were not bricks purchased from Patey; rather they were smuggled out of the lot by construction workers and curiosity-seekers. It was said that from these bricks, too, come the legends of misfortune and bad luck. Are these bricks authentic? The owners say they are, but the reader will have to judge for himself.

HAUNTINGS ON CLARK STREET

Whatever the legend of the bricks, and whether or not they were somehow "haunted" by the horrific murders, there is little doubt that the massacre site on Clark Street was haunted – at least for awhile.

For many years, people walking along the street, or who lived nearby, reported hearing the sounds of screams, moans, muffled voices and even the unmistakable thump-thump-thump of Tommy gun fire. The garage is long gone now, demolished in a misguided attempt by city officials to erase all vestiges of Chicago's gangster past. A portion of the block was taken over by the Chicago Housing Authority and a fenced-in lawn that belongs to a senior citizens' development now marks the area where the garage once stood. Five trees are scattered about the site and the one in the center actually marks the point where the rear wall once stood, where Moran's men were lined up and mercilessly gunned down. The apartment building where Jeanette Landesman lived and where she heard the sound of the terrified German shepherd barking in the garage still stands but all remnants of the SMC Cartage Company have vanished.

Or have they?

According to reports, residents of the senior housing complex built on one end of the lot have had strange encounters in the building, especially those who live on the side that faces the former massacre site. A television reporter from Canada interviewed a woman who once lived in an apartment that overlooked the small park area. She often complained that, at night, she would hear strange voices, sounds and knocking on her door and her window. She complained to the management, who dismissed her claims

THE SITE OF THE MASSACRE TODAY IS AN EMPTY, PARK-LIKE LOT NEXT TO THE ASSISTED LIVING FACILITY ON CLARK STREET.

as imagination but assigned her another apartment. A new tenant moved into the rooms and she also complained of odd happenings, including knocking sounds on her door at night. When she opened the door to see who was there, she never found anyone nearby. One night, the tenant stated that she saw a dark figure wearing an old fashioned-looking hat. He remained in place for a few moments and then faded away. Most of the strange phenomena experienced by the new tenant also faded away and soon eerie events either stopped completely or she became so used to them that they no longer bothered her anymore.

Outside, along Clark Street, passersby occasionally reported strange sounds, like weeping and moaning, and the indescribable feeling of fear as they walked past the former site of the garage. Skeptics tried to laugh this off, saying that the sounds were nothing more than the overactive imaginations of those who knew what once occurred on the site, but based on the reports of those who had no idea of the history of the place, something strange was apparently occurring.

Those who were accompanied by their dogs also reported their share of weirdness. The animals seemed to be especially bothered by the section of lawn where the garage's rear wall once stood, sometimes barking and howling, sometimes whining in fear. Their sense of the tragedy that happened there many years ago seemed to be much greater than that of humans.

However, many believe that what dogs sensed at the site was not the human trauma experienced in the massacre, but rather the trauma that must have been experienced by Johnny May's German Shepherd, Highball. The poor animal must have been terrified by what occurred that morning, from the deafening sounds of the Tommy guns to the bloody slaying of his beloved owner. Tied to the front bumper of the truck, Highball had nowhere to run. It should be noted again that it was not the sound of machine-gun fire that alerted Mrs. Landesman to the horror inside the garage: it was the howling and barking of the dog.

Tragically, Highball was so traumatized by the events of that morning that he had to be put down after the massacre. *Chicago Sun* reporter Russell V. Hamm, one of the first newsmen on the scene, said that the dog was never the same again. His bizarre behavior left the police no choice but to put him to death.

Could the animals that subsequently passed by this empty lot have sensed the trauma suffered by Highball so many years ago? As any ghost buff can tell you, it's the events of yesterday that create the hauntings of today and sometimes, those who lived in the past can leave a little piece of themselves behind to be experienced over and over again.

While the site of the St. Valentine's Day Massacre seems to be quiet today, the violent events of the city's gangster era still reverberate over time. Men like Al Capone, whether city officials want to admit it or not, left an indelible mark on Chicago. It seems that the events of St. Valentine's Day 1929 left one, too.

The ghosts of the massacre may not be still around today – but one of them made his presence known for many years after his death. He had a reason for staying behind and, according to his victim, haunted him to the grave.

19. THE RETURN OF JIMMY CLARK

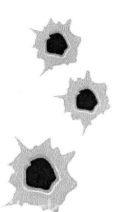

Capone remained in Florida during the early months of 1929, staying as far away from the trouble in Chicago that had been caused by the massacre as he could. He finally returned in the early days of May, likely against his better judgment. What brought him back, however, was an unsettling rumor that was making the rounds that claimed that Anselmi and Scalise, the two Sicilian gunmen that had previously been fiercely loyal to Capone, had shifted their loyalties to the new head of the Unione Siciliane, Joseph "Hop Toad" Giunta. Giunta, Capone also learned, had formed an alliance with another of his enemies, Joe Aiello. Worse yet, Capone heard that Scalise had taken to boasting, "I am the most powerful man in Chicago." With the complex mix of blood oaths and loyalties in the Sicilian culture, such words could only be seen as a direct challenge to Capone's control over the city's underworld. Capone had always been careful to keep the volatile Unione Siciliane on his side. Any disagreement with the Sicilians had the possibility of being lethal and Scalise and Anselmi were particularly dangerous. Capone would be lucky to survive any attempt they made on his life.

Before Capone acted on what were only rumors at this point, he decided to test the loyalties of his two assassins. He invited the two men to dinner, along with Frank Rio, a Capone captain of unquestioned devotion. At the dinner, Capone and Rio pretended to get into a fierce argument and to the astonishment of Scalise and Anselmi, the shouting turned violent when Rio actually slapped Capone across the face before rushing out of the restaurant. Impressed by his daring, the Sicilians secretly met with Rio the next day, offering to involve him in a plot they had cooked up to kill Capone and seize control of all of his rackets. They had unwittingly taken Capone's bait.

Rio spent the next three days negotiating with Scalise and Anselmi and then reported their treachery to the boss. Capone didn't have to think long about how he would dispose of the two gunmen and their associate, Giunta – he would throw a banquet in their honor.

On May 7, Capone, his inner circle and the three traitors gathered for a banquet at a roadhouse called the Plantation in Hammond, Indiana. That Capone wanted to cross state lines for the gathering should have sent up a red flag to the invited guests; anyone who committed a crime, like murder, in Indiana and quickly slipped across the state line into Illinois would be considerably more difficult to arrest. But the guests were compelled to attend since they knew their absence would be a sign they were plotting betrayal.

The guest list that night was large, consisting of nearly one hundred of Capone's closest allies in Chicago. Capone had planned the evening as an object lesson for anyone else who might consider betraying him. Eating and drinking went on long into the night, until Al's jovial mood began to darken. As he addressed his guests – playfully holding a baseball bat to illustrate his lecture on team spirit – he

POLICE OFFICERS AT THE SITE NEAR WOLF LAKE WHERE THE BODIES OF SCALISE, ANSELMI AND GIUNTA WERE FOUND. THE COAT -- AND WHITE "X" -- IS WHERE ANSELMI'S BODY WAS DISCOVERED ON THE GROUND.

suddenly turned on Scalise, Anselmi and Giunta. "This is how we deal with traitors," he growled and before the men could move, Capone soldiers bound them into their chairs. Capone beat each of the men to within an inch of their lives with the baseball bat. But he didn't kill them. As he stepped away, gunmen approached with their weapons drawn and began firing. Scalise threw up a hand to cover his face and a bullet severed his little finger and slammed into his eye. Another bullet crashed into his jaw and he fell out of his chair. Anselmi's right arm was broken by a bullet. Giunta's chest opened up with the force of the slugs, showering the table in front of him with blood. When the men fell out of their chairs and onto the floor, their assailants stood over them and fired more bullets into their backs.

It was not a subject open for debate – Capone was still the most powerful man in Chicago.

The next morning, the three broken corpses were found on a road along the shore of Wolf Lake, an isolated area of water, grasslands and swamps on Chicago's Southeast Side, straddling the border of Illinois and Indiana. In the early 1920s, Wolf Lake was dubbed a "gangland graveyard" by the newspapers and by the police, who frequently found the bodies of gangsters dumped there. The desolate and lonely place was a popular spot for hiding corpses and had earned notoriety in 1924 when the body of kidnapped schoolboy Bobby Franks was discovered there. His killers, Nathan Leopold and Richard Loeb, had been tried during a sensational court case just five years before.

Scalise and Giunta were found in the back of an abandoned car and Anselmi's body lay nearby. Dr. Francis McNamara, who examined the bodies, stated that never in his thirty years as a jail physician had he seen that much damage done to a human body. Scalise and Anselmi were sent back home to Sicily for burial while Giunta, like so many other Chicago gangsters and their victims, was laid to rest in Mt. Carmel Cemetery.

THE SWAMPY AREAS AROUND WOLF LAKE WERE KNOWN AS A "GANGSTER'S GRAVEYARD" IN THE 1920S. THERE ARE A NUMBER OF GHOST STORIES TOLD ABOUT THE AREA.

The question remains whether these men remain peacefully in their graves.

The numerous deaths in the vicinity of Wolf Lake – from swimmers drowning to the gangsters' "one-way rides" --- seem to have left a vivid impression on the place. There are many tales of haunting cries in the woods, eerie screams and even the ghost of a woman in a blue dress who has been seen wandering the shoreline. But perhaps the strangest story is that of the "walking man" who has been seen along nearby Avenue O. This long stretch of roadway goes through the most secluded and remote areas on the Southeast Side, passing closer to Wolf Lake than any other road. It offers just about the only access to the lake to fisherman and outdoorsmen ---- and to the swamps that came to be dubbed the "gangland cemetery."

According to the legend, the ghost of a man in a suit and tie, wearing an old-style fedora, walks the edge of the road, apparently trying to flag down cars that pass by him at night. He is described as looking very ordinary and not ghost-like at all. Most people who have seen him assume that he is someone whose car was broken down on this isolated roadway. The stories say that if a driver stops to offer him assistance, he always disappears.

One witness claimed that he had encountered the man in 1999. He was driving south on Avenue O when he spotted a man in a gray suit and hat walking north in the opposite direction. The man waved at him, apparently trying to get his attention. The driver had just reached an entrance to the conservation area at Wolf Lake, so he pulled in and turned around to see if the man needed help. As he started driving back north, he kept an eye out for the man in the suit. It was starting to get very dark by this time but he knew there was nowhere to go but on the road and that he would quickly come up on the man as he walked along. But strangely, the walking man was nowhere to be seen. The driver slowed down, came to a stop and honked his horn a couple of times --- but the man had vanished.

In 2004, another driver told of an encounter with the walking man. "I was driving north on Avenue O and was traveling alongside Wolf Lake when I saw this man in a suit and hat on the side of the road," he said. "As I passed by him, he turned halfway around and waved both of his arms, as if he wanted me to stop.

"Normally, I would never do this, especially at night, but this guy just looked so normal and well-dressed that I had to think that his car had just broken down somewhere and he needed a ride or a phone," the witness recalled.

"Anyway, I stopped and pulled over to the side of the road. It was maybe thirty yards past where I had seen the man but it took me a little distance to slow down. I figured that since the guy was so intent on waving me down that he would hurry and catch up to me but he never came. I looked in my rearview mirror but there was no one behind me. I waited a minute or so and then got out of the car. All that I can say is that there was no one back there. I have no idea where the guy went but he was definitely gone," he said.

"I don't think that I have driven that way after dark since then," he chuckled a little nervously. "And if I ever do, I am never stopping for a hitchhiker again."

Who is this mysterious man? Despite the number of other slain gangsters that were dumped in this area during the days of Prohibition, many believe that he may be a member of the treacherous trio that Capone killed at the Plantation roadhouse in May 1929. Could the man be Scalise, Anselmi or Giunta? It certainly seems possible. If anyone had a reason to leave a restless ghost behind, it would be one of these traitorous mobsters, each of whom met death much sooner than he planned.

Three days after taking as baseball bat to Scalise, Anselmi and Giunta, Capone left Chicago, supposedly to attend a prizefight in Atlantic City, New Jersey. The fight served as a pretext to Capone's real mission, which was to attend a meeting between racketeers from all over the country who planned to form a commission to resolve disputes among members in a peaceful, business-like fashion. At least, this was the

MEYER LANSKY

CHARLES "LUCKY" LUCIANO

DUTCH SCHULTZ

MEMBERS OF THE PURPLE GANG FROM DETROIT HIDE THEIR FACES FROM THE CAMERA.

stated reason for the gathering. As Capone would discover over the course of the next few days, there was hidden agenda — to strip him of his power and profits because of the publicity and heat that had been generated by what newspapers were calling the "St. Valentine's Day Massacre."

The guests at this gathering included Capone, Jake Guzik, Frank Rio and Frank Nitti from Chicago; "Boo-Hoo" Hoff and Nig Rosen from Philadelphia; Abe Bernstein from the Purple Gang in Detroit; Leo Berkowitz and Moe Dalitz from Cleveland; John Lazia from Kansas City; Longy Zwillman from New Jersey; and Daniel Walsh from Rhode Island. The New York contingent was the most formidable and the angriest at Capone. It was made up of Meyer Lansky, Dutch Schultz, Charles "Lucky" Luciano, Albert Anastasia, Louis Buchalter, Ben Siegel, Joe Adonis and Frank Costello. They also brought with them Johnny Torrio. All of them were upset with Capone for killing Frankie Yale without permission — and for having the gall to do it on their home territory.

The delegates talked for three days, often walking on the beach, where they could be far away from prying ears. They adopted a series of resolutions, some designed to cut Capone down to size and others to lay a groundwork for organized crime after Prohibition. The delegates also formed a commission, with retired Torrio as the head, which would deal with all disagreements between members. Capone managed to maintain his power in Chicago. In fact, the smaller North and South Side gangs were to be merged under his leadership. He did have to agree to some concessions, though, namely that there would be no more killing and that the new head of the Chicago Unione Siciliana would be Capone's enemy, Joe Aiello.

Other resolutions adopted were to have serious consequences for organized crime in the future. There were two men who were conspicuously absent from the Atlantic City conference: Joe Masseria and Salvatore Maranzano, rival Mafia leaders in New York, who were at war over which of them would be the leader. For Luciano, Lansky and the others, such Mafia battles were a thing of the past, a holdover from the days of the ethnic gangs. They wanted a Syndicate in which each member controlled his own territory and no one person was in charge. Thanks to the bloodshed and the publicity that the war was generating, they decided that Masseria and Maranzano had to be removed. The old Sicilian Mafia would be replaced by a new American version.

It was also decided that it would be a good idea for Capone to go to jail. Not only would it allow the heat from the St. Valentine's Day Massacre to continue to cool, but it might be just the thing to save Capone's life. George Moran had not attended the Atlantic City conference. He, along with a few scattered remnants of his gang, was still plotting to kill Capone. Also, as Capone knew, a number of Chicago Sicilians had sworn to avenge Scalise, Anselmi and Giunta. Threatened by killers and harassed by other members of the new Syndicate, he decided on the same course that Torrio had taken when he was in fear of his life from O'Banion and his North Side gang – Capone had himself jailed.

Capone had become friendly at the Hialeah racetrack the year before with a Philadelphia detective named James "Shooey" Malone, so as soon as the conference ended on May 16, he telephoned a friend in Philadelphia and asked him to get a message to Malone. He and Frank Rio then drove to the city and decided to go to the movies at a theater on Market Street. When they came out around 9:00 p.m., Malone and another detective, John Creedon, were waiting for them.

"You're Al Capone, aren't you?" Malone asked.

"My name's Al Brown," Capone replied, "but you can call me Capone if you want to. Who are you?" The detectives flashed their badges. "Oh, bulls, eh? Ah, here's my gun." He handed over a .38 caliber revolver, thereby establishing the grounds to arrest and convict him for carrying a concealed weapon. He elbowed Rio, who also handed over a revolver.

The police magistrate before whom they were arraigned shortly after midnight fixed bail at $35,000 each. They only had a few thousand bucks between them and the two lawyers that Capone had sent for, Bernard L. Lemisch and Cornelius Haggerty, Jr., accused the police of railroading their clients into jail. Capone just smiled – railroading was exactly what he wanted.

The judge imposed the maximum sentence of one year. As Capone was led off with the unlucky Frank Rio to Philadelphia's Holmesburg County Prison, he took a diamond ring from his finger and handed it to his attorney, instructing him to get it to his brother Ralph. Between arrest and imprisonment, only sixteen hours had passed.

Holmesburg, with more than 1,700 prisoners jammed into cells built to hold 600, was one of the country's worst county jails. A few weeks before Capone entered it, the prisoners, rioting over bad food and brutal guards, set fire to their mattresses. The word went out from Chicago that

ALBERT ANASTASIA

BEN SIEGEL

FRANK COSTELLO

EASTERN STATE PENITENTIARY

a $50,000 fee awaited any attorney that could get Capone out of Holmesburg. None succeeded. The same fee was offered to the district attorney in Philadelphia, John Monoghan, as a bribe to procure Capone's release, but he turned it down.

Luckily for Capone, he was transferred in August to the city's larger and more orderly Eastern State Penitentiary. There, Warden Herbert B. Smith made him more comfortable, giving him a private cell and letting him furnish it with Oriental rugs, pictures, a chest of drawers, double bed, bookshelf, lamps and a $500 radio console. As his work assignment, he drew the comfortable job of library file clerk. Capone continued to conduct business from prison. He was allowed to make long-distance telephone calls from the warden's office and to meet with his lawyers and his brother, Ralph, along with Frank Nitti and Jake Guzik, all of whom made frequent trips to Philadelphia. For ordinary inmates, visiting hours were limited to Sunday, but Capone's family and friends could come and see him any day. He also met often with reporters, who kept their readers up to date on Capone's schedule, daily life and reading habits.

He bought $1,000 worth of arts and crafts made by his fellow inmates and mailed them to friends as Christmas presents. He also donated $1,200 to a Philadelphia orphanage. Such seemingly good-hearted deeds aroused a great deal of sympathy for Capone. A civil engineer from Chicago, a total stranger to Capone, who was in Philadelphia on business, got permission to visit him. He warmly shook his hand and told him, "Al, we're with you."

Shortly after arriving at Eastern State, Capone had to have his tonsils removed. The surgeon who performed the operation, Dr. Herman Goddard of the Pennsylvania State Board of Prison Inspections, could barely contain the admiration that he felt for his infamous patient. "In my seven years experience," he said,

"I have never seen a prisoner so kind, so cheery and accommodating."

But Capone was not always "cheery and accommodating" at Eastern State, especially at night, after the lights had gone out. It was at Eastern State Penitentiary, during those dark nights while he tossed and turned in the cot in his cell, that a terrifying memory of the St. Valentine's Day Massacre came back to visit Al Capone.

That memory's name was James Clark.

It was while he was incarcerated at Eastern State that Capone first began to be haunted by the ghost of James Clark, a member of the North Side gang and one of the men killed during the St. Valentine's Day Massacre. While in prison, other inmates reported that they could hear

THE COMFORTS OF CAPONE'S CELL HAD HIM SERVING ANYTHING BUT HARD TIME AT EASTERN STATE AND YET THE ISOLATION AND FORBIDDING SURROUNDINGS WERE MADE EVEN MORE TERRIFYING BY THE PRESENCE OF JAMES CLARK, WHO FIRST BEGAN TO MANIFEST AS A HAUNTING WHILE CAPONE WAS INCARCERATED.

Capone screaming in his cell, begging someone whom he called "Jimmy" to go away and leave him alone. No one had any idea what he was talking about; Capone was alone in his cell. During the daylight hours, he refused to speak about it.

Later, that would change. After his return to Chicago, Capone would speak often about the ghost and about the "curse" that haunted his life. He even went so far as to hire a spirit medium to try and convince the ghost to leave. Was the ghost real? Did Capone imagine the whole thing, or was he already showing signs of the psychosis that would haunt him after his release from Alcatraz years later?

Capone certainly believed the ghost was real and over the course of the next few years, the haunting would become more intense, reaching a point when Capone was not the only person to encounter the vengeful spirit of James Clark.

Good behavior earned Capone a two-month reduction in sentence and it was announced that he would leave Eastern State on March 17, 1930. Warden Smith's helpfulness in prison followed him after his release. With help from the Philadelphia police and Pennsylvania's governor, John S. Fisher, he fooled the reporters, cameramen, curiosity-seekers, and possible assassins waiting for him outside the prison by slipping out the day before. The police aided in the deception on March 17 by roping off an opening at the main gate and patrolling all of the approaches to the prison. Motorcycle officers waited to escort Capone's car to a nearby airfield, where a small plane was stationed to take him north, or so the pilot said. From Warden Smith's office, periodic updates were issued to reporters – Capone was eating scrambled eggs for breakfast; he was restless and ready to leave; release papers that had been signed by the governor were expected to arrive from Harrisburg at any time....

But Capone was long gone. He had been cleared by the parole board several days before. He had been smuggled out of the prison in the warden's car on March 16 and had been driven to the town of Graterford, about twenty miles northwest of Philadelphia. There he remained in custody until his official release the following day. Some of his men had driven to Graterford to pick him up. At 8:00 p.m. on March 17, when was already on his way back to Chicago, Warden Smith emerged from the prison with a grin on his face and announced to reporters: "We stuck one in your eye. The big guy's gone."

Capone vanished and didn't turn up again for four days. Captain John Stege announced that he was going to arrest Capone and run him out of town as soon as he showed his face. Even though he had no legal grounds for doing so, Stege set up a round-the-clock watch at Capone's house on South Prairie Avenue. He placed 25 policemen on duty and told them to arrest Capone on sight. But instead of coming into Chicago, Capone went to Cicero and spent his first night back in Illinois at the Western Hotel, raging drunk. During the early morning hours of March 18, wiretaps set up by federal agents intercepted a call from an unidentified gang member to Ralph Capone. "Listen Ralph," said the caller, "we're up in Room 718 at the Western and Al is getting out of hand. He's in terrible shape. Will you come up, please? You're the only one who can handle him when he gets like this. We've sent for a lot of towels."

"I'll be up a little later," Ralph told him. "Just take care of things the best that you can for now."

After he sobered up, Capone went over to his old headquarters at the Hawthorne Inn and spent the next three days reviewing his financial situation with Jake Guzik. There was little to be happy about. The Depression, which began after the stock market crash five months before, was sharply reducing their profits. The big spenders of the Jazz Age had little money left to spare for booze, girls and gambling.

On Capone's fourth day of freedom, Capone and his attorneys brazenly walked into the detective bureau and the office of Captain Stege. Capone had found out that there were no arrest warrants or indictments that had been issued for him and as much as the cops wanted to push him out of town, they had no legal standing to do so. As Capone passed the press corps waiting for him outside the detective bureau, he chuckled. "I guess nobody wants me," he said, and headed straight for the Lexington Hotel.

His first interview at the Lexington was with *Chicago Tribune* reporter Genevieve Forbes Herrick, to whom he delivered a lengthy tirade of self-justification. Capone probably never considered himself an actual criminal. His way of doing business was, after all, only slightly worse than the methods considered standard practice by big businessmen, such as stock manipulators who stole millions from the public or factory owners who hired thugs to beat up union organizers. He told Miss Herrick that he had been unfairly treated by the law because his name was Capone. If he had been John Smith from Oshkosh, he wouldn't have served even as much time in prison as he had for carrying a gun. Now that he had done his time, and had gotten his parole for good behavior, he deserved to be left alone.

He pressed a buzzer on his desk, summoning an aide, and asked to have his wife and sister brought into his office. A few minutes later, Mae and Mafalda, who were sharing a suite for a few days, came in and chatted with the reporter. After they left, Capone asked Miss Herrick if she had noticed his wife's hair. The reporter smiled and complimented Mrs. Capone's her hairstyle. "No, I mean the streaks of gray," Capone said. "She's only 28 and she's got gray hair worrying over the things here in Chicago. I've been blamed for crimes that happened as far back as the Chicago Fire."

20. ANOTHER WAY TO "GET" CAPONE

After Capone returned to Chicago, one of the pieces of bad news that awaited him was the fact that his brother, Ralph, who had been left in charge of operations while he was in prison, had been indicted for income tax evasion. As far as Capone was concerned, this was one of his least important concerns. It seemed unlikely that anyone would be convicted of a crime as trivial as not paying taxes. Murder, racketeering, gambling, bootlegging – those were crimes for which a gangster went to prison. Nobody gets locked up for a bookkeeping error, right?

But Capone couldn't have been more wrong. Income tax evasion and bootlegging were both crimes that he had committed that fell under the purview of the federal government. And there was one man within the government who definitely wanted to get Capone – President Herbert Hoover. He had his own reasons, albeit mysterious ones, for wanting to close down the Capone operations, but he had also recently been visited by a delegation from Chicago, led by *Chicago Daily News* publisher Colonel Frank Knox, looking for help. The delegation knew that nothing was going to be done to bring down Capone by the city or state authorities, so they had come to Washington to ask Hoover to intervene. Capone was a perfect target when it came to bootlegging and tax evasion. The man had never filed a return in his life. Following Knox's appeal, a two-pronged attack was launched against Al Capone. One operation, led by agents from the Justice Department, would try and wreck him financially while the other, led by IRS agents, would work to send him to prison.

The Prohibition agents from the Justice Department were led by a young man named Eliot Ness, who had become something of a rising star in the division. Ness has been born in Chicago in 1903 and was raised in the city. He graduated from the University of Chicago and in 1928, joined the Bureau of Prohibition, working under the District Attorney, George E.Q. Johnson. Ness began working undercover, posing as a corrupt official, an investigation that resulted in 81 indictments and the destruction of a bootlegging operation that was bringing in almost thirty-six million dollars a year.

"UNTOUCHABLE" ELIOT NESS

After the new initiative against Capone was launched, Ness was promoted and tasked with trying to dismantle the gang's operation. However, he found that the Prohibition Bureau was so riddled with corruption that little progress was being made. Determined to change that, he began searching the personnel files of the agents in his command, looking for men, as he later put it, "with no Achilles' heels in their make-ups." He selected and led a small team of honest agents whose resistance to the Capone organization's efforts to buy them off led to them being dubbed the "Untouchables" by the newspapers. The destruction coordinated by Ness --- and it was substantial despite what revisionists have written to try and downplay his efforts --- was managed by just nine, "untouchable" agents.

During the time that Capone was serving his sentence at Eastern State Penitentiary and Ralph was in charge of operations, Ness managed to tap Ralph's telephone and learn the locations of some of the secret breweries that supplied the Capone organization. He raided a large brewery on South Wabash Avenue, ramming through the front door with a snowplow, and shut the place down, seizing hundreds of cases of beer. The team also managed to trace beer barrels on their journey from speakeasy back to the brewery and was able to locate and raid six Capone breweries and five distribution plants. They seized 25 delivery trucks and confiscated beer worth about nine million dollars. To humiliate Capone, Ness paraded the trucks down Michigan Avenue past Capone's headquarters at the Lexington Hotel after first calling the mob boss and telling him to look out the window.

Ness managed to arrest 69 Capone bootleggers and his raids caused substantial damage to the organization. He survived several attempts on his life, once discovering a bomb in his car. In the end, it may not have been Ness' sole efforts that caused Capone's downfall, but they certainly contributed to it.

President Hoover did not start the investigation into Capone's tax delinquencies, but he did manage to speed things up. As early as 1927, Elmer L. Irey, the chief of the IRS's enforcement branch, was given a powerful weapon to use against gangsters. The U.S. Supreme Court handed down a decision that year on an appeal by a bootlegger named Manley Sullivan, who had failed to file tax returns on the grounds that illegal transactions were not taxable. A criminal did not have to declare his income, his attorneys argued, because he was protected from self-incrimination by the Fifth Amendment. The Supreme Court ruled against him, finding no reason "why the fact that a business is unlawful should exempt it from paying taxes that if lawful, it would have to pay." The court also ruled that the Fifth Amendment had not been written to

ELMER L. IREY

protect criminals from stating the income that they had obtained during the commission of a crime. And thus, the Sullivan Law was born, which would make it possible for law enforcement officials to legally prosecute gangsters for tax evasion, even though they had managed to elude punishment for bootlegging, murder and other crimes.

Irey chose Chicago as a testing ground for the new Sullivan Law. His first targets were Terry Druggan, Frank Lake and their Standard Beverage Corporation. For the years between 1922 and 1924, the IRS had already hit them with hefty fines but they had disregarded the demands for payment until the Supreme Court ruling. They then tried to offer a compromise payment, submitting a statement of their assets with the lower offer. The IRS quickly rejected it. Irey set a group of his special agents, headed by Frank J. Wilson, to work investigating the assets statement. Wilson was transferred in from Washington specifically to work on the mob cases. Poker-faced and serious, he had no fear of reprisals and colleagues jokingly said that he was known to "sweat ice water." Wilson and his men uncovered concealed assets of Druggan and Lake that included an apartment house, five race horses, several Cadillacs and Rolls-Royces, a farm and assorted other real estate. In March 1928, they were indicted for filing false returns and in 1929, for falsifying the statement of their assets. They entered guilty pleas but legal maneuvering delayed their sentences until 1932, when they were sent to Leavenworth, Druggan for two and a half years and Lake for eighteen months.

Irey next turned his attention to Ralph Capone, seeing it as a rehearsal for the major battle that was coming against his brother. Ralph was less shrewd and less careful than his brother and his petty greed made the investigation a relatively simple one. In practice, the IRS did not then prosecute tax delinquents if they voluntarily paid what they owed before the investigation began. In Chicago, a zealous young IRS agent named Eddie Waters assigned himself the task of lecturing gangsters, whenever he found them, on the dangers of holding out against the government. Waters was a likable man and he

FRANK J. WILSON

knew Ralph Capone well. He kept after him for three years until Ralph finally weakened in 1926. He still resisted the hassle of filling out the forms and Waters offered to do it for him, as long as Ralph supplied the figures. So Ralph offered a modest estimate of $70,000 grossed between 1922 and 1925. Waters dutifully filled out the forms, acknowledging a tax obligation of $4,065.75 and Ralph signed it. But that was all he did, he never paid. Even though he actually made hundreds of thousands of dollars, he could not bring himself to part with a little over $4,000.

The following January, the IRS obtained warrants that allowed it to seize Ralph Capone's property. Ralph immediately went to the tax collector and pleaded poverty. But, he said, if the government would accept $1,000 as a full settlement, he would borrow the money and make sure his debt was paid. His lawyer explained the situation: "My client has sustained considerable loss as the result of the sickness and

death of his race horses throughout the past year. He has also lost a great deal gambling. All he has left is a half-interest in two race horses and at the present time he is using up practically all his income trying to get them into shape."

Irey had been hoping for some sort of lie from Capone and he was not disappointed. He instructed agent Arthur P. Madden to prove that Ralph was lying. Madden assigned the task to Archie Martin, another agent with an almost encyclopedic knowledge of the enterprises that the Capone gang owned and controlled, and Nels E. Tessem, an accounting genius. When Ralph learned that he was under investigation, he raised his offer to $2,500 and then, when the government rejected it, agreed to pay the full amount that he owed. By then, it was too late.

RALPH CAPONE WITH HIS ATTORNEYS DURING HIS TAX FRAUD TRIAL

Around this same time, a police raid had taken place at the Subway, one of the Capone outfit's gambling houses in Cicero. According to records that were seized and turned over to federal agents, its apparent owner was a man named Oliver Ellis. To save himself from the tax audit that was surely coming if he continued to claim ownership of the place, Ellis told Archie Martin about an account that he kept under an alias at Cicero's Pinkert State Bank. Among the canceled checks in the account, which Tessem was analyzing, was one for $3,200 drawn to a James Carroll. Carroll had also had an account at the Pinkert State Bank, but had closed it at some time before. Ellis refused to disclose Carroll's identity and the bank officers insisted they knew nothing about him. Tessem turned the bank upside-down. He examined thousands of clearance sheets before he found a clue – Carroll opened his account with an amount that was identical to what was in a James Carter's account when he had closed his. In addition, the Carter account contained the same amount at the start that was in the account of a James Costello on the day it was closed. Tessem also noticed another curious thing about all of the different accounts: most of the deposited amounts could be divided by 55. Interestingly, the wholesale price of a barrel of beer was $55.

The series of apparently connected accounts continued with those of Harry Roberts and finally an account closed on October 27, 1925 with the balance transferred to a Harry White. The name of the original depositor was Ralph Capone – all of the other names were aliases used by Ralph to conceal his assets. On the day he pleaded poverty, "James Carter" had more than $25,000 in his account. It was later learned that between 1925 and 1929, more than eight million dollars had passed through the series of accounts at the Cicero bank. Ralph had opened the account in 1925 and had never come into the bank again. The deposits were always made by a messenger boy who was accompanied by a man that bank employees identified from mug shots as Ralph's bodyguard, Tony Arresso. Martin and Tessem made their case by going to the merchants to whom checks were written, including a jeweler, various shopkeepers and saloon owners, and convincing them that it was in their best interests to identify the man who wrote the checks. All of them named Ralph Capone. In October 1929, seven indictments were returned against him by a grand jury and Ralph was arrested as he sat in the front row of a Chicago prizefight on October 8 by Special Agent Clarence Converse. He was released the next day on $35,000 bond. Although his lawyers managed to delay things for quite some time, he finally went to trial – and lost – six months later. Ralph was fined $10,000 and sentenced to three years in prison.

"I don't understand this at all," he muttered, hoping his lawyers could get him off on appeal.

His brother Al didn't understand any of it either. He couldn't imagine getting away with a decade of blood and violence, only to go to jail for withholding money from the government. He thought the Sullivan Law was "bunk" and was overheard stating that the government should not be allowed to collect legal taxes from illegal money. His lawyers advised him to pay what he owed before he was investigated like his brother, but Al ignored them. It wasn't until Ralph was actually indicted that he began to get nervous. After he was released from prison in Philadelphia, he retained a Washington, D.C., tax attorney named Lawrence P. Mattingly.

Even then, it was too late.

The Pinkert State Bank turned out to be a rich source of evidence against other tax-dodging Capone gangsters. Between 1927 and 1929, the bank had issued almost $250,000 worth of cashier's checks to "J.V. Dunbar." The chief teller was evasive when asked to describe "Dunbar" (Tessem found out that he used to tip him $15 a week) but a former Pinkert teller revealed that Dunbar's real name was Fred Ries. A former cashier for a number of Capone gambling houses, Ries used to bring gunnysacks full of cash to the bank and purchase cashier's checks. The teller added a weird little detail – Ries was terrified of insects. Once when a cockroach crawled out of one of the sacks at the bank counter, Ries turned ashen and went into a panic.

From an informer, Frank Wilson learned that Ries had moved to St. Louis and he drove down there with Tessem. On the chance that he was receiving mail under his own name, they enlisted the help of postal inspectors. When a special delivery letter arrived for Ries, the agents followed the postman to Ries' house. Ries was reading the letter, which had come from Jake Guzik's brother-in-law, when they rang his doorbell. The letter revealed that Guzik had been paying Ries to hide out in Miami and St. Louis and now wanted him to go to Mexico. When questioned, Ries swore that he had never heard of the Pinkert Bank and had never even been to Cicero. Wilson arrested him anyway and on his way back to Chicago, dropped Ries off at a small, dirty jail in Danville, Illinois. Remembering Ries' fear of insects, he was pretty sure that he could get the cashier to talk. He was right. Ries held out for four days and then sent a message to Wilson. "The bedbugs are eating me alive! I'll explain the cashier's checks but for god's sake, get me away from these bugs."

Using Ries' testimony, a grand jury indicted Guzik on October 3. It was not that, like Capone, he had filed no tax returns at all, but the income he did report over a three-year period was about $980,000 short of what it actually was.

At his trial in November, Ries admitted that Guzik was his boss, as were Al and Ralph Capone and Frank Nitti. He also admitted that he had used cash from the gambling houses to purchase cashier's checks that were given to Guzik's driver. The prosecutor produced the checks, endorsed by Guzik, and he drew a fine of $17,500 and a five-year prison sentence.

The next important Capone gangster indicted by a federal grand jury was Frank Nitti. On December 20, he entered a guilty plea to evading $158.823 in taxes. His sentence was a $10,000 fine and an eighteen-month stretch in prison.

Following these successes, Irey now set his sights on Al Capone. By this time, President Hoover had made Capone a top priority and Irey put Frank Wilson in charge of the case, offering him any men that he wanted for his assistants. He asked for Nels Tessem, William Hodgins, Clarence Converse, James Sullivan, and Michael F. Malone, or "Mysterious Mike Malone," as his colleagues referred to him. Malone was an undercover agent who hailed from New Jersey. He was an Irishman but thanks to his dusky complexion and dark eyes was able to pass as an Italian, Jew, Greek or whatever type the job demanded. Malone had been in an airplane crash during World War I and had married the nurse who cared for him. They had one child, a little girl, who was killed by a truck at the age of three. After that, Malone and his wife drifted apart and Mike went into undercover work. He seemed to lose interest in everything else, Wilson later wrote, and it became his entire life.

The challenge ahead of Wilson and his men was to find Capone's gross income over $5,000 (the standard exemption at the time) for years in which he didn't file a return. This was quite a task since Al, unlike his brother, never had a bank account or bought property in his own name, endorsed no checks, signed no receipts and paid cash for everything. To trap taxpayers who concealed income, the IRS had developed two methods of indirect proof that were based on circumstantial evidence involving their net worth and their net expenditure. According to the first method, the taxpayer's manner of living and outward indication of wealth was investigated. If it didn't seem to match an income of only a few thousand dollars, the IRS assumed that his net worth had increased by an unreported amount. According to the second methods, investigators compared the taxpayer's daily expenses to the amount of assets he supposedly had. In Capone's case, the agents used both methods to delve into his life and finances.

Internal Revenue Service agents blanketed stores in Chicago and Miami, calculating the cost of Capone's furniture, his automobiles, tableware and clothing, right down to his underwear. He spent thousands on jewelry, parties, food, prizefights, cars, groceries, doctor bills, home renovations, two new docks and a boathouse for the Palm Island estate and much more. After interviewing hundreds of people and looking over thousands of receipts, it was clear that his income was vastly greater than what he stated. All told, the investigators uncovered about $165,000 of taxable income.

But this wasn't enough for Wilson. This was a trivial sum when compared to the millions that Capone made from illicit sources. To be able to ensure the kind of prison sentence that President Hoover wanted for Capone, Wilson needed evidence that proved that the crime boss actually owned his breweries and distilleries, gambling parlors and brothels.

Special Agent Sullivan began investigating Capone's brothels. The local police customarily chose Saturday nights to raid the sporting houses because it was the busiest night of the week. After a federal grand jury began investigating gangster enterprises, the girls who were arrested were taken before the jury and questioned. None dared testify, however. It occurred to Sullivan that by combining sympathy and cash, he might be able to get some of the women to speak to him privately. So, on Saturday nights, he took to hanging out at the Federal Court Building and checking out the girls as the cops brought them in. Following a raid at the Harlem Inn, he took note of a beaten-down older prostitute in her fifties, nearing the end of career. He sensed a potential informer and he was right. For $50 a week, a fortune compared to what she normally earned, she went to work for him.

Meanwhile, a new guest had arrived at the Lexington Hotel. A dark-haired fellow with an Italian accent had checked in, signing the register "Michael Lepito – Philadelphia." He was given Room 724, next door to Capone gunman Phil D'Andrea. For hours each day, Lepito sat in the lobby and read the newspapers, not looking around and speaking to no one. His main interest seemed to be gambling and there were plenty of opportunities for it in the hotel. He liked shooting craps and he played for sizable stakes. Capone's men checked out the stranger, searching his room and looking at the labels on his clothes to see that they came from Philadelphia. They also intercepted his mail, which was postmarked from Philadelphia and filled with slang and underworld lingo. One day, a Capone gunman named Michael Speringa approached Lepito and bluntly asked him his business. "Keeping quiet," Lepito answered, which translated to him being a fugitive outlaw. A few days later, Speringa bought him a drink and a few days later, Lepito returned the favor. Over their drinks, he confided that he was wanted by the Philadelphia cops for burglary. The gang liked Lepito and befriended him, inviting him to sit in on private poker games and asking him to dinner at the New Florence Restaurant around the corner.

Lepito was, of course, undercover agent Mike Malone.

Malone and Sullivan fed Wilson invaluable background information. When Capone threw a birthday party at the Lexington for Frank Nitti, Malone was on the guest list and was given a close look at the gang in its most unguarded moments. From his source, Sullivan was given a detailed picture of the brothels under Capone's control. The two agents gathered important information for the Guzik and Nitti cases but hard evidence directly connecting Capone to his sources of income continued to elude them.

Wilson, who was living at the Sheridan Plaza Hotel with his wife while in Chicago, was faring no better. He visited dozens of banks and credit agencies, looking for records of any financial transactions that involved Capone. Month after month, he searched through the city and through Cicero, looking for any sign of Capone ownership or indications of how money was being channeled from the speakeasies and gambling parlors into his pockets. It was impossible to find anyone who would talk. Possible witnesses were either hostile to the authorities, gave perjured testimony to protect their bosses, or were simply too scared of the Capone organization. Evidence was mostly gathered by Malone, Sullivan and Converse, who faced certain death if their identities were found out.

More than a year passed with no real results.

In April, Capone's tax lawyer, Lawrence Mattingly, contacted Wilson and told him that his client wished to clear up any outstanding debts that he might have with the IRS and would be happy to furnish information about his business activities. Wilson set up a meeting on April 17 and Capone showed up with a brace of bodyguards, who remained on watch outside the building. Wilson greeted him politely but when Capone held out a hand for him to shake, Wilson pretended not to notice it. In addition to Wilson, Ralph Herrick, the tax agent in charge of the Chicago enforcement unit was also present, as was agent William

Hodgins and a stenographer. Herrick advised Capone and his lawyer that any statements made during the meeting could be used against him, but Mattingly assured the two agents that Capone wanted to cooperate.

Herrick asked Capone if he kept any business records or checking accounts but Capone replied that he never had. "How long, Mr. Capone," Herrick questioned, "have you enjoyed a large income?"

"I never had much of an income," Capone said.

"I will state it differently – an income that might be taxable?"

Capone smirked. "I would rather let my lawyer answer that question."

Mattingly spoke up. "Well, I tell you, prior to 1926, John Torrio, who happens to be a client of mine, was the employer of Mr. Capone and up to that point it is my impression his income wasn't there; he was in the position of an employee, pure and simple. That is the information that I get from Mr. Torrio and Mr. Capone."

Wilson took over the questioning. "Did you furnish any money to purchase real estate which was placed in the name of others?

"Does your wife or any relatives keep brokerage accounts?

"Do they keep safe-deposit boxes?

"What about wire transfers sent to you in Miami?

"Were you ever connected to the Hawthorne Kennel Club?"

The list of questions went on, but to almost all of them, Capone's response was the same: "I would rather not answer that question." As the questioning wore on, he became more agitated and angry. "They're trying to push me around," he barked at his lawyer at one point, "but I'll take care of myself."

Finally, Capone was finished. Refusing to answer anything else, he picked up his coat and hat and got ready to leave. Before he did, though, he turned back to Wilson and spoke in a low voice. "How's your wife, Wilson? You be sure to take care of yourself."

When they were alone, Hodgins turned to Wilson with a worried look. "Frank, watch your step from now on," he said.

Two months later, Mike Malone passed on some new information. He told Wilson that Frankie Pope, the manager of the Hawthorne Smoke Shop, had gotten into an argument with Capone because he felt that he had been cheated out of a lot of money by the outfit. Malone felt that Pope might be talked into informing on the gang. However angry he might have been, though, Pope wasn't interested in becoming a snitch. But when Wilson spoke with him, he did drop a hint. A reporter named Jake Lingle knew more about gang activities than any other reporter in Chicago and had a relationship with Capone that was far closer than anyone knew.

Wilson made arrangements to speak with Lingle confidentially on the morning of June 10--- but Lingle never showed up.

21. DEATH CALLS FOR JAKE LINGLE

Despite a few setbacks within the organization, harassment by the IRS and the efforts of the "Untouchables," Capone was still at the height of his power in 1930, a year after the St. Valentine's Day Massacre had taken place. The Atlantic City Commission never enforced its sanctions against him and when Capone returned from prison, he was able to take back control of the organization and continue things just as they had been before. Capone even went to the trouble of rubbing the commission's nose in the fact that they could do nothing to stop him by killing their appointed head of the Unione Siciliana, Joe Aiello.

Several Aiello associates were wiped out in 1930 and by October, Joe was hiding out in the Chicago home of Unione Siciliane treasurer Pasquale Prestogiacomo. Fearing for his life, Aiello was making plans to flee to Mexico but when he left Prestogiacomo's building on October 23, a gunman in a second-floor window across the street started firing a machine gun at Aiello. Aiello toppled off the building steps and moved around the corner, out of the line of fire. Unfortunately for Aiello, he stumbled into the range of a second machine gun nest on the third floor of another apartment block. It was a classic Capone-style set-up. Aiello was taken to Garfield Park Hospital, but was pronounced dead on arrival. The coroner eventually removed 59 bullets from his body.

The commission took no action against Capone for the hit and for a brief time, at the age of 31, he remained the most powerful man in Chicago.

The final months of 1929 were relatively quiet in Chicago. The St. Valentine's Day Massacre, which took place earlier in the year, had produced an eerie calm in the city. The Capone organization was now firmly in control and few dared to

THE LAST PUBLIC APPEARANCE OF DOMINICK AIELLO

challenge him, even if he was locked up in a prison cell in Philadelphia. By the latter months of 1929, there had been only 53 gangland murders in Chicago, which, while still nothing for city leaders to brag about, were far below the numbers of the previous year. There was, during that summer, even time for relaxing and social life, allowing the gangsters to come out of hiding and mix with their friends and families. When a relative of Capone partner Jake Guzik was married, there was a great gathering at the church that included Bathhouse John Coughlin, alderman of the First Ward, William V. Pacelli, alderman of the Twentieth Ward, Captain of Police Hugh McCarthy, and Ralph Capone. Al himself, of course, was unable to attend.

Only a couple of bloody incidents marred the early months of 1930. In January, a gun battle occurred in which Frank McErlane received partial payback for the murders of at least nine victims of gangland slayings for which he was reportedly responsible. Coroners had often listed him as a cause of death and he was also indicted for the double killing of George Bucher and George Meeghan, but the charges were dismissed. McErlane had been recently restless. He had fought over shares with his partner Joe Saltis and had transferred his allegiance to the South Side O'Donnells.

On the night of January 28, he was attacked and his right leg was fractured by a bullet. While recovering at the German Deaconess Hospital, he had two unexpected visitors, who walked into his room and opened fire. McErlane, imprisoned by splints, did the best he could. He reached under his pillow and pulled out a .38 caliber revolver, which he fired five times. The intruders ran, leaving McErlane still alive. Two full chambers had been fired at him but McErlane was only hit three times and none of the wounds were fatal.

He was interviewed by the police but, of course, did not name his attackers. He did, however, hint angrily that this would not be the end of the matter. One of the shooters had been John "Dingbat" O'Berta, a ferocious little man who was Saltis' chief gunman. On March 5, O'Berta and his driver, Sam Malaga, were taken for a ride in Dingbat's own Lincoln sedan. He had been shotgunned to death. O'Berta's funeral was a two-day affair, attended by 15,000 admirers from the Back-of-the-Yards district on the South Side, where O'Berta had earned a name for himself as an influential young politician.

Dingbat's widow had previously been the wife of Big Tim Murphy, the racketeer controller of the Street Sweepers' Union. Big Tim had been machine-gunned in front of his Rogers Park home in

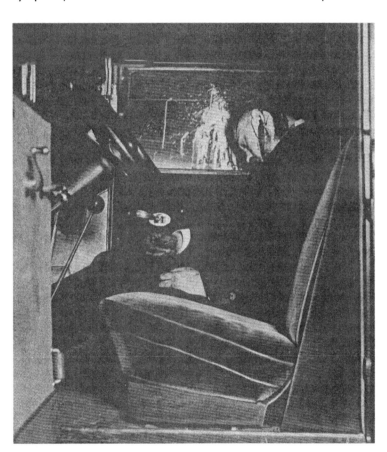

THE LAST RIDE OF "DINGBAT" O'BERTA

June 1928. She and O'Berta had met at Murphy's funeral. She had her second husband buried next to her first in Holy Sepulchre Cemetery, each with a rosary in his gun hand. She told reporters, "They were both good men."

Then, in the last week of May 1930, the guns roared again, kicking off what some wags would dub "Slaughter Week." On Saturday, Peter Gnolfo, who had once worked for the defunct Genna operation and had enlisted with the Aiellos, was shotgunned to death in a spiteful murder that was carried out by the Druggan-Lake gang and attributed to orders from Capone. Within hours, the Aiellos struck back and three died in the reprisal. A party of five was sitting on the terrace of a small resort hotel on Piskatee Lake during the early hours of Sunday morning. They were Joseph Bertsche, who since being released from the Atlanta Penitentiary had been working for the Druggan-Lake mob; Micheal Quirk, a labor racketeer and beer runner; George Druggan, Terry Druggan's brother; Sam Peller, an election strong-arm man from the Twentieth Ward; and Vivian McGinnis, the wife of a Chicago lawyer. A full drum of machine gun bullets shattered the glass and slaughtered the group at the table. Peller, Quirk and Bertshe died on the spot. Druggan and Mrs. McGinnis were both injured. The assailants vanished into the darkness.

No arrest was made and newspapers explained the attack as a quarrel that had developed because some of the Druggan-Lake boys were muscling in on the Fox Lake area, which was then supplied by Aiello and Moran breweries.

The reprisals continued and on Tuesday, with Thomas Somnerio, an Aiello man, found dead in an alley at the rear of 831 West Harrison Street in Chicago. He had been garroted and a deep line around his neck indicated that it had been done slowly in an effort to make him talk. His wrists had been bound with wire.

Four days later, a tugboat passing along the drainage canal at Summit, on the Southwest Side, bumped into the body of Eugene "Red" McLaughlin, a Druggan-Lake gunman who had been named four times as a murderer and twice as a diamond thief and yet had never seen the inside of a prison. He had been shot twice in the head and dumped in the river. His wrists had been tied behind his back with telephone wire and 75 pounds of iron had been stuffed in his pockets. It hadn't been enough to keep him from floating up from the bottom of the canal.

Two weeks later, his body was identified by his brother, Bob McLaughlin, who was president of the Chicago Checker Cab Company. He had taken over the office from Joe Wokral, who had run into a nasty accident while running for re-election – he had been shot in the head. Before he died, he named Red McLaughlin as his attacker, a lead that was ignored by the police. A mournful Bob McLaughlin spoke to reporters after the grim task of identifying his brother's corpse. He said, "A better kid never lived. He was friendly with all the boys, the West Side outfit, the North Siders, and the bunch on the South Side, Capone, too... I don't know, I don't know..."

On the day after the tugboat nosed McLaughlin's body out of the water, a car driven by a man named Frank R. Thompson steered erratically into a filling station in the small town of New Milford, about ninety miles northwest of Chicago. The door opened and Thompson, covered in blood, fell out onto the ground at the feet of the service station attendant, begging the stunned man to call a doctor. Little was known about Thompson. He was a gun dealer who – ballistics tests suggested – had supplied at least one of the machine guns used in the St. Valentine's Day Massacre and the gun used in the killing of Capone enemy Frankie Yale in New York. He was taken, gravely wounded, to Rockford Hospital, where he was interviewed by Sherriff Harry Baldwin. Thompson's dying words were: "Listen, Harry. I've seen everything, done everything and got everything and you're smart enough to know I won't talk. Go to hell."

 For most Chicagoans, such a string of murders and violence was commonplace but on Monday, June 9, a new and apparently different incident became the talk of the town. It was an outrage that was splashed across the front page of every newspaper in the city. This was the murder of Alfred L. "Jake" Lingle, a crime reporter for the *Chicago Tribune*, who was shot to death while walking, smoking a cigar, and reading the racing news in the crowded underpass at Randolph Street and Michigan Boulevard during the lunch hour.

It would become the most sensational murder of 1930, even though prior to his death, the general public had no idea who Lingle was. In spite of this, his murder created a furor. In those days, newspaper reporters were not well paid, but they had a place in public regard that was generated by glamour, respect and authority. The murder of Lingle immediately assumed the importance of that of a public official – and was publicized by every newspaper in town.

Lingle's duties on the police beat for the *Tribune* earned him $65 a week, which was not a princely sum. He had no aptitude for writing and could only transmit the facts. For eighteen years he had been a "leg man" who gathered crime news and phoned it in to the to the city editor's desk. For writers at the *Tribune,* he was a great asset. Crime was front page news in the Chicago of the 1920s and every paper relied heavily on its in-house crime expert. In that category, Lingle had no equal. He frequently scooped the competition, for not only did he enjoy easy access to Capone, he was on intimate terms with both Police Commissioner Russell and Deputy Commissioner Stege.

ALFRED "JAKE" LINGLE

Lingle never had a by-line in the paper and his name was unknown to most readers. To the public, he became much more famous in death than he ever was in life. And soon, he became notorious as details about his lifestyle began to be revealed. The supposedly humble reporter owned a chauffeur-driven Lincoln limousine and had just bought a $16,000 house at Long Beach on Lake Michigan, where his wife and two children were planning to spend the summer months. He also owned a house on the West Side but had recently taken a suite at the Stevens, one of Chicago's most stylish hotels. He was an avid gambler at the horse and greyhound tracks, but his lavish way of life couldn't be bought with winnings at the track.

On the day of his death, Lingle was on his way to the races. He had left his wife packing for her departure to the lake house and he planned to spend the afternoon at Washington Park in Homewood. Later that night, he planned to go to the Sheridan Wave Tournament Club, a society gambling parlor on Waveland Avenue, where the champagne, whisky and food were distributed with the management's compliments during play. It was due to re-open that evening and Lingle wanted to be there.

In retrospect, it seems that Lingle knew he was in trouble. Attorney Louis B. Piquett later volunteered to the police that 24 hours before Lingle's death, he had met with the reporter in the Loop. They stood on Randolph Street talking about the discovery of Red McLaughlin's body in the canal. Lingle was giving Piquett his theory about the crime when a blue sedan with two men in it pulled alongside them and stopped at the curb. Lingle stopped talking in mid-sentence and looked at the men in a startled way. The two men simply stared at him. Lingle never finished what he was saying to Piquett. He simply told the attorney goodbye and walked into a nearby store. Also, on the day of his murder, after lunching at the Sherman Hotel he met Sergeant Thomas Alcock of the detective bureau and told him that he was being tailed.

And apparently, he was. After buying cigars at the Sherman Hotel kiosk, he walked the four blocks to Michigan Avenue to catch the 1:30 p.m. train to the Washington Park racetrack. He descended into the underground walkway that led to the Illinois Central suburban electric railroad in Grant Park. At that time of day, the subway was very crowded, filled with a steady stream of shoppers and office workers.

Oddly, though, even though he knew he was being followed, Lingle acted unconcerned. According to witnesses, he arrived at the entrance to the subway walking between two men. One had blonde hair and wore a straw boater hat and a gray suit. The other was dark-haired and wore a blue suit. At the entrance, Lingle paused and bought a racing edition of the evening newspaper. As he did so, a man in a roadster on the south side of Randolph Street blew his horn to attract Lingle's attention. There were two men in the automobile and one of them called out, "Play Hy Schneider in the third!" According to a Yellow Cab superintendent who heard the exchange, Lingle grinned, waved at the man and called back, "I've got him!"

Lingle walked on into the subway, where where he was seen by Dr. Joseph Springer, a former coroner's physician and a long-time acquaintance. Springer later reported, "Lingle didn't see me. He was reading the race information. He was holding it before him with both hands and smoking a cigar."

Lingle had almost reached the end of the subway. He stopped across from the newsstand about 25 feet short of the east exit and the dark man who had been walking next to him moved away as if to buy a paper. As he did, the blonde man stepped behind Lingle, pulled out a snub-nosed .38 colt, and fired a single shot into the back of Lingle's head. The single bullet drove upward into his brain and exited his forehead. Lingle pitched forward, cigar still clenched in his teeth and newspaper still in his hands.

The blonde killer tossed away the gun and ran forward into the crowds. Then, for some reason, he doubled back past Lingle's body and ran up the eastern staircase. He jumped a fence, changed his mind again, ran west on Randolph Street, through a passage (where he tossed away a left-hand silk glove, probably used to prevent leaving fingerprints) and, pursued by a policeman, ran onto Wabash Avenue, where he disappeared into the crowd.

Meanwhile in the subway, a bystander named Patrick Campbell saw the dark-haired man who had been walking with Lingle and the killer hurrying towards the west exit. He moved to try and catch him, but

DEATH CALLS FOR JAKE LINGLE

his movement was blocked by a priest, who bumped into him. The priest delayed Campbell just long enough for the accomplice to escape. He told Campbell that he was getting out of the subway because someone had been shot. Later, Lieutenant William Cusack of the detective bureau commented gruffly, "He was no priest. A priest would never do that. He would have gone to the side of the stricken person."

Slowly, the method of Lingle's murder became clear. He had walked into a trap that had been formed by perhaps as many as a dozen men. But what was never put forward as a theory, and which seems the most likely explanation, was that during his progress into the subway between the two men, he was eased along at gunpoint, under orders to keep walking naturally and keep reading the paper.

COLONEL ROBERT MCCORMICK OF THE
CHICAGO TRIBUNE

That evening, Colonel Robert R. McCormick, publisher of the *Chicago Tribune*, summoned his news staff together and addressed them about the death of a reporter that he had never met and whose name he had likely never heard before. He spoke for 45 minutes and pledged to solve the murder of the martyred journalist. The next morning, the front page of the paper blared with an eight-inch banner headline that announced the dead of Lingle. The story read: "Alfred L. Lingle, better known in the world of newspaper work as Jake Lingle, and for the last eighteen years a reporter on the *Tribune*, was shot to death yesterday in the Illinois Central subway at the east side of Michigan Avenue, at Randolph Street.

The *Tribune* offered $25,000 as a reward for information which will lead to the conviction of the slayer or slayers. An additional reward of $5,000 was announced by the *Chicago Evening Post*, making a total of $30,000."

The next morning, not to be outdone by the *Tribune*, Hearst's *Chicago Herald & Examiner* also offered up a $25,000 reward, bringing the total up to $55,000.

Colonel McCormick, meanwhile, continued to take Lingle's death as an affront to him personally and an attack on the press. He regarded it as being much more serious than the other hundreds of cases of violence that plagued Chicago. He announced that Lingle's murder was committed in reprisal and as an attempt to intimidate the newspapers into suppressing stories about the dealings of the underworld. But, he declared, this was now a war and the *Tribune* and Chicago's other newspapers would not rest until Lingle's killers had been brought to justice.

What was especially shocking was that up to that point, gangsters had taken a "hands-off" policy toward harming reporters. Lingle was hailed as a hero who died in the service of the public and over 25,000 people attended his funeral.

Police Commissioner Russell was forced into making a statement. "I have given orders to the five deputy police commissioners to make this town so quiet that you will be able to hear a consumptive canary cough," he said colorfully, but then added, as a preliminary explanation for the lack of further action, "Of course, most of the underworld has scuttled off to hiding places. It will be hard to find them, but we will never rest until the criminals are caught and Chicago is free of them forever."

The next day, a newspaper editorial remarked sadly, "These gangs have run the town for many months and have strewn the streets with the lacerated bodies of their victims. Commissioner Russell and Deputy Commissioner John P. Stege have had their opportunity to break up these criminal gangs, who have made the streets hideous with bleeding corpses. They have failed."

POLICE COMMISSIONER WILLIAM RUSSELL, A LIFELONG FRIEND OF LINGLE, WHO ALLOWED THE REPORTER TO USE HIS INFLUENCE WITH HIM TO BROKER BACK ROOM DEALS FOR GANGSTERS AND POLITICIANS ALIKE

Russell replied to the charges, "My conscience is clear. All I ask is that the city will sit tight and see what is going to happen."

All that actually happened was that Russell and Stege, in the words of the newspaper, "staged a mock heroic battle with crime by arresting every dirty-necked ragamuffin on the street corners, but carefully abstained from taking into custody any of the men who matter."

Meanwhile, some of the blanks that had remained in the accounts of Lingle's character and lifestyle began to be filled in. It is fair to say that the management at the *Tribune* was unaware of them, or they likely would not have turned Lingle into the martyr that they did. Some of the facts that had remained so far unmentioned were that he had himself hinted that he was the man who fixed the price of beer in Chicago; that he was a close friend of Al Capone and had stayed with him at his Florida estate; that when he died he was wearing a diamond-studded belt buckle that had been a gift from Capone; that he was on improbably friendly terms, for a newspaper reporter of his lowly status, with millionaire businessmen, judges, and county and city officials, and that he spent golfing holidays and shared stock market tips with the police commissioner – a boyhood chum whom Lingle had helped elevate to his current position in 1928.

By the time a week had passed, certain reservations had started to temper the anger about the newspaperman's slaying that had been displayed on the front page and in the editorial columns of the *Tribune*. As more details about Lingle's extracurricular activities began to emerge, McCormick and his editorial executives began to back-pedal away from their earlier statements and demands. Rumors about Lingle's background and liaisons were racing around Chicago, supported by muckraking stories in other newspapers, and the *Tribune* began to take a different stance. They admitted that Lingle was apparently involved in some unsavory activities but they noted that the gangsters who killed him were still out there – and they still needed to be brought to justice.

McCormick's investigators, as well as the police, had learned a lot about the background of Jake Lingle, a semiprofessional baseball player from the slums who had wormed his way into the lowest levels of Chicago journalism. His first job after leaving a West Jackson Boulevard elementary school was as an office boy at a surgical supply house. He was playing semiprofessional baseball at the time and he met William Russell, at that time a police patrolman, with whom he struck up a friendship. Lingle was hired as a *Tribune* copyboy in 1918. He had no aptitude for writing, but it was his long list of contacts (mostly made through Russell) and timely telephone calls to the city desk that made him indispensable to editors and rewrite men. The brash and cocky reporter cultivated acquaintances in the courts, the jails and in the gin mills of the North and South sides. Relying on the word of informants and friendships, he became one of the city's least-known but cleverest crime reporters. He also became one of the wealthiest but whether this was from his dealings in the stock market, his investments in gambling clubs on the North Side, or from some other source is unknown.

Some believed that Lingle operated as a liaison between the underworld and the city's political machine. Many out of town newspapers were referring to the slain reporter as the "unofficial Chief of Police," who, for a sum, was able to "put the fix" in for gamblers, bootleggers, and anyone else who was having a problem involving law enforcement. Among the city hall insiders with whom he maintained a close relationship wias attorney Samuel A. Ettleson, the corporation counsel for Chicago and an operator in city government.

Al Capone confirmed that Lingle was "one of the boys" during an interview in Florida in July 1930. He said that Lingle was a friend and that he didn't have any sort of disagreement with him that led to his death. Capone also stated, "The Chicago police know who killed him."

The question of who killed Jake Lingle was temporarily forgotten during exposure of his fascinating financial affairs. In addition to the secret bank account that Lingle kept with the Lake Shore Trust and Savings Bank, he was also known for carrying large sums of cash in his pocket. He had $9,000 dollars on him the day that he was killed. Another interesting branch of his activities that came to light were his "loans" from gamblers, politicians, and businessmen. He had "borrowed" $2,000 from Jimmy Mondi, a Capone gambling operator in Cicero and the Loop, -- a loan that had never been paid back. He had also borrowed $5,000 from Alderman Berthold A. Cronson, nephew of Samuel Ettleson, who later stated that the loan was a "pure friendship proposition." That loan, too, had never been repaid He also had $5,000 from Ettleson himself, who only said that he had never loaned money to Lingle but often gave him some small remembrance at Christmas. He had a loan of $2,500 from Carlos Ames, president of the Civil

"JAKE WAS ONE OF THE BOYS", CAPONE TOLD NEWSPAPER REPORTERS. "THE CHICAGO POLICE KNOW WHO KILLED HIM." AL CLAIMED THAT HE AND LINGLE WERE FRIENDS -- HE HAD BEEN ONE OF THE RECIPIENTS OF A DIAMOND-STUDDED BELT BUCKLE -- AND HAD NO REASON TO WANT HIM DEAD. BUT WAS THIS TRUE?

Service Commission, that Ames stated was a "purely personal affair." He had $300 from Police Lieutenant Thomas McFarland, who said that he had given Lingle the money because they had been close friends for many years. It was also alleged that Sam Hare, a roadhouse and gambling parlor operator, had "loaned" Lingle $20,000. Hare denied it.

Investigations also revealed that Lingle had been in an investment partnership with his old friend, William Russell. The account, used for stock market speculation, was opened in November 1928 with a $20,000 deposit. On September 20, 1929 – preceding the market crash in October – their joint paper profits were $23,696. Later, a loss of $58,850 was shown. Lingle showed paper profits at a peak of $85,000 that, after the crash, were converted to a loss of $75,000. Russell's losses were variously reported as $100,000 and $250,000.

As to the source of the money put up by Lingle and deposited by him into his bank account, investigators noted, "We have thus far been able to come to no conclusion."

But the press and the public had come to conclusions – and they were painfully obvious ones, which again confirmed that they were the residents of a city that was governed by dishonorable leaders and corrupt officials. The newspapers theorized about why Lingle had been murdered, but the fervor, and righteous anger, had waned. The unofficial verdict was that Lingle had "asked for it," so to speak, by becoming involved with gangsters and dirty politicians.

Most theories of his death identified Lingle as a favor-seller and most placed the blame on Capone's opposition, the Moran-Aiello merger. One story that made the rounds in gangland was that Lingle had been given $50,000 to secure protection for a West Side dog track, that he had failed to do so and kept the money.

Another story implicated him in the re-opening of the Sheridan Wave Tournament Club, which had been operated by the Weiss-Moran gang, but which, after the St. Valentine's Day Massacre, had closed. Moran worked for eighteen months to try and find sympathetic officials to help him re-open the club, giving the job to Joe Josephs and Julian "Potatoes" Kaufman. It was said that Kaufman, an old friend of Lingle, had approached the reporter and asked him to use his influence with the police to get the club open again. Allegedly, Lingle agreed to do so – but only if he were cut in on the action. He demanded fifty percent of the profits but Kaufman refused. Lingle then allegedly retorted, "If this joint is opened up, you'll see more squad cars in front ready to raid it than you ever saw in your life before." In spite of this, the story said, the club was permitted to re-open anyway. It was widely advertised that it would be opening on June 9 – the day on which Lingle set out for the races for the final time.

An equally plausible story stated that he got too deeply involved in the struggle for money and power in the gambling syndicate. For years, there had been a bitter war between the General News Bureau, a racing news wire service that existed entirely for the purposes of betting, and the independent news services. As an appointed intermediary, Lingle brought the two opposed factions together in January 1930 and a two-year truce was agreed upon. The truce, it was said, may not have extended to Lingle.

Perhaps some of these stories were true, or perhaps all or none of them were. Whatever the reason behind his murder, Lingle likely just got mixed up in the violence and bloodshed of gangland, an arena where even the most experienced can sometimes be torn apart.

The Lingle case so intrigued the public that it was the basis for the 1931 Warner Brothers film, *The Finger Points*.

The biggest question remained – who pulled the trigger that ended the reporter's life?

Weeks, then months passed before the police produced a suspect. The serial number on the handgun that the killer had dropped had been filed off, but ballistics expert Colonel Calvin Goddard traced the origin

of the gun to a sporting goods store owned by Peter Von Frantzius on Diversey Parkway. Records showed that the gun had been sold to Frankie Foster, a member of the North Side Moran gang. Foster fled to Los Angeles after the Lingle shooting, but was indicted in Chicago as an accessory before the fact to murder. Foster, whose real name was Frank Citro, was eventually extradited to Chicago and was held in the county jail for four months before the evidence against him was deemed inconclusive and the charges against him were dropped.

A short time later, a new suspect was named. Leo Vincent Brothers, a labor union slugger from St. Louis, was arrested in New York and indicted for the Lingle murder. Brothers had started out as a member of Egan's Rats and soon graduated into labor racketeering and contract murder. Dodging a 1929 murder indictment, Brothers fled to Chicago, where he found work with Al Capone. Brothers was convicted and sentenced to fourteen years in prison for killing Lingle on April 2, 1931.

"I can do that standing on my head!" Brothers quipped after the sentence was handed down. Most observers, then and now, believe that Brothers was handed up to the state by Al Capone as a sacrifice, taking the fall for Jack Zuta, a racketeer who ran a string of whorehouses. Zuta was already dead by the time the trial wrapped up.

It seemed that just about everyone had a motive to kill Jake Lingle, but crime historians are in general agreement that Brothers took the rap and served time for a substantial cash payoff – but we'll never really know for sure.

After his release in 1940, Brothers returned to St. Louis, beat his original murder case, and became hooked up with the local mob. Three months after an abortive attempt on his life, Leo Brothers died of heart disease in St. Louis on December 23, 1950. He took the secrets of the Lingle murder with him to the grave.

22. FOLK HERO

At the height of Capone's power, the Chicago Crime Commission published a list of the most prominent criminals in the city. The first name on the list was, of course, Al Capone. The idea of "public enemies" was picked up across the country and J. Edgar Hoover, head of the FBI, created a "Most Wanted" list that still adorns the walls of U.S. Post Offices today.

Capone was bothered by the list, since it seemed to show how far his popularity had slipped in the eyes of the general public. He began making efforts to try and undo some of the damage that had been done by the St. Valentine's Day Massacre. Capone needed to be liked, especially by the general public, who had always seen him as the "public benefactor" that he believed himself to be. Everybody who drank violated the Prohibition law. They weren't any worse than Al Capone, were they?

At the Charlestown, Indiana, racetrack, thousands stood and cheered when Capone strode in with his bodyguards, his hands clasped above his head like a prizefighter. At the American Derby in Washington Park, the band struck up in Capone's honor as the gangster, dressed in a bright yellow suit and tie, took his seat. On another occasion, at a Cubs game at Wrigley Field, he sat with State Senator (later U.S. Congressman) Roland V. Libonati. A news photographer snapped him smiling and chatting with Capone and Jack McGurn. When called on the photo later, Libonati replied, "I was very proud when he asked me to speak to his son. I would still be proud to speak to any man's son."

But not every punlic appearance went well and the gradual erosion of Capone's carefully crafted image was starting to become obvious. During a football game between Northwestern and Nebraska universities in Evanston, an enthusiastic cry of "Yaaay, Al!" went up when Capone arrived. The cheers came from a group of Boy Scouts whose tickets Capone had provided. Other spectators were not so friendly. When Capone left with McGurn after the third quarter, a crowd of about four hundred students followed them to the gate,

CAPONE TAKES IN A BALL GAME

booing in derision. McGurn paused long enough to turn and snarl at them and then the gunman and his boss fled the stadium. In the next issue of the student newspaper, the editor wrote under a headline of GET THIS, CAPONE: "You are not wanted at Dyche Stadium nor at Soldier Field when Northwestern is host. You are not getting away with anything and you are only impressing a moronic few who don't matter anyway."

It would be the Great Depression that would bring

Capone his best press in the fall of 1930. Chicago was reeling under the impact of the Depression and no American city suffered more, for the nationwide economic disaster was compounded by the disastrous third Thompson administration. That year saw the city spending $23 million more than it collected in taxes. Outraged citizens organized a tax strike. More than 1,500 municipal employees, including teachers, firemen and policemen, lost their jobs and those who kept them went weeks without pay. With city, state and county treasuries running dry, private groups took up collections to try and keep the schools open. Teachers used their own savings to help feed their students.

A drought in the Midwest made things worse. Homeless families slept in underpasses and tunnels. Communities of shacks called

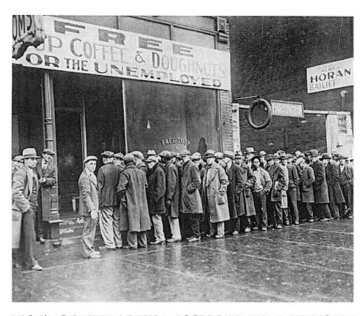

CAPONE'S SOUP KITCHENS GARNERED HIM GOOD PUBLICITY, WHICH HE NEEDED TO FIGHT OFF HIS "PUBLIC ENEMY" STATUS AND CONTINUED PROBLEMS FROM THE IRS AND THE ST. VALENTINE'S DAY MASSACRE.

"Hoovervilles" made of packing cases, tin, tarpaper and cardboard began springing up in empty lots and on the outskirts of the city. The shantytowns were named for President Hoover, who was blamed for allowing the country to slide into a depression.

As public relief funds dwindled, bills were introduced in the state legislature and Congress to raise taxes, a prospect that brought an angry response from those who still had money. For tax purposes, Colonel McCormick publisher of the *Chicago Tribune* reported his income as no more than $25,250 --- and yet Al Capone was being pursued by the government as a tax cheat.

Capone tried to shrug off his "Public Enemy" image by opening a soup kitchen on South State Street during the winter months. He fed nearly 3,000 unemployed people every day, costing him more than $12,000 a week. On Thanksgiving, he fed more than 5,000 families by giving away free turkeys. At Christmas, he gave a huge party for the poor of Little Italy during which an old woman knelt before him and kissed his hand. The goodwill created by his generosity did a great deal to soften Capone in the eyes of the ordinary Chicagoan, but it did nothing to help his image with the federal government; they wanted to know where he got the money to pay for all of that generosity.

The Capone legend grew both at home and abroad, fed by a multitude of reporters, writers, radio hosts, preachers, playwrights and moviemakers. The Hawthorne Inn became a featured location on guided bus tours around Chicago, since visitors always asked to see where Capone lived. Tour operators knew better than to venture past the Lexington or Capone's home on Prairie Avenue.

Seven books devoted largely or entirely to Capone were published between 1929 and 1931. Fawcett publications put out a profusely illustrated one-shot magazine on the newsstands, priced at 50 cents, called *Al Capone on the Spot*. The title page carried a quote by Judge John H. Lyle: "We will send Al Capone to the chair if it is possible to do so!" The anonymous author of the booklet attributed most of the murders described in the text to Capone, though in many cases there was no connection. According to rumor, the

BEN HECHT

executive at Fawcett who put out the magazine went on a long vacation at coincidentally the same that it hit newsstands. He didn't return for several weeks. Apparently, though, Capone was more flattered than offended by the lavish magazine – he bought 100 copies.

In Howard Hughes' Hollywood studios, work began on a film called *Scarface*, starring Paul Muni. It was written by former Chicago reporter Ben Hecht. One night (as Hecht told the story years later) he answered a knock on his Hollywood hotel room door to find two hard-eyed strangers waiting to speak to him. They had a copy of his screenplay for the movie.

"You the guy who wrote this?" asked the man with the script.

Hecht admitted that he was.

"We read it."

"How did you like it?" Hecht nervously asked.

"Is this stuff about Al Capone?"

"God, no!" Hecht quickly replied. "I don't even know Al." He named a few other gangsters that he had known while working in Chicago, like Colosimo, O'Banion, Hymie Weiss and a few others.

The man at the door seemed to consider this for a moment. "Okay then, we'll tell Al this stuff you wrote is about them other guys." As they started to leave, the other man seemed to have a thought. "If this stuff isn't about Al Capone, why are you calling it *Scarface*? Everybody'll think it's him."

"That's the reason," Hecht told them honestly. "Al is one of the most famous and fascinating men of our time. If you call the movie *Scarface*, everybody will want to see it, figuring it's about Al. That's part of the racket we call showmanship."

"I'll tell Al. Who's this fellow Howard Hughes?"

"He's got nothing to do with it. He's the sucker with the money."

"Okay, the hell with him." And the two men left, apparently satisfied with what they heard.

GEORGE JESSEL

The prominent people who wanted to meet Capone ranged from movie, music and stage celebrities to wealthy Chicagoans who looked down on the rest of the city from the windows of their lakeshore mansions. When the Metropolitan Opera diva Lucrezia Bori learned that George Jessel, who had been introduced to her in a New York restaurant, knew Capone, she asked him if he could arrange a meeting the next time she was in Chicago. Jessel wrote to the opera-loving gang leader. Whether or not the meeting ever took place is unknown, but one summer opera season at Ravinia Park, she did receive a case of champagne with a note that read "with the compliments of Al Capone."

A number of Chicago gangsters, Capone among them, had been George Jessel fans since 1926, when he won them over in with his role in *The Jazz Singer*. In the last week of Hymie Weiss' life, he took his mother to the Harris Theater for the show and by the third act was weeping openly. Capone, equally moved, sent Terry Druggan backstage to tell Jessel how much he wanted to shake his hand. He was told to call Capone "Snorky" when curiosity brought the actor to the Metropole Hotel three nights later. Capone took him to supper and told him, "Anything happens to you or any of your friends, you let me know."

It was not an offer to be taken lightly. With Moran's North Side gang reduced by bullets and jail sentences to a skeleton crew and the Aiellos either dead or vanished, there was no serious challenge remaining for Capone. Few gangsters now operated in Chicago without his knowledge and even less without his approval. Thanks to this, he was able to intervene when Jessel appealed to him on behalf of a colleague. Show business people were the natural prey of extortionists, who threatened them with injury or disfigurement if they didn't pay a regular tribute, and of hold-up men, who waited for them when they left the theater at night. Chicago victims included Lou Holtz, Georgie Price, Rudy Vallee, Harry Richman, and many others.

Richman presented a particularly attractive target to thieves since he wore a fortune in jewelry and always carried at least one $1,000 bill on him because it amused him to pay a restaurant or speakeasy tab with it and see the shocked face of the waiter. During a theater run in Chicago in 1927 he was robbed while walking between the Erlanger Theater and his hotel not once, but several times. The next day, he would replace his jewelry and gold cigarette case, only to be robbed again. He finally went to see Capone, who he heard was an admirer. After whispering an order to one of his men, Capone took the actor on a drive along the lakeshore. When they got back to the Lexington, there was a package on Capone's desk. It contained all of Richman's missing jewelry and several thousand dollars. Capone handed Richman a note and told him, "Put this in your pocket and if you get into trouble, use it." The note read: "To Whom It May Concern – Harry Richman is a very good friend of mine. Al Capone." Richman had occasion to use the note a few nights later. The hold-up man, embarrassed, apologized for the trouble and quickly left.

While the impressionist Georgie Price was playing a Chicago vaudeville engagement, his hotel room was robbed of jewelry and cash. After Jessel spoke to Capone, that loot was also returned.

Perhaps the most dramatic return of stolen goods that Capone arranged followed an appeal from a woman who had done him a small service, Mary Lindsay, the manager of a Washington, D.C. hotel. While in the Midwest on vacation, she had come upon a Chicago-bound train stalled just outside of the city. Among the passengers waiting alongside the track was Al Capone, who she didn't recognize when he asked her for a lift in her car into the city. She drove him to the Lexington and it was not until she looked at the card he gave her when he urged her to call on him for any help that she might need in Chicago that she realized who her passenger was. A few days later, her purse, which contained all of her money and traveler's checks, was snatched. She called Capone. That night, following his instructions, she had dinner in a West Side restaurant, taking the table facing the first of a line of stone columns. Halfway through her meal, he purse suddenly appeared on the chair next to the column. None of her money was missing.

ATTORNEY CHARLES F. RATHBUN

Capone may have been riding a wave of "folk hero" status for a time, but by the latter part of 1930, things were starting to crumble. After the murder of Jake Lingle, the police, casting a dragnet over the Chicago underworld, hauled in and questioned more than 700 criminals of record. Attorney Charles F. Rathbun and chief investigator for the state's attorney's office, Patrick T. Roche, were placed on

JUDGE JOHN H. LYLE

the payroll of the *Chicago Tribune* and given investigative powers that rivaled even those of the police department. They followed dozens of trails in the Lingle murder to dead ends, always finding, however, that things seemed to lead them back to Capone. Rumor had it that the reporter had taken $50,000 from Capone as the price of official sanction for a new dog track on the West Side but had never delivered. The reporter's considerable knowledge of Capone's financial transactions – if, as Frank Wilson thought possible, he could have been persuaded to share them with the government – would have given Capone another reason to have him killed. But Rathbun and Roche could find no evidence to prove either theory.

Still hoping for a lead, the two investigators began a campaign of relentless, daily harassment of Chicago's gangland, hoping that somebody somewhere would eventually crack under the pressure. Detectives assigned to them by the state's attorney, armed with axes, sledgehammers and crowbars, proceeded to raid and wreck every brothel, gambling parlor and speakeasy they could find in Chicago and the suburbs and arrest everyone they found on the premises. At the same time, Rathbun and Roche began using legal files to have old charges against a number of gangsters revived, paroles revoked and pending cases brought to trial. Judge John Lyle worked with them, setting bail so high that offenders couldn't pay and had to wait for their trials in jail. In just this way, many important members of the Capone organization ended up behind bars.

Judge Lyle also invoked a long-unused vagrancy law that defined a vagrant as a person without visible means of support. The law carried a penalty of up to six months imprisonment, a fine of $200, or both. Lyle desperately wanted to find Capone in violation of the law. If he was fined and tried to pay the fine, he would have to explain where the money came from. If he admitted a source of income, then he could be investigated on tax evasion charges, which would figure into the government's case. Lyle issued a warrant for Capone in felony court on September 16, 1930. He never showed up for his hearing.

Capone was feeling the pressure from the arrests and the raids on his places of business. He tried to arrange a sit-down with Rathbun and Roche but they refused to meet with him. They sent a unnamed go-between to the meeting and Capone tried to convince him that he knew nothing about the Lingle murder. He was agitated and upset about the crackdown on his operation, telling the agent, "I can't stand the gaff of these raids and pinches. If it's going to keep up, I'll have to pack up and get out of Chicago." He continued to insist that he had nothing to do with the Lingle murder, that other crime interests in the city had set him up to look responsible. When the go-between reported this back to Rathbun and Roche, they weren't buying it.

"You can tell Capone," Roche said, "that he can go to hell."

But if the murmurings of Al Capone on the subject are to be believed, he was already in "hell" at this point in his life. The haunting that had begun while he was locked up at Eastern State Penitentiary had grown progressively worse during the months since he had been out. James Clark, Capone swore, was constantly hounding him, refusing to let him sleep many nights and had become a "curse" on his business, dragging him down.

Capone's empire was falling apart and he was now subject to increasing pressure from the police and from IRS agents. Moody and ill-tempered, friends often heard him speak of the "curse" and "something evil that I can't fight." Hoping to ease his mind, some of his closest associates put him in touch with a Chicago clairvoyant named Alice Britt, a Spiritualist who maintained that she could make contact with the dead. Capone told her that he wanted "to get rid of this thing which is bothering me."

During his meeting with Mrs. Britt, Capone admitted that he often woke up at night and saw the face of Jimmy Clark. Invariably, Clark always had the same message for him: "I'll send you mad, Capone."

At a séance in early 1931, Mrs. Britt said that she could see the image of a "tall, sallow man with a black scarf around his throat" lurking behind Capone. Al told her, "That's Clark. He just won't quit bothering me."

Mrs. Britt advised him to mend his ways and then perhaps the spirit would stop haunting him. Capone permitted himself a smile. "I guess it's a bit late for that," he said.

Capone was living at the Lexington Hotel at this time and there were many times when his bodyguards would hear him begging to be left him in peace. On several occasions, they broke into his suite, fearing that someone had gotten to the boss. Capone would tell them that Clark's ghost had been there, delivering his same vile threat.

Not long after the séance with Alice Britt, Hymie Cornish, Capone's valet, also believed that he saw the ghost. He entered the lounge of Capone's suite and spotted a tall man standing near the window. He demanded that the man's identify himself and state his business but the shadowy figure slipped behind a curtain and out of sight. Cornish immediately summoned two of Capone's bodyguards, but a search of the room revealed that no one was there. Cornish told one of the bodyguards that he was sure that the man he had seen was James Clark. He was warned not to mention the incident to Capone.

"The boss will have you shot if you mention that name," he was told.

But Capone certainly knew that Clark was still lingering near him. Years later, he would insist that Jimmy Clark led him to the grave.

23. DEATH & TAXES

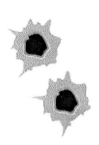

By 1931, things looked bad for Al Capone. He was hiding out in Florida, worried about a warrant that had been issued for him when he failed to appear in court after being subpoenaed. He decided to take a stab at clearing things up – not legally, of course – in typical Capone manner. He submitted a proposal through George "Red" Barker of the Teamsters' Union to Judge John P. McGoorty, offering to surrender on the vagrancy warrant that had been issued by Judge Lyle and was still pending. He further offered to quit labor racketeering, leave Chicago and operate his other enterprises from a distance. His conditions: dismissal of the vagrancy charge the moment he surrendered and no interference in his liquor business."

What the judge told Barker was not recorded, but he told a grand jury: "[Capone's] most formidable competitors have been ruthlessly exterminated and his only apparent obstacle towards undisputed sway is the law. Such a trade is unthinkable. The time has come when the public must choose between the rule of the gangster and the rule of the law."

Things were not looking much better for Frank Wilson at this point either. The office space that had been given to him in the old Federal Building was so cramped that he could hardly move without bumping into a file cabinet or another agent. He had been closeted there for well over a year, combing through mountains of papers seized by the police on Capone establishments dating back to 1924. He searched bank records and memoranda filed by his assistant agents and yet they could still not prove enough to take Capone down. Between them, Wilson, Tessem and Hodgins had examined close to 1.7 million separate items – but they refused to give up.

One night, near midnight, Wilson finally found what he was looking for. Exhausted and discouraged, he was gathering papers that had been strewn all over the office and returning them to a file cabinet. Bending over to retrieve a bundle of checks, he bumped into a file cabinet drawer and it slammed shut, locking automatically. He couldn't find the key so he decided to store all of the papers that he had in his arms in one of the old file cabinets in the corridor outside his office. The drawer that he opened was partially filled by a large package that was tied up in brown paper, one of many turned over to him by the state's attorney, which he had overlooked until now. He broke the string and three black ledgers with red corners tumbled out of the paper wrapping. They were dated 1924-1926. Leafing through them, he stopped, his heart pounding, at a page in the second ledger. The columns were headed BIRD CAGE; 21; CRAPS; FARO; ROULETTE; HORSE BETS.

No longer exhausted, Wilson took the ledger to his desk and began scanning the entries. They showed net profits totaling, in an eighteen-month period, more than $500,000. Every few pages, a balance had been taken and divided among "A" (for Al, Wilson surmised), "R" (Ralph Capone), "J" (Jake Guzik) and others. A balance of $36,687 on December 2, 1924 had been divided:

TOWN: $6,537.42
RALPH: $1634.35
PETE: $1634.35
FRANK: $5720.22
J & A: $5720.22
LOU: $5720.22
D: $5720.22

Wilson assumed that "Town" meant Cicero officials; "Pete" was probably Pete Penovich, the first smoke shop manager; "Frank", Frankie Pope; "J & A:" Jake and Al; "Lou" was perhaps Louis La Cava. He didn't know who "D" might be. There was a notation at the foot of the page that read: "Frank paid $17,500 for Al."

Wilson hurried to the state's attorney's office the next morning and learned that the ledgers had been seized from the raid on the Hawthorne Smoke Shop after the McSwiggin murder in 1926. The entries were written in three different hands. Wilson and his men began the laborious task of matching the handwriting in the ledgers to gangsters' handwriting samples collected from places like the motor vehicle bureau, banks, bail bondsmen and the criminal courts. Eventually, a bank deposit slip turned up a signature that matched the writing in many of the ledger entries recorded between 1924 and 1926. It belonged to Leslie Alderbert "Lou" Shumway, who had been the cashier at The Ship gambling house before Fred Ries.

Wilson also continued to meet with Mattingly, Capone's tax attorney, who now conceded that his client's enterprises had produced an income, although a relatively modest one. Wilson asked him to specify how much of an income in writing. Mattingly wrote back:

Taxpayer became active as a principal with three associates at about the end of the year 1925. Because of the fact that he had no capital to invest in their various undertakings, his participation during the year 1926 and the greater part of 1927 was limited. During the years 1928 and 1929, the profits of the organization of which he was a member were divided as follows: one-third to a group of regular employees and one-sixth to taxpayer and three associates...

I am of the opinion that his taxable income for the years 1926 and 1927 might be fairly fixed at not to exceed $26,000 and $40,000, respectively, and for the years 1928 and 1929, not to exceed $100,000 per year.

Wilson knew that the figure was laughable – Capone spent more than $100,000 every year on his lavish lifestyle alone. But no matter how far it was from the truth, here was a written admission of tax delinquency. Mattingly wrote that the statement was "without prejudice to the rights of the above named taxpayer in any proceedings that might be instituted against him. The facts stated are upon information and belief only." But he made a fatal blunder because no such stipulation was legally binding. Wilson happily added it to the growing case against Capone.

The statement from Capone's tax attorney made it very apparent that the gangster was getting nervous about the evidence that the IRS was continuing to gather against him. Wilson had reason to recall the veiled threat that Capone had made against him – "you be sure to take good care of yourself" – when he received a telephone call from a secret informant that he had within the Capone organization, warning him that a contract had been taken out on his life. According to the informant, Capone had, acting against the judgment of cooler heads, imported five gunmen from New York to not only kill Wilson, but also Arthur Madden, the chief of the Chicago tax intelligence unit, Pat Roche and U.S. Attorney George Johnson. Mike Malone confirmed the informant's tip – the contract was for $25,000 and the gunmen had arrived in a blue

Chevrolet sedan with New York plates.

The informant told him: "They know where you keep your automobile, what time you go home at night and what time you leave in the morning." Wilson and his wife moved to another hotel right away. He told the staff at the front desk of the Sheridan Plaza that they were going to Kansas. The couple drove to Union Station, then circled back and took a room at the Palmer House. A 24-hour police guard was assigned to each of the intended victims.

Pat Roche ordered his detectives to bring in Capone, but warned by Cook County officers, Capone eluded them. Hearing that John Torrio was in Chicago, Arthur Madden called Torrio and gave a message to the former Chicago gang leader, knowing that he was much more level headed than Capone. "If those hoodlums are not out of town by tonight," Madden said, "I'm going after them myself with two guns." With the murder plot known to the authorities, Capone's closest circle prevailed on him to call things off. Torrio telephoned Madden to tell him the hitmen had been called off. "They left an hour ago," he said.

Wilson dodged a bullet, thanks to the timely tip from his secret informant. But who was this man, who had risked his life to warn the IRS agent? That information would not come out for several years and when it did, it turned out to be fatal. Wilson's secret ally was lawyer and dog track operator Eddie O'Hare. He had been hopelessly entangled in the affairs of the mob for years and he wanted nothing more than to get out of them. So, unbeknownst to his gangster friends, O'Hare became a secret government informant. For nearly eight years, he funneled information about Capone to Wilson and his IRS agents. A mutual friend, a writer named John Rogers of the *St. Louis Post-Dispatch*, had brought the two men together. They first met over lunch at the Missouri Athletic Club so that O'Hare could look the government agent over and decide if he was really the man to get Capone. "He's satisfied," Rogers told Wilson after the meeting.

O'Hare decided to inform against Capone for paternal reasons. His son, Butch, was determined to attend the U.S. Naval Academy at Annapolis and O'Hare wanted to smooth the way for him by helping the government bring down Capone and his organization.

Wilson asked Rogers if O'Hare understood the risks involved with helping to nail Capone.

"If O'Hare had ten lives," Rogers told him, "he would gladly risk them all for the boy."

Wilson heard from O'Hare frequently after that, either directly or through Rogers. It was O'Hare who told him about the structure of the Capone dog track management and verified that more than half of the profits went directly into Capone's pockets. He was also the one who called to warn Wilson about the gunmen who had been brought to Chicago to kill him.

Capone went to prison but O'Hare's undercover activity didn't end with the Capone case. Despite his long and profitable association with gangsters, O'Hare had detested them from the start, and he went on informing against them to both county and state police, undaunted by Wilson's warning that some policeman in the pay of mobsters would betray him. And Wilson was right – O'Hare's secret would not remain hidden for long.

Ensign Henry "Butch" O'Hare graduated from Annapolis in 1937 and was sent overseas just after the attack on Pearl Harbor, which marked the United States' entry into World War II. On February 20, 1942, he single-handedly saved the U.S. Navy carrier *Lexington* from certain destruction. The lone pilot attacked a wing of Japanese fighters and wreaking havoc on the enemy craft, he prevented an aerial bombardment of the fleet. For his bravery, President Franklin Delano Roosevelt awarded him with the Congressional Medal of Honor. More than a year later, in November 1943, Butch O'Hare vanished near Tarawa Island while establishing night radar flights. No trace of him or his plane was ever found. On September 18, 1949, Orchard Depot, an isolated airfield on the far Northwest Side of Chicago was formally re-named O'Hare Field in honor of the brave fighter pilot.

Unfortunately, the hero's father never lived to see the recognition that was given to his son. The word had leaked out that Eddie O'Hare was an informant, just as Wilson feared that it would. A team of gunmen was recruited from the Egan's Rats gang of St. Louis and plans were set in motion to kill O'Hare.

It is thought that perhaps Frank Wilson's warnings had made an impression on O'Hare. He was still enjoying considerable success in his professional life as the president of the Sportsman's Park racetrack in Stickney, as a developer of legal dog racing tracks, manager of the Chicago Cardinals football team, real estate investor, and the owner of an insurance company and two advertising agencies. But in spite of his wealth and the respect that he earned as a business leader, he became very paranoid. Remembering Wilson's words, O'Hare began carrying a gun with him every day. But on the day he was murdered he never even had a chance to draw it from its holster.

On November 8, 1939, O'Hare was driving from the dining room at the Illinois Athletic Club on Michigan Avenue to his office at the racetrack. He had no idea that his assassins were waiting for him at Twenty-Second Street and Ogden Avenue. As O'Hare drove past the intersection, a car pulled out and followed close behind him. Moments later, they pulled alongside him as he approached 2601 West Ogden. O'Hare clumsily tried to draw his gun, but it was too late. Two men fired shotguns from the other car and Eddie was hit in the face and the head. The new Lincoln Zephyr automobile

IT TOOK A FEW YEARS BUT WORD EVENTUALLY LEAKED THAT EDDIE O'HARE WAS A GOVERNMENT INFORMANT. GUNMEN CAUGHT UP WITH HIS DRIVING SOUTH ON OGDEN AVENUE AND SHOT HIM TO DEATH.

that he was driving swerved sharply, jumped the curb, rattled over the streetcar tracks, and smashed into a trolley pole in the center lane. The second car roared away and O'Hare's killers were never found.

After abandoning murder as the solution to his tax problems, Capone tried bribery. In New York, Joseph H. Callan, former special assistant to the Commissioner of Internal Revenue and now an executive with the Crucible Steel Company, received a visit from an emissary called "Smith." He brought an offer from Capone for Elmer Irey and asked Callan to pass it on — $1.5 million if there was no conviction in his case. Callan brusquely showed the man to the door.

In February 1931, a few months after Lou Shumway had been identified as the keeper of The Ship's books, John Rogers passed on a message from Eddie O'Hare that sent Wilson to Miami. Shumway was working there as a cashier at a dog or horse track, O'Hare didn't know which. Wilson eventually tracked him down at the Biscayne Kennel Club. When Shumway, trembling with terror, denied any knowledge of the ledgers, Wilson gave him two choices: he could go on pretending ignorance, in which case a deputy sheriff would publicly hand him a subpoena and let the Capone gang know that he had been found, or he could cooperate with the government and get the same protection as Fred Ries, who was now living anonymously in South America. Wilson added that the gang would probably kill him to ensure his permanent silence if he was served with the subpoena. Shumway decided to cooperate.

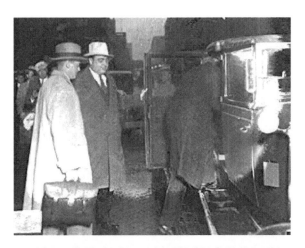

CAPONE SHOWED UP FOR HIS CONTEMPT OF COURT TRIAL, WAS FOUND GUILTY AND SENTENCED TO SIX MONTHS AT THE COOK COUNTY JAIL. HE SKATED ON THE VAGRANCY CHARGE, MUCH TO THE CHAGRIN OF JUDGE LYLE.

Shumway confessed that while all of the orders relating to his work were given to him by Frank Pope and Pete Penovich, the only other person that he recognized as the owner of the business was Al Capone. He also described a raid that the West Suburban Citizen's Association had forced the county police to stage against the Smoke Shop in 1925. This led Wilson to interview Reverend Henry Hoover and Chester Bragg, the vigilante who had guarded the entrance to the gambling parlor during the raid. Bragg swore to the self-incriminating words that Capone accidentally blurted out in anger that morning – "I own the place."

On February 25, with a contempt of court citation hanging over him, Al Capone entered the Chicago Federal Courts Building. His arrival caused the place to literally shut down. Hundreds of clerks and stenographers abandoned their desks to catch a glimpse of him. Capone strolled in, a tight grin on his face, dressed in a bright blue suit, a blue and white striped tie and gray spats. He was heavier than ever before, blown up to over 250 pounds. Phil D'Andrea walked warily next to him, his hands plunged deep into the pockets of his overcoat.

Capone had waived a jury trial and he entered a guilty plea before Judge James H. Wilkerson. The short, often testy judge listened to seven prosecution witnesses who swore that Capone was lying when he claimed that he had been in bed with bronchial pneumonia and couldn't travel from Miami to Chicago to answer a subpoena that had been issued for him.

As Capone left the courtroom for the lunch recess, two police sergeants arrested him on the vagrancy warrant that had been issued by Judge Lyle. They took him to the detective bureau, gave him a sandwich and coffee, then fingerprinted and photographed him. When they asked him his occupation, Capone smirked and replied, "Real estate." A new hearing was set for March 2.

At the contempt trial, Judge Wilkerson found him guilty and later fixed the penalty as six months in the Cook County Jail. He was released on bond, pending appeal. "I ain't worrying about a cell," Capone told reporters. "I'm not there yet. There are other courts."

In the vagrancy case, he turned out to be right. While Judge Lyle was on temporary assignment in another court, Capone managed to get his case heard by a judge who had been a severe critic of Lyle's high bond policy. The case was continued three times and then dismissed."

Before Wilson sent Shumway into hiding, a federal grand jury secretly convened to hear the cashier's testimony. It was in Wilson's best interests to get Shumway in front of the jury as soon as possible. The majority of Capone's disclosures about his income referred to the year 1924. Together with figures supplied by Fred Ries and Eddie O'Hare, they showed a tax liability, not counting penalties of $32,488.81 on a net income of $123,102.89, but under a six-year statute of limitations, tax offenses committed in 1924 would be barred from prosecution after March 15.

The grand jury returned an indictment on March 13 but at the request of U.S. Attorney Johnson, it agreed not to make its verdict public until the investigation into the period between 1925 and 1929 could be completed.

In April, an era came to an end with the final defeat of Capone's political ally, Big Bill Thompson. In the Republican primary, he had won over Judge Lyle (which highly amused Capone) but Thompson lost the election to Anton J. Cermak, a Democrat who won with the biggest majority in the history of Chicago mayoral elections.

Cermak never intended to purge Chicago of gangsters – he only wanted to get rid of the Capone gang in favor of other mobsters who supported his campaign. After Capone went to prison, Cermak declared war on the gang – a move that would have fatal consequences for him.

On June 5, the federal grand jury convened again, this time openly, and returned its earlier indictment against Capone, adding another 22 counts for the years 1925-1929. The IRS had been able to come up with an income of $1,038,655.84 during those years with a tax assessment that came to $219,20.12 and penalties of $164,455.09.

A week later, the grand jury returned another indictment. Based on evidence gathered by Eliot Ness and the Untouchables, it charged Capone and 68 members of his gang with conspiring to violate the Volstead Act. An additional 5,000 separate offenses were cited, 4,000 of them consisting of beer truck deliveries -- 32 barrels to a truck. They went all of the way back to 1922, when Capone bought a used truck for Torrio.

The income tax case, however, was the priority for prosecutors.

If Capone was found guilty on every count in the indictments, he faced a possible prison sentence of 34 years. Of course, Capone didn't want to spend a single day behind bars but figured in the worse case, he might end up serving a year or two. He had complete faith in his attorney, Thomas Nash, and the rest of his firm, which included Michael J. Ahern and Albert Fink. They offered U.S. Attorney Johnson a compromise: their client would plead guilty if assured a light sentence. After consulting with Wilson, Irey, Attorney General William Mitchell and Secretary of the Treasury Ogden Mills, Johnson agreed to recommend a sentence of two and a half years. There was always a risk that threats from the gang might prevent witnesses from testifying and there was also no certainty that the Supreme Court would uphold the six-year statute of limitations. If only a three-year limit was applied to tax evasion, as a U.S District Court of Appeals had recently ruled, it would, in Capone's case, prevent them from prosecuting anything under the first indictment.

On June 16, Capone returned to Judge Wilkerson's courtroom and entered a guilty plea. As he entered the elevator in the Federal Courts Building, a judge who tried to enter at the same time was waved back and told, "You can't use this, bud. It's reserved for Al Capone." After the plea, Judge Wilkerson adjourned the hearing until July 30.

It was taken for granted in the press that Capone was going to get off with a light sentence. Newspapers across the country condemned not only Chicago, but also the criminal courts, which allowed gangsters to get away with all sorts of murder and mayhem, but then only prosecuted them for failing to pay taxes on their ill-gotten gains. A cartoon by Daniel Fitzpatrick in the *St. Louis Post-Dispatch* showed a burglar breaking into a safe while Uncle Sam reminds him: "Don't fail to report this on your income tax."

On July 29, the day before he was to return to Judge Wilkerson's court, Capone, wearing white-bordered, black silk pajamas, chatted with reporters in his suite at the Lexington. He appeared relaxed about his upcoming imprisonment, saying: "I've been made an issue and I'm not complaining. But why don't they go after these bankers who took the savings of thousands of poor people and lost them in bank failures? How about that? Isn't it a lot worse to take the last few dollars some small family has saved— perhaps to live on while the head of the family is out of a job – than to sell a little beer? Believe me, I can't see where the fellow that sells it is any worse off than the fellow who buys and drinks it."

When asked what would become of the gang while he was in prison, Capone replied, "It's really a shame to disabuse the public, to destroy one of their most popular myths, but honestly, there is not, nor has there ever been what might be called a Capone gang."

That evening, Capone threw a farewell dinner at the New Florence Restaurant. Mike Malone, still undercover with the gang, was invited to attend. "Sorry you're going away, Al," he told the gang boss. But Capone was not all that unhappy. A two and one-half year sentence with reduction for good behavior, was not too bad, especially considering the alternatives. John Torrio, who had come from New York for his pal's send-off, had been tasked with watching over things while Capone was away.

Capone showed up in the courtroom the next day wearing a pea-green suit. He grinned at the spectators as he waited to hear his sentence. It never came. Instead, Judge Wilkerson, tense with anger, announced that he would not accept the sentence recommendation that had been offered by the prosecution.

Capone's attorney, Michael Ahern, jumped to his feet. "We were led to believe that the recommendation would be approved by the Court," he exclaimed. "Unless we had been confident that the Court would act according to the recommendation agreed upon, the plea of guilty would never have been entered."

The judge grew angrier. "The Court will listen to the recommendation of the district attorney and listen to the recommendation of the attorney general, but the thing the defendant cannot think, must not think, is that in the end the recommendation of the attorney general and the secretary of the treasury, all considered, the Court is bound to enter judgment according to that recommendation. It is time for somebody to impress upon the defendant that it is utterly impossible to bargain with a federal court."

Judge Wilkerson allowed Capone to withdraw his guilty plea and plead not guilty. He scheduled the trial for October.

A week before the trail, Frank Wilson heard from Eddie O'Hare again. Capone, he reported, had gotten hold of the list from which the jurors in his trial would be chosen and his men were busy trying to bribe them with prizefight tickets, cash, and job offers. Those they couldn't bribe, they were threatening to kill or injure. O'Hare had managed to copy ten names from the list --- numbers 30 to 39. Wilson showed them to Johnson and they took them to Judge Wilkerson, who sent for the complete list. The names matched up with those that O'Hare had jotted down. His information was accurate.

"Bring your case to the court as planned, gentlemen," the judge told them. "Leave the rest to me."

CAPONE IN COURT WITH HIS ATTORNEYS

Jury selection began on October 6. Squad cars carrying fourteen detectives escorted Capone from the Lexington Hotel to the Federal Courts Building. The lead car paused at an intersection while its occupants surveyed the side streets for any friends or foes that might try and rescue or kill Capone. Approaching the Federal Building, the motorcade turned into a tunnel that was normally used only by delivery trucks. It ended at a basement entrance. The detectives took Capone through a series of underground passages to a freight elevator. The sixth-floor corridor was kept clear until he entered the courtroom.

When the first name on the potential jury list was called, Capone's face clouded with confusion. This was not a name on the copy of the list that he had obtained. At the last minute, Judge Wilkerson had switched lists with a fellow judge, using a jury pool that had not been tainted by Capone's men.

By 4:00 p.m., Judge Wilkerson, Capone's attorneys and the prosecution had empanelled a jury made up of small-town tradesmen, mechanics and farmers, each having sworn that they held no prejudice against the defendant. Judge Wilkerson was satisfied with the outcome, as was U.S. Attorney George E.Q. Johnson. Four Assistant U.S. Attorneys were seated at his table – William J. Froelich, Samuel G. Clawson, Jacob I. Grossman, and Dwight H. Green (the last a future governor of Illinois) – and during the trial, Johnson entrusted them with the examination of the witnesses, content to plot strategy from behind the scenes.

The person who seems most worried about the jury was Capone – and for good reason.

On October 7, the government's first witness, an IRS clerk, testified that Capone filed no returns for the years between 1924 and 1929. Chester Bragg followed him to the stand and repeated Capone's admission of ownership of the Hawthorne Smoke Shop during the raid. A pale, nervous Lou Shumway then tabulated the profits of the smoke shop during the two years that he served as the cashier. They exceeded $550,000.

The next day, Assistant U.S. Attorney Clawson submitted into evidence the letter that IRS agents had from Mattingly, Capone's tax attorney, admitting that he had shown a profit from his enterprises. Capone's attorney, Fink, objected. "A lawyer cannot confess for his client. When my client conferred power of attorney in this case to enable him to keep out of the penitentiary, it did not imply the power or authority to make statements that may get him into the penitentiary."

"It might have that effect ultimately," the judge remarked.

Fink fumed. "This is the last toe. They have got him nailed to the cross now. This is putting the last toe on him."

Ahern spoke up: "The Supreme Court has often held that it is human nature to avoid tax. We had a Boston tea party..."

Judge Wilkerson interrupted him. "I suppose this is a Boston tea party?"

But Capone was still hopeful, despite the advantages that seemed to be stacked against him. He still had faith in his lawyers and still couldn't quite grasp the idea of going to jail for not paying taxes. At the Lexington that evening, a tailor measured him for two new suits.

"You don't need to be ordering fancy duds," Frank Rio snorted. "You're going to prison. Why don't you have a suit made with stripes on it?"

"The hell I am!" Capone shot back. "I'm going to Florida for a nice long rest and I need some new clothes before I go."

On October 9, a story appeared in the *Chicago Herald-Examiner* that claimed the wholesale price of a five-gallon can of bootleg liquor had jumped from $30 to $32 to help defray the cost of Capone's defense. Capone didn't comment.

In court, Dwight Green called the government's first Florida witness, hotel owner Parker Henderson. Squirming under the gaze of Capone and Phil D'Andrea, he testified to the Western Union money orders that he picked up for Capone and to the purchase of the Palm Island house, the landscaping done at the estate, the addition of the boat dock and the swimming pool. Henderson was followed on the stand by a small, pale, agitated man named John Fotre, the manager of the Western Union office at the Lexington Hotel, from which many of the money orders were sent. Although cooperative before the trial, he claimed on the stand that he didn't know who sent them. Judge Wilkerson told Fotre that he had better think about his testimony and adjourned for the day.

After court recessed, Wilson reproved the reluctant witness. "What do you expect," Fotre said, "when they let one of Capone's hoodlums sit there with his hand on his gun?"

Fotre was talking about Phil D'Andrea, who had been sitting directly behind Capone for the entire trial. Wilson detailed Sullivan and Mike Malone, who was no longer undercover, to verify the claim. The next day, when they entered the Federal Building, the two agents entered a crowded elevator behind D'Andrea. Malone brushed against him and nodded at Sullivan. He had felt the hard steel of a revolver in a holster under his arm. Reporting to Judge Wilkerson, he told them that they could not cause a scene in the courtroom, which might affect witnesses who hadn't testified yet. Instead, they needed to handle D'Andrea outside. At a prearranged signal, a bailiff notified D'Andrea that a messenger was waiting for him in the hallway with a telegram. As the bodyguard left the courtroom, the agents followed closely, hustled him into a nearby office, seized his revolver and handed him over the police. Claiming the right to carry a concealed weapon, D'Andrea flourished deputy sheriff's credentials, like those carried by several of Capone's men. Judge Wilkerson wasn't impressed. He found D'Andrea in contempt of court and sent him to jail for six months.

A long procession of witnesses started on the stand, each whom had sold things to Capone and could contribute to the puzzle of what his net worth, and net expenditures, truly were. Their testimony took up two full days of the trial and included butchers, grocers, real estate agents, decorators, furniture dealers, building contractors, jewelers, tailors and more.

One of the contractors from Miami, Curt Otto Koenitzer, took the witness chair while smoking a cigar. A deputy marshal took it away from him, to the amusement of the courtroom spectators. After testifying that Mrs. Capone paid him $6,000 to work on their bathhouse and garage he retrieved his cigar to a chorus of laughter and exited the courtroom with a grin. Another witness, a former IRS agent, admitted that in the course of investigating Capone he drank beer with him in a Cicero speakeasy. "It was good beer, too," he admitted without embarrassment.

The last important prosecution witness was Fred Ries, who implicated Pete Penovich, Jimmy Mondi, Frank Pope, Jake Guzik, Ralph Capone and the defendant in the running of the Hawthorne Smoke Shop.

The defense began presenting its case on October 15. Their principal argument centered on Capone's misfortunes at the racetracks. Fink made it sound like no unluckier gambler had ever placed a bet. Capone nearly always lost, he said, and in this case, his pronouncements were true. His friends knew how badly he fared at gambling and eight different bookmakers were brought in to estimate the large sums that Capone paid to them every year, ranging from $12,000 in 1924 to $110,000 in 1929. It seemed that almost all of the money that the government claimed that Capone made from his business, the bookies took away.

Oscar Gutter, a Chicago bookie, testified to a $60,000 loss by Capone in 1927. Asked how he remembered the amount under cross-examination, he stated that it was in his ledger at the end of the month.

"I thought you didn't keep books," Green said.

"Well, I kept them from month to month so I could pay my income tax," Gutter replied, to laughter in the courtroom.

"Why didn't you keep them permanently?"

"Well, it was an illegitimate business."

Joe Yario, a self-styled gambling broker who operated from a Chicago "soft-drink parlor" (speakeasy) said that Capone had "two or three $10,000 losses" but couldn't remember any individual bets. He explained that he "never kept no books."

Budd Gentry, a Miami bookmaker, was asked by Dwight Green to name the horses that Capone backed in 1929 for an alleged loss of about $10,000 each. He shook his head, unable to do so.

"Can you give the name of just one horse the defendant bet on?"

"I have five or six in mind," Gentry answered, "but they just won't come out."

The defense was futile. They were grasping at straws became tax payers could deduct gambling losses only from gambling winnings and Capone's lawyers insisted that he hardly ever won. All that the testimony from the bookies showed was that he did receive income totaling, during one year, at least $200,000. For the additional income, evidenced by his possessions and his expenditures, they offered no plausible explanation.

Torrio, who had been in the courtroom since the first day, sat quietly, expecting to be called once the defense started its case, but he never was. They never called Capone either. Instead, they wrapped up their defense and closing arguments were set for the next day.

On October 16, Fink led off the summation for the defense. "Suppose Capone believed the money he received from so-called illegal transactions was not taxable," he asked the jury, "suppose he discovered to the contrary and tried to pay what he owed, would you say he ever had an intent to defraud the government?" He paused and looked over at his client. "No, and neither would I. Capone is the kind of man who never fails a friend."

"If the defendant's name was not Al Capone," Fink continued, "there would be no case and we would die laughing at the evidence." There wasn't, he maintained, a scrap of evidence to say that Capone made a single dollar in 1924. In 1928, the government had shown that he had expenses but again, no income. He paid for furniture with checks signed by Jake Guzik, but maybe that was a loan. As for 1929, Capone had started trying to pay his taxes two days after he was released from Eastern State. The government was prosecuting him "merely because his name is Al Capone."

Johnson, speaking at length for the first time during the trial, wound up the summation for the government. He urged the jurors to use common sense. Where did the Western Union money orders come from? Where did he get the money to pay for them, and all of his other expenses? Gifts? Insurance settlements? An inheritance? He told the jurors to "draw your own conclusions."

The jury retired at 2:40 p.m. and considering the bizarre nature of the verdict, it's a wonder that it took eight hours to reach it. But one juror had been a holdout, and the verdict ended up being a compromise – a messy, confusing compromise, but a compromise nonetheless.

Capone had returned to the Lexington after leaving the courthouse and he was summoned back that night at 11:00 p.m. The first words that he heard when the verdict was read were "not guilty" on a single count of the indictment covering 1924. After that, though, the verdict became such a muddle that it confused both the prosecution and the defense. On three of the 22 counts in the second indictment – charging tax evasion in 1925, 1926 and 1927 – they voted guilty. He was also found guilty on counts that charged him with failure to file a return in 1928 and 1929. On the remaining counts, all charging tax evasion, they found him not guilty.

The verdict left the prosecution befuddled. How could Capone be guilty of failing to file when he wasn't guilty of tax evasion? They needed a minute to talk things over and asked for a short recess. They returned to court fifteen minutes later and agreed to accept the verdict as rendered. Capone stood guilty of three felonies in the second indictment, each carrying a possibly of a five-year sentence and a $10,000 fine. He was also guilty of two misdemeanors, which called for a one-year sentence and a $10,000 fine.

The defense counsel immediately announced that they planned to appeal.

On October 24, Capone returned to the courtroom for sentencing. Judge Wilkerson began to read the sentence: "It is the judgment of his court on count one that the defendant shall go to the penitentiary for five years, pay a fine of $10,000 and pay the cost of prosecution." On the next two counts, the judge imposed the same sentence and on the final two, a year each in the county jail, plus the same fines and court costs. The sentence added up to eleven years in prison, fines that totaled $50,000 and court costs of $30,000 – the stiffest penalty ever given to a tax evader at the time. The indictments based on evidence provided by Ness and the Untouchables were never pursued.

Judge Wilkerson denied bail, pending the appeal, and asked U.S. Marshal Henry Laubenheimer when he could remove Capone to Leavenworth. Capone audibly gasped at the reply: "At 6:15 tonight, your honor." But following a plea from Ahern, Wilkerson agreed to let Capone stay temporarily in the Cook

CAPONE NEVER BELIEVED THAT IT COULD ACTUALLY HAPPENED -- HE WAS CONVICTED OF TAX EVASION AND SENTENCED TO FEDERAL PRISON IN 1931.

County Jail. Sheriff's deputies escorted him out of the courtroom. As he was leaving, a man walked up to him with an official-looking document. He handed it to Capone. "Internal Revenue," he said. "I have a demand for liens on the property of Alphonse and Mae Capone." To prevent Capone from selling or transferring any assets before satisfying the tax claim the bureau had frozen them with what it called a "jeopardy assessment." Capone turned red, hurled an obscenity at the man and drew back a foot to kick him. Before he could, the deputy sheriffs took him away for fingerprinting. Away from the man, he recovered his self-control.

In the freight elevator, he found himself next to the man whom he knew for two years as "Mike Lepito," now revealed as Special Agent Mike Malone. "The only thing that fooled me was your looks," he said good-naturedly. "You look like a wop." He gave Malone a half grin. "You took your chances and I took mine. I lost."

As he was marched out of the courthouse, he cried out to the news photographers waiting outside. "Get enough, boys," he told them. "You won't see me again for a long time."

A deputy who had been assigned to take Capone to jail in an unmarked car hung back, fearful of some sort of rescue attempt. He confided to Agent Sullivan that, "I wouldn't get into that car for all the money in the world." So Sullivan and a man from the narcotics bureau assumed the risk.

Reporters followed him to the jail and Capone told them that his trial was a blow below the belt, but "what can you expect when the whole community is prejudiced against you?" Photographers asked him to pose behind the bars of the receiving cell. "Please don't take my picture here, fellas," he pleaded with them, backing away from the bars. "Think of my family."

His temper erupted when, on his way to his fourth-floor cell, he heard a camera click. Spinning around, he grabbed a tin bucket and lunged at the offending photographer. "I'll knock your block off," he raged at the man.

The jail guards subdued him and rushed him off to his cell, the reporters still following. As the turnkey opened the cell door, Capone founds two other occupants sitting on the cots. One was a black man who had violated his parole and the other was a skid-row bum who was unable to pay a $100 fine for disorderly conduct. After questioning the bum, who was too awed by being in the presence of Capone to utter a word, Capone peeled a $100 bill off the roll in his pocket and handed it to the man. "I'm going to help this guy out if I can," he announced.

After the reporters left, guards took Capone to the jail hospital for a routine shower and medical examination. Humiliated and alone, the bleakness of his situation was starting to set in.

Capone remained incarcerated at the Cook County Jail while he appealed his sentence. Needless to say, this was still Chicago and many public officials were now capable of repaying favors for past kindnesses that had been shown to them by Capone. Warden David Moneypenny installed him in a one-man cell on the fifth floor with a private shower. He was allowed to make telephone calls and send telegrams and continue running his operation from behind bars. Capone's old political cronies also managed to arrange visitor's passes for Joe Fusco, Murray Humphreys, John Torrio and Jake Guzik. Torrio raised the cash needed for lawyers' fees and other expenses for Capone didn't dare draw on any of his hidden cash reserves. If the IRS found them, they would impound everything.

In December, anonymous telegrams were sent to the Department of Justice, describing Capone's privileged life in jail, and that put an end to it. After an investigation, Moneypenny was ordered to ban all visitors except the prisoner's wife, mother, son, and lawyers. Capone was transferred to the hospital ward with a detail of deputy U.S. marshals assigned to 24-hour guard duty. On February 27, Capone learned that the District Court had rejected his appeal.

Then, three days later, there occurred one of the most atrocious crimes in American history – the kidnapping of Charles Lindbergh's baby from the family's home in rural New Jersey. Americans were shocked and saddened by the crime but to Capone, it presented the possibility of regaining his freedom.

Ten days after the Lindbergh kidnapping, a columnist for the Hearst newspapers, Arthur Brisbane, was given special permission to visit Capone. Capone had sent a message to Brisbane that stated he "could do as much as anybody alive in getting the baby back."

Capone told Brisbane, "I don't want any favors if I am able to do anything for that baby. If they will let me out of here, I will give any bond they require." He told the reporter that he would even leave his brother in jail in his place if he could get out and assist in the search for the kidnapped child.

He explained to Brisbane what he hoped to accomplish. "I have a good many angles and anybody that knows anything would know that he could trust me. There isn't a mob that wouldn't trust me to pay that money, if the relations of the kidnapped child wanted me to pay it, and there isn't anybody would think I would tell where I got the child, or who had it... I would know if whether the child is in the possession of any regular mob that I can connect with or in the possession of any individual working his own racket that would have sense enough to know he could trust me, and know that it might not be a bad idea to do me a good turn," he said.

The newspaper printed a screaming headline that was picked up all over the country. Al Capone wanted to help search for the Lindbergh baby! The story claimed that Capone could do what others could not and Brisbane wrote that he believed that Capone, whether he failed or not, would honor his promise to return to his cell. The article touched off a public clamor to free Capone but no federal court would even discuss Capone's proposition. Charles Lindbergh himself had the final word on the subject: "I wouldn't ask for Capone's release even if it would save a life."

24. BEHIND THE WALLS IN ATLANTA

Capone's next appeal attempt was made with the U.S. Supreme Court, which rejected his application on May 2. On May 4, he was taken from the Cook County Jail. His original destination had been Leavenworth but since so many of Capone's men were already incarcerated there, officials decided that he should go to the Atlanta Penitentiary instead.

As Capone was taken from the jail, both prisoners behind the fence and the crowd gathered outside called out to him. They wished him well and assured him that he had gotten a bum break. Darkness had fallen and flares were lit to brighten the scene so that officers would spot any trouble that might be coming. It was a constant fear for law enforcement officials that elements of Capone's mob might make an attempt to break him out.

At 10:00 p.m., a U.S. marshal's car, accompanied by fifteen police cars, pulled out of the jail yard. Capone sat in the back, between a secret service agent and a car thief named Vito Morici, to whom he had been handcuffed. U.S. Marshal Henry Laubenheimer and a deputy marshal sat facing them on jump seats. At the Dearborn Station, where another crowd had gathered, Capone gestured at Morici's overcoat and told him to throw it over his arm so that no one could see the handcuffs. Capone's brothers, Matt and Mimi, walked with the prisoners as far as the train gate.

CAPONE AND CAR THIEF VITO MORICI ON BOARD THE DIXIE FLYER, WHICH WOULD DELIVER CAPONE TO THE ATLANTA PENITENTIARY.

The entourage boarded the Dixie Flyer, which carried five day coaches and three Pullman cars. In Car 48, second to last, Drawing Room A and an upper berth had been reserved for Capone and Morici, a thin-faced youth in an old suit and worn-out shoes who was going through to Tampa, Florida, to stand trial for transporting a stolen car across state lines. Five deputy marshals, in addition to Laubenheimer, rode the train. As soon as the prisoners took their seat, they were locked into leg irons. The Dixie Flyer left on time at 11:30 p.m.

Morici barely said a word during the trip but Capone talked most of the time. He mostly talked about Chicago and how his organization, he explained to Laubenheimer, had been a boon for the city. It had given jobs to men who otherwise might have been out committing crimes.

The handcuffs and leg irons were removed while the prisoners prepared for bed. Capone slipped into a pair of sky-blue silk pajamas and Laubenheimer insisted on putting the handcuffs back on, which meant the prisoners had to share the same berth. The small, thin car thief lay awake all night, clinging fearfully to the edge of the bunk, terrified that Capone might roll over and smother him.

At every station during the trip, a crowd of two or three hundred turned out, hoping to catch a glimpse of Capone through the window. The sight of this always lifted his spirits. As they continued southward, the temperature started to climb, finally reaching the low 90s. Capone drank quarts of lemonade that he purchased from the dining car and he bought soda pop for Morici.

The train arrived at Atlanta's Union Station at 7:46 p.m., just eleven minutes late. After Morici was transferred to another car for the rest of the trip to Atlanta, Car 48 was moved to a side track to avoid reporters. From there, Laubenheimer and his prisoner were driven four miles to the penitentiary.

In the receiving cell, Capone was stripped to the skin and his posh clothing was replaced with a blue denim uniform. Fingerprinted and photographed, his hair was shaved close to the skull. Then he was transferred to the hospital ward for a three-week stay while the penitentiary physician, Dr. William Ossenfort, determined whether he carried any communicable diseases. A Wasserman test, which Capone took under protest, proved negative. Capone admitted that he had once been exposed to syphilis but believed that he had been cured of it three years before. More tests were ordered, which included a spinal tap, but Capone refused them.

The overcrowded Atlanta Penitentiary had no single cells, only two-man and eight-man cells. Capone was assigned to an eight-man cell, whose occupants included an oil-well promoter, a former judge who had been convicted of mail fraud, a criminal from Ohio and four mail robbers serving 25-year sentences. One of the mail robbers turned out to be Red Rudensky, a mechanic whom Capone knew from his early bootleg days. Rudensky thought highly of Capone and the two of them sat up talking during Capone's first night, as

THE ATLANTA PENITENTIARY

CELLS - ATLANTA PENITENTIARY   626

CAPONE'S RECORDS FROM ATLANTA, INCLUDING A NEW PRISON MUGSHOT.

THE PENITENTIARY WAS OVERCROWDED AND WITH NO SMALL CELLS AVAILABLE, CAPONE WAS ASSIGNED TO AN EIGHT-MAN CELL.

the gangland boss was unable to sleep.

The other prisoners mostly admired Capone and when Rudensky, who stage-managed most of the entertainment at the theater, introduced him to the captive audience, Capone received a standing ovation. But things didn't always go that smoothly. Rudensky later recalled, "I sent word to lay off Big Al, but while 99 percent would always go along with anything I asked, there was always the creepy 25 or 30 cons waiting for a chance to make trouble. They had a healthy respect for Al, and figured that between us anyone who gave him trouble would get it back fast. Still, two hillbillies, both in on a morals charge, decided to put our strength to the test. I got the neck chop and the knee one day out in the yard. Al was roughed up at chow. But inside 24 hours, I had a revenge team take it out in spades. The two jackasses were pounded into bloody pulps during work hours. One wound up with a broken cheekbone and a fractured skull. The other never used his right arm again for work."

Rudensky remained close with Capone. He arranged cash to be smuggled to him from the gang by way of a trusty who drove a supply truck. With this money, Capone bought privileges from certain guards and loyalty and protection from other prisoners. He usually a band of bodyguards who surrounded him at work and during recreation times in the yard.

Sleeping in the same cell as Capone, Rudensky also recalled his frequent nightmares and the times when he seemed to be shouting at nothing, urging the darkness, "Go away, Jimmy, leave me alone!" The same visions of the vengeful specter of James Clark apparently followed Capone to Atlanta. He swore that he saw the specter hanging above his bed at night, always with a sinister grin on his face. One night, he woke everyone on the cell block with his screams – crying out that an intruder was in his cell. His cellmates saw nothing out of the ordinary, but Capone had.

Jimmy Clark was still with him and would never leave until Capone, too, was dead.

Not long after he entered the penitentiary, his brothers bought bitter news – his longtime friend John Torrio had formed a partnership with mobster Dutch Schultz. While Capone had been incarcerated at the Cook County Jail, Schultz had visited him with Charles "Lucky" Luciano. Torrio had brought them at Capone's insistence. Schultz had been challenging Luciano's claims to certain territories, endangering a general peace that existed, and Capone cast himself in the role of an arbitrator. He wanted the two men to put aside their differences and work with other gang leaders to revitalize the national organization that had been talked about in Atlantic City. Capone planned to play a leading role in it when he was released from prison.

RED RUDESNKY, PHOTOGRAPHED AT LEAVENWORTH IN 1923

But the outcome of the meeting was troubling. Capone was infuriated by Schultz's sweeping demands and behaved as if all of New York belonged to him. Capone said years later, "If I'd had him outside, I'd have shoved a gun in his guts."

The meeting broke up with nothing settled but what troubled Capone more was that Torrio, for some reason, seemed to favor Schultz. Before his old mentor returned to New York, he urged him to have nothing to do with him. Torrio was noncommittal at the time and now Capone learned that he had gone into business with Schultz. Capone sent Torrio a message, urging him to end the partnership, return to Chicago and resume leadership of the organization. There was no reply. Capone never forgave him and he ordered his wife to tear up the bonds that Torrio had been buying for Sonny on every birthday, now worth more than $80,000.

Capone had the last laugh when it came to Dutch Schultz, though. He died in 1935, two days after being gunned down in the bathroom of the Palace Chop House and Tavern in Newark, New Jersey.

Over the course of the next several months, Capone's family continued his legal battles on the outside, attempting to appeal his case. In August, Teresa Capone retained the services of one of the country's leading attorneys, William E. Leahy. He attempted to re-open Capone's case, stating that the statute of limitations had run out on the original indictment. This was a problem that the government feared might come up at trial although, strangely, Capone's counsel had failed to delve into it. That was an omission that reportedly lost the Nash-Ahern firm all of its gangster clientele. He based his arguments on a similar case that had been decided in Boston, maintaining that Capone's case was parallel and that his client was being imprisoned illegally. Capone appeared before federal Judge E. Marvin Underwood, who took the petition under advisement.

On December 5, Capone was still waiting for the judge's decision when an announcement came that President Franklin D. Roosevelt had ratified the repeal of the Eighteenth Amendment. Prohibition had come to an end. This was, perhaps, a bad omen for Capone. Prohibition had allowed him to make all of the money that he had gone to prison for and now it was over, just like Capone's final court case. The judge dismissed the petition and Capone remained in jail. And to make matters worse, word had just come from the Justice Department that he was going to be transferred to the new, brutal "escape-proof" prison, Alcatraz.

25. CAPONE ON "THE ROCK"

"The Rock," the name given to Alcatraz Penitentiary, was the ultimate American prison. It was the place where scores of the country's worst criminal offenders, blood-letters, tough guys and escape artists called the end of the line. For 29 years, the damp, fog-enshrouded prison kept America's most notorious lawbreakers isolated from the rest of the world on a small island in San Francisco Bay. The heavy mist, the cold wind, freezing water and wailing foghorns made Alcatraz the loneliest of prisons. During its almost three decades as a federal prison, its steel doors clanged shut on more than a 1,000 convicts. It was a place of total punishment and minimum privilege. Those who survived Alcatraz often did so at the cost of their sanity --- and in the case of a few of the men, like Al Capone, even their souls.

Alcatraz Island, located in the mist off the coast of San Francisco, received its name in 1775 when the Spanish explorers charted San Francisco Bay. They named the rocky piece of land La Isla de los Alcatraces, or the Island of Pelicans. The island was totally uninhabited, plagued by barren ground, little vegetation and

ALCATRAZ ISLAND -- AMERICA'S "ESCAPE-PROOF" PRISON

surrounding water that churned with swift currents. In the late 1840s, the grim island was taken over by the U.S. military. It was a prime location for the establishment of a fort and a lighthouse was desperately needed there because of the all of the ships that were coming to San Francisco during the Gold Rush. Topographical engineers began conducting geological surveys and by 1853, a military fortress was started. One year later, a lighthouse was established (the first on the Pacific Coast) to guide ships through the Golden Gate.

A few years later, a military fort was erected on the island and in 1859, Alcatraz saw its first prisoners, a contingent of court-martialed, military convicts. Then in 1861, Alcatraz started to receive Confederate prisoners, thanks to its natural isolation created by the surrounding waters. Until the end of the Civil War, the prison population varied, consisting of soldiers, Confederate privateers and southern sympathizers. They were confined in the dark basement of the guardhouse and conditions were grim. The men slept side-by-side, head to toe, lying on the stone floor of the basement. There was no running water, no heat and no latrines. Disease and infestations of lice spread from man to man and not surprisingly, overcrowding was a serious problem. They were often bound by six-foot chains attached to iron balls, fed bread and water and confined in sweatboxes as punishment.

After the war ended, the fort was deemed obsolete and was no longer needed. The prison continued to be used, though, and soon, more buildings and cell houses were added. In the 1870s and 1880s, Indian chiefs and tribal leaders who refused to give in to the white man were incarcerated on Alcatraz. They shared quarters with the worst of the military prisoners. The island became a shipping point for incorrigible deserters, thieves, rapists and repeated escapees.

In 1898, the Spanish-American War sent the prisoner population from less than 100 to over 450. The Rock became a holding pen for Spanish prisoners brought over from the Philippines. Around 1900, Alcatraz again became a disciplinary barracks for military prisoners. Ironically, it also served as a health resort for soldiers returning from the Philippines and Cuba with tropical diseases. The overcrowding caused by a combination of criminals and recovering soldiers resulted in pardons to reduce the number of men housed on the island.

By 1902, the Alcatraz prison population averaged around 500 men per year, with many of them serving sentences of two years or less. The wooden barracks on the island had fallen into a ramshackle state, thanks to the damp, salt air so in 1904, work was begun to modernize the facility. Prisoner work crews began extending the stockade wall and constructing a new mess hall, kitchen, shops, a library and a washhouse. Work continued on the prison for the next several years and it even managed to survive the Great Earthquake of 1906. The disaster left San Francisco in shambles and a large fissure opened up on Alcatraz, but left the buildings untouched. Prisoners from the heavily damaged San Francisco jail were temporarily housed on the island until the city's jail could be rebuilt.

Construction of the new buildings was completed a few years later and, in 1911, the facility was officially named the "United States Disciplinary Barracks." In addition to Army prisoners, the Rock was also used to house seamen captured on German vessels during the First World War. Alcatraz was the Army's first long-term prison and it quickly gained a reputation for being a tough facility. There were strict rules and regulations with punishments ranging from loss of privileges to solitary confinement, restricted diet, hard labor and even a twelve-pound ball and ankle chain.

Despite the stringent rules, Alcatraz was still mainly a minimum-security facility. Inmates were given various work assignments, depending on how responsible they were. Many of them worked as general servants, cooking and cleaning for families of soldiers housed on the island. In many cases, the prisoners were even entrusted to care for officers' children. However, this lack of security led to a number of attempted escapes. Most of those who tried to swim for freedom never made it to the mainland and were forced to turn back. Many others were never seen again. They had either made it to shore – or had drowned in the harsh waters of the bay.

ALCATRAZ WARDEN JAMES A. JOHNSTON

During the 1920s, Alcatraz gradually fell into disuse. The lighthouse keeper, a few Army personnel and the most hardened of the military prisoners were the only ones who remained on the island. The mostly empty buildings slowly crumbled but this period would not last for long. A change was coming to Alcatraz that would make it the most formidable prison in American history.

The social upheaval that began in America during Prohibition and continued into the Great Depression brought new life to Alcatraz. President Roosevelt and the newly empowered FBI began a national "War on Crime" to deal with the gangsters, kidnappers and bandits that were "terrorizing" the country. Attorney General Homer Cummings supported J. Edgar Hoover and the FBI in creating a new, escape-proof prison that would strike fear into the hearts of criminals. They decided that Alcatraz would be the perfect location for such a penitentiary. In 1933, the facility was officially turned over to the Federal Bureau of Prisons and the Attorney General asked James A. Johnston of San Francisco to take over as warden of the new prison. He implemented a strict set and rules and regulations for the facility and selected the best available guards and officers from the federal penal system.

The Rock became largely Warden Johnston's creation. New construction was started on the project and practically the entire cellblock building was built atop the old Army fort. Part of the old Army prison was used but the rusting iron bars were replaced by bars of hardened steel. Gun towers were erected at various points around the island and the cellblocks were equipped with catwalks, gun walks, electric locks, metal detectors, a well-stocked arsenal, barbed and cyclone wire fencing and even tear gas containers that were fitted into the ceiling of the dining hall and elsewhere. Apartments for the guards and their families were built on the old parade grounds and the lighthouse keeper's mansion was taken over to become the warden's residence. Alcatraz had been turned into an impregnable fortress.

Wardens from prisons all over the country were polled and were permitted to send their most incorrigible inmates to the Rock. These included inmates with behavioral problems, those with a history of escape attempts and even high-profile inmates who were receiving privileges because of their status or notoriety. Each train that came from the various prisons seemed to have a "celebrity" on board. Among the first groups were Al Capone, Doc Barker, George "Machine Gun" Kelly, Robert Stroud (who would later become notorious as the Birdman of Alcatraz), Bonnie and Clyde driver Floyd Hamilton and kidnapper and bank robber Alvin Karpis. When each of these men arrived on Alcatraz, they ceased to exist as the people they once were and simply became numbers.

When Warden Johnston conceived of the idea behind Alcatraz prison, he did not even pay lip service to the principle of rehabilitation. This was a place of punishment, plain and simple, and nothing that these men had done or accomplished in the past mattered now. Inside, there would be no rewards for good behavior, it was simply expected and demanded. There were no trustees, only punishment for breaking the rules. Johnston believed that a policy of maximum security, combined with few privileges and total isolation would serve as a deterrent to America's public enemies and those who emulated them. In the end, though, it would deter them no more than the electric chair, the hangman or the gas chamber did. In fact, despite the propaganda coming from the Attorney General's office, comparatively few big-time gangsters ever went to Alcatraz. There were not enough of them who were captured alive to fill the cells. What the FBI called a "notorious mail robber" was more likely to be a small-time loser who broke into some postal boxes.

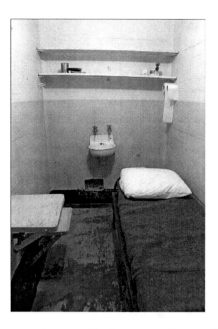

ALCATRAZ CELL BLOCK

(RIGHT) A TYPICAL ONE-MAN CELL AT ALCATRAZ

Unbelievably, some inmates were first-time offenders. If the new prison profited anyone, it was the wardens who were able to empty some of their cells to populate Alcatraz. No court could sentence criminals to Alcatraz. Only those already serving terms could be transferred there, if the warden recommended it and the Bureau of Prisons approved.

Alcatraz was a brutal place of penitence, as the Quakers who had devised the American prison system intended all prisons to be. It was a place where the inmates had only five rights – food, clothing, a private cell, medical care and a shower once each week. Any, and all, of those rights could be taken away for even a minor infraction.

Each of the cells in Alcatraz measured four by eight feet and had a single fold-up bunk, toilet, desk, chair and a sink. A prisoner's day began at 6:30 a.m. with the clanging of a bell and bright electric lights. He had twenty minutes in which to dress and make his bed. If he wanted to shave, he had to shove a matchbox through the bars of his cell. A guard would place a razor blade in it and allow three minutes before returning to reclaim it. At 6:50 a.m. the bell sounded again and the floor guard took the morning count. A third bell would clang when all prisoners were accounted for. A fourth bell sounded when it was time for breakfast. The turnkeys, standing inside locked cages, pulled back a lever and all of the heavy steel cell door locks pulled back simultaneously. The prisoners then marched in a single file line to the mess hall. The prisoners ate ten men to a table, with the black prisoners segregated. They all sat facing the same direction and all of them ate in silence. The first years of Alcatraz were known as the "silent years" and during this period, the rules stated that no prisoner was allowed to speak to another, or to sing, hum or whistle. Talking was forbidden in the cells, in the mess hall and even in the showers. The inmates were allowed to talk for three minutes during the morning and afternoon recreation yard periods and for two hours on weekends. This rule of silence was later relaxed.

Food was served cafeteria-style from a steam table. Bad food had caused more prison riots than anything else so Warden Johnston was determined to serve three palatable meals each day. Typical breakfast fare consisted of oatmeal with milk, fried bologna sausage, cottage fried potatoes, toast with margarine and coffee. Prisoners were required to clean their plates and if they did not, they received no food the following day. Johnston also issued three packs of cigarettes each week, and for heavy smokers, he installed tobacco and paper dispensers in each cell so that inmates could roll their own. However, he did not approve a commissary, which most prisons had, where the men could buy items like candy, chewing gum and soda pop with the few cents they earned each day in the prison workshops.

After breakfast, the prisoners were lined up again and marched back to their cells for another count. No prisoner was allowed to wear a watch. Bells told the time and they rang almost every half hour for one reason or another. After the post-breakfast count, prisoners were lined up again according to their assigned workshop. Aside from breaks and lunch, the prisoners worked for most of the day, until 9:30 p.m. when lights were turned out. The methodical routine never varied, except on weekends. On Sunday mornings, time was allowed for religious worship and on Saturday, the men were allowed their weekly shower. Both days offered two hours of free time that could be used exercising in the yard or pursuing indoor hobbies.

In their cells, before lights out, prisoners could read books or magazines borrowed from the prison library, but to intensify their isolation, Johnston denied them newspapers or radios. Correspondence was also severely limited. A prisoner could write one letter a week to a relative and could receive no more than three letters, also from his family. He could correspond with no one outside of his family except for his lawyer. Censors read all incoming and outgoing mail, deleted any part of it that did not confine itself to family affairs, and sent a typed copy of what remained. There were no set visiting days. Each monthly visit, limited to 45 minutes, had to be arranged through Johnston. The warden would issue a pass and give instructions on where and when to board the boat to the island. A sheet of plate glass, which ran from floor to ceiling, separated the visitors from the inmates. At head level were two strips of steel, a few inches apart, which had small holes drilled into them. Visitors and prisoners could speak through these holes but they were designed to be so small that nothing could be passed through them. Guards were also present and could hear every word that was exchanged. They interrupted if forbidden topics were broached.

The guards at Alcatraz were almost as hardened as the prisoners. There was one guard for every three inmates, which was stunning considering that most prisons assigned one guard to every twelve inmates. Gun galleries had been placed at each end of the cell blocks and as many as twelve counts each day allowed the guards to keep very close tabs on the men on their watch. Because of the small number of inmates at Alcatraz, the guards generally knew everyone by name. Although Warden Johnston forbid corporal punishment as a general rule, the guards did not hesitate, when met with any resistance, to knock a man senseless with water from a high pressure hose, or to break and arm or a leg with their clubs, or truss a prisoner up for days in a straitjacket. The usual punishment, though, was solitary confinement in the punishment cells. While the cells in which the prisoners lived were barren at best, they must have seemed like luxury hotel suites compared to the punishment cells. Here, the men were stripped of all but

THE ENTRANCE TO ONE OF THE PITCH-DARK SOLITARY CONFINEMENT CELLS

their basic right to food and even then, what they were served barely sustained the convict's life, let alone his health.

One place of punishment was the single strip cell, which was dubbed "the Oriental." This dark, steel-encased cell had no toilet and no sink. There was only a hole in the floor that could be flushed from the outside. Inmates were placed in the cell naked and were given little food. The cell had a standard set of bars, with an expanded opening to pass food through, but a solid steel door enclosed the prisoner in total darkness. Men were usually kept in this cell for one or two days. It was cold and completely bare, save for a straw mattress that the guards removed each morning. This cell was used as punishment for the most severe violations and was feared by the prison population.

The "Hole" was a similar type of cell. There were several of them and they were all located on the bottom tier of cells and were considered to be a severe punishment by the inmates. Mattresses were again taken away each morning and prisoners were sustained by bread and water, supplemented by a solid meal every third day. Steel doors also closed these cells off from the daylight, although a low-wattage bulb was suspended from the ceiling. Inmates could spend up to nineteen days here, completely silent and isolated from everyone. Time in the hole usually meant psychological and sometimes even physical torture. Usually, convicts who were thrown into the hole for anything other than a minor infraction were beaten by the guards. The screams from the men being beaten in one of the four holes located on the bottom tier of D Block echoed throughout the block as though being amplified through a megaphone. Sometimes when men emerged from the darkness and isolation of the hole, they would be totally disoriented and would end up in the prison's hospital ward, devoid of their sanity. Others came out with pneumonia and arthritis after spending days or weeks lying naked on the cold cement floor.

And there were even worse places to be sent than the hole. Located in front of the unused A Block was a staircase that led down to a large steel door. Behind the door were catacomb-like corridors and stone archways that led to the sealed-off gun ports from the days when Alcatraz was a fort. Fireplaces located in several of the rooms were not used for warmth, but to heat up cannonballs so that they would start fires after reaching their targets. Two of the other rooms located in this dank, underground area were dungeons. Prisoners who had the misfortune of being placed in the dungeons were not only locked in, but also chained to the wall. Their screams could not be heard in the main prison. The only toilets they had were buckets, which were emptied once each week. For food, they received two cups of water and one slice of bread each day. Every third day, they would receive a regular meal. The men were stripped of their clothing and their dignity as guards chained them to the wall in a standing position from morning until night. In the darkest hours, they were given a blanket to sleep on. Thankfully, the dungeons were rarely used, but the dark cells of D Block, were regularly filled.

Alcatraz could test the limits of men's endurance, both physically and mentally. Over the years, a number of inmates attempted suicide, and a few succeeded. Those who failed always wound up in the hole. A counterfeiter named John Standig tried to kill himself before he even got to Alcatraz by jumping from the train taking him there, but he survived. At the prison, where he made another attempt, he told a fellow inmate, "If you ever get out of here, tell them I wasn't trying to escape. I was trying to kill myself." An inmate named Jimmy Grove, a former soldier imprisoned after raping an officer's daughter, was saved by a blood transfusion after he cut the arteries in both arms. In April 1936, a prisoner named Joe Bowers was taken to the hole after he broke his eyeglasses and tried to cut his own throat with the glass. When he was released from solitary, he scaled the fence surrounding the work area, knowing that the guards would shoot him. They did, and his body fell 75 feet into the waters of the bay below. Ed Wutke, a former merchant marine who was serving 27 years for murder at sea, was found dead in his cell one day after severing his own jugular vein with the blade from a pencil sharpener.

In 1937 alone, fourteen prisoners at Alcatraz went rampantly insane. That number does not include the men who slowly became "stir crazy" from the prison's brutal conditions. To Warden Johnston, mental

(LEFT) HENRY YOUNG AND (RIGHT) RUFUS MCCAIN

illness was nothing more than an excuse to get out of work. If he was capable of functioning physically, without disruption to the general population, a madman was ignored. If he was uncontrollable, he was confined to the hospital ward. A consulting psychiatrist visited the island at irregular intervals but offered little help to the inmates. One prisoner from Leavenworth screamed every time an airplane flew over the island. Another kept his head wrapped in towels to protect him from invisible assailants. Another one, nicknamed "Rabbit," was a docile prisoner until he scooped up every object in his third-tier cell, wrapped them in a bundle, and then hurled it all over the railing when his cell door was opened again. He was dragged, clawing and howling, to the medical ward and never returned to the cellblocks.

And then there was prisoner no. 284, Rube Persefal. A former gangster and bank robber, Persefal was assigned to work on the dock detail. One day, he picked up a hatchet, placed his left hand on a block of wood and, laughing maniacally, began hacking off the fingers on his hand. He then placed his right hand on the block and pleaded with a guard to chop off those fingers as well. Persefal was placed in the hospital, but was never declared insane.

In 1941, inmate Henry Young went on trial for the murder of fellow prisoner Rufus McCain, his accomplice in a failed escape attempt. The two men, along with three other inmates – Doc Barker, William Martin and Dale Stamphill – had slipped out of the prison on the foggy night of January 13, 1939. An alarm sounded and the men were discovered on the beach trying to fabricate a crude raft. Two of the men started to flee and guards fired, killing Barker and wounding Stamphill. Young and McCain surrendered peacefully and were kept in solitary for almost a year. After they were returned to their cells in November 1940, the two argued on several occasions. McCain was assigned to the tailor shop and Young to the furniture shop, located directly downstairs. On December 3, Young waited until just after a prisoner count and then when a guard's attention was diverted, he ran downstairs and stabbed McCain, who went into shock and he died five hours later.

Young refused to say why he had killed his former partner but his attorney had a ready explanation. During the trial that followed, his attorney claimed that, because of the terrible conditions at the prison, Young could not be held responsible for his actions. He stated that the Alcatraz guards frequently beat his client and that he had endured long periods of extreme isolation. This cruel and inhumane treatment had caused Young to become insane and his responses to hostile situations had become desperately violent. The attorney literally put Alcatraz itself on trial. He subpoenaed Warden Johnston to testify about the prison's conditions and policies and in addition, several inmates were also called to recount the state of daily life in Alcatraz. The prisoners told of being locked in the dungeons and of being beaten by the guards. They also testified to knowing several inmates who had gone insane because of such treatment. The jury ended up sympathizing with Young's case and he was convicted of a manslaughter charge that only added a few years onto his original sentence.

After the trial, Young was transferred to the Medical Center for Federal Prisoners in Springfield, Missouri. After serving his federal sentence, he was sent to the Washington State Penitentiary and was paroled in 1972. He had spent nearly forty years in prison. After his release, Young vanished into history and whatever became of him is unknown.

Al Capone arrived at the prison in August 1934. He quickly learned that while he may have once been famous, on Alcatraz, he was only a number. He made attempts to flaunt the power that he had enjoyed at the federal prison in Atlanta, where he was used to the special benefits that he was awarded by guards and wardens alike. He was arrogant and unlike most of the other prisoners, was not a veteran of the penal system. He had only spent a short time in prison and his stay had been much different than that of most other convicts. Capone had possessed the ability to control his environment through wealth and power, but he was soon to learn that things were much different at Alcatraz.

After Capone and the prisoners who arrived with him were unloaded from the train, they were taken to a barge that brought them across the water to Alcatraz. The guards who had transferred him from Atlanta took off his leg irons, but not his handcuffs. Capone hobbled along with the rest of the men onto the boat, across the bay and then up the steep, spiraling roadway to the top of the island.

Warden Johnston had a custom of meeting new prisoners when they arrived to give them a brief orientation. When Capone entered the rear of the cell house, Johnston sat at a desk. When he called out the names of the prisoners, a guard removed their handcuffs and brought them to the desk. Johnston later wrote in his memoirs that he had little trouble recognizing Capone when he saw him. Capone was grinning and making comments to other prisoners as he stood in the lineup. When it became his turn to approach the warden, Johnston ignored him and simply gave him a standard prison number, just like all of the other men. Johnston wrote: "It was apparent that he wanted to impress other prisoners by asking me questions as if he were their leader. I wanted to make sure that he didn't get any such idea. I handed him a ticket with his number, gave him the instructions I had given every other man, and told him to move along."

(ABOVE) CAPONE'S CELL AT ALCATRAZ. USED TO BEING ABLE TO PURCHASE FAVORS AND HAVE THE RUN OF WHATEVER JAIL THAT HE WAS STUCK IN, CAPONE FOUND THE NEW PENITENTIARY TO BE A HARSH AND BRUTAL PLACE.

(RIGHT) CAPONE'S PRISON RECORDS FROM ALCATRAZ. AS CAN BE SEEN BY THE SMIRKING PHOTOGRAPH, THE MUGSHOT WAS TAKEN SOON AFTER CAPONE'S ARRIVAL, WHEN HE THOUGHT THAT THE NEW PRISON WAS GOING TO BE JUST LIKE EASTERN STATE AND ATLANTA. HE SOON FOUND OUT THAT IT WASN'T.

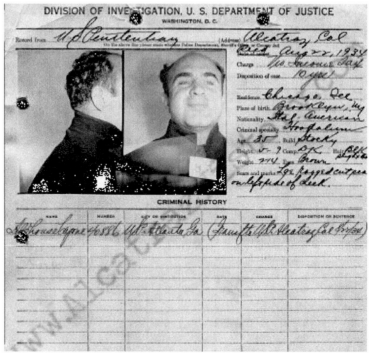

The guards led Capone to the bathhouse to be stripped, medically examined, and his ears, nose, mouth and rectum probed for contraband. For weekday wear, he was issued pants and a shirt made of gray denim and for Sunday, a blue denim uniform. For cold weather, he was given a wool-lined pea coat. The fronts and backs of his clothing were stamped with Capone's number, 85, that could be seen from twenty yards away. He was then given sheets, a pillowcase, towel, comb, and a toothbrush and taken to his cell, where he would spend about fourteen hours out of every day, seven days a week. Capone drew the fifth cell from the right, third tier, Block B. The entire process must have been quite a shock to the crime boss, from the clothing to the accommodations. Even in Atlanta, he had been used to special treatment. He was allowed to wear his own clothing, given special food and drink and even permitted to keep his silk underwear. He quickly discovered that Alcatraz was not the same sort of prison.

Warden Johnston had a policy to listen to any prisoner who wanted to speak with him and when, on the day after he arrived, Capone requested an interview, Johnston had him brought to his office. He asked what Capone wanted and the gangster explained, "Well, I don't know how to begin but you're my warden now and I just thought I better tell you that I have a lot of friends and expect to have lots of visitors and I want to arrange to see my wife and mother and my son and brothers."

Johnston explained to him that, like all of the other inmates, Capone would have very limited visiting privileges, extending to blood relatives only, except for his brother, Ralph, who had a prison record and was not allowed to visit. None of his "friends and business associates" could visit. No rules were going to be bent for any inmate, no matter who he was.

Capone allegedly smiled feebly as he said, "It looks like Alcatraz has got me licked."

Johnston granted another interview request from Capone the following week, where Capone again tried to plead his case for special visitors. He explained that among his important friends were big businessmen who depended on him for help and advice. Johnston again sent him on his way.

Capone may have struck out with the warden but he was determined to try and gain the kind of leadership within the prison that he had enjoyed at Atlanta. Capone tried to dispense favors to his fellow prisoners, offering to have money sent to their relatives and to buy musical instruments for those who, like himself, wanted to play in the prison band. Johnston thwarted all of his efforts. When it became apparent that Capone could not obtain even the smallest consideration, he lost respect, as Johnston intended, among the inmates, especially among the minor criminals who made up the majority of the prison population. He soon found that his safety was in danger.

It was deprivation of news from the outside world that led to Capone's first punishment. He spent a full nineteen days in the hole for attempting to bribe a guard to bring him a newspaper. He also did two ten-day stretches in the hole for talking to other inmates when the rule of silence was in effect. Each time that Capone was sent to the hole, he emerged a little the worse for wear.

Capone was assigned to work in the prison's basement laundry room, to which the army posts around the bay area sent their wash. The laundry room was damp and badly ventilated and when an army transport ship anchored in the bay with an accumulation of wash, the workload became backbreaking. In January 1935, Capone was at his usual station when 36 of his co-workers walked off the job in protest. The strikers were quickly surrounded, separated and sent to the hole. Because Capone took no part in the action, he aroused a great deal of hostility from the other workers. A month later, one of the strikers, Bill Collier, was catching laundry as Capone fed it into the machine. He complained that it was coming to him too fast, but Capone ignored him. Finally, Collier picked up a sopping bundle and flung it into Capone's face. Before the guards could stop the fight, Capone blacked both of his attacker's eyes. Both men spent eight days in the hole for the altercation.

Another strike, this time a general one, took place without Capone in January of the following year. The immediate provocation was the death of a prisoner with a stomach ulcer, whom Johnston had refused medical treatment because he thought he was pretending to be sick. Capone stuck to his post again, once more incurring the wrath of the strikers. But it was not cowardice that kept him from striking; he knew the odds and knew there was nothing to be gained by going up against the guards. He asked to be excused from work and allowed to remain in his cell until the strike ended. Capone was not alone in this. Nearly all of the prison's high-profile inmates – felons like Doc Barker, George "Machine Gun" Kelly, kidnappers Albert Bates and Harvey Bailey, and train robber and escape artist Roy Gardner – shared Capone's prudence and likewise incurred the hatred of the strikers.

Capone's request was granted. On his first day back at work, the strikers having been starved into submission, an unknown person hurled a sash weight at his head. Roy Gardner saw it coming and

(LEFT) ROY GARDNER AND (RIGHT) ALVIN KARPIS, TWO OTHER HIGH PROFILE INMATES AT ALCATRAZ AND TWO MEN THAT CAPONE DEVELOPED FRIENDSHIPS WITH.

threw himself at Capone, shoving the other man aside. The weight still managed to strike Capone's arm, inflicting a deep cut. After that, he was transferred to the bathhouse cleaning crew. The bathhouse adjoined the barbershop. On the morning of June 23, five months after the second strike, Jim Lucas, a Texas bank robber, reported for his monthly haircut. When he left, he grabbed a pair of scissors, slipped up behind Capone, who was mopping the bathhouse floor, and drove the blades into his back. Capone recovered after a week in the hospital and Lucas went to the hole.

After this incident, Mae Capone hired a San Francisco lawyer, who appealed to the Attorney General to have Capone incarcerated elsewhere, but all of the requests were refused. Other attempts followed to kill or maim the "wop with the mop," as his enemies now referred to him. His friends exposed a plan to doctor his coffee with lye one morning and on his way to the dentist, he was jumped and almost strangled before he broke his attacker's hold and knocked the man down.

During this time, Capone still longed for news from outside. The best way to get it was from new arrivals. Most of the inmates would work tirelessly to get close to and befriend the newcomers. If they succeeded, they had to hold their conversations out of the earshot of the guards. A new man whom Capone managed to befriend was Alvin Karpis and the two had an initial conversation one day while sitting in the recreation yard with their banks against the wall. Capone asked him if he needed money and Karpis told him that he didn't. They discussed their personal lives and since Karpis was able to play guitar, he joined the prison band at Capone's suggestion. Capone had become quite adept at the tenor banjo. The two men talked for the next few Sundays, as they bent their heads together over a music stand, pretending to study the sheet music that had been placed on it. Karpis turned out to be the first of several new arrivals who kept Capone abreast of recent developments in the underworld.

Capone learned about the death of one of his favorite bodyguards, Jack McGurn, who had been shot to death in a bowling alley on the eve of St. Valentine's Day, 1936. A comical valentine had been left behind at the scene, hinting at revenge for the murders on Clark Street seven years before.

The organization that Capone had created was still largely intact and was now growing in new directions. Jake Guzik, released from Leavenworth in 1935, and Ralph Capone had picked up where things left off as, respectively, general business manager and director of gambling and vice. Capone's brother Mitzi was handling horse betting at a new Cicero spot, the Hi Ho Club, and acting as a contact man for loan sharks. Phil D'Andrea had become the president of the Italo-American National Union (once called the Unione Siciliane) and with Guzik and others had infiltrated a Hollywood-based movie theater union and extorted millions of dollars by threatening labor trouble. Tony Accardo and Paul Ricca, once lowly Capone soldiers, were now joining the ranks of respected organized crime leaders.

The news that Capone received from his family in the fall of 1936 mostly concerned his wife's struggle to retain the Palm Island house. After the payment of her husband's lawyers' fees and part of the fines, court costs and taxes owed, she didn't have much left. Capone's sister, Mafalda, wrote to say that Ralph was taking care of everything and not to worry. Ralph wrote a short time later and Mae and Matt visited Alcatraz soon after to try and set his mind at ease. In November, Ralph paid off everything that was still owed on the house and obtained a complete release in Mae's name.

In September 1937, another mutiny, which Capone again did not take part in, broke out and nearly cost Warden Johnston his life. When a majority of the prisoners refused to work unless they could choose their jobs, Johnston gave them a simple choice: obedience or starvation. About two-thirds of them grudgingly returned to their jobs, while 100 others remained locked in their cells. From the start of his administration, Johnston had observed a dangerous custom. At the end of each meal, he would wait by the exit, alone and unarmed, with his back to the prisoners until the last of them marched out of the mess hall. During the 1937 mutiny, a prisoner named Barton "Whitey" Phillips, a young bank robber serving a life sentence, didn't march out. As he passed close to Johnston, he hit him hard with a right fist to the jaw. The warden went down and before the guards could reach him, Phillips had stamped on his chest several times and kicked him in the head. Johnston survived, minus a few of his teeth, but the beating that Phillips took, followed by weeks in the hole, left him a permanently broken man

In late January 1938, Capone's fourth year on Alcatraz, he received a visit from a man he knew, Special Agent James Sullivan. He brought with him U.S. Attorney Seymour Klein from New York, who had obtained permission to question Capone about John Torrio.

A predictable outcome from Capone's conviction had been a rush of gangsters to the tax collector to pay up before the law caught up with them, too. The lesson was only partially learned, however. Many of them, aided by accountants and lawyers, concocted what they imagined to be unbeatable schemes to hide income. Torrio, usually a very careful man, adopted such a scheme after the repeal of Prohibition. While detailed, it was simple enough in essence: he would only declare a small part of his income and the bulk of it would be invested with dummy partners in a legitimate New York wholesale liquor firm.

Sullivan and Klein were the first visitors ever allowed near an Alcatraz prisoner without supervision. At the start of the afternoon work periods, guards admitted them to Capone's cell, brought him back from his work, locked the cell door, and left the three of them alone. Klein, a small man, grew increasingly nervous as the bulky Capone, with his notorious temper, paced the small cell. He stayed as far away as possible and let Sullivan conduct the interview. Capone and Sullivan got along well and Al talked – then talked some more. In his hunger for communication with the outside world, he talked all afternoon and convinced the two men to return the next day. He talked about his whole life, from his early days in Brooklyn right up to his conviction. He mentioned Torrio frequently, telling Sullivan that "I carried a gun for him" and "I'd go to the limit for him." He couldn't forgive him for his partnership with Dutch Schultz (whom Luciano had since had murdered) but he couldn't betray him either. Most of the questions that Sullivan asked about Torrio were answered with generalities. Torrio made his money the same way Capone did; he's been in the rackets for twenty years longer, but no information that Capone gave could be used in a courtroom. The investigators left Alcatraz empty handed, yet filled with stories of Capone and the underworld.

A year passed before Torrio stood trial, charged with evading taxes for the years 1933-1935. The trial went badly for him and halfway through, Torrio changed his plea to guilty. He went to Leavenworth for two and a half years.

The attempts on his life, the days of silence, the trips to the hole, the grinding daily routine and likely what was, by now, an advanced case of syphilis began to take their toll on Capone. Eventually, he stopped going into the recreation yard and practiced his banjo instead. Once practice was over, he returned immediately to his cell, avoiding all of the inmates except for a few of his closest friends. Occasionally, guards reported that he would refuse to leave his cell to go to the mess hall and eat. They would often find him crouched down in the corner like an animal. On other occasions, he would mumble to himself or babble in baby talk or simply sit on his bed and strum little tunes on the banjo. Years later, another inmate recalled that Capone would sometimes stay in his cell and make his bunk over and over again.

When the guards decided that the weather was cold enough for the inmates to wear their pea coats, they indicated the decision with three blasts of a whistle. The morning of February 5, 1938, started off unseasonably warm and no whistle blew. Capone nevertheless put on his pea coat. For a year, he had been on library duty, delivering and collecting books and magazines. Alvin Karpis, who occupied the second cell to the left of Capone and always followed him in the line to the mess hall, had a magazine to return and he tossed it into Capone's cell as he passed it. Seeing Capone standing there in his winter coat, including a cap and gloves, he called to him that he didn't need his jacket that day. Capone seemed to neither hear nor recognize him. He simply stood there, staring vacantly into space.

He failed to fall into line when ordered to do so, a breach of discipline ordinarily punished by a trip to the hole, but the guards sensed something was seriously wrong and watched without disturbing him. He finally left his cell and entered the mess hall, last in line. A thread of drool dripped down his chin. As he moved mechanically toward the steam table, a deputy warden, Ernest Miller, spoke to him quietly and patted his arm. Capone grinned strangely and for some reason, pointed out the window. Then, suddenly, he started to choke and retch. Miller led him to a locked gate across the hall and called to the guard on the other side to unlock it. They helped Capone up a flight of stairs to the hospital ward.

To the prison physician, and a consulting psychiatrist for whom he sent, Capone's symptoms suggested central nervous system damage characteristic of advanced syphilis. When Capone, after a return to lucidity, understood this, he finally agreed to the spinal puncture and the other tests that he had refused in Atlanta. The fluid was rushed to the Marine Hospital in San Francisco for analysis. Warden Johnston later stopped by his bed to ask him what had happened to him that morning. Capone replied, "I dunno, they tell me that I acted like I was a little whacky."

The report from the Marine Hospital confirmed the doctors' diagnosis. Word of it reached the press and newspapers from coast to coast painted a picture of Capone as a man driven insane by the horrors of Alcatraz. Mae Capone pleaded with Warden Johnston by telephone, imploring him to free her husband, an act that was far beyond his power. The hardened warden must have taken some pity on the former gangland boss, though. Capone was never returned to the cellblock and spent the remainder of his sentence in the hospital ward, subjected to injections of arsphenamine, shock treatments and induced fever. His disease was slowed down but not stopped. He alternated between lucidity and confusion, often at the brink of total insanity. He spent most of his time sitting by himself, plucking at the strings of his banjo, sometimes completely unaware of his surroundings.

Capone was discharged from Alcatraz on January 6, 1939 but still owed another year's sentence for the misdemeanor offense of failing to file a tax return. Reducible by good behavior, he still had about ten months to serve. Due to his deteriorated state, officials decided not to ship him to Chicago to serve out the sentence at the Cook County Jail. Instead, they sent him to the newly opened federal prison at Terminal Island, just outside Los Angeles. He was taken there by Deputy Warden Miller and three armed guards, with extra weights added to his leg chains, which was rather pointless since he was partially paralyzed.

The following November, after the last of his fines were paid through a Chicago gang lawyer, Capone was transferred to the U.S. Penitentiary at Lewisburg, Pennsylvania. He arrived on November 16 and was met by Ralph and Mae Capone, who drove him to Baltimore's Union Hospital. Until spring, he lived with Mae

in Baltimore as an outpatient of the hospital under the care of Dr. Joseph Moore, a syphilis specialist from Johns Hopkins.

In Chicago, reporters asked Jake Guzik if Capone was now going to return to Chicago and take command of the mob again. Jake, despite being one of Al's closest and most loyal friends replied, "Al is nuttier than a fruitcake."

The story of Al Capone and Alcatraz is not quite over...

There are many who believe that the old prison is a very haunted place. If ghosts return to haunt the places where they suffered traumatic experiences when they were alive, then Alcatraz must be loaded with spirits. There have been claims made that many of the guards who served at the prison between 1946 and 1963 experienced strange happenings on Alcatraz. The guards often spoke to one another of voices sobbing and moaning, inexplicable smells, cold spots and spectral apparitions of prisoners and soldiers inhabiting every part of the island, from the cellblocks to the prison yard and on down to the caverns beneath the buildings. Phantom gunshots were known to send seasoned guards ducking to the ground in the belief that some of the prisoners had escaped and had obtained weapons. There was never an explanation for the sounds. A deserted laundry room would sometimes fill with the smell of smoke, even though nothing was burning. The guards would be sent running from the room, only to return later and find that the air clear.

Even Warden Johnston, who did not believe in ghosts, once encountered the unmistakable sound of a person sobbing while he accompanied some guests on a tour of the prison. He swore that the sounds came from inside the dungeon walls. The strange sounds were followed by an ice-cold wind that swirled through the entire group. He could offer no explanation for the weird events.

Alcatraz was closed as a penitentiary in 1963 and years later, was taken over by the National Park Service. Since that time, the ghostly happenings seem to have intensified. Weird noises and eerie apparitions continue to be encountered and one of the most prominent ghosts still lingering on the island may be that of one of the most famous men to have served time there: Al Capone. It's not uncommon for rangers and guides to sometimes hear the sound of banjo strings being plucked on the cell block or in the bathhouse, where Capone once cleaned and became known by the derogatory nickname of the "wop with the mop." Many who have experienced these strange sounds have no idea that Capone once played the banjo and one ranger even surmised that perhaps it was a ghostly echo from the time when Alcatraz was a military fort. Others have come to believe that the sound of the banjo is the only lingering part of a man who left his sanity behind on the island. Is it merely an imprint from the past, or is Al Capone still imprisoned on Alcatraz, a lonely and broken spirit still plucking the strings of a spectral banjo and still serving time on The Rock?

26. THE LAST DAYS OF AL CAPONE

Capone's final years were lived out on his estate near Miami. He continued to cry at night, claiming that the ghost of James Clark was still haunting him and the sight of an automobile, especially one carrying men, would throw him into a panic. No outsiders were ever allowed into the compound or near Al because, Ralph cautioned, in his foggy mental state, he might talk about the organization.

The household on Palm Island was made up of Al, Mae, and Sonny; Mae's sister, Muriel; her husband, Louis Clark; and an old but alert fox terrier that barked ferociously at any stranger. Two servants, "Brownie" Brown, cook and general handyman, and Rose, the family's maid, lived off the premises. There were a variety of gunmen who came and went, all there to protect Capone, and Steve from Steve's Barber Shop at the Grand Hotel, a Miami hangout for gangsters, came once each month to cut Capone's hair. Mae's brother, Danny Coughlin, and his wife, Winifred, operated two nearby establishments frequented by resident and visiting mobsters: Winnie's Waffle Shop and Winnie's Little Club, which grossed between $500 and $700 a day. Danny was also the business agent for the Miami Bartenders' and Waiters' Union.

At least four times each week, Mae attended mass at St. Patrick's Cathedral in Miami Beach. Capone never accompanied her because he claimed that he would embarrass the pastor, Monsignor William Barry. Capone's boy, Sonny, had gone to the private preparatory school run by the monsignor, who took a special interest in the shy, semi-deaf boy, helping him to rise above the problems caused by his family name. In 1937, Sonny had entered Notre Dame under his father's alias, Al Brown. He withdrew after his freshmen year, when his real identity became known. He eventually earned a business degree from the University of Miami.

Probably because Capone slept so badly, haunted by what he believed were visitations from a slain gunman, the household kept strange hours. They often retired around 10:00 p.m. and were up again by 3:00 a.m. Most of the day was spent next to the pool. Capone, wearing pajamas and a dressing gown, would spend hours on the dock, smoking cigars and holding a fishing rod. Occasionally, he would hit a tennis ball over the net that had been strung across the yard. He hated to be alone and always wanted people around him, provided that he recognized them as trusted friends. He had grown obese and looked much older than his years. He also enjoyed playing gin rummy and pinochle; but the mental effort was usually too much for him and his friends let him win.

In 1940, the family received some stunning news. They heard from the firstborn Capone brother, Jim, who had vanished 35 years before. He was living in the town of Homer, Nebraska, under his adopted name of Richard James Hart. He had no money, was missing an eye and had a wife and children to support.

Desperate, he had written to Ralph for help. Ralph sent him $250 and invited him to Racap Lodge, his country house near Mercer, Wisconsin. From there, Jim traveled to Miami and stayed with Al for a month. After he returned to Homer, Ralph sent him a check every month.

According to the long-lost Capone brother, Jim had devoted most of his life to law enforcement. Many Nebraskans knew him as "Two-Gun Hart" because he carried a gun on each hip and at one time, could shoot the cap off a beer bottle at 100 feet. He lost an eye, he explained, in a gunfight with gangsters. Newspaper writers loved the story and published it without question – he was a cop in a family of mobsters.

However, government agents looked into the story and found that it did not quite ring true. After running away from his boyhood home in Brooklyn, Jim had joined up with a traveling circus and went all over the country and Central America. In 1919, he hopped off a freight train passing through Homer and decided to settle there. He set up shop as a painter, but was never any good at it. He became friendly with a grocer named Winch and his daughter, Kathleen, whose lives he saved during a flash flood. He told them that he came from Oklahoma, had left home as a boy, and had worked on a railroad gang until he accidentally killed a man in a fight, at which point he said he fled to Nebraska. He further lied, saying he had enlisted during World War I and had fought overseas. Thanks to this claim, the local American Legion post elected him as commander. Near the end of 1919, he married Kathleen and they later had four sons.

For two years, he served as Homer's town marshal, then for a year as a state sheriff. In 1922, he became a special officer for the Indian Service, investigating the sale of liquor to Winnebago and Omaha Indians, among whom he earned a reputation for brutality. Transferred to Sioux City, Iowa, he was arrested for the murder of an Indian in a bar fight but when the victim turned out to be a bootlegger, Jim was set free. Soon after, he was ambushed by the victim's relatives, which is how he lost an eye. He was then transferred to Coeur D'Alene, Idaho, and charged with a second murder, but was never tried.

After his return to Homer, he was once again named town marshal, which involved being entrusted with keys to various stores in town so that he could enter them, if necessary, when patrolling the town at night. Soon, store owners began missing all sorts of merchandise and even Jim's father-in-law began finding his stock of canned goods mysteriously depleted. Jim was eventually relieved of both the keys and his marshal's badge. As an American Legion official, he had often traveled to conventions, but when the increasingly suspicious local legion members finally asked him for proof of his war service and he was unable to produce it, they expelled him. Evicted from one house after another for non-payment of rent, the family went on relief.

Apparently this Capone wasn't so different from his brothers after all.

Jim died of a heart attack on October 1, 1952.

On December 30, 1941, Capone overcame his reluctance and went to church to witness his son's marriage to Diana Ruth Casey, a girl whom Sonny had first met in high school. After the honeymoon, the newlyweds remained in Miami, where Sonny had opened a florist shop. During World War II, Sonny was classified as 4-F because of his defective hearing but he volunteered for civilian employment with the War Department and was assigned to the Miami Air Depot as a mechanic. His wife bore him four children, all girls, on whom their grandfather doted, constantly buying them expensive gifts and playing with them in the Palm Island swimming pool.

The course of Capone's syphilis was unpredictable. At times, he seemed normal but at other times, his speech was slurred, he became disoriented and he suffered from tremors and seizures. Even at the best of times, Capone lacked mental and physical coordination and he skipped abruptly from subject to subject, humming, whistling and singing as he chatted about nothing. By 1942, penicillin had become available, but in an extremely limited supply due to the war. Dr. Moore at Johns Hopkins was able to procure dosages for Capone, who became one of the first syphilitics to be treated with antibiotics. His condition stabilized somewhat after that, but no therapy could reverse the extensive damage that had been done to his brain.

On January 19, 1947, at just after 4 a.m., Capone collapsed from a brain hemorrhage. Dr. Kenneth Phillips arrived, followed by Monsignor Barry, who administered the last rites. The newspapers announced that Capone was dead, but he rallied and Dr. Phillips pronounced him out of danger. The following week, though, he developed bronchial pneumonia and reporters began to gather outside the compound's locked gates. As the hot day wore on, Ralph let them inside and offered them cold beer.

On Saturday night, January 25, witnesses claim that Capone was lucid. In fact, at 6:30 p.m., an hour before he died, he was said to have told Ralph that he saw the ghost of Clark standing in the

AL CAPONE'S GRAVE IN MOUNT CARMEL CEMETERY, WHICH IS OFTEN COVERED WITH CIGARS, LIQUOR BOTTLES AND PLASTIC TOMMY GUNS.

doorway of the guest bedroom where Capone had been staying during his final illness so as not to disturb Mae. The fearful specter had tormented Capone for eighteen years but on this occasion, he stood smiling, beckoning to Capone to follow him. The ghost gestured urgently and then disappeared.

At 7:30 p.m., Al Capone took James Clark up on his invitation and followed him to the grave.

Capone's body was dressed in a new blue suit, white shirt, black tie and two-tone black and white twp-tone shoes. He was placed in a $2,000 bronze casket and returned to Chicago for burial. Two drivers took turns behind the wheel of a Cadillac hearse for the 48-hour trip. Meanwhile, an empty coffin had been loaded aboard a train bound for Chicago in order to fool the press.

Capone was buried on a cold, winter's day in Mount Olivet Cemetery, sharing a black granite marker with this father, Gabriele, and his brother, Frank, who had been killed by police in Cicero. This was no typical "gangland funeral;" it was a simple affair with only family and Al's closest remaining friends in attendance, although a number of lavish floral arrangements were delivered to the funeral home and the graveside. Among them was a seven-foot-tall floral cross.

When Capone's mother died in 1952, Capone's body was moved to Mount Carmel Cemetery, where he now lies in the same burial ground with Dion O'Banion, Hymie Weiss, the Genna brothers, Jack McGurn and Sam Giancana.

It was a quiet end to the life of the man who had once ruled Chicago.

27. CHICAGO AFTER CAPONE

When Al Capone had arrived in Chicago in 1921, the city was a confusion of ethnic gangs, battling one another for control of the vice and prostitution rackets. Ten years later, after Capone had gone to prison, the city had completely changed. After Prohibition was repealed in 1933, the old ethnic gangs vanished, the members either absorbed into the Capone organization, the civilian world, the penitentiary, or the graveyard.

Many expected that with Capone behind bars at Alcatraz, his organization would fall apart. The press had created the impression that Capone was the sole criminal mastermind behind the organization, single-handedly responsible for corruption in politics and the police force and for the violence and mayhem on Chicago's streets. His prosecutors also thought that, once he was imprisoned, organized crime in the city would fade away. It was not long before they realized that things were not going to be so simple.

Capone had inherited an efficient operation from John Torrio and went on to transform it into a modern corporation that would outlive its creator. Prohibition had provided the organization with the money to diversify and to create a network that linked the Chicago mob to other crime groups across the country and into Canada and the Caribbean. All of the cities involved had been part of a network of illegal liquor production, smuggling, and shipping operations. Groups that would have had no contact otherwise were now in almost daily communication. Capone had created a system that rivaled nearly any legitimate businesses of the time.

In Chicago, with Capone gone, the mob was taken over by a "board of directors" made up of Jake Guzik, Frank Nitti, Johnny Roselli, Paul "The Waiter" Ricca and Murray Llewellyn Humphreys with Antonio "Joe Batters" Accardo as the head. These men were insulated from the operational end of the business by layers of "managers," each with an area of authority, from bootlegging to prostitution. At the street level were the collectors, enforcers and gunmen. The organization was dubbed the "Outfit" and remains a viable entity in Chicago today, although downsized and changed greatly from what it was in the 1930s.

The Outfit had a number of rules. It tried to discourage flamboyant dress (so-called "gangster chic") and urged its members, from the managers on down to the gunmen to avoid drawing attention. The members were asked to dress well, but in somber business suits, and to not make a spectacle of themselves when dining out or socializing. Mild social drinking was allowed but anything more was frowned upon. Most of the members worked twelve-hour days and no drug dealing was allowed. Anyone who broke

that rule was killed. Wives and families were sacrosanct and, if possible, were to have no knowledge of Outfit operations. Widows of Outfit members were paid pensions. Mae Capone, for example, received monthly payments until her death in 1986.

The Chicago organization was no longer creating mayhem on the streets of the city. Massacres and gang assassinations were, for the most part, a thing of the past. But there would be more trouble to come in the Windy City.

THE MURDER OF ESTELLE CAREY

On the early afternoon of February 2, 1943, firefighters responding to an alarm rushed into a trendy Gold Coast apartment at 512 West Addison Street. Inside, they found a scene of carnage and horror. In a third-floor apartment, they found the body of a 34-year-old woman partly concealed beneath an overturned chair, her feet and legs consumed by the flames. Someone had vented a great deal of rage on her; she had been battered with an eight-inch-long blackjack, a kitchen rolling pin and a whiskey bottle. As if that were not enough, she had also been slashed by a ten-inch-long bread knife, and strangled. Horrifyingly, the coroner later determined that she had not died from the assault, but from second- and third-degree burns caused by a flammable liquid being poured over her body and set alight.

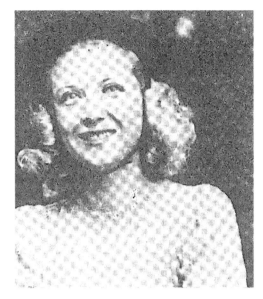

ESTELLE CAREY

Detectives called to the scene found matted hair next to the corpse, but the police lab could not determine whose hair it was. It was obvious that the young woman had fought for her life because signs of a violent struggle were everywhere. There were bloodstains all over the apartment – on the stove, on the rear door through which the killer likely fled (the front door was still locked), on cabinet doors, and all over the living room.

Found scattered throughout the apartment were the bloody bread knife, an electric iron that was coated with blood, the blackjack, and a broken whiskey bottle, its jagged edges streaked with gore. There were bloody smudges everywhere, but not a single fingerprint was found, other than those of the victim and her roommate, Maxine Buturff, who was fortunate enough to be elsewhere at the time of the killing.

Investigators quickly learned that the name of the victim was Estelle Carey, who grew up on the city's northwest side. Her father died when she was two and a half and her mother, finding herself impoverished, placed Estelle in an orphanage. She did not return home until 1916, by which time her mother had married a man named Carey. Estelle, who was very pretty but not one for studying, dropped out of school and took a job in a factory that made silk thread. She did occasional modeling work, became a telephone operator and then a waitress in a North Side restaurant. It was at that point

ESTELLE'S LAKEVIEW APARTMENT BUILDING AT 512 WEST ADDISION

that she met a nightclub owner named Nicholas Dean Circella, also known as Nick Dean. Circella hired her to work in his swanky Rush Street club. Soon, the girl from the orphanage was wearing furs and lavish gowns. Her life must have seemed like something out of a fairy tale, until the doorbell rang that winter afternoon.

According to her cousin, Phoebe, Estelle had been home alone on the afternoon of February 2. With her roommate out for the day, Estelle decided to make a few telephone calls. She was chatting on the phone with Phoebe when the doorbell rang. Phoebe remembered hearing Estelle's little dog barking in the background, but Estelle did not seem concerned. Ending the call, she had apparently gone to the door and opened it to her killer.

When the cops interviewed Estelle's neighbors, they found Mrs. Jessie Lovrein, who lived in the same building and said that she was looking out her back window at about 2:30 p.m. when she saw a man going down the rear stairs. She gave a vague description of the man, stating that after he left the rear of the apartment building, he walked across a snow-covered lot toward Lake Shore Drive. She added that he was carrying two fur coats. A check of Estelle's wardrobe revealed that a sable and a mink coat were missing.

Strangely, more than $2,500 in jewelry that Estelle kept in a shoebox was untouched, along with the key to her safe deposit box. The box later yielded about $2,000 in cash, bonds, and jewelry. Whatever the killer had been looking for, it had apparently not been money.

The initial police investigation focused on jealous lovers. She had plenty of suitors from working at the club, evidenced by a pile of steamy letters found stashed in her bedroom. With the coats missing, the police surmised that the fire had been set to cover a robbery. But if robbery was the motive, why leave the jewelry behind? As more digging was done into Estelle's background, they began to uncover her strong connections to Chicago's underworld, notably to a local hood named Nick Circella, a.k.a Nick Dean. It would be because of Circella that Estelle Carey would become involved in one of the most deadly mob scandals of the early 1940s.

When Al Capone was convicted of income-tax evasion and sent off to prison, the Chicago Outfit expanded in a number of directions. Prohibition was over and the mob began looking toward gambling, prostitution, and extortion as major rackets. One extortion scheme stretched all the way to Hollywood.

During the Great Depression, one of the only thriving industries in America was the movie business. Needless to say, this attracted the attention of gangsters, who were looking to diversify into new markets. In the early 1930s, two minor Chicago labor racketeers, Willie Bioff and George E. Browne, began extorting money from local theater owners. Under the guise of donating money to area soup kitchens to feed the city's Depression victims, the two men hit up one theater chain for $20,000. While celebrating this coup, Bioff and Browne got drunk and bragged about the scheme in front of Nick Circella. The two loudmouths soon became "employees" of the Chicago Outfit and were allowed take over trade unions like the Motion Picture Operators' Union and set up a protection racket on movie theater chains, often demanding up to fifty percent of their take. Another Chicago gangster, Johnny Roselli, broke into Hollywood as a result of the 1933 strike by the International Alliance of Stage Employees (IATSE). The studios went to Roselli to break the strike, which he did by hiring thugs to intimidate the strikers.

Meanwhile, in Chicago, the board of the Outfit had summoned George Browne to a meeting. Browne was a candidate to become the next president of the IATSE. The membership consisted of motion picture employees, from stagehands and technicians in Hollywood to projectionists at local movie houses. The Outfit told him that they would guarantee his election in return for control of the union. Browne, already in trouble with the Outfit for running a protection racket in their territory, quickly agreed. He was elected president in a race where no other candidate was even nominated to run.

Browne and Bioff were sent to New York, where they were introduced to Lucky Luciano and Frank Costello, Syndicate gangsters with control of New York. Soon afterward, Browne was able to demonstrate his power by calling for a strike against the RKO and Loew theater chains. He then went to the chairman of RKO and offered to call it off for the sum of $87,000. It was quickly handed over. The president of Loew, Nick Schenk, then paid Browne and Bioff $250,000 for a no-strike deal that would last for a period of seven years. In exchange, Browne agreed to reduce worker wage increase demands by two-thirds.

Bioff was put in charge of the Hollywood branch of the IATSE in 1936. He and Browne levied a two percent surcharge on paychecks as "strike insurance." This levy generated more than six million dollars, a hefty percentage of which went directly to the Outfit.

With the major unions under control, the mob then moved against the film studios. By controlling the unions, they could cripple any studio that refused to pay protection against strikes. They could close down all of the theaters in the country with a single telephone call. They went to Nick Schenk first and demanded two million dollars, finally settling for a million before they started making the rounds to other studios. They were soon extorting, and dictating to, the biggest names in Hollywood's motion picture industry including Louis B. Mayer and the Warner brothers.

The Outfit was in control of Hollywood but it was not meant to last. Unfortunately for them, Bioff was the weak link in the organization. He made a down payment on piece of property using a $100,000 check from Twentieth Century Fox, run by Nick Schenk's brother, Joe. The check proved to be Bioff's undoing. A breakaway organization from the IATSE, the International Alliance Progressives, was determined to remove the underworld control of the union. They began to convince workers to defy Bioff. At the same time, Bioff tried to take over the Screen Actor's Guild, which started to investigate Bioff's activities. The California State Legislature became interested in him, as well. The $100, 000 check and Bioff's past history as a Chicago pimp came to light. Even worse was to come. The press discovered from Chicago police files that, in 1922, Bioff had been convicted of beating a prostitute. He was still wanted on that charge and a warrant was issued for his arrest. He ended up serving five months in jail.

In New York, Joe Schenk was indicted for fraud. In return for a suspended sentence, he agreed to tell everything that he knew about Bioff and Browne.

On May 24, 1941, Bioff and Browne were indicted on federal racketeering charges in New York City, where many of the movie moguls maintained their business offices. The two were found guilty five months later, on October 30. Bioff was sentenced to ten years in prison, Browne to eight. Each was fined $20,000. Nick Circella, who was indicted at the same time, pled guilty and received an eight-year sentence.

Prosecutors weren't satisfied with locking up men whom they saw as only minor players in the mob. They wanted the top men in the organization, but the only way to get them was to convince Browne, Bioff, and Circella to talk. Browne and Bioff were questioned relentlessly, but refused to name names. Prosecutors then went after Nick Circella, who had originally gone to prison rather than submit to questioning and give up his associates. However, prosecutors found that prison life had eroded his determination and he agreed to talk. Circella refused to spell out everything for them, but he did agree to cooperate and spent part of January 1943 in front of a New York grand jury. The Outfit soon got word that Circella was talking.

The Outfit immediately began damage control procedures. First, mob emissaries approached Mrs. Circella and asked her to talk to her husband for them. In mid-January, while on a trip to New York, she met with Nick and pleaded with him not to say anything else. But his wife's appeals had little effect and word came back to Frank Nitti and Paul Ricca in Chicago that Circella planned to continue testifying for the grand jury. Nitti and Ricca were seen conferring with associates in a downtown hotel room in late January. The mob decided not to act against Mrs. Circella, but there was someone else they could make an example out of...

Circella had been cozy with beautiful Estelle Carey since the middle 1930s. She worked for him at the Yacht Club, managing one of several "26" dice tables, a simple form of gambling. Usually, an attractive woman like Estelle sat behind a green felt table, chatting and joking with patrons who wagered less than $1 at a time. A "26" game was really just a come-on for potential gamblers. A client first selected his target number, one through six, from the dice cube. He placed his bet, then took a leather cup containing ten cubes and rolled them out thirteen times. Each time, the hostess counted and marked the number of times his payoff number came up. The payoff odds depended on the final tally -- totals of 10 or less and 30 or more paid the highest, while odds with 12 or any number between 14 and 25 were losers. If the sum of the dice came to 26, the player won a free drink.

The key to Estelle's job was her ability to work while bantering with flirtatious gentlemen and lonely drunks, building a rapport and ensuring their future return, while also relieving them of $10 or more each night. The latter was achieved through skillful manipulation of the dice, which usually meant switching loaded dice into the game or marking a false tally in the house's favor. Estelle quickly proved to be quite good at this, allegedly scamming at least $800 from one customer. She also had a good eye for the high rollers and steered them away from the small games and directed them to the upstairs casino, where much more damage could be done.

Estelle became such a moneymaker for Circella that he made her the manager of all of the "26" games and reportedly gave her 25 percent of the take. Later, he moved her over to the ritzy Colony Club, 744 N. Rush Street, where she increasingly handled a considerable portion of Circella's funds, some of it thought to be extortion and payoff money for which Nick was responsible. The two became lovers and he moved her into a high-class Lakeview apartment, providing her with an income of more than $500 a week. Investigators later found that none of the many dresses in her closet cost less than $130, a sum that translates into over $1,000 in today's money.

Estelle's good fortune should have come to an end in 1940 when police raids shuttered the Colony Club. After that, her benefactor was indicted in the Hollywood extortion case in 1941. When the FBI nabbed him, it seemed likely that Estelle had given away his location. Seemingly unbothered by this, Estelle continued to be seen with several men about town, with one of whom she vacationed in Florida. She remained well dressed, apparently not hurting financially after Circella was arrested. Talk turned to money that had gone missing and one writer surmised that Estelle was safeguarding Nick's extortion money while he was away. Any mob suspicions regarding her role with the FBI in building the extortion case were well founded because the feds intended to call her as a prospective witness. Further rumors of collaboration with the IRS didn't help her position.

Then, on February 2, 1943, Estelle Carey was brutally murdered. Had the mob finally caught up with her?

Police investigators thought so. Dozens of underworld suspects were interrogated and released. Two of the main suspects were Ralph Pierce and his friend, Les "Killer" Kruse, but lacking solid evidence, the police had to release them.

Detectives came to believe that Estelle knew the location of Circella's syndicate money and was either keeping it for him or had hidden it somewhere for herself. Her death involved torture and they suspected that perhaps her attacker had tried to get her to give up the location of the money. Did she tell what she knew? No one would ever know and what transpired between Estelle Carey and her killer in the apartment afternoon became a matter of endless speculation. The pretty young girl's killer was never found.

The mob's strategy in killing Estelle Carey initially seemed to work. When the news of her death made it to New York, prosecutors lost Circella as a witness. One of them later recalled, "As soon as she was killed, that was the end of it. He turned off, boom! Just like an electric light."

The murder had a completely different effect on Bioff and Browne. Bioff especially was enraged. He immediately called in prosecutors, "We sit around in jail for those bastards and they go killing our families. To hell with them! What do you want to know?"

On March 18, 1943, another New York City grand jury handed up indictments on Frank Nitti, Paul "the Waiter" Ricca, Louis "Little New York" Campagna, Phil D'Andrea, and others.

Nitti, rumored to be despondent at the possibility of returning to prison, committed suicide the day after the indictments were announced. If Nitti had ordered the death of Estelle Carey, as many seemed to believe, then perhaps this tragic woman got one last bit of revenge from the other side. Her murder had led to the death of the man who sent her to an early grave.

FRANK NITTI'S LAST WALK

On the evening of March 19, 1943, a lone figure walked out of his home in Riverside, Illinois, and began strolling along the streets of the quiet neighborhood. It was a cool, early spring night and the man seemed to have not a care in the world as he walked along, his hands tucked into his pockets and a soft whistle on his lips. His casual manner gave no hint to the turmoil he felt inside. Or that he had a loaded handgun weighting down the pocket of his coat.

The man left the street and began walking along the Illinois Central Railroad tracks that ran west of Harlem Avenue and around Cermak Avenue. He carefully picked his way over the railroad ties and walked along until the shadows seemed to envelope him. Darkness was just beginning to fall and this seemed as good a time as any for one last look at the world. The man took the gun from his pocket and raised it to his head. His hand began to tremble as he squeezed the trigger and then a deafening roar filled his ears and echoed in the stillness of the city around him.

When the first shot was fired, railroad workers who were doing routine maintenance a little father up the line, looked up to see the walking man. His hands shook as he held the pistol and a thin ribbon of smoke curled from its barrel. The gun had been aimed at his head but the first shot had somehow missed. One of the railroad men started to call out to the man as he saw him calmly lift the gun again. Before the words could leave the railroader's lips, the man pulled the trigger again. This time, when the gun went off, the bullet did not miss. It blew apart the top of the man's head and he stumbled over the railroad ties and collapsed against the fence that ran next to the tracks. Blood began to seep into the grass, looking black in the fading light.

Frank Nitti, once thought of as one of the most powerful men in Chicago and an enforcer for Al Capone, lay dead on the ground, slain by his own hand.

Frank Nitti (or Nitto, which was the preferred family spelling) was a man of mystery. Intensely private and quiet, he is only scarcely remembered today as being part of the legendary Capone gang. If not for the television series based on the exploits of Eliot Ness and his "Untouchables," it's possible that he would only be known to the most dedicated gangster buffs and researchers and not to the general public at all. Nitti was a small man but one with incredible will. He maintained discipline in the ranks and acted as Capone's enforcer and troubleshooter. He was also one of the only gangsters in the organization who never used an assumed name, which got him into trouble when investigators discovered a check he had endorsed. This put him into prison for eighteen months in the early 1930s, an experience that had a lasting effect on him.

Nitti was born on January 27, 1881 in the small town of Angri, in the province of Salerno, Campania, Italy. He was the second child of Luigi and Rosina Nitto. His father died when Frank was very young and a year later his mother married Francesco Dolendo. In July 1890, Dolendo emigrated to American and the rest of the family followed in June 1893 when Nitti was 12. They settled at 113 Navy Street in Brooklyn and Frank worked numerous odd jobs to help support the family. He left school in the seventh grade and

FRANK NITTI

worked as a bowling alley pinsetter, a factory worker and a barber. Al Capone's family lived nearby but the Capone brothers were much too young to be known to Nitti.

Frank left home at age 19, unhappy with his stepfather, and wanting to make it on his own. Starting in 1900, he worked in a number of factories and finally, in 1910, he left Brooklyn. Little is known about his life over the course of the next few years but he probably moved to Chicago around 1913, working as a barber and making the acquaintance of gangsters Alex Louis Greenberg and Dion O'Banion.

He married a woman from Chicago, Rosa Levitt, in Dallas, Texas, on October 18, 1917. The couple's movements after their marriage remain uncertain. He is known to have become a partner in the Galveston crime syndicate run by "Johnny" Jack Nounes and is reported to have stolen a large sum of money from Nounes and mobster Dutch Voight, after which Nitti returned to Chicago. By 1918, he had moved into an apartment at 914 South Halsted Street. He soon renewed his contact with Greenberg and O'Banion, becoming a jewel thief, liquor smuggler, and fence. Through his liquor smuggling activities, Nitti came to the attention of Chicago crime boss John Torrio and, later, to his successor, Al Capone.

ALTHOUGH NITTI WAS PUBLICLY SEEN AS THE HEAD OF THE OUTFIT AFTER CAPONE, MOST BELIEVE THAT THE REAL FORCE BEHIND THE ORGANIZATION WAS PAUL "THE WAITER" RICCA (ABOVE).

Under Capone, Nitti gained a fearsome reputation as an enforcer. Originally working as a bodyguard, Capone began tasking Nitti with the planning and execution of some of the gang's most notable assassinations, like that of Hymie Weiss in 1926. He also ran Capone's liquor smuggling and distribution operation, importing whisky from Canada and selling it through a network of speakeasies around Chicago. Known as one of Capone's top captains, he was trusted for his leadership and business skills but he never wanted leadership of the gang.

However, after Capone went to prison, newspaper reporters began looking for a new face for the head of the gang and somehow, Nitti ended up as that man. While an efficient organizer under Capone, it had been his job to make sure that Capone's orders had been carried out, not to give them himself. Nitti was only supposed to be a member of the board of directors of the new Outfit, not the man in charge. When Lucky Luciano and Meyer Lansky established their national crime syndicate, they dealt with Paul "The Waiter" Ricca as the leader of the Chicago mob and not with Nitti.

However, Ricca and the others used Nitti's high profile with the press to keep the heat off the real inner workings of the Outfit. He became a valuable man to take the heat. Chicago mayor Anton Cermak even dispatched his own police "hit men" to try and take out Nitti so that he could replace him with other gangsters who kept him on the payroll.

On December 19, 1932, a team of Chicago police, headed by Detective Sergeants Harry Lang and Harry Miller, raided Nitti's office in Room 554 of the LaSalle Building. Lang shot Nitti three times in the back and neck. He then shot himself in the finger to make the shooting look like self-defense, claiming that Nitti had shot him first. Nitti was badly wounded during the attempt on his life. He lingered near death for a time, but recovered only to end up standing trial for the shooting of one of the cops during the gun battle. Court testimony claimed that the murder attempt was personally ordered by newly elected Mayor Anton Cermak, who supposedly wanted to eliminate the Outfit in favor of Ted Newberry, who had taken over the remnants of the O'Banion/Moran mob, and redistribute the Capone territories. During the trial, Miller testified that Lang received $15,000 to kill Nitti. Another uniformed officer who was present at the shooting testified that Nitti was shot while unarmed. Nitti's trial ended with a hung jury. Harry Lang and Harry Miller were both fired from the police force and each fined $100 for assault.

This was not the end of story, though. Most believe that Nitti managed to get his revenge on Cermak

CHICAGO MAYOR ANTON CERMAK, WHO TARGETED NITTI IN AN ATTEMPT TO PAVE THE WAY FOR TED NEWBERRY.

(RIGHT) CERMAK AFTER BEING SHOT IN MIAMI. LEGEND HAS IT THAT NITTI GOT HIS REVENGE.

a few months later.

On February 15, 1932, Cermak was shot in Bayfront Park in Miami. Cermak was on the reviewing stand and, after President-elect Franklin Roosevelt made a short speech from an open car, he waved over Cermak to join him. As Roosevelt's car was about to start, shots rang out and Cermak and four others were hit. They were shot by a man named Giuseppe Zangara, whose intention had been to kill the president.

Cermak was rushed to the hospital, where he died a short time later. As he was taken away by ambulance, Cermak was supposed to have said to the president, "I am glad that it was me instead of you." They became the most famous words that Cermak ever uttered -- or they would have been, if he had really said them. A reporter who was there that day, Ed Gilbreth, stated that the phrase was created by William Randolph Hearst's *Chicago Herald-American* to make a good headline and sell papers. Cermak never said anything before he died.

Although some words uttered by another reporter who was standing nearby might have provided more of a clue in the shooting than officials would admit. Just as the shots rang out, a reporter who was nearby allegedly joked to Cermak, "Just like Chicago, eh Mayor?" Rumors have persisted ever since the shooting that Cermak had not been an accidental target that day.

As the IRS began cracking down on the mob, Nitti served prison time for an income tax charge related to a check that was discovered bearing his name. In spite of this, he stayed out of the newspapers until November 1940, when he was indicted for influencing the Chicago Bartenders and Beverage Dispensers' Local of the AFL. Nitti was accused of putting mob members into positions of power in the union and then forcing the sale of beer from mob-owned breweries. The trial rested on the testimony of one man, George McLane, the president of the union. He allegedly was forced to follow Nitti's orders but the pressure got to him and he went to the authorities and explained what the mob was doing. McLane was all set to testify until two mob soldiers showed up at his door and told him that if he talked in court, his wife would be mailed to him in small pieces. When the day came, McLane pleaded for his right to remain silent under the Fifth Amendment and the case was dropped.

The heat was on Nitti again in 1943 during what came to be called the "Hollywood Extortion case."

After Bioff and Browne decided to talk, indictments were brought against Nitti, Paul Ricca and several others. A meeting was called at Nitti's home in Riverside and Ricca decided that it was the perfect time to take advantage of Nitti's perceived top position in the mob. He ordered Nitti to plead guilty in the extortion case and to take the rap for everyone. He would be taken care of when he got out, as long as he kept his mouth shut while he was inside.

But there was no "inside" for Nitti. He refused to go back to prison. His earlier jail time had so traumatized the gangster that he now had a terrible fear of small, confined spaces. He urged Ricca to come up with another plan or to allow some of the others to share the responsibility with him. Ricca was enraged and demanded that Nitti be a "stand-up guy." When Nitti still refused, Ricca told him that, "he was asking for it." Nitti took these words to mean his death sentence but he simply couldn't face another stretch in prison. He made a last-ditch effort to try and bribe the prosecutor in the case, M.F. Correa, but his attempt was coldly rebuffed.

So, on March 19, the day after the meeting, Frank Nitti placed a gun in his pocket and went for one last stroll through his neighborhood. When he made it as far as the Illinois Central Railroad tracks, his journey came to an end -- or did it?

Nitti was laid to rest in Mount Carmel Cemetery, not far from the grave of Al Capone. His simple stone is marked with his family name of "Nitto" and bears a direct and ominous inscription: "There is no life except by death." Many believe that Nitti does not rest there in peace.

For years, it has been a local legend in the North Riverside and Forest Park areas that the ghost of Frank Nitti still walks along the railroad tracks where he committed suicide back in 1943. There are many who claim to have not only sensed his last anguished moments but who also state that they have seen the eerie figure of a man here, as well. The figure often appears along the railroad tracks at Cermak Avenue and begins walking west, plainly visible under the harsh lights of a nearby shopping center. The tracks, which are seldom used these days, can be found next to a toy store, a restaurant and a large shopping mall. The place that marks Nitti's suicide is isolated from the activity of the retail stores.

POLICE DETECTIVES EXAMINED THE FALLEN BODY OF FRANK NITTI

I spoke to a man who became curious about this area after reading about it in a Chicago crime book. He decided to go out there one night and have a look for himself. Although a believer in ghosts, this had nothing to do with his survey of the railroad tracks. He was more interested in Nitti's exploits while alive and he never expected to see anything out of the ordinary.

The man parked his car at the nearby toy store and walked over to the tracks. As he stood there, he tried to imagine what had been going through Nitti's thoughts during his last journey. Rumor had it that, in addition to facing prison time, Nitti was also suffering from stomach cancer. This may have contributed to his decision to end his life.

As the man walked slowly along the tracks, he froze for a moment at what he saw ahead of him. Up ahead, about fifteen yards down the tracks, he saw the dark silhouette of a man. He watched as the figure stepped high to avoid the rails and stumble once or twice as it moved along. He was unable to clearly describe what he saw and only said, "It gave the impression of a man who was wearing a thigh-length coat." The witness followed the figure for a short distance and then he described to me that it seemed to "spin" around and fall toward the ground. Moments later, it was gone.

The startled observer blinked once or twice, unable to believe what he had seen. Could he have just witnessed a re-enactment of the last moments of Frank Nitti? He wrote to me a few months after this encounter took place: "I never went there expecting to see anything. And while I believed that some places and people might be haunted, I never thought I would ever see anything like that. I am sure that it must have been Frank Nitti's ghost that I saw that night. It's up to you whether you want to believe me or not but I am sure about what I saw. I think he [Nitti] is haunting those railroad tracks."

THE OUTFIT

Although seen as the leader of the Outfit, Nitti was little more than a figurehead to the real man behind the organization, Paul "The Waiter" Ricca. After being caught shaking down the movie industry, Ricca wanted Nitti to take the fall for the entire gang. Nitti committed suicide instead. Ricca then became the boss in name as well as in fact, with his enforcement captain, Tony Accardo, as underboss.

In late 1943, Ricca went to prison for his part in the Hollywood extortion plan. He was joined by several other members of the Outfit who, although receiving sentences of ten years, were out in three, thanks largely to the efforts of Murray Humphreys. As a condition of his parole, Ricca could not associate with any known felons. This left Accardo to take over the day-to-day operations, but to all indications, Ricca continued behind the scenes as a "consultant." He and Accardo shared the leadership of the organization for the next thirty years.

Accardo joined Ricca in semi-retirement in 1957. By then, Accardo was being harassed by the IRS over back taxes and he stepped aside to let others --- Sam Giancana, Joseph "Joey Doves" Aiuppa, William "Willie Potatoes" Daddano, Felix "Milwaukee Phil" Aderiso and "Jackie "The Lackey" Cerone --- serve as the front men. Operations continued as usual and Accardo and Ricca were always consulted when it came to any major business transactions or murders. Ricca died in 1972, leaving Accardo as the sole power behind the organization.

THE LEADERSHIP OF THE OUTFIT INTO THE 1950S: (LEFT TO RIGHT) SAM GIANCANA, JOSEPH "JOEY DOVES" AIUPPA, FELIX "MILWAUKEE PHIL" ADERISO AND "JACKIE "THE LACKEY" CERONE

The Outfit reached the height of its post-Capone power in the 1960s. With assistance from Meyer Lansky, Accardo used the Teamsters' Union pension fund to engage in large-scale money laundering in conjunction with the Outfit's illegal casinos, but it didn't last long. By the 1970s and

1980s, law enforcement had begun to penetrate the Outfit and off-track betting and legitimate casinos had started to inroads on illegal operations. Full-scale operations by the FBI ended the Outfit's skimming and control of their Las Vegas casinos, severely damaging the organization's finances. Money from auto theft, prostitution and professional sports betting did not replace the lost profits.

Tony Accardo, lowly Capone soldier turned mob boss, died in 1992. Despite having an arrest record that dated back to 1922, he never spent a single night in jail.

And despite the best efforts of both national and Chicago authorities, the Outfit has never gone away. Just as it did when Prohibition came to an end, the Outfit had adapted successfully to changing times. They have become heavily engaged in stock market fraud, cyber crime, Internet pornography, banking fraud and have continued their interests in gambling, which has become even more legitimate than in the heyday of the Las Vegas casinos. A conquest of the drug trade is the only thing that has managed to elude them. It is simply too large and too diversified to be controlled by any one organization. The Outfit (and other American Mafia families) realized this long ago and have confined themselves to financing drug deals and laundering money for the cartels. They leave the production and distribution of the drugs to the specialists.

Globalization has opened up new markets and has also revived old trades like white slavery and smuggling of illegal aliens. The emergence of carjacking in recent years was a direct result of globalization, supplying distant markets with cars that are stolen in New York and Canada. There are markets that would have stunned men like Al Capone and John Torrio, like global trades in forged airplane parts, fake pharmaceuticals and a wide range of counterfeit consumer items.

The Outfit may have become big business but this has not stopped the government from trying to shut them down.

In April 2005, the U.S. Department of Justice launched "Operation Family Secrets," which indicted fourteen Outfit members and associates under the Racketeer Influenced and Corrupt Organizations Act (RICO). U.S. District Court Judge James Zagel presided over the Family Secrets trial. The federal prosecutors were Mitchell A. Mars, T. Markus Funk, and John Scully. The jury found James Marcello, Joseph Lombardo, Frank Calabrese, Sr., Paul Schiro, and Anthony Doyle guilty of extortion, illegal gambling, tax fraud, loan sharking and murder on September 10, 2007. Paul Schiro was sentenced to twenty years in prison. Frank Calabrese, Sr. was sentenced to life in prison on January 28. On February 2, 2009, Joseph Lombardo was sentenced to life imprisonment. James Marcello also received life imprisonment on February 5, 2009. On March 12, 2009, Anthony Doyle, who was not convicted of murder, received twelve years of prison. Nicholas Calabrese was sentenced to twelve years, four months of imprisonment. This lenient sentence was due in part to Calabrese's cooperation with the government.

As had become typical in Mafia trials by this time, Nick Calabrese had turned government witness in the early 2000s and became the star witness in the "Family Secrets" trial. Gone were the days of gangsters who refused to talk or to admit who had shot them.

Damage had been done to one of the most prominent organized crime outfits in the county, but it has never gone away. Organized crime will always be a part of America's checkered landscape. As long as they are out there, just as in the days of Al Capone, "giving the people what they want," there will always be a place for the Mafia.

EPILOGUE:
WHATEVER HAPPENED TO...?

Al Capone died quietly in his bed. The once-powerful mob boss who ruled Chicago was a broken man when the end finally came for him. Many of his friends and associates were not even as lucky as he was. Gunned down, imprisoned, wracked with disease and worse, many of them came to terrible ends. Others passed peacefully to the other side. Many of their fates have already been chronicled in these pages. Others will be presented here.

In almost every case, they left part of the era's story untold.

MAE CAPONE

After the death of her husband, an event that shattered her emotionally and caused family members to seek medical help for her, Mae returned to the mostly anonymous life that she had maintained during her marriage to Al Capone. Few saw her, most never heard from her again and outside of immediately family gatherings, she almost ceased to exist. She wanted nothing do with the press, turned down numerous offers to write a book about her life with Capone and lived a quiet, peaceful existence that was supported by the "pension" that she received from the Outfit.

Only once after Capone's death did his widow emerge from anonymity. In 1959, CBS televised *The Untouchables*, a two-part film that sensationalized Eliot Ness' account of Chicago during the waning days of Prohibition. Mae, Sonny and Mafalda jointly brought a million-dollar lawsuit against the network, the producer of the film, Desilu Productions, and the sponsor, Westinghouse, complaining that the dead man's name, likeness and personality were being used for profit. They lost the suit and in the fall, ABC launched *The Untouchables* as a weekly series starring Robert Stack. A film version of the series, starring Kevin Costner, further blurred the line between reality and fiction in 1987.

Capone's last lawyer, Abraham Teitelbaum, did not exaggerate much when he said that Capone died "penniless." Capone never kept the sources of his vast wealth for himself; he shared them with partners – the organization – and when he could no longer run them, the sources reverted to the organization. The Outfit provided the means for him to live out his life comfortably – Ralph and Jake Guzik saw to that – but his personal properly was heavily mortgaged and most of the family cash went to paying off taxes. Mae sold both the Palm Island and Prairie Avenue houses and for a time, she and Sonny operated a restaurant in Miami Beach, but the venture failed.

Later in life, she divided most of her time between Miami, Chicago and Ralph's home in Wisconsin. Mafalda and her husband ran a delicatessen in Chicago and died in Michigan in March 1988.

Mae died on April 16, 1986 at the Hollywood Hills Nursing Home in Florida.

Sonny Capone

Albert Francis "Sonny" Capone drifted along in Miami after the death of his father. He worked for a period of time as a used car salesman, but he reportedly disliked some of the fraudulent practices that were rampant among used car dealers of the 1950s, like setting back the odometers on cars. He avoided the temptation to get into the rackets out of respect for his mother, although his name alone would have guaranteed him a position. At one point, a representative from the Outfit approached him about taking a more active role, but when he told his mother, she wouldn't hear of it. "Your father broke my heart," she said. "Don't you do it, too."

In need of money, Sonny opened a restaurant in Miami with Mae's help. He was often seen in the kitchen, preparing the sauces. The FBI kept him under quiet scrutiny and learned that he was not as removed from the Outfit as his mother would have liked. He receives a modest annual allowance from Chicago, as Mae did. It was the policy of the Outfit at the time to make sure that the widows and orphans of valued members had something to keep them going. In return, the Outfit demanded loyalty and silence. There was a limit to how much they offered, though. At one point, Sonny asked for a loan of $24,000 to expand his restaurant but his request was refused.

Like his mother, Sonny avoided the press and any mention of his infamous father. Unfortunately, whatever privacy he had was stripped away in August 1965, when a store detective spotted him shoplifting at a Kwik Chek supermarket in North Miami Beach. He was a regular at the store and well known to the managers, but for some reason, he stole two bottles of aspirin and a package of transistor radio batteries, the value of which came to $3.50.

"Everybody has a little larceny in them," was his only explanation to the judge.

With the Capone name made popular again by *The Untouchables* television show, Sonny's appearance in court before Judge Edward S. Klein on a minor shoplifting charge generated more interest than it should have. Neatly dressed, balding and looking older than his 45 years, Sonny pleaded no contest and received two years probation. At the time of Sonny's pathetic foray into the world of crime, he was in the midst of his second divorce and was a very unhappy man. The incident seemed to be a cry for help, but help never came. Sonny responded by legally changing his name from Albert Francis Capone to Albert Francis, a name he kept for the rest of his life.

Albert Francis died in 2004 in Florida. He was buried in California.

Ralph Capone

Following his brother's imprisonment for tax evasion in 1931, Ralph "Bottles" Capone remained with the Outfit. He hosted several high-level Outfit conferences at the Palm Island house and was deeply involved in the operation of syndicate gambling and vice, even after being convicted for tax evasion himself in 1935. In actuality, Ralph held relatively little power in the Outfit and the National Crime Syndicate. This finally became evident during his testimony before a Senate committee in 1950. Ralph and John Capone were both summoned to Washington to testify before Senator Estes Kefauver's widely publicized special committee investigating organized crime.

During his testimony, Ralph admitted being a bootlegger during Prohibition but stated that his gang consisted of "two fellows and myself" who sold beer on consignment. He was less forthcoming when the committee asked him to name other members of the Capone gang. When Ralph balked, they supplied some names for him. He admitted that he and his late brother, Al, knew Jake Guzik "very well," along with Murray Humphreys and former Capone bodyguards Phil D'Andrea and Louis Campagna. The committee wanted to know how he spent his time in Miami and Ralph admitted that it was at the dog tracks.

"When you showed up they rolled out the red carpet for you, didn't they?" a committee member asked sarcastically.

"Not necessarily," Ralph replied. "When I was there they were out of red carpet."

After Ralph stepped down, John, who also had some marginal interests with the Outfit, took a seat before the committee. He spent hours parrying Kefauver's questions. It made for good theater — hauling in the Capone boys — but Ralph and John could tell them little that was new.

In spite of what was now Ralph's minor role in the Outfit, the name Capone kept him in the firing line of government investigations. He hoped that his appearance before the Kefauver committee would earn him some breathing room, but it didn't. To make matters worse, his son Ralph, Jr., who preferred to call himself Ralph Gabriel, committed suicide in his Chicago apartment. He swallowed a bottle of cold tablets that had the potential of being lethal when mixed with alcohol and washed them down by a half-quart of scotch. As the lethal mixture took effect, he wrote a pathetic note to his girlfriend, a nightclub singer named Jeanne Kerin. "Jeanie, my sweetheart," he scrawled, "I love you. I love you. Jeanie only you I love. Only you. I'm gone...."

Soon after this, Ralph Capone, Sr., faced new legal challenges. On March 16, 1951, the government leveled new charges of tax evasion against him. Since he had already been convicted of that charge in the past, the new indictment posed a serious threat for him. Ralph's attorneys attempted to arrive at a compromise but the IRS refused to even discuss the matter. They claimed that Ralph owed $96,679 in taxes and that they had 25 agents continuing to work on the case, who would surely come up with even more evidence against him.

Ralph was now retired and spending most of his time at his lodge in Wisconsin. He continued to deal with the IRS, keeping them at arm's length, throughout the 1950s. The interest and penalties on the taxes more than doubled what he owed, but in the end he paid them off and retained his freedom and a measure of privacy.

On November 22, 1974, Capone died of natural causes in Hurley, Wisconsin. He was cremated at Park Hill Cemetery in Duluth, Minnesota. His ashes were buried at the Capone Family gravesite at Mt. Carmel Cemetery by his granddaughter Deirdre Marie Capone, in June 2008.

OTHER CAPONE FAMILY MEMBERS

All of Capone's brothers continued in the rackets, with loose connections to the Outfit, for most of the remainder of their lives. Albert, who began using the name Bert Novak, operated out of the suburb of Hickory Hills into the 1970s.

It was Matt Capone who turned out to be the biggest disappointment to his family. Al had sent him to college with the belief that he could make something of himself in the legitimate world, but it was never meant to be. In the spring of 1944, the Capones' relatively quiet life in Florida was shattered by the news that Matt had gotten into trouble in Cicero. He was running the Hall of Fame Tavern in that city and on April 18, two of the tavern's employees, Jens Larrison and Walter Sanders, got into a brawl about a $5 bill that was supposedly missing from the till. There were perhaps twenty people in the bar at the time and as they later told the police, they saw Sanders push Larrison into a back room while Matt looked for something in a drawer. Soon after, they heard gunshots from the back. Matt took off and the cops found Larrison's body in an alley not far from the tavern.

Wanted for questioning, Matt made things worse by going into hiding and this gave law enforcement officials the excuse to go digging into the Capone family's affairs all over again. They turned up nothing of interest and the case against Matt went away when Sanders, the star witness, also disappeared. Matt turned up again a year later and the possibility that he committed murder shadowed him for the rest of his life.

Matt died of heart failure in February 1967 and was buried at Mount Carmel Cemetery.

Teresa Capone, Al's mother, died in 1952 at the age of 85. She had remained living at the Prairie Avenue house during Capone's time at Atlanta and Alcatraz. In 1947, ownership of the house was transferred to Mafalda, but Teresa continued to live there almost up until the time she died. Mafalda sold the house to William Petty in January 1953. It has passed through many owners since then, but remains one of the last remaining relics of Capone's Chicago.

At the time of Teresa's death, she was buried at Mount Carmel Cemetery, instead of at Mount Olivet, where Al had been laid to rest in 1947. Over the years, the family was disturbed by the streams of tourists coming to see Al's grave, some of whom left cigars, bottles of liquor and toy Tommy guns behind in a kind of twisted tribute. When someone stole the photographs of Gabriele and Frank from the front of the black marble monument, it was the last straw. The Capones bought another plot in Mount Carmel on the opposite side of the city and had all of the caskets moved there. A grey shaft bearing the name Capone is discreetly hidden behind some bushes. Small black marble stones mark the individual Capone graves, each bearing the words "My Jesus Mercy."

The original black marble shaft bearing the Capone names still stands in Mount Olivet, left behind to deceive curiosity seekers.

John Torrio

After leaving Chicago, Torrio went into retirement. Despite the fact that law enforcement officials and the press often expressed doubts that he had retired, Torrio largely kept to himself. His main involvement with the underworld was as a sort of elder statesman who dispensed advice on the rackets and in the formation of Lucky Luciano and Meyer Lansky's national Syndicate. At the landmark gang conference in Atlantic City in 1929, Torrio was chosen to head the commission that would deal with disputes between the various organizations. He came out of retirement briefly to testify at Capone's tax trial, but he was never called to the stand. Unfortunately, his long friendship with Capone ended over Torrio's backing of volatile mobster Dutch Schultz. However, when Schultz was killed a short time later, it was allegedly done with Torrio's approval.

In April 1957, Torrio suffered a heart attack while sitting in the chair of a Brooklyn barbershop. He lingered in the hospital for several days afterward, but never recovered. He was 75 years old.

Ironically, a few months later, another mob figure, Albert Anastasia, was assassinated in a barbershop in Manhattan. He had been relaxing with his eyes closed when the killers struck. Anastasia should have known that he was a potential target. Torrio, in contrast, had nothing to fear and yet he always kept his eyes open while having his hair cut and chose the chair facing the door, just in case of trouble.

He had spent too much time in Chicago not to have learned his lesson.

Jack McGurn

The last years of Jack "Machine Gun" McGurn's life are a perfect example of what happened to gangsters who outlived their time. Life was never the same for McGurn after the St. Valentine's Day Massacre. The press that he received after the murders led to his necessary estrangement from Capone and many of the duties that he had taken care of began to be handled by Phil D'Andrea. After Capone went to prison, McGurn no longer enjoyed the patronage of the organization and he fell on hard times. Most of his nightclubs went under during the Depression and Louise Rolfe, the "Blonde Alibi," whom he had married to escape prosecution for his role in the massacre, abandoned him.

McGurn met his end on February 13, 1936, the eve of the anniversary of the St. Valentine's Day Massacre. He was in the middle of his third frame at the Avenue Recreation Parlor, an amusement establishment with a couple of bowling lanes located at 805 North Milwaukee Avenue, when remnants from the old Moran gang finally caught up with him. Five men burst into the bowling alley and while three of them pretended to rob the place, the other two machine-gunned McGurn to death on the hardwood lanes.

A calling card – a comic valentine – was left behind at the desk with McGurn's name on it. The card showed a couple who had literally lost their shirts, gazing sadly at a sign reading "Sale of Household Goods."

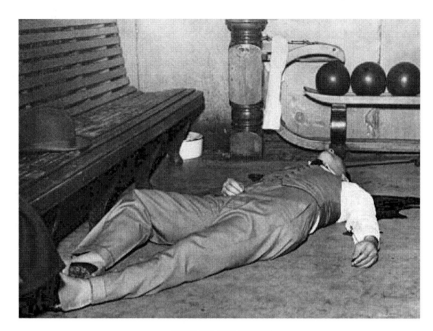

DEATH OF JACK MCGURN

The accompanying verse read:

YOU'VE LOST YOUR JOB.
YOU'VE LOST YOUR DOUGH,
YOUR JEWELS AND HANDSOME HOUSES.
BUT THINGS COULD BE WORSE, YOU KNOW.
YOU HAVEN'T LOST YOUR TROUSERS.

GEORGE MORAN

Although the St. Valentine's Massacre greatly diminished the power of George Moran and the North Side gang, it did not completely destroy it. Moran managed to keep control of most of his territory and what remained of his gang through the end of Prohibition and into the early 1930s. But with the repeal of Prohibition, the North Side gang declined along with almost everyone else and Moran decided to leave Chicago. One of his parting acts may have been the murder of Jack McGurn. Because of the comic valentine left behind at the scene, it was commonly assumed that the prank-loving Moran had ordered the murder in retaliation for the slaughter of his gang seven years before.

Many crime writers believe that Moran's biggest liability as a gang boss was Moran himself -- he was simply not very smart in the ways of long-term survival as a mob leader. While Capone was a master at planning his operations several steps in advance (thanks to his mentoring by Torrio), Moran operated almost like an ordinary street fighter, doing everything by cause and effect. So, having been squeezed out of Chicago at the end of Prohibition, he reverted back to his early life of pulling common crimes like safecracking and robbery. Moran went from being one of the wealthiest gangsters in Chicago to a penniless crook in less than two decades.

In July 1946, Moran was arrested in Ohio for robbing a bank messenger of $10,000, a paltry sum compared to his ill-gotten gains during the Prohibition days. He was convicted and sentenced to ten years in the Ohio Penitentiary. Shortly after his release, Moran was again arrested for an earlier bank raid, receiving another a ten-year sentence, this time in Leavenworth. Only a matter of days after arriving there, most of which were spent in the prison hospital, Moran died of lung cancer on February 25, 1957. He was buried in the prison cemetery.

JAKE GUZIK

Jake "Greasy Thumb" Guzik was perhaps one of the most loyal men to ever work for Capone. After Capone's death, the only serious problems Guzik ever had were with the IRS and he eventually served a few years for tax evasion. He quietly did his time and then returned to his bookkeeping duties for the mob. At the Kefauver hearings in 1950, Guzik made an interesting – but uncommunicative – witness. He often pled the Fifth Amendment on the grounds that any response to the questions might "discriminate against me."

Even after Capone's death, Guzik's position in the Outfit was never questioned and all of the bosses gave him complete authority when it came to financial and legal matters. They knew Guzik's loyalty was firm to the gang that Capone built. Guzik was much admired and protected by Capone while Capone was alive, partially because of his complete loyalty and fiscal honesty, and partially because of his quiet, businesslike and low-profile way of taking care of gang affairs. While not known for certain, it is frequently reported that Guzik never carried a gun.

Jake Guzik died of a heart attack on February 21, 1956. Fittingly, he was dining at St. Hubert's Old English Grill and Chop House when he died, a place where he spent many years passing out payoffs to Chicago cops. At his funeral service, more Italians were at in attendance at the synagogue that day than in any other time in the place's history.

LOUIS CAMPAGNA

Following Capone's conviction, Louis "Little New York" Campagna rose through the ranks of the Outfit as an extortionist and labor racketeer, mentored by Paul Ricca. In 1935, Campagna participated in the Outfit infiltration of the Chicago Bartenders and Beverage Dispensers' Union, which would lead to an injunction being filed by the union head to keep Campagna out of the union's business five years later. However, when the case went to trial, the union leader refused to testify and the case was dismissed. In 1943, Campagna and his associates stole about $900,000 from the treasury of Retail Clerks International Protective Association, Local 1248. The funds were never recovered.

Campagna was also deeply involved in the Hollywood extortion case with Willie Bioff and George Browne. When Bioff was arrested, he sent word to Campagna that he wanted to leave the Outfit. Campagna visited Bioff in prison and gave him the following ultimatum: "Anybody who resigns, resigns feet first." Bioff rebelled and later assisted the government when Campagna was convicted for extortion. His trial ended in a guilty verdict and he received a ten-year sentence at the Atlanta Federal Penitentiary.

In August 1947, after only three years in prison, Campagna was released on parole. Rumors flew that Tony Accardo had bribed a district attorney for the release of Campagna and other Outfit associates that had been caught up in the case and this created a storm of protest in Chicago. The Department of Justice went to court to revoke the parole, but was unsuccessful. After his release, Campagna returned to working for the Outfit under boss Sam Giancana.

In 1950, he was called to testify at the Kefauver hearings and apart from revealing the income from his former illegal gambling operations, he didn't provide any useful testimony. In his later years, Campagna spent most days at his farms in Fowler, Indiana, and in Berrien Springs, Michigan, and at his suburban house in Berwyn.

On May 30, 1955, Campagna was fishing on his lawyer's boat in Biscayne Bay, off the Florida coast. Campagna had just finished reeling in a thirty-pound grouper when he suffered a fatal heart attack. He was buried at Mount Carmel Cemetery in Chicago's Hillside section, taking his place among a host of other mobsters of the era.

FRANK RIO

The Capone bodyguard and captain had high aspirations for himself after the boss went to federal prison. Along with a small faction of gunmen and lieutenants, Rio tried to get himself named as Capone's successor. Opposed by many of the higher-level men in the organization because he lacked leadership experience, Rio was passed over and Frank Nitti came to be acknowledged as the top man.

Although Rio never really left the Outfit, his association with it dwindled over the next several years. In 1932, he was sent to New Jersey to offer the mob's assistance in helping Charles Lindbergh find his kidnapped son. He was refused.

Rio's health began to deteriorate. He suffered from heart disease, which caused severe shortness of breath and physical weakness. After 1933, he rarely left his Oak Park home even though he maintained financial interests in a number of cafes, nightclubs and casinos.

Frank Rio died at noon on February 23, 1935 from a heart attack. The police were never notified. Instead, friends and fellow gang members removed the body from his home and took it straight to Rago's funeral home at 624 North Western Avenue. The police would later claim the hasty funeral had been arranged so that gang members could divide up Rio's assets before news of his death hit the streets. There is, as they say, no honor among thieves.

Rio was denied a church burial but prayers for the dead were read at the funeral parlor. Three automobiles filled with flowers and more than one hundred carloads of mourners accompanied his body for burial at Mount Carmel Cemetery.

MURRAY HUMPHREYS

Murray "The Camel" Humphreys, one of the men responsible for getting Capone imbedded within the Chicago labor unions, continued in the rackets after Al went to prison. In 1933, Humphreys was also indicted and went on the run for eighteen months. He finally gave himself up near Whiting, Indiana, and entered a guilty plea. He was sentenced to serve eighteen months at Leavenworth but was out in just over a year.

Humphreys likely had a hand in arranging the 1933 fake kidnapping of John "Jake the Barber" Factor, a British con artist wanted in England for stock swindling. Factor, a Capone friend, was facing extradition proceedings when the Outfit staged a fake disappearance and framed Capone rival Roger "Terrible" Touhy for allegedly kidnapping Factor. Touhy received a 99-year prison sentence but was released in 1959, only to be murdered several weeks later. Six months after Touhy's death, Humphreys supposedly bought several shares of an insurance company and eight months later redeemed the shares for $42,000. An IRS investigation determined that the shares had been originally owned by John Factor. The IRS claimed that the $42,000 was a payment from Factor to Humphreys for the fake 1933 kidnapping. They forced Humphreys to declare the money as income and pay taxes on it.

In 1947, Humphreys was assigned the difficult task of securing paroles for the Outfit members who had been caught up in the Hollywood Extortion case. A deal was made with the U.S. Attorney General at the time, Tom C. Clark, promising him that if he arranged the paroles he would be appointed to the Supreme Court. The Outfit allegedly extorted President Harry Truman to arrange the appointment. Clark delivered and on October 3, 1949, Clark was nominated to the Supreme Court.

When Jake Guzik died in 1956, Humphreys became the Outfit's chief political fixer and financial manager, working directly under Sam Giancana. Both men topped the FBI's Top Hoodlum list, a program that was created to target organized crime figures. When Chicago FBI agents, under the leadership of William F. Roemer, discovered that a second-floor tailor shop on North Michigan Avenue was a frequent meeting place for such Outfit notables as Humphreys, Tony Accardo and Sam Giancana, the FBI installed a hidden microphone in the shop after hours. It remained in place undetected for five years, and gave the FBI invaluable knowledge about the inner workings of the Outfit.

In 1965, Chicago boss Sam Giancana was jailed by Federal Judge William J. Campbell for his refusal to answer questions regarding the syndicate's activities. Three weeks after Giancana's arrest, Humphreys was issued a subpoena to appear before the same grand jury. When FBI Agent William Roemer came to Humphreys' Marina Towers apartment to deliver the subpoena he was met at the door by Ernest Humphreys, who told Roemer that his brother had just left for parts unknown. Roemer, knowing that increasing blindness in one of Humphrey's eyes meant that he always traveled by train to visit his family in Oklahoma, notified agents to stop the train and arrest Humphreys. He was picked up in Norman, Oklahoma, and claimed that he had no idea that a subpoena had been issued for him. Roemer gathered evidence that this was not true and three agents were sent to arrest Humphreys on a charge of perjury.

Roemer, who had grown to like Humphreys in the course of dealing with him (on one occasion, FBI agents who were assigned to follow Humphreys were surprised when the genial mobster climbed into their car with them and said "We're all going to the same place; I'll just ride with you." He even bought them lunch that day), was not among the agents that were sent to arrest him. When the agents knocked on the door of Humphreys' apartment it was opened by Humphreys, with a 38-caliber revolver in his hand. One of the agents is quoted as saying: "Murray, for Christ's sake, you know we're FBI agents, put down the gun." The agents overpowered the aging mobster without much difficulty and handcuffed him. Humphreys was taken downtown and a friend, restaurant owner Morrie Norman, posted bail for him later that day.

That night, at approximately 8:30 p.m., Ernest Humphreys found his brother lying fully clothed and face down on the floor of the same room where he and the agents had fought earlier that day. Humphreys had apparently been vacuuming the room and had suffered a fatal heart attack.

A private service was held at the Donnellan Funeral Home, where Humphreys' remains were cremated, despite his wish to have his body donated for medical research. FBI Agent William Roemer later wrote: "I had clearly developed an affinity for Hump – more so by far than for anyone else in the mob. The man had killed in the Capone days on the way up. He had committed my cardinal sin, corruption, many times over. But there was a style about the way he conducted himself. His word was his bond... Without question, I preferred working against a despised adversary such as a Giancana rather than a respected adversary such as a Humphreys. Each was a challenge – the difference being that I enjoyed the fruit of my success so much more against Giancana than I did against 'The Camel'... in Chicago there would be plenty more mobsters to choose as targets. But none like Hump."

WILLIAM "BIG BILL" THOMPSON

Even after losing to Anton Cermak in 1931, Big Bill Thompson was not quite finished with Chicago – although Chicago was certainly finished with Thompson. In 1936, he made a failed attempt to run for the Illinois governor's seat and in 1939 made another attempt at the Chicago mayor's office. He lost out to Edward J. Kelly and finally took the hint and went into retirement.

On March 19, 1944, Thompson, who had been ill for seven week with a severe chest cold, died in his luxurious suite at the Blackstone Hotel. It was thought that at the time of his death that his estate amounted to about $150,000, which would have indicated that, despite the rumors, his claims of being honest were true and that it had been the newspapers creating scandalous tales about corruption in the mayor's office all along. However, when his safe-deposit boxes were opened, cash literally came tumbling out. One box held $1,466,250 in cash, plus stocks, bonds and gold certificates. Another had $112,000 in stocks and bonds and two other boxes contained nearly $250,000 in stocks and cash made up of $50 and $100 bills. In the end, his estate totaled well over two million dollars. No one had any idea how the money had gotten there -- but there were plenty of theories, which have continued to this day.

To make matters worse, his death also sparked a battle between his mistress of a dozen years, Ethabelle Green, who settled for $250,000 and his wife, Maysie, who got most of the estate. By the time that she paid off all of her attorney bills, she managed to end up with just $100,000.

The *Daily News* sounded the last note on Thompson in that he "was not a great man, he was highly successful in his field. He was not a statesman; he was a consummate politician. His success was based on deception and distraction. He was the most amazingly unbelievable man in Chicago's history."

As a final note, it has been claimed that Thompson's former hotel suite at the Blackstone is haunted. Subsequent tenants and guests have claimed to hear the sounds of heavy, plodding footsteps in the bedroom and the sound of a man's labored breathing – as if the final days of Big Bill Thompson have left an impression behind. Perhaps this is only fitting based on the indelible mark that he left on the city of Chicago.

FRANK J. WILSON

Frank Wilson – the man who really caught Capone using income tax evasion charges – had an illustrious career after sending the mob boss to prison. During the Lindbergh kidnapping in 1932, Wilson's insistence that the serial numbers on the gold certificates in ransom money be recorded would lead to the 1934 arrest of Bruno Richard Hauptmann, who was later convicted and executed for the kidnapping. The method devised by Wilson of recording serial numbers, and later "marked bills," would eventually become commonly used to prosecute criminals.

In 1936, Wilson was named chief of the Secret Service. Over the course of the next eleven years he successfully resisted attempts by J. Edgar Hoover to transfer the Secret Service to the Justice Department and the jurisdiction of the FBI. He made it much more difficult for counterfeit money to be produced and distributed. During his administration, he also initiated practices in presidential security that have since become standard procedure. He retired in 1947.

Wilson died in Washington, D.C., on June 22, 1970 at the age of 83.

In the 1987 film, *The Untouchables*, the character Oscar Wallace (played by Charles Martin Smith) is loosely based upon Wilson.

ELIOT NESS

Popular culture has, over time, tied the two names of Al Capone and Eliot Ness together in such a way that we almost can't think of the Prohibition era in Chicago without thinking of them as matching symbols of good and evil. Al Capone was the sinister mob boss who ruled the city and Ness was a hard-working Prohibition agent who swore to bring him down. Their paths collided when Ness began destroying mob breweries and gathering evidence of Prohibition violations. This special unit, formed in August 1929, was called "the Untouchables." But how much of that was real, and how much was the work of press-savvy Ness working in conjunction with the Chicago newspapers of the day?

Capone's men really did try to kill Ness, once planting a bomb in his car. They also tried to bribe him. When Ness and two of his agents refused to accept money to turn their backs on Capone's illicit activities, a newspaper columnist called them "Untouchable." The nickname faded into history, but it was resurrected as the title of a book Eliot Ness and a professional writer, Oscar Fraley, co-authored in 1956-57.

It may not have been the evidence gathered by Ness that sent Capone to prison, but they did have an overwhelming case of Prohibition law violations against Capone and his associates. However, it was never prosecuted. Instead, Capone was charged with tax evasion, went to prison, and then spent the rest of his life in seclusion.

After Prohibition was reps director in December 1935. Mayor Harold Burton wanted an independent director who was not afraid to do battle with corrupt police officials and organized crime. He got all of that and more. Eliot Ness rooted out corruption and inefficiency in the police department, smashed gambling and extortion rings, tamed violent youth gangs, upgraded fire protection and traffic safety, and instituted other reforms.

Some of Ness' most impressive work against organized crime was done in Cleveland. At the time he took over as public safety director, it was one of the most corrupt cities in the country with a police force that, like Chicago's, was notorious for graft. A vicious gang called the Mayfield Road Mob, made up of Jewish and Italian mobsters, preyed on the city, blighting every neighborhood with gambling and prostitution rackets. Violence was commonplace and murders occurred on a regular basis. Ness was given a free hand at cleaning up the city and he ordered mass transfers and fired officers for taking bribes and being drunk while on duty.

Over the course of six years, Ness was shot, beaten, threatened and dodged an attempted frame-up by dirty cops. In the end, he managed to transform Cleveland, in the worlds of one writer, "from the deadliest metropolis to the safest big city in the USA." The Mayfield Road Mob was put out of business and a number of gambling operations were forced to move into outlying counties and eventually, thanks to continued pressure, as far away as Northern Kentucky.

Despite his professional accomplishments, Ness had many personal problems. His commitment to law enforcement and long hours away from his home were largely responsible for his two failed marriages. Ness also developed a drinking habit, which would haunt him for the rest of his life.

It would finally be his failure to apprehend one of the nation's early serial killers, the so-called "Mad Butcher of Cleveland," that ended his law enforcement career. Despite hard work and help from dedicated detectives, Ness was unable to stop the murders. This not only frustrated him, it made him the object of public criticism. The murders continued for years and were never solved.

Criticism of Ness intensified in March 1942, thanks to an early morning traffic accident in which he was involved on an ice-covered Cleveland street. The fact that Ness had been drinking and tried to persuade the investigating officers to look the other way turned the tide of public opinion against him. He resigned as public safety director to become national director of the government's Social Protection Program. In that role, Ness worked with police agencies and community leaders near military bases, in an effort to stamp out prostitution and curb venereal disease. It was a big step down from the exciting life that he led as an "Untouchable" and as the man who cleaned up Cleveland.

Ness's career took another bizarre twist when he was installed as chairman of the board of directors for Diebold, Inc. of Canton, Ohio, one of the world's largest manufacturers of vaults and safes. At the same time, Ness helped form an export-import company that sent American steel and manufactured goods abroad while bringing silk, tea and other products into this country. He also teamed with General Claire Lee Chennault, famous leader of the "Flying Tigers" air squadron, to set up a separate export-import firm dealing exclusively with China.

A badly mangled run for the Cleveland mayoral office in 1947 began a downward spiral that continued for the final years of Ness' life. He drifted from one failing business enterprise to another. Finally, he accepted an executive position with North Ridge Industrial Corporation in 1956. The company had the worthy idea of a unique method for watermarking checks and other important documents as protection against counterfeiting. However, due to market trends and internal strife, North Ridge was teetering on the brink of bankruptcy when Ness died of a heart attack in his Coudersport, Pennsylvania, home on May 16, 1957 at the age of 54.

At the time of his death, Eliot Ness was depressed, disillusioned and deeply in debt. He never knew that the book manuscript he and Oscar Fraley had produced would create the legend that still endures today. The book itself was a poor seller, but Hollywood was attracted to the glorified accounts of Ness's Chicago days. "The Untouchables" took on a life of its own and created a story that continues to live on.

AFTERWORD:

I wanted to end this book with a short note -- a "thank you" if you will, to all of the people who have stuck with it this far and finished the book to the end. This was an exciting book for me to write and one that I feel a touch of sadness about as it comes to an end. I always wanted to write a book about Al Capone, ever since I was introduced to his story many years ago as a teenager. He was a compelling, fascinating man who lived in a troubled, violent time -- a time that many of us have both glorified and memorialized with our stories, our writings and in my case, our tours of Chicago. Many would question the idea of "glorifying" such a bloody, crime-ridden era but I don't think that those of us who write about the "Roaring 20s" are as much glorifying the era as we are making sure that it's not forgotten.

I didn't write this book because I'm an "expert" on Al Capone, far from it. I wrote it for myself and my love for the history of Chicago in the Prohibition period and if you read it, and liked it, so much the better. There are so many people that I can thank for instilling in me a great passion for the era written about in this book, but any mistakes within these pages are certainly my own.

TROY TAYLOR
SUMMER 2010

BIBLIOGRAPHY

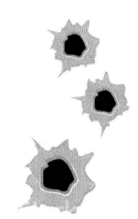

Adler, Jeffrey S. – *First in Violence, Deepest in Dirt*; 2006
Allsop, Kenneth – *The Bootleggers;* 1961
Asbury, Herbert - *Gem of the Prairie*; 1940
Bergreen, Laurence – *Capone: The Man & The Era*; 1994
Bilek, Arthur J. – *The First Vice Lord*; 2008
Binder, John J. – *The Chicago Outfit;* 2003
Burns, Walter Noble – *The One-Way Ride;* 1931
Chicago Public Library
Chicago Historical Society
Demaris, Ovid – *Captive City*; 1969
Eghigian, Jr., Mars – *After Capone;* 2006
Engelmann, Larry – *Intemperance;* 1979
Enright, Richard T. -- *Capone, On the Spot;* 1931
Farr, Finis – *Chicago*; 1973
Gomez, Mario – *Al Capone Museum* (website)
Goulart, Ron – *Line up Tough Guys;* 1966
Halper, Albert – *The Chicago Crime Book*; 1967
Heimel Paul – *Eliot Ness: The Real Story;* 1997
Helmer, William – *Public Enemies*; 1998
---------- & Arthur J. Bilek, *The St. Valentine's Day Massacre*; 2004
Humble, Ronald – *Frank Nitti;* 2007
Johnson Curt with R. Craig Sautter – *Wicked City*; 1994
Keefe, Rose --- *Guns and Roses*; 2003
-------------- --- *The Man who Got Away*; 2005
Kobler, John – *Ardent Spirits: Rise and Fall of Prohibition;* 1973
--------------- – *Capone*; 1971
Lait, Jack and Lee Mortimer – *Chicago Confidential*; 1950
Landesco, John – *Organized Crime in Chicago*; 1968
Lesy, Michael – *Murder City*; 2007
Lewis, Lloyd & Henry Justin Smith – *Chicago*; 1929
Lindberg, Richard - *Chicago by Gaslight*; 1996
---------- - *Return to the Scene of the Crime*; 1999
---------- - *Return Again to the Scene of the Crime*; 2001
Lunde, Paul – *Organized Crime;* 2004
Lyle, Hudge John – *The Dry and Lawless Years;* 1960
Mark, Norman – *Mayors, Madams & Madmen*; 1979
McPhaul, Jack – *Johnny Torrio: First of the Ganglords*; 1970
Moore, Lucy – *Anything Goes;* 2010
Murray, George – *The Legacy of Al Capone*; 1975

Nash, Jay Robert - *Bloodletters and Bad Men*, 1995
-------------- - *Open Files*, 1983
Ness, Eliot & Oscar Fraley – *The Untouchables;* 1957
Olla, Roberto -- *Godfathers; 2003*
Repetto, Thomas -- *American Mafia; 2004*
Sann, Paul – *The Lawless Decade;* 1957
Shmelter, Richard J. – *Chicago Assassin*, 2008
Sifakis, Carl - *Encyclopedia of American Crime*, 1982
------------ -- *Mafia Encyclopedia;* 1987
Spiering, Frank – *The Man who Got Capone;* 1976
Spot Publishing Company -- *X Marks the Spot: Chicago Gang War in Pictures;* 1930
Taylor, Troy – *Bloody Chicago*, 2006
---------- - *Bloody Illinois*, 2008
----------- - *Dead Men Do Tell Tales*, 2008
------------ *Murder & Mayhem in Chicago's Downtown;* 2009
------------ *Murder & Mayhem in Chicago's Vice Districts;* 2009
------------ *Murder & Mayhem on Chicago's North Side;* 2009
------------ *Murder & Mayhem on Chicago's South Side;* 2009
------------ *Murder & Mayhem on Chicago's West Side;* 2009
Waugh, Daniel – *Egan's Rats;* 2007
Weir, William - *Written with Lead;* 1992
Whittington-Egan, Richard -- *Weekend Book of Ghosts;* 1975
Winer, Richard & Nancy Osborn – *Haunted Houses;* 1979
Wright, Sewell Peaslee – *Chicago Murders*, 1945

Newspapers & Photographs
Chicago American
Chicago Daily News
Chicago Herald & Examiner
Chicago Historical Society
Chicago Herald-American
Chicago Inter-Ocean
Chicago Sun-Times
Chicago Times
Chicago Tribune
Library of Congress

Special Thanks to:
Jill Hand – Editor
Mike Schwab – Cover Design
Ken Berg
Adam Selzer
Paul Barile
Clarence Goodman
John Winterbauer
Jim Graczyk
Richard Lindberg
Mario Gomez
Crusty & Herbie
Helayna Taylor
& Haven Taylor

ABOUT THE AUTHOR

Troy Taylor is an occultist, crime buff, supernatural historian and the author of nearly 80 books on ghosts, hauntings, history, crime and the unexplained in America.

He is also the founder of the American Ghost Society and the owner of the American Hauntings Tour company.

Taylor shares a birthday with one of his favorite authors, F. Scott Fitzgerald, but instead of living in New York and Paris like Fitzgerald, Taylor grew up in Illinois. Raised on the prairies of the state, he developed an interest in "things that go bump in the night" at an early age and as a young man, began developing ghost tours and writing about hauntings and crime in Chicago and Central Illinois. His writings have now taken him all over the country and into some of the most far-flung corners of the world.

He began his first book in 1989, which delved into the history and hauntings of his hometown of Decatur, Illinois, and in 1994, it spawned the Haunted Decatur Tour -- and eventually led to the founding of his Illinois Hauntings Tours (with current tours in Alton, Chicago, Decatur, Lebanon, Springfield & Jacksonville) and the American Hauntings Tours, which travel all over the country in search of haunted places.

Along with writing about the unusual and hosting tours, Taylor has also presented on the subjects of ghosts, hauntings and crime for public and private groups. He has also appeared in scores of newspaper and magazine articles about these subjects and in hundreds of radio and television broadcasts about the supernatural. Taylor has appeared in a number of documentary films, several television series and in one feature film about the paranormal.

Troy and his wife, Haven -- when they are not traveling -- currently reside in Chicago.

WHITECHAPEL PRESS

Whitechapel Productions Press is a division of Dark Haven Entertainment and a small press publisher, specializing in books about ghosts and hauntings. Since 1993, the company has been one of America's leading publishers of supernatural books and has produced such best-selling titles as *Haunted Illinois, The Ghost Hunter's Guidebook, Ghosts on Film, Confessions of a Ghost Hunter, The Haunting of America, Sex & the Supernatural* the *Dead Men Do Tell Tales* crime series and many others.

With more than a dozen different authors producing high quality books on all aspects of ghosts, hauntings and the paranormal, Whitechapel Press has made its mark with America's ghost enthusiasts.

You can visit Whitechapel Productions Press online and browse through our selection of ghostly titles, plus get information on ghosts and hauntings, haunted history, spirit photographs, information on ghost hunting and much more. by visiting the internet website at:

WWW.AMERICAN HAUNTINGS.ORG

AMERICAN HAUNTINGS TOURS

Founded in 1994 by author Troy Taylor, the American Hauntings Tour Company (which includes the Illinois Hauntings Tours) is America's oldest and most experienced tour company that takes ghost enthusiasts around the country for excursions and overnight stays at some of America's most haunted places.

In addition to our tours of America's haunted places, we also offer tours of Illinois' most haunted cities, including Chicago, Alton, Decatur, Lebanon, Springfield and Jacksonville. These award-winning ghost tours run all year around, with seasonal tours only in some cities.

Find out more about tours, and make reservations online, by visiting the internet website at:

WWW.AMERICAN HAUNTINGS.ORG

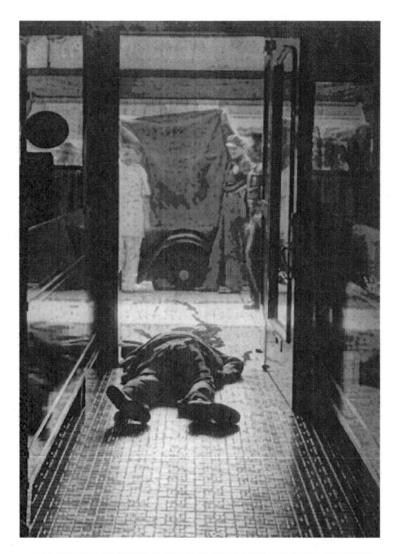

OF COURSE I KNOW WHO SHOT ME, BUT I DIDN'T THINK THE RUNT HAD
ENOUGH NERVE TO DO IT.
PADDY "PADDY THE BEAR" RYAN